ACCA

S
T
U
D
Y
T
E
X
T

PAPER F5

PERFORMANCE MANAGEMENT

BPP Learning Media is the **sole ACCA Platinum Approved Learning Partner – content** for the ACCA qualification. In this, **the only Paper F5 study text to be reviewed by the examiner**:

- We **discuss** the **best strategies** for studying for ACCA exams

- We **highlight** the **most important elements** in the syllabus and the **key skills** you will need

- We **signpost** how each chapter links to the syllabus and the study guide

- We **provide** lots of **exam focus points** demonstrating what the examiner will want you to do

- We **emphasise key points** in regular **fast forward summaries**

- We **test your knowledge** of what you've studied in **quick quizzes**

- We **examine your understanding** in our **exam question bank**

- We **reference all the important topics** in our **full index**

BPP's **i-Pass** product also supports this paper.

FOR EXAMS IN 2011

First edition 2007
Fourth edition November 2010

ISBN 9780 7517 8921 8
(Previous ISBN 9870 7517 6367 6)

British Library Cataloguing-in-Publication Data
A catalogue record for this book
is available from the British Library

Published by

BPP Learning Media Ltd
BPP House, Aldine Place
London W12 8AA

www.bpp.com/learningmedia

Printed in the United Kingdom

We are grateful to the Association of Chartered Certified
Accountants for permission to reproduce past
examination questions. The suggested solutions in the
exam answer bank have been prepared by BPP Learning
Media Ltd, except where otherwise stated.

Your learning materials, published by BPP
Learning Media Ltd, are printed on paper
sourced from sustainable, managed forests.

ii

Contents

A note about copyright

Dear Customer

What does the little © mean and why does it matter?

Your market-leading BPP books, course materials and e-learning materials do not write and update themselves. People write them: on their own behalf or as employees of an organisation that invests in this activity. Copyright law protects their livelihoods. It does so by creating rights over the use of the content.

Breach of copyright is a form of theft – as well as being a criminal offence in some jurisdictions, it is potentially a serious breach of professional ethics.

With current technology, things might seem a bit hazy but, basically, without the express permission of BPP Learning Media:

- Photocopying our materials is a breach of copyright
- Scanning, ripcasting or conversion of our digital materials into different file formats, uploading them to facebook or emailing them to your friends is a breach of copyright

You can, of course, sell your books, in the form in which you have bought them – once you have finished with them. (Is this fair to your fellow students? We update for a reason.) But the e-products are sold on a single user licence basis: we do not supply 'unlock' codes to people who have bought them second-hand.

And what about outside the UK? BPP Learning Media strives to make our materials available at prices students can afford by local printing arrangements, pricing policies and partnerships which are clearly listed on our website. A tiny minority ignore this and indulge in criminal activity by illegally photocopying our material or supporting organisations that do. If they act illegally and unethically in one area, can you really trust them?

Helping you to pass – the ONLY F5 Study Text reviewed by the examiner!

NEW FEATURE – the PER alert!

Before you can qualify as an ACCA member, you do not only have to pass all your exams but also fulfil a three year **practical experience requirement** (PER). To help you to recognise areas of the syllabus that you might be able to apply in the workplace to achieve different performance objectives, we have introduced the '**PER alert**' feature. You will find this feature throughout the Study Text to remind you that what you are **learning to pass** your ACCA exams is **equally useful to the fulfilment of the PER requirement**.

Tackling studying

Studying can be a daunting prospect, particularly when you have lots of other commitments. The **different features** of the text, the **purposes** of which are explained fully on the **Chapter features** page, will help you whilst studying and improve your chances of **exam success**.

Developing exam awareness

Our Texts are completely **focused** on helping you pass your exam.

Our advice on **Studying F5** outlines the **content** of the paper, the **necessary skills** the examiner expects you to demonstrate and any **brought forward knowledge** you are expected to have.

Exam focus points are included within the chapters to highlight when and how specific topics were examined, or how they might be examined in the future.

Using the Syllabus and Study Guide

You can find the syllabus and Study Guide on page xi of this Study Text

Testing what you can do

Testing yourself helps you develop the skills you need to pass the exam and also confirms that you can recall what you have learnt.

We include **Questions** – lots of them - both within chapters and in the **Exam Question Bank**, as well as **Quick Quizzes** at the end of each chapter to test your knowledge of the chapter content.

Chapter features

Each chapter contains a number of helpful features to guide you through each topic.

Topic list

Topic list	Syllabus reference

Tells you what you will be studying in this chapter and the relevant section numbers, together the ACCA syllabus references.

Introduction

Puts the chapter content in the context of the syllabus as a whole.

Study Guide

Links the chapter content with ACCA guidance.

Exam Guide

Highlights how examinable the chapter content is likely to be and the ways in which it could be examined.

Knowledge brought forward from earlier studies

What you are assumed to know from previous studies/exams.

FAST FORWARD

Summarises the content of main chapter headings, allowing you to preview and review each section easily.

Examples

Demonstrate how to apply key knowledge and techniques.

Key terms

Definitions of important concepts that can often earn you easy marks in exams.

Exam focus points

Tell you when and how specific topics were examined, or how they may be examined in the future.

Formula to learn

Formulae that are not given in the exam but which have to be learnt.

This is a new feature that gives you a useful indication of syllabus areas that closely relate to performance objectives in your Practical Experience Requirement (PER).

 Question

Give you essential practice of techniques covered in the chapter.

 Case Study

Provide real world examples of theories and techniques.

Chapter Roundup

A full list of the Fast Forwards included in the chapter, providing an easy source of review.

Quick Quiz

A quick test of your knowledge of the main topics in the chapter.

Exam Question Bank

Found at the back of the Study Text with more comprehensive chapter questions. Cross referenced for easy navigation.

Studying F5

The F5 examiner wants candidates to be able to apply management accounting techniques in business environments. The key question you need to be able to answer is 'what does it all actually mean?' Modern technology is capable of producing vast amounts of management accounting information but it has to be used to help managers to make good decisions and manage effectively. The emphasis in this paper is therefore on practical elements and application to the real world. The examiner does not want to trick you and papers will be fair.

The F5 examiner

The examiner for this paper is **Ann Irons**, who replaced Geoff Cordwell from the December 2010 sitting onwards. Ann Irons has written several articles in *Student Accountant*, including one on how to approach the paper (September 2010 issue). Make sure you read these articles to gain further insight into what the examiner is looking for.

Syllabus update

The F5 syllabus has been updated for the June 2011 sitting onwards. The full syllabus and study guide can be found in this Study Text on pages xi to xviii. The main changes are the omission of backflush accounting and the inclusion of environmental accounting and cost volume profit (CVP) analysis. The syllabus order has also been changed, which has been reflected in this Study Text.

A full summary of the changes to the F5 syllabus is given on the next page.

SUMMARY OF CHANGES TO F5

RATIONALE FOR CHANGES TO STUDY GUIDE PAPER F5

ACCA periodically reviews its qualification syllabuses so that they fully meet the needs of stakeholders such as employers, students, regulatory and advisory bodies and learning providers. As a result of the latest review, ACCA is making changes to the ACCA Qualification effective from June 2011. With each syllabus is included a specific rationale for these changes as far as each examination syllabus and study guide is concerned.

Due to planned changes in the F2 syllabus, the F5 syllabus and study guide has changed to include

areas that the new F2 is no longer covering, such as short term decisions.

Additionally, as a result of feedback regarding the intellectual gap between F5 and P5 papers. Some items in the study guide of F5 which were considered to be of higher intellectual level have been removed from F5 and included in either P5 or P3.

Finally the syllabus has been updated to include areas that are considered important but not explicitly covered in the management accounting stream of papers

The main changes to the F5 syllabus are as shown in Tables 1 and 2 below:

Table 1 – Additions to F5

Section and subject area	Syllabus content
A3- Life cycle costing	b) Derive a life cycle cost in manufacturing and service industries.[2] c) Identify the benefits of life cycle costing.[2]
A5- Environmental accounting	a) Discuss the issues business face in the management of environmental costs.[1] b) Describe the different methods a business may use to account for its environmental costs.[1]
B1- Relevant cost analysis	a) Explain the concept of relevant costing.[2]. b) Identify and calculate relevant costs for a specific decision situations from given data.[2] c) Explain and apply the concept of opportunity costs .[2]
B2- cost volume analysis	a) Explain the nature of CVP analysis.[2] b) Calculate and interpret break even point and margin of safety.[2] c) Calculate the contribution to sales ratio, in single and multi-product situations, and demonstrate an understanding of its use.[2]. d) Calculate target profit or revenue in single and multi-product situations, and demonstrate an understanding of its use.[2] e) Prepare break even charts and profit volume charts and interpret the information contained within each, including multi-product situations.[2] f) Discuss the limitations of CVP analysis for planning and decision making.[2]
B3 limiting factors	b) Determine the optimal production plan where an organisation is restricted by a single limiting factor

B4- pricing decisions	(d) Determine prices and output levels for profit maximisation using the demand based approach to pricing (both tabular and algebraic methods).[1]
B6- dealing with risk and uncertainty	e) Draw a decision tree and use it to solve a multi-stage decision problem f) Calculate the value of perfect information
D 4- Sales mix and quantity variances	a) Calculate, identify the cause of, and explain sales mix and quantity variances.[2] b) Identify and explain the relationship of the sales volume variances with the sales mix and quantity variances.[2]

Table 2 – Deletions to F5

Section where deletions arise	Subject areas where deletions are proposed
A1d	Explain the implications of switching to ABC for pricing, sales strategy, performance management and decision-making.[2]
A2c	Explain the implications of using target costing on pricing, cost control and performance management.[2]
A3b	Explain the implications of lifecycle costing on pricing, performance management and decision-making.[2]
A4 Back flush accounting	a) Describe the process of back-flush accounting and contrast with traditional process accounting.[2] b) Explain the implications of back-flush accounting on performance management and the control of a manufacturing process.[2] c) Identify the benefits of introducing back-flush accounting.[2] d) Evaluate the decision to switch to back-flush accounting from traditional process control.

Please note that the learning curve formula on the standard ACCA formula sheet is changed. Currently, it shows the formula as related to costs rather than time which leads to a lot of mistakes by students in the exams. It now reads as follows:

$Y = ax^b$

Where:

Y = cumulative average time per unit to produce x units.

a = the time taken for the first unit of output

x = the cumulative number of units

b the index of learning (log LR/log 2)

LR = the learning rate as a decimal

There is also a new formula added to the formula sheet and reads as follows:

$MR = a - 2bQ$

1 What F5 is about

The aim of this syllabus is to develop knowledge and skills in the application of management accounting techniques. It covers modern techniques, decision making, budgeting and standard costing, concluding with how a business should be managed and controlled.

F5 is the middle paper in the management accounting section of the qualification structure. F2 concerns just techniques and P5 thinks strategically and considers environmental factors. F5 requires you to be able to apply techniques and think about their impact on the organisation.

2 What skills are required?

- You are expected to have a core of management accounting knowledge from Paper F2
- You will be required to carry out calculations, with **clear workings** and a logical structure
- You will be required to **interpret** data
- You will be required to **explain** management accounting techniques and **discuss** whether they are appropriate for a particular organisation
- You must be able to **apply** your skills in a practical context

3 How to improve your chances of passing

- There is no choice in this paper, all questions have to be answered. You must therefore study the **entire syllabus**, there are no short-cuts
- Practising questions under timed conditions is essential. BPP's **Practice and Revision Kit** contains 20 mark questions on all areas of the syllabus
- Questions will be based on simple scenarios and answers must be **focused** and **specific** to the organisation
- **Answer plans** will help you to focus on the requirements of the question and enable you to manage your time effectively
- **Answer all parts** of the question. Even if you cannot do all of the calculation elements, you will still be able to gain marks in the discussion parts
- Make sure your answers focus on **practical applications of management accounting**, common sense is essential!
- Keep an eye out for **articles** as the **examiner** will use **Student Accountant** to communicate with students
- Read journals etc to pick up on ways in which real organisations apply management accounting and think about your own organisation if that is relevant

4 Brought forward knowledge

You will need to have a good working knowledge of basic management accounting from Paper F2. Chapter 1 of this Study Text revises costing and brought forward knowledge is identified throughout the text. If you struggle with the examples and questions used to revise this knowledge, you must go back and revisit your previous work. The examiner will assume you know this material and it may form part of an exam question.

The exam paper

Format of the paper

The exam is a three-hour paper containing **five** compulsory 20 mark questions. You also have 15 minutes for reading and planning.

There will be a mixture of calculations and discussion and the examiner's aim is to cover as much of the syllabus as possible.

Syllabus and Study Guide

The F5 syllabus and study guide can be found on the next page.

Syllabus

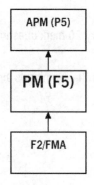

AIM

To develop knowledge and skills in the application of management accounting techniques to quantitative and qualitative information for planning, decision-making, performance evaluation, and control

On successful completion of this paper, candidates should be able to:

A Explain and apply cost accounting techniques

B Select and appropriately apply decision-making techniques to facilitate business decisions and promote efficient and effective use of scarce business resources, appreciating the risks and uncertainty inherent in business and controlling those risks

C Identify and apply appropriate budgeting techniques and methods for planning and control

D Use standard costing systems to measure and control business performance and to identify remedial action

E Assess the performance of a business from both a financial and non-financial viewpoint, appreciating the problems of controlling divisionalised businesses and the importance of allowing for external aspects

MAIN CAPABILITIES

RELATIONAL DIAGRAM OF MAIN CAPABILITIES

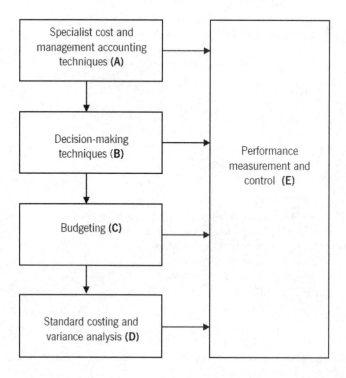

RATIONALE

The syllabus for Paper F5, *Performance Management*, builds on the knowledge gained in Paper F2, *Management Accounting*. It also prepares candidates for more specialist capabilities which are covered in P5 *Advanced Performance Management*.

The syllabus begins by introducing more specialised management accounting topics. There is some knowledge assumed from Paper F2 – primarily overhead treatments. The objective here is to ensure candidates have a broader background in management accounting techniques.

The syllabus then considers decision-making. Candidates need to appreciate the problems surrounding scarce resource, pricing and make-or-buy decisions, and how this relates to the assessment of performance. Risk and uncertainty are a factor of real-life decisions and candidates need to understand risk and be able to apply some basic methods to help resolve the risks inherent in decision-making.

Budgeting is an important aspect of many accountants' lives. The syllabus explores different budgeting techniques and the problems inherent in them. The behavioural aspects of budgeting are important for accountants to understand, and the syllabus includes consideration of the way individuals react to a budget.

Standard costing and variances are then built on. All the variances examined in Paper F2 are examinable here. The new topics are mix and yield variances, and planning and operational variances. Again, the link is made to performance management. It is important for accountants to be able to interpret the numbers that they calculate and ask what they mean in the context of performance.

The syllabus concludes with performance measurement and control. This is a major area of the syllabus. Accountants need to understand how a business should be managed and controlled. They should appreciate the importance of both financial and non-financial performance measures in management. Accountants should also appreciate the difficulties in assessing performance in divisionalised businesses and the problems caused by failing to consider external influences on performance. This section leads directly to Paper P5.

DETAILED SYLLABUS

A   Specialist cost and management accounting techniques

1.   Activity-based costing

2.   Target costing

3.   Life-cycle costing

4.   Throughput accounting

5.   Environmental accounting

B   Decision-making techniques

1.   Relevant cost analysis

2.   Cost volume analysis

3.   Limiting factors

4.   Pricing decisions

5.   Make-or-buy and other short-term decisions

6.   Dealing with risk and uncertainty in decision-making

C   Budgeting

1.   Objectives

2.   Budgetary systems

3.   Types of budget

4.   Quantitative analysis in budgeting

5.   Behavioural aspects of budgeting

D   Standard costing and variances analysis

1.   Budgeting and standard costing

2.   Basic variances and operating statements

3.   Mix and yield variances

4. Planning and operational variances

5. Behavioural aspects of standard costing

E   Performance measurement and control

1. The scope of performance measurement

2. Divisional performance and transfer pricing

3. Performance analysis in not-for-profit organisations and the public sector

4. External considerations and behavioural aspects

APPROACH TO EXAMINING THE SYLLABUS

Paper F5, *Performance Management,* seeks to examine candidates' understanding of how to manage the performance of a business.

The paper builds on the knowledge acquired in Paper F2, *Management Accounting,* and prepares those candidates who choose to study Paper P5, *Advanced Performance Management,* at the Professional level

The syllabus is assessed by a three-hour paper-based examination.

The examination will contain five compulsory 20-mark questions. There will be calculation and discursive elements to the paper with the balance being broadly in line with the pilot paper. The pilot paper contains questions from four of the five syllabus sections. Generally, the paper will seek to draw questions from as many of the syllabus sections as possible.

Study Guide

A SPECIALIST COST AND MANAGEMENT ACCOUNTING TECHNIQUES

1. Activity based costing

a) Identify appropriate cost drivers under ABC.[1]

b) Calculate costs per driver and per unit using ABC.[2]

c) Compare ABC and traditional methods of overhead absorption based on production units, labour hours or machine hours.[2]

2. Target costing

a) Derive a target cost in manufacturing and service industries.[2]

b) Explain the difficulties of using target costing in service industries.[2]

c) Suggest how a target cost gap might be closed.[2]

3. Life-cycle costing

a) Identify the costs involved at different stages of the life-cycle.[2]

b) Derive a life cycle cost in manufacturing and service industries.[2]

c) Identify the benefits of life cycle costing.[2]

4. Throughput accounting

a) Calculate and interpret a throughput accounting ratio (TPAR).[2]

b) Suggest how a TPAR could be improved.[2]

c) Apply throughput accounting to a multi-product decision-making problem.[2]

5. Environmental accounting

a) Discuss the issues business face in the management of environmental costs.[1]

b) Describe the different methods a business may use to account for its environmental costs.[1]

B DECISION-MAKING TECHNIQUES

1. Relevant cost analysis

a) Explain the concept of relevant costing.[2].

b) Identify and calculate relevant costs for a specific decision situations from given data.[2]

c) Explain and apply the concept of opportunity costs .[2]

2. Cost volume profit analysis

a) Explain the nature of CVP analysis.[2]

b) Calculate and interpret break even point and margin of safety.[2]

c) Calculate the contribution to sales ratio, in single and multi-product situations, and demonstrate an understanding of its use.[2].

d) Calculate target profit or revenue in single and multi-product situations, and demonstrate an understanding of its use.[2]

e) Prepare break even charts and profit volume charts and interpret the information contained within each, including multi-product situations.[2]

f) Discuss the limitations of CVP analysis for planning and decision making.[2]

3. Limiting factors

a) Identify limiting factors in a scarce resource situation and select an appropriate technique.[2]

b) Determine the optimal production plan where an organisation is restricted by a single limiting factor, including within the context of "make" or "buy" decisions.[2].

c) Formulate and solve multiple scarce resource problem both graphically and using simultaneous equations as appropriate.[2]

d)   Explain and calculate shadow prices (dual prices) and discuss their implications on decision-making and performance management. [2]

e)   Calculate slack and explain the implications of the existence of slack for decision-making and performance management.[2]
(Excluding simplex and sensitivity to changes in objective functions)

4.   **Pricing decisions**

a)   Explain the factors that influence the pricing of a product or service.[2]

b)   Explain the price elasticity of demand.[1]

c)   Derive and manipulate a straight line demand equation. Derive an equation for the total cost function(including volume-based discounts).[2]

d)   Calculate the optimum selling price and quantity for an organisation, equating marginal cost and marginal revenue[2]

e)   Evaluate a decision to increase production and sales levels, considering incremental costs, incremental revenues and other factors.[2]

f)   Determine prices and output levels for profit maximisation using the demand based approach to pricing (both tabular and algebraic methods) .[1]

g)   Explain different price strategies, including: [2]
   i)   All forms of cost-plus
   ii) Skimming
   iii) Penetration
   iv) Complementary product
   v)   Product-line
   vi) Volume discounting
   vii) Discrimination
   viii) Relevant cost

h)   Calculate a price from a given strategy using cost-plus and relevant cost.[2]

5.   **Make-or-buy and other short-term decisions**

a)   Explain the issues surrounding make vs. buy and outsourcing decisions.[2]

b)   Calculate and compare make" costs with "buy-in" costs.[2]

c)   Compare in-house costs and outsource costs of completing tasks and consider other issues surrounding this decision.[2]

d)   Apply relevant costing principles in situations involving shut down, one-off contracts and the further processing of joint products.[2]

6.   **Dealing with risk and uncertainty in decision-making**

a)   Suggest research techniques to reduce uncertainty e.g. Focus groups, market research.[2]

b)   Explain the use of simulation, expected values and sensitivity.[1]

c)   Apply expected values and sensitivity to decision-making problems.[2]

d)   Apply the techniques of maximax, maximin, and minimax regret to decision-making problems including the production of profit tables.[2]

e)   Draw a decision tree and use it to solve a multi-stage decision problem

f)   Calculate the value of perfect information.

C   **BUDGETING**

1.   **Objectives**

a)   Outline the objectives of a budgetary control system.[2]

b)   Explain how corporate and divisional objectives may differ and can be reconciled.[2]

c)   Identify and resolve conflicting objectives and explain implications.[2]

2.   **Budgetary systems**

a)   Explain how budgetary systems fit within the performance hierarchy.[2]

b) Select and explain appropriate budgetary systems for an organisation, including top-down, bottom-up, rolling, zero-base, activity-base, incremental and feed-forward control.[2]

c) Describe the information used in budget systems and the sources of the information needed.[2]

d) Explain the difficulties of changing a budgetary system.[2]

e) Explain how budget systems can deal with uncertainty in the environment.[2]

3. Types of Budget

a) Indicate the usefulness and problems with different budget types (zero-base, activity-based, incremental, master, functional and flexible).[2]

b) Explain the difficulties of changing the type of budget used.[2]

4. Quantitative analysis in budgeting

a) Analyse fixed and variable cost elements from total cost data using high/low and regression methods.[2]

b) Explain the use of forecasting techniques, including time series, simple average growth models and estimates based on judgement and experience. Predict a future value from provided time series analysis data using both additive and proportional data.[2]

c) Estimate the learning effect and apply the learning curve to a budgetary problem, including calculations on steady states [2]

d) Discuss the reservations with the learning curve.[2]

e) Apply expected values and explain the problems and benefits.[2]

f) Explain the benefits and dangers inherent in using spreadsheets in budgeting.[1]

5. Behavioural aspects of budgeting

a) Identify the factors which influence behaviour.[2]

b) Discuss the issues surrounding setting the difficulty level for a budget.[2]

c) Explain the benefits and difficulties of the participation of employees in the negotiation of targets.[2]

D STANDARD COSTING AND VARIANCES ANALYSIS

1. Budgeting and standard costing

a) Explain the use of standard costs.[2]

b) Outline the methods used to derive standard costs and discuss the different types of cost possible.[2]

c) Explain the importance of flexing budgets in performance management.[2]

d) Prepare budgets and standards that allow for waste and idle time.[2]

e) Explain and apply the principle of controllability in the performance management system.[2]

f) Prepare a flexed budget and comment on its usefulness.[2]

2. Basic variances and operating statements

a) Calculate, identify the cause of and interpret basic variances: [1]
   i) Sales price and volume
   ii) Materials total, price and usage
   iii) Labour total, rate and efficiency
   iv) Variable overhead total, expenditure and efficiency
   v) Fixed overhead total, expenditure and, where appropriate, volume, capacity and efficiency.

b) Explain the effect on labour variances where the learning curve has been used in the budget process.[2]

c) Produce full operating statements in both a marginal cost and full absorption costing environment, reconciling actual profit to budgeted profit.[2]

d) Calculate the effect of idle time and waste on variances including where idle time has been budgeted for.[2]

e) Explain the possible causes of idle time and waste and suggest methods of control.[2]

f) Calculate, using a simple situation, ABC-based variances.[3]

g) Explain the different methods available for deciding whether or not too investigate a variance cause.[2]

3. **Material mix and yield variances**

a) Calculate, identify the cause of, and explain material mix and yield variances.[2]

b) Explain the wider issues involved in changing material mix e.g. cost, quality and performance measurement issues.[2]

c) Identify and explain the relationship of the material price variance with the material mix and yield variances.[2]

d) Suggest and justify alternative methods of controlling production processes.[2]

4. **Sales mix and quantity variances**

a) Calculate, identify the cause of, and explain sales mix and quantity variances.[2]

b) Identify and explain the relationship of the sales volume variances with the sales mix and quantity variances.[2]

5. **Planning and operational variances**

a) Calculate a revised budget.[2]

b) Identify and explain those factors that could and could not be allowed to revise an original budget.[2]

c) Calculate planning and operational variances for sales, including market size and market share, materials and labour.[2]

d) Explain and discuss the manipulation issues involved in revising budgets.[2]

6. **Behavioural aspects of standard costing**

a) Describe the dysfunctional nature of some variances in the modern environment of JIT and TQM.[2]

b) Discuss the behavioural problems resulting from using standard costs in rapidly changing environments.[2]

c) Discuss the effect that variances have on staff motivation and action.[2]

E **PERFORMANCE MEASUREMENT AND CONTROL**

1. **The scope of performance measurement**

a) Describe, calculate and interpret financial performance indicators (FPIs) for profitability, liquidity and risk in both manufacturing and service businesses. Suggest methods to improve these measures.[2]

b) Describe, calculate and interpret non-financial performance indicators (NFPIs) and suggest method to improve the performance indicated.[2]

c) Explain the causes and problems created by short-termism **and financial manipulation of results** and suggest methods to encourage a long term view.[2]

d) Explain and interpret the Balanced Scorecard, and the Building Block model proposed by Fitzgerald and Moon.[2]

e) Discuss the difficulties of target setting in qualitative areas.[2]

2. **Divisional performance and transfer pricing**

a) Explain and illustrate the basis for setting a transfer price using variable cost, full cost and the principles behind allowing for intermediate markets.[2]

b) Explain how transfer prices can distort the performance assessment of divisions and decisions made.[2]

c) Explain the meaning of, and calculate, Return on Investment (ROI) and Residual Income (RI), and discuss their shortcomings.[2]

d) Compare divisional performance and recognise the problems of doing so.[2]

3. **Performance analysis in not for profit organisations and the public sector**

a) Comment on the problems of having non-quantifiable objectives in performance management.[2]

b) Explain how performance could be measured in this sector.[2]

c) Comment on the problems of having multiple objectives in this sector.[2]

d) Outline Value for Money (VFM) as a public sector objective.[1]

4. **External considerations and behavioural aspects**

a) Explain the need to allow for external considerations in performance management, including stakeholders, market conditions and allowance for competitors.[2]

b) Suggest ways in which external considerations could be allowed for in performance management.[2]

c) Interpret performance in the light of external considerations.[2]

d) Identify and explain the behaviour aspects of performance management [2]

READING LIST
This section only contains examiner suggested reading which is in addition to the study texts and/or revision materials and/or other reading listed within the learning content provider directory.

Additional examiner suggested reading:

C. Drury, Management and Cost Accounting (7th edition), Thomson, 2008

C.T. Horngren, A. Bhimani, S.M Datar and G. Foster, *Management and Cost Accounting* (4th Edition), FT Prentice-Hall. 2008.

C. Emmanuel, D Otley, *Accounting for Management Control,* Chapman and Hall, ISBN 186152218

Further details on reading lists and Approved Learning Content can be found in the first few sections of this guide and on the following link.

http://www.accaglobal.com/learningproviders/alpc/content_provider_directory/search/

Analysis of past papers

The table below provides details of when each element of the syllabus has been examined and the question number in which each element appeared. Further details can be found in the Exam Focus Points in the relevant chapters.

Covered in Text chapter		June 2010	Dec 2009	June 2009	Pilot Paper
	SPECIALIST COST AND MANAGEMENT ACCOUNTING TECHNIQUES				
2a	Activity based costing	1			1
2b	Target costing		2		
2c	Life cycle costing				
2d	Throughput accounting			1	
2e	Environmental accounting				
	DECISION-MAKING TECHNIQUES				
3	Cost-volume-profit analysis				
4	Multi-limiting factors and the use of linear programming and shadow pricing	3			
5	Pricing decisions	1, 4		4	
6	Make-or-buy and other short-term decisions			4	
7	Dealing with risk and uncertainty in decision-making				
	BUDGETING				
8	Objectives				
9	Budgetary systems				
9	Types of budget				
10	Quantitative analysis in budgeting		3	5	3
8	Behavioural aspects of budgeting	5			
	STANDARD COSTING AND VARIANCE ANALYSIS				
11	Budgeting and standard costing				
12	Basic variances and operating systems	2	1	3	2
12	Material mix and yield variances	2			2
13	Planning and operational variances		1		
13	Behavioural aspects of standard costing				
	PERFORMANCE MEASUREMENT AND CONTROL				
14	The scope of performance measurement		4	2	4
15	Divisional performance and transfer pricing	4			
16	Performance analysis in not-for-profit organisations and the public sector				

Exam formulae

Set out below are the **formulae you will be given in the exam**. If you are not sure what the symbols mean, or how the formulae are used, you should refer to the appropriate chapter in this Study Text.

Chapter in Study Text

Learning curve

10

$Y = ax^b$

Where Y = cumulative average time per unit to produce x units
a = the time taken for the first unit of output
x = the cumulative number of units
b = the index of learning (log LR/log 2)
LR = the learning rate as a decimal

Regression analysis

10

$y = a + bx$

$$b = \frac{n \sum xy - \sum x \sum y}{n \sum x^2 - (\sum x)^2}$$

$$a = \frac{\sum y}{n} - \frac{b \sum x}{n}$$

$$r = \frac{n \sum xy - \sum x \sum y}{\sqrt{(n \sum x^2 - (\sum x)^2)(n \sum y^2 - (\sum y)^2)}}$$

Demand curve

5

$P \quad = a - bQ$

$$b \quad = \frac{\text{change in price}}{\text{change in quantity}}$$

$a \quad$ = price when $Q = 0$

$MR = a - 2bQ$

Specialist cost and management accounting techniques

1

Costing

Introduction

Part A of this Study Text looks at specialist cost and management accounting techniques. This chapter serves as a revision of concepts you will have covered in your previous studies.

In the following chapter we will be looking at more complex techniques so it is important that you are familiar with the key concepts and terminology in this chapter.

Exam guide

This chapter serves as an introduction to your study of cost and management accounting techniques, as knowledge is assumed from Paper F2 Management Accounting and is still examinable at this level. Questions in this paper will focus on interpretation rather than doing calculations.

1 Costing

Costing is the process of determining the costs of products, services or activities.

Cost accounting is used to determine the cost of products, jobs or services (whatever the organisation happens to be involved in). Such costs have to be built up using a process known as **cost accumulation.**

In your earlier studies you will have learnt how to accumulate the various cost elements which make up total cost.

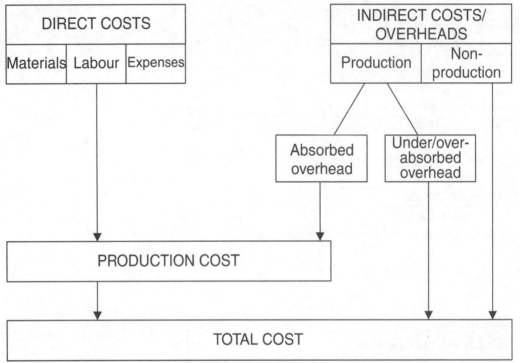

Absorption costing cost accumulation system

2 The problem of overheads

Indirect costs, or **overheads**, are costs incurred in making a product or providing a service, but which cannot be traced directly to the product or service. **Absorption costing** is a means of incorporating a fair share of these costs into the cost of a unit of product or service provided.

If a company manufactures a product, the cost of the product will include the cost of the raw materials and components used in it and cost of the labour effort required to make it. These are **direct costs** of the product. The company would, however, incur many other costs in making the product, which are not directly attributable to a single product, but which are incurred generally in the process of manufacturing a large number of product units. These are **indirect costs** or **overheads**. Such costs include the following.

- Factory rent and rates
- Machine depreciation
- Supervision costs
- Heating and lighting

A **direct cost** is a cost that can be traced in full to the product, service or department that is being costed.

An **indirect cost** or **overhead** is a cost that is incurred in the course of making a product, providing a service or running a department, but which cannot be traced directly and in full to the product, service or department.

In some companies, the overheads cost might greatly exceed the direct production costs.

It might seem unreasonable to ignore indirect costs entirely when accumulating the costs of making a product, and yet there **cannot be a completely satisfactory way of sharing out indirect costs** between the many different items of production which benefit from them.

2.1 Using absorption costing to deal with the problem of overheads

Traditionally, the view has been that a fair share of overheads should be added to the cost of units produced. This fair share will **include a portion of all production overhead expenditure** and possibly administration and marketing overheads too. This is the view embodied in the principles of **absorption costing**.

2.1.1 Theoretical justification for using absorption costing

All production overheads are incurred in the production of the organisation's output and so each unit of the product receives some benefit from these costs. Each unit of output should therefore be charged with some of the overhead costs.

2.1.2 Practical reasons for using absorption costing

(a)   **Inventory valuations**

Inventory in hand must be valued for two reasons.

(i)   For the closing inventory figure in the statement of financial position
(ii)   For the cost of sales figure in the income statement

The valuation of inventories will affect profitability during a period because of the way in which the cost of sales is calculated.

Cost of goods sold =   cost of goods produced + the value of opening inventories
                          – the value of closing inventories

(b)   **Pricing decisions**

Many companies attempt to set selling prices **by calculating the full cost of production or sales** of each product, and then adding a margin for profit. 'Full cost plus pricing' can be particularly useful for companies which do jobbing or contract work, where each job or contract is different, so that a standard unit sales price cannot be fixed. Without using absorption costing, a full cost is difficult to ascertain.

(c)   **Establishing the profitability of different products**

This argument in favour of absorption costing states that if a company sells more than one product, it will be difficult to judge **how profitable each individual product is**, unless overhead costs are shared on a fair basis and charged to the cost of sales of each product.

2.2 Using marginal costing to deal with the problem of overheads

For many purposes absorption costing is less useful as a costing method than marginal costing. In some situations, **absorption costing can be misleading** in the information it supplies.

Advocates of **marginal costing** take the view that only the variable costs of making and selling a product or service should be identified. **Fixed costs should be dealt with separately** and treated as a cost of the accounting period rather than shared out somehow between units produced. Some overhead costs are, however, variable costs which increase as the total level of activity rises and so the marginal cost of production and sales should include an amount for variable overheads.

3 A revision of absorption costing

FAST FORWARD

Absorption costing is a traditional approach to dealing with overheads, involving three stages: allocation, apportionment and absorption.

Apportionment has two stages, general overhead apportionment and service department cost apportionment.

Key term

Absorption costing is a method of product costing which aims to include in the total cost of a product (unit, job and so on) an appropriate share of an organisation's total overhead, which is generally taken to mean an amount which reflects the amount of time and effort that has gone into producing the product.

You should have covered absorption costing in your earlier studies. We will therefore summarise the simpler points of the topic but will go into some detail on the more complex areas to refresh your memory.

Knowledge brought forward from earlier studies

Absorption costing

- Product costs are built up using absorption costing by a process of **allocation**, **apportionment** and **overhead absorption**.
- **Allocation** is the process by which whole cost items are charged directly to a cost unit or cost centre. **Direct costs** are allocated directly to cost units. **Overheads** clearly identifiable with cost centres are allocated to those cost centres but costs which cannot be identified with one particular cost centre are allocated to general overhead cost centres. The cost of a warehouse security guard would therefore be charged to the warehouse cost centre but heating and lighting costs would be charged to a general overhead cost centre.
- The **first stage of overhead apportionment** involves sharing out (or apportioning) the overheads within **general overhead cost centres** between the other cost centres using a fair basis of apportionment (such as floor area occupied by each cost centre for heating and lighting costs).
- The **second stage of overhead apportionment** is to apportion the costs of **service cost centres** (both directly allocated and apportioned costs) to production cost centres.
- The final stage in absorption costing is the **absorption** into product costs (using overhead absorption rates) of the overheads which have been allocated and apportioned to the production cost centres.
- Costs allocated and apportioned to non-production cost centres are usually deducted from the full cost of production to arrive at the cost of sales.

Question

Cost apportionment

Briefly discuss the type of factors which could affect the choice of the bases an organisation can use to apportion service department costs.

(a) The type of service being provided
(b) The amount of overhead expenditure involved
(c) The number of departments benefiting from the service
(d) The ability to be able to produce realistic estimates of the usage of the service
(e) The resulting costs and benefits

Question

More cost apportionment

A company is preparing its production overhead budgets and determining the apportionment of those overheads to products. Cost centre expenses and related information have been budgeted as follows.

	Total $	Machine shop A $	Machine shop B $	Assembly $	Canteen $	Mainten-ance $
Indirect wages	78,560	8,586	9,190	15,674	29,650	15,460
Consumable materials	16,900	6,400	8,700	1,200	600	–
Rent and rates	16,700					
Buildings insurance	2,400					
Power	8,600					
Heat and light	3,400					
Depreciation (machinery)	40,200					
Value of machinery	402,000	201,000	179,000	22,000	–	–
Power usage (%)	100	55	40	3	–	2
Direct labour (hours)	35,000	8,000	6,200	20,800	–	–
Machine usage (hours)	25,200	7,200	18,000	–	–	–
Area (sq ft)	45,000	10,000	12,000	15,000	6,000	2,000

Required

Using the direct apportionment to production departments method and bases of apportionment which you consider most appropriate from the information provided, calculate overhead totals for the three production departments.

Answer

	Total $	A $	B $	Assembly $	Canteen $	Main-tenance $	Basis of apportionment
Indirect wages	78,560	8,586	9,190	15,674	29,650	15,460	Actual
Consumable materials	16,900	6,400	8,700	1,200	600	–	Actual
Rent and rates	16,700	3,711	4,453	5,567	2,227	742	Area
Insurance	2,400	533	640	800	320	107	Area
Power	8,600	4,730	3,440	258	–	172	Usage
Heat and light	3,400	756	907	1,133	453	151	Area
Depreciation	40,200	20,100	17,900	2,200	–	–	Val of mach
	166,760	44,816	45,230	26,832	33,250	16,632	
Reallocate	–	7,600	5,890	19,760	(33,250)	–	Direct labour
Reallocate	–	4,752	11,880	–	–	(16,632)	Mach usage
Totals	166,760	57,168	63,000	46,592	–	–	

4 Overhead absorption

FAST FORWARD

After apportionment, overheads are **absorbed** into products using an appropriate **absorption rate** based on budgeted costs and budgeted activity levels.

Having allocated and/or apportioned all **overheads**, the next stage in absorption costing is to **add them to, or absorb them into**, the cost of production or sales.

4.1 Use of a predetermined absorption rate

Knowledge brought forward from earlier studies

Step 1	The overhead likely to be incurred during the coming year is estimated.
Step 2	The total hours, units or direct costs on which the overhead absorption rates are based (activity levels) are estimated.
Step 3	Absorption rate = estimated overhead ÷ budgeted activity level

4.2 Choosing the appropriate absorption base

Question   Absorption bases

List as many possible bases of absorption (or 'overhead recovery rates') as you can think of.

Answer

(a)   A percentage of direct materials cost
(b)   A percentage of direct labour cost
(c)   A percentage of prime cost
(d)   A percentage of factory cost (for administration overhead)
(e)   A percentage of sales or factory cost (for selling and distribution overhead)
(f)   A rate per machine hour
(g)   A rate per direct labour hour
(h)   A rate per unit

The choice of an absorption basis is a **matter of judgement and common sense**. There are no strict rules or formulae involved. But the basis should realistically reflect the characteristics of a given cost centre, avoid undue anomalies and be 'fair'. The **choice will be significant in determining the cost of individual products, but the total cost of production overheads is the budgeted overhead expenditure, no matter what basis of absorption is selected**. It is the relative share of overhead costs borne by individual products and jobs which is affected.

Question   Absorption rates

Using the information in and the results of the question on page 7, determine budgeted overhead absorption rates for each of the production departments using appropriate bases of absorption.

Machine shop A:	$57,168/7,200	= $7.94 per machine hour
Machine shop B:	$63,000/18,000	= $3.50 per machine hour
Assembly:	$46,592/20,800	= $2.24 per direct labour hour

4.3 Over and under absorption of overheads

Under-/over-absorbed overhead occurs when overheads incurred do not equal overheads absorbed.

The rate of overhead absorption is based on estimates (of both numerator and denominator) and it is quite likely that either one or both of the estimates will not agree with what actually occurs. Actual overheads incurred will probably be either greater than or less than overheads absorbed into the cost of production, and so it is almost inevitable that at the end of the accounting year there will have been an over absorption or under absorption of the overhead actually incurred.

- **Over absorption** means that the **overheads charged to the cost of sales are greater than the overheads actually incurred**.
- **Under absorption** means that **insufficient overheads have been included in the cost of sales**.

Suppose that the budgeted overhead in a production department is $80,000 and the budgeted activity is 40,000 direct labour hours, the overhead recovery rate (using a direct labour hour basis) would be $2 per direct labour hour. Actual overheads in the period are, say $84,000 and 45,000 direct labour hours are worked.

	$
Overhead incurred (actual)	84,000
Overhead absorbed (45,000 × $2)	90,000
Over-absorption of overhead	6,000

In this example, the cost of production has been charged with $6,000 more than was actually spent and so the cost that is recorded will be too high. The over-absorbed overhead will be an adjustment to the profit and loss account at the end of the accounting period to reconcile the overheads charged to the actual overhead.

Question

Under and over-absorption

The total production overhead expenditure of the company in the questions above was $176,533 and its actual activity was as follows.

	Machine shop A	Machine shop B	Assembly
Direct labour hours	8,200	6,500	21,900
Machine usage hours	7,300	18,700	–

Required

Using the information in and results of the previous questions, calculate the under- or over-absorption of overheads.

Answer

		$	$
Actual expenditure			176,533
Overhead absorbed			
Machine shop A	7,300 hrs × $7.94	57,962	
Machine shop B	18,700 hrs × $3.50	65,450	
Assembly	21,900 hrs × $2.24	49,056	
			172,468
Under-absorbed overhead			4,065

4.4 The reasons for under-/over-absorbed overhead

The overhead absorption rate is predetermined from budget estimates of overhead cost and activity level. Under or over recovery of overhead will occur in the following circumstances.

- Actual overhead costs are different from budgeted overheads.
- The actual activity level is different from the budgeted activity level.
- Actual overhead costs **and** actual activity level differ from those budgeted.

Question   Over and under-absorption

Elsewhere has a budgeted production overhead of $180,000 and a budgeted activity of 45,000 machine hours.

Required

Calculate the under-/over-absorbed overhead, and note the reasons for the under-/over-absorption in the following circumstances.

(a)   Actual overheads cost $170,000 and 45,000 machine hours were worked.
(b)   Actual overheads cost $180,000 and 40,000 machine hours were worked.
(c)   Actual overheads cost $170,000 and 40,000 machine hours were worked.

Answer

The overhead recovery rate is $180,000/45,000 = $4 per machine hour.

		$
(a)	Actual overhead	170,000
	Absorbed overhead (45,000 × $4)	180,000
	Over-absorbed overhead	10,000

Reason: Actual and budgeted machine hours are the same but actual overheads cost less than expected.

		$
(b)	Actual overhead	180,000
	Absorbed overhead (40,000 × $4)	160,000
	Under-absorbed overhead	20,000

Reason: Budgeted and actual overhead costs were the same but fewer machine hours were worked than expected.

		$
(c)	Actual overhead	170,000
	Absorbed overhead (40,000 × $4)	160,000
	Under-absorbed overhead	10,000

Reason: A combination of the reasons in (a) and (b).

5 Marginal costing

In **marginal costing**, inventories are valued at variable production cost whereas in absorption costing they are valued at their full production cost.

Key terms

Marginal cost is the cost of one unit of a product/service which could be avoided if that unit were not produced/provided.

Contribution is the difference between sales revenue and variable (marginal) cost of sales.

Marginal costing is an alternative to absorption costing. Only variable costs (marginal costs) are charged as a cost of sales. Fixed costs are treated as period costs and are charged in full against the profit of the period in which they are incurred.

Knowledge brought forward from earlier studies

Marginal costing

- In **marginal costing**, closing **inventories are valued at marginal (variable) production cost** whereas, in **absorption costing**, inventories are **valued at their full production cost** which includes absorbed fixed production overhead.
- If the opening and closing inventory levels differ, the **profit reported** for the accounting period **under the two methods** of cost accumulation **will therefore be different**.
- But **in the long run, total profit for a company will be the same** whichever is used because, in the long run, total costs will be the same by either method of accounting. Different accounting conventions merely affect the profit of individual periods.

Question

Absorption and marginal costing

A company makes and sells a single product. At the beginning of period 1, there are no opening inventories of the product, for which the variable production cost is $4 and the sales price $6 per unit. Fixed costs are $2,000 per period, of which $1,500 are fixed production costs. Normal output is 1,500 units per period. In period 1, sales were 1,200 units, production was 1,500 units. In period 2, sales were 1,700 units, production was 1,400 units.

Required

Prepare profit statements for each period and for the two periods in total using both absorption costing and marginal costing.

Answer

It is important to notice that although production and sales volumes in each period are different, over the **full period, total production equals sales volume**. The total cost of sales is the same and therefore the **total profit is the same by either method** of accounting. **Differences** in profit in any one period are merely **timing differences** which cancel out over a longer period of time.

(a) **Absorption costing.** The absorption rate for fixed production overhead is $1,500/1,500 units = $1 per unit. The fully absorbed cost per unit = $(4+1) = $5.

	Period 1		Period 2		Total	
	$	$	$	$	$	$
Sales		7,200		10,200		17,400
Production costs						
Variable	6,000		5,600		11,600	
Fixed	1,500		1,400		2,900	
	7,500		7,000		14,500	
Add opening inventory b/f (300×$5)	–		1,500		1,500	
	7,500		8,500		16,000	
Less closing inventory c/f (300×$5)	1,500		–		1,500	
Production cost of sales	6,000		8,500		14,500	
Under-absorbed o/hd	–		100		100	
Total costs		6,000		8,600		14,600
Gross profit		1,200		1,600		2,800
Other costs		(500)		(500)		(1,000)
Net profit		700		1,100		1,800

(b) **Marginal costing**

The marginal cost per unit = $4.

	Period 1		Period 2		Total	
	$	$	$	$	$	$
Sales		7,200		10,200		17,400
Variable production cost	6,000		5,600		11,600	
Add opening inventory b/f (300×$4)	–		1,200		1,200	
	6,000		6,800		12,800	
Less closing inventory c/f (300×$4)	1,200		–		1,200	
Variable prod. cost of sales		4,800		6,800		11,600
Contribution		2,400		3,400		5,800
Fixed costs		2,000		2,000		4,000
Profit		400		1,400		1,800

Question

Marginal and absorption costing

RH makes and sells one product, which has the following standard production cost.

		$
Direct labour	3 hours at $6 per hour	18
Direct materials	4 kilograms at $7 per kg	28
Production overhead	Variable	3
	Fixed	20
Standard production cost per unit		69

Normal output is 16,000 units per annum. Variable selling, distribution and administration costs are 20 per cent of sales value. Fixed selling, distribution and administration costs are $180,000 per annum. There are no units in finished goods inventory at 1 October 20X2. The fixed overhead expenditure is spread evenly throughout the year. The selling price per unit is $140. Production and sales budgets are as follows.

	Six months ending 31 March 20X3	Six months ending 30 September 20X3
Production	8,500	7,000
Sales	7,000	8,000

Required

Prepare profit statements for each of the six-monthly periods, using the following methods of costing.

(a) Marginal costing
(b) Absorption costing

Answer

(a) **Profit statements for the year ending 30 September 20X3**
     Marginal costing basis

	Six months ending 31 March 20X3		Six months ending 30 September 20X3	
	$'000	$'000	$'000	$'000
Sales at $140 per unit		980		1,120
Opening inventory			73.5	
Std. variable prod. cost (at $49 per unit)	416.5		343.0	
	416.5		416.5	
Closing inventory (W1)	73.5		24.5	
		343		392
		637		728
Variable selling and so on costs		196		224
Contribution		441		504
Fixed costs: production (W2)	160		160	
selling and so on	90		90	
		250		250
Net profit		191		254

(b) **Profit statements for the year ending 30 September 20X3**
     Absorption costing basis

	Six months ending 31 March 20X3		Six months ending 30 September 20X3	
	$'000	$'000	$'000	$'000
Sales at $140 per unit		980		1,120
Opening inventory			103.5	
Std. cost of prod. (at $69 per unit)	586.5		483.0	
	586.5		586.5	
Closing inventory (W1)	103.5		34.5	
	483.0		552.0	
(Over-)/under-absorbed overhead (W3)	(10.0)		20.0	
		473		572
Gross profit		507		548
Selling and so on costs				
Variable	196		224	
Fixed	90		90	
		286		314
Net profit		221		234

Workings

	Six months ending 31 March 20X3	Six months ending 30 September 20X3
	Units	Units
Opening inventory		1,500
Production	8,500	7,000
	8,500	8,500
Sales	7,000	8,000
Closing inventory	1,500	500
Marginal cost valuation (× $49)	$73,500	$24,500
Absorption cost valuation (× $69)	$103,500	$34,500

2 Budgeted fixed production o/hd = 16,000 units × $20 = $320,000 pa = $160,000 per six months

3

	Six months ending 31 March 20X3		Six months ending 30 September 20X3	
Normal output (16,000 ÷ 2)	8,000	units	8,000	units
Budgeted output	8,500	units	7,000	units
Difference	500	units	1,000	units
× std. fixed prod. o/hd per unit	× $20		× $20	
(Over-)/under-absorbed overhead	($10,000)		$20,000	

6 Absorption costing and marginal costing compared

FAST FORWARD If opening and closing inventory levels differ profit reported under the two methods will be different. In the long run, total profit will be the same whatever method is used.

6.1 Reconciling the profit figures given by the two methods

The **difference in profits** reported under the two costing systems is due to the **different inventory valuation methods** used.

(a) **If inventory levels increase** between the beginning and end of a period, **absorption costing will report the higher profit** because some of the fixed production overhead incurred during the period will be carried forward in closing inventory (which reduces cost of sales) to be set against sales revenue in the following period instead of being written off in full against profit in the period concerned.

(b) **If inventory levels decrease, absorption costing will report the lower profit** because as well as the fixed overhead incurred, fixed production overhead which had been carried forward in opening inventory is released and is also included in cost of sales.

6.2 Example: Reconciling profits

The profits reported for period 1 in the question on page 11 would be reconciled as follows.

	$
Marginal costing profit	400
Adjust for fixed overhead in inventory (inventory increase of 300 units × $1 per unit)	300
Absorption costing profit	700

Exam focus point

Remember that if opening inventory values are greater than closing inventory values, marginal costing shows the greater profit.

6.3 Marginal versus absorption costing: reporting to management

Marginal costing is more **useful** for **decision-making** purposes, but absorption costing is needed for **financial reporting** purposes to comply with accounting standards.

We know that the reported profit in any period is likely to differ according to the costing method used, but does one method provide a more reliable guide to management about the organisation's profit position?

With marginal costing, contribution varies in direct proportion to the volume of units sold. Profits will increase as sales volume rises, by the amount of extra contribution earned. Since fixed cost expenditure does not alter, marginal costing gives an accurate picture of how a firm's cash flows and profits are affected by changes in sales volumes.

With absorption costing, in contrast, **there is no clear relationship between profit and sales volume**, and as sales volume rises the total profit will rise by the sum of the gross profit per unit plus the amount of overhead absorbed per unit. Arguably this is a confusing and unsatisfactory method of monitoring profitability.

If sales volumes are the same from period to period, marginal costing reports the same profit each period (given no change in prices or costs). In contrast, using absorption costing, profits can vary with the volume of production, even when the volume of sales is constant. **Using absorption costing there is therefore the possibility of manipulating profit, simply by changing output and inventory levels.**

6.4 Example: Manipulating profits

Gloom Co budgeted to make and sell 10,000 units of its product in 20X1. The selling price is $10 per unit and the variable cost $4 per unit. Fixed production costs were budgeted at $50,000 for the year. The company uses absorption costing and budgeted an absorption rate of $5 per unit. During 20X1, it became apparent that sales demand would only be 8,000 units. The management, concerned about the apparent effect of the low volume of sales on profits, decided to increase production for the year to 15,000 units. Actual fixed costs were still expected to be $50,000 in spite of the significant increase in production volume.

Required

Calculate the profit at an actual sales volume of 8,000 units, using the following methods.

(a)   Absorption costing
(b)   Marginal costing

Explain the difference in profits calculated.

Solution

(a)   **Absorption costing**

	$	$
Sales (8,000 × $10)		80,000
Cost of production (15,000 × $9)	135,000	
Less: over-absorbed overhead (5,000 × $5)	(25,000)	
		(110,000)
		(30,000)
Closing inventory (7,000 × $9)		63,000
Profit		33,000

(b)   **Marginal costing**

	$	$
Sales		80,000
Cost of sales		
Cost of production (15,000 × $4)	60,000	
Closing inventory (7,000 × $4)	(28,000)	
		32,000
Contribution		48,000
Fixed costs		50,000
Loss		(2,000)

The difference in profits of $35,000 is explained by the **difference in the increase in inventory values** (7,000 units × $5 of fixed overhead per unit). With absorption costing, the expected profit will be higher than the original budget of $10,000 (10,000 units × ($10 – 9)) simply because $35,000 of fixed overheads will be carried forward in closing inventory values. By producing to absorb overhead rather than to satisfy customers, inventory levels will, of course, increase. Unless this inventory is sold, however, there may come a point when production has to stop and the inventory has to be sold off at lower prices. Marginal costing would report a contribution of $6 per unit, or $48,000 in total for 8,000 units, which fails to cover the fixed costs of $50,000 by $2,000.

The argument above is not conclusive, however, because marginal costing is not so useful when **sales fluctuate from month to month because of seasonal variations in sales demand**, but production per month is held constant in order to arrange for an **even flow of output** (and thereby prevent the cost of idle resources in periods of low demand and overtime in periods of high demand).

Question	Absorption v marginal costing

A clothing manufacturer makes a specific brand of jeans which it sells at a standard price of $100 per pair. The manufacturer's costs are as follows.

Standard variable production cost: $16 per pair

Total fixed production cost per month: $240,000 (10,000 pairs are planned to be produced per month)

Total fixed non-production costs: $300,000 per month

In Month 1, when the opening inventory is 1,000 pairs, production of 10,000 pairs is planned and sales of 8,000 pairs are expected.

In Month 2, sales are planned to be 9,000 pairs and production is still 10,000 pairs.

Required

(a)   What would be the net profit for Months 1 and 2 under

    (i)   Absorption costing
    (ii)   Marginal costing

(b)   What comments could you make about the performance of this business?

(a) Absorption standard cost per unit = $16 + 240,000/10,000
                                        = $40

	Absorption costing					Marginal costing			
	Month 1		Month 2			Month 1		Month 2	
	$'000	$'000	$'000	$'000		$'000	$'000	$'000	$'000
Sales 8,000 @$100		800		900			800		900
Cost of sales									
Opening inventory									
(1,000 @ $40)	40		120		1,000 @ $16	16		48	
Production									
(10,000 @ $40)	400		400		10,000 @ $16	160		160	
Less: closing inventory*									
(3,000 @ $40)	(120)		(160)		3,000 @ $16	(48)		(64)	
		(320)		(360)			(128)		(144)
Gross profit		480		540					
Contribution							672		756
Less other costs									
Fixed production						(240)		(240)	
Fixed non-production		(300)		(300)		(300)		(300)	
							(540)		(540)
		180		240			132		216

* Closing inventory = 1,000 + 10,000 – 8,000

(b) The absorption costing net profit is higher than the marginal costing net profit in both months because **inventories are rising**. Under absorption costing, where inventories are increasing, a greater amount of the fixed production cost is carried forward in the closing inventory valuation than was brought forward in the opening inventory valuation.

This means that the impact of these costs on profit is **delayed** under absorption costing. Under marginal costing, the full impact of the fixed production costs on profit is immediate.

The business is profitable and sales have increased. However, a build up of inventories in the clothing manufacturing industry is unwise as demand is subject to tastes and fashion. The business needs to **respond rapidly** to changes in demand or it will become rapidly **uncompetitive**.

Chapter Roundup

- **Costing** is the process of determining the costs of products, services or activities.

- **Indirect costs**, or **overheads**, are costs incurred in making a product or providing a service, but which cannot be traced directly to the product or service. **Absorption costing** is a means of incorporating a fair share of these costs into the cost of a unit of product or service provided.

- **Absorption costing** is a traditional approach to dealing with overheads, involving three stages: allocation, apportionment and absorption.

- **Apportionment** has two stages, general overhead apportionment and service department cost apportionment.

- After apportionment, overheads are **absorbed** into products using an appropriate **absorption rate** based on budgeted costs and budgeted activity levels.

- **Under-/over-absorbed overhead** occurs when overheads incurred do not equal overheads absorbed.

- In **marginal costing**, inventories are valued at variable production cost whereas in absorption costing they are valued at their full production cost.

- If opening and closing inventory levels differ profit reported under the two methods will be different.

  In the long run, total profit will be the same whatever method is used.

- Marginal costing is more **useful** for **decision-making** purposes, but absorption costing is needed for **financial reporting** purposes to comply with accounting standards.

1   Here are some terms you should have encountered in your earlier studies. *Match the term to the definition.*

Terms	Definitions
Direct cost	(a) Specific costs of, say, an activity, which would not be incurred if the activity did not exist
Prime cost	
Overhead	(b) Total of direct costs
Classification by function	(c) Future cash flow which will be changed as the result of a decision
Fixed cost	(d) Product produced by an organisation
Variable cost	(e) Dividing costs into production, administration, selling and distribution, research and development and financing costs
Product cost	
Avoidable cost	(f) Cost that can be traced in full to whatever is being costed
Controllable cost	(g) Organisation's departments
Relevant cost	(h) A cost that varies with the level of output
Cost centre	(i) A cost that is incurred in the course of making a product but which cannot be traced directly and in full to the product
Cost unit	(j) Cost that is incurred for a particular period of time and which, within certain activity levels, is unaffected by changes in the level of activity
	(k) Cost identified with goods produced or purchased for resale and initially included in the value of inventory
	(l) Cost which can be influenced by management decisions and actions

2   .... is the process of determining the costs of products, activities or services.

3   How is an overhead absorption rate calculated?

   A   Estimated overhead ÷ actual activity level
   B   Estimated overhead ÷ budgeted activity level
   C   Actual overhead ÷ actual activity level
   D   Actual overhead ÷ budgeted activity level

4   Over absorption means that the overheads charged to the cost of sales are greater than the overheads actually incurred.

   ☐ True   ☐ False

5   *Fill in the blanks in the statements about marginal costing and absorption costing below.*

   (a)   If inventory levels .... between the beginning and end of a period, absorption costing will report the higher profit.

   (b)   If inventory levels decrease, ... costing will report the lower profit.

6   *Fill in the following blanks with either 'marginal' or 'absorption'.*

   (a)   Using .... costing, profits can be manipulated simply by changing output and inventory levels.

   (b)   Fixed costs are charged in full against the profit of the period in which they are incurred when .... costing is used.

   (c)   .... costing fails to recognise the importance of working to full capacity.

   (d)   .... costing could be argued to be preferable to .... costing in management accounting in order to be consistent with the requirements of accounting standards.

   (e)   .... costing should not be used when decision-making information is required.

Answers to Quick Quiz

1		
Direct cost	(f)
Prime cost	(b)
Overhead	(i)
Classification by function	(e)
Fixed cost	(j)
Variable cost	(h)
Product cost	(k)
Avoidable cost	(a)
Controllable cost	(l)
Relevant cost	(c)
Cost centre	(g)
Cost unit	(d)

2 Costing

3 B

4 True

5 (a) Increase
  (b) Absorption

6 (a) absorption
  (b) marginal
  (c) marginal
  (d) absorption, marginal
  (e) absorption

Now try the questions below from the Exam Question Bank

Number	Level	Marks	Time
Q1	Introductory	10	18 mins

Activity based costing

2a

Topic list	Syllabus reference
1 Activity based costing	A1 (a), (b)
2 Absorption costing versus ABC	A1 (c)
3 Merits and criticisms of ABC	A1 (c)

Introduction

Chapter 2 covers Part A of the syllabus, specialist cost and management accounting techniques. It has been divided into five sub-chapters to reflect the examiner's emphasis that all five techniques are equally important and equally examinable.

In this chapter we will be looking at the first alternative method of cost accumulation, **activity based costing (ABC).** ABC is a modern alternative to absorption costing which attempts to overcome the problems of costing in a modern manufacturing environment.

Study guide

		Intellectual level
A1	**Activity based costing**	
(a)	Identify appropriate cost drivers under ABC	1
(b)	Calculate costs per driver and per unit using ABC	2
(c)	Compare ABC and traditional methods of overhead absorption based on production units, labour hours or machine hours	2

Exam guide

There was a question on ABC in the Pilot Paper for F5. It was also examined in June 2008 and June 2010 and is therefore a crucial topic to understand.

1 Activity based costing

6/08, 6/10

FAST FORWARD

An alternative to absorption costing is **activity based costing (ABC)**.

ABC involves the identification of the factors **(cost drivers)** which cause the costs of an organisation's major activities. Support overheads are charged to products on the basis of their usage of an activity.

- For costs that vary with production level in the short term, the cost driver will be volume related (labour or machine hours).
- Overheads that vary with some other activity (and not volume of production) should be traced to products using transaction-based cost drivers such as production runs or number of orders received.

1.1 Reasons for the development of ABC

The traditional cost accumulation system of **absorption costing** was developed in a time when most organisations produced only a **narrow range of products** (so that products underwent **similar operations** and consumed **similar proportions of overheads**). And **overhead costs were only a very small fraction of total costs**, direct labour and direct material costs accounting for the largest proportion of the costs. The **benefits** of more accurate systems for **overhead allocation** would probably have been relatively **small**. In addition, **information processing costs were high.**

In recent years, however, there has been a **dramatic fall** in the costs of processing information. And, with the advent of **advanced manufacturing technology (AMT)**, **overheads** are likely to be far **more important** and in fact direct labour may account for as little as 5% of a product's cost. It therefore now appears difficult to justify the use of direct labour or direct material as the basis for absorbing overheads or to believe that errors made in attributing overheads will not be significant.

Many resources are used in **non-volume related support activities**, (which have increased due to AMT) such as setting-up, production scheduling, inspection and data processing. These support activities assist the efficient manufacture of a wide range of products and are **not, in general, affected by changes in production volume**. They tend to **vary in the long term according to the range and complexity** of the products manufactured rather than the volume of output.

The wider the range and the more complex the products, the more support services will be required. Consider, for example, factory X which produces 10,000 units of one product, the Alpha, and factory Y which produces 1,000 units each of ten slightly different versions of the Alpha. Support activity costs in the factory Y are likely to be a lot higher than in factory X but the factories produce an identical number of units. For example, factory X will only need to set-up once whereas Factory Y will have to set-up the production run at least ten times for the ten different products. Factory Y will therefore incur more set-up costs for the same volume of production.

Traditional costing systems, which assume that all products consume all resources in proportion to their production volumes, tend to **allocate too great a proportion of overheads to high volume products** (which cause relatively little diversity and hence use fewer support services) and **too small a proportion of overheads to low volume products** (which cause greater diversity and therefore use more support services). Activity based costing (ABC) attempts to overcome this problem.

1.2 Definition of ABC

Key term

> **Activity based costing (ABC)** involves the identification of the factors which cause the costs of an organisation's major activities. Support overheads are charged to products on the basis of their usage of the factor causing the overheads.

The major ideas behind activity based costing are as follows.

(a)   **Activities cause costs**. Activities include ordering, materials handling, machining, assembly, production scheduling and despatching.

(b)   **Producing products creates demand for the activities.**

(c)   Costs are assigned to a product **on the basis of the product's consumption of the activities.**

1.3 Outline of an ABC system

An ABC system operates as follows.

Step 1   Identify an organisation's major activities.

Step 2   Identify the factors which determine the size of the costs of an activity/cause the costs of an activity. These are known as **cost drivers.**

Key term

> A **cost driver** is a factor which causes a change in the cost of an activity.

Look at the following examples.

Costs	Possible cost driver
Ordering costs	Number of orders
Materials handling costs	Number of production runs
Production scheduling costs	Number of production runs
Despatching costs	Number of despatches

Step 3   Collect the costs associated with each cost driver into what are known as **cost pools**.

Step 4   Charge costs to products on the basis of their usage of the activity. A product's usage of an activity is measured by the number of the activity's cost driver it generates.

Question   Cost driver

Which of the following definitions best describes a cost driver?

A   Any activity which causes an increase in costs
B   A collection of costs associated with a particular activity
C   A cost that varies with production levels
D   Any factor which causes a change in the cost of an activity

D   Any factor which causes a change in the cost of an activity.

ABC is a popular exam topic.

Questions on activity based costing often require a comparison with more traditional methods. The implications for the business of each approach is often required.

2 Absorption costing versus ABC   6/08, 6/10

The following example illustrates the point that traditional cost accounting techniques result in a misleading and inequitable division of costs between low-volume and high-volume products, and that ABC can provide a more meaningful allocation of costs.

2.1 Example: Activity based costing

Suppose that Cooplan manufactures four products, W, X, Y and Z. Output and cost data for the period just ended are as follows.

	Output units	Number of production runs in the period	Material cost per unit $	Direct labour hours per unit	Machine hours per unit
W	10	2	20	1	1
X	10	2	80	3	3
Y	100	5	20	1	1
Z	100	5	80	3	3
		14			

Direct labour cost per hour	$5

Overhead costs	$
Short run variable costs	3,080
Set-up costs	10,920
Expediting and scheduling costs	9,100
Materials handling costs	7,700
	30,800

Required

Prepare unit costs for each product using conventional costing and ABC.

Solution

Using a **conventional absorption costing approach** and an absorption rate for overheads based on either direct labour hours or machine hours, the product costs would be as follows.

	W $	X $	Y $	Z $	Total $
Direct material	200	800	2,000	8,000	
Direct labour	50	150	500	1,500	
Overheads *	700	2,100	7,000	21,000	
	950	3,050	9,500	30,500	44,000
Units produced	10	10	100	100	
Cost per unit	$95	$305	$95	$305	

* $30,800 ÷ 440 hours = $70 per direct labour or machine hour.

Using **activity based costing** and assuming that the number of production runs is the cost driver for set-up costs, expediting and scheduling costs and materials handling costs and that machine hours are the cost driver for short-run variable costs, unit costs would be as follows.

	W	X	Y	Z	Total
	$	$	$	$	$
Direct material	200	800	2,000	8,000	
Direct labour	50	150	500	1,500	
Short-run variable overheads (W1)	70	210	700	2,100	
Set-up costs (W2)	1,560	1,560	3,900	3,900	
Expediting, scheduling costs (W3)	1,300	1,300	3,250	3,250	
Materials handling costs (W4)	1,100	1,100	2,750	2,750	
	4,280	5,120	13,100	21,500	44,000
Units produced	10	10	100	100	
Cost per unit	$428	$512	$131	$215	

Workings

1	$3,080 ÷ 440 machine hours =	$7 per machine hour
2	$10,920 ÷ 14 production runs =	$780 per run
3	$9,100 ÷ 14 production runs =	$650 per run
4	$7,700 ÷ 14 production runs =	$550 per run

Summary

Product	Conventional costing unit cost	ABC unit cost	Difference per unit	Difference in total
	$	$	$	$
W	95	428	+ 333	+3,330
X	305	512	+ 207	+2,070
Y	95	131	+ 36	+3,600
Z	305	215	− 90	−9,000

The figures suggest that the traditional volume-based absorption costing system is flawed.

(a) It **underallocates overhead costs to low-volume products** (here, W and X) and **over-allocates overheads to higher-volume products** (here Z in particular).

(b) It **underallocates overhead costs to smaller-sized products** (here W and Y with just one hour of work needed per unit) and **over allocates overheads to larger products** (here X and particularly Z).

2.2 ABC versus traditional costing methods

Both traditional absorption costing and ABC systems adopt the two stage allocation process.

2.2.1 Allocation of overheads

ABC establishes separate cost pools for support activities such as despatching. As the costs of these activities are assigned directly to products through cost driver rates, reapportionment of service department costs is avoided.

2.2.2 Absorption of overheads

The principal difference between the two systems is the way in which overheads are absorbed into products.

(a) Absorption costing most commonly uses two **absorption bases** (labour hours and/or machine hours) to charge overheads to products.

(b) ABC uses many **cost drivers** as absorption bases (eg number of orders or despatches).

Absorption rates under ABC should therefore be more closely linked to the causes of overhead costs.

2.3 Cost drivers

The principal idea of ABC is to focus attention on **what causes costs to increase,** ie the cost drivers.

(a) The **costs that vary with production volume**, such as power costs, should be traced to products using production **volume-related cost drivers**, such as direct labour hours or direct machine hours.

Overheads which do not vary with output but **with some other activity** should be traced to products using **transaction-based cost drivers**, such as number of production runs and number of orders received.

(b) Traditional costing systems allow overheads to be related to products in rather more arbitrary ways producing, it is claimed, less accurate product costs.

Question	Traditional costing versus ABC

A company manufactures two products, L and M, using the same equipment and similar processes. An extract of the production data for these products in one period is shown below.

	L	*M*
Quantity produced (units)	5,000	7,000
Direct labour hours per unit	1	2
Machine hours per unit	3	1
Set-ups in the period	10	40
Orders handled in the period	15	60

Overhead costs	$
Relating to machine activity	220,000
Relating to production run set-ups	20,000
Relating to handling of orders	45,000
	285,000

Required

Calculate the production overheads to be absorbed by one unit of each of the products using the following costing methods.

(a) A traditional costing approach using a direct labour hour rate to absorb overheads
(b) An activity based costing approach, using suitable cost drivers to trace overheads to products

Answer

(a) **Traditional costing approach**

	Direct labour hours
Product L = 5,000 units × 1 hour	5,000
Product M = 7,000 units × 2 hours	14,000
	19,000

$$\therefore \text{Overhead absorption rate} = \frac{\$285,000}{19,000}$$

$$= \$15 \text{ per hour}$$

Overhead absorbed would be as follows.

Product L	1 hour × $15	=	$15 per unit
Product M	2 hours × $15	=	$30 per unit

(b) **ABC approach**

		Machine hours
Product L	= 5,000 units × 3 hours	15,000
Product M	= 7,000 units × 1 hour	7,000
		22,000

Using ABC the overhead costs are absorbed according to the cost drivers.

	$			
Machine-hour driven costs	220,000	÷	22,000 m/c hours	= $10 per m/c hour
Set-up driven costs	20,000	÷	50 set-ups	= $400 per set-up
Order driven costs	45,000	÷	75 orders	= $600 per order

Overhead costs are therefore as follows.

		Product L		Product M
		$		$
Machine-driven costs	(15,000 hrs × $10)	150,000	(7,000 hrs × $10)	70,000
Set-up costs	(10 × $400)	4,000	(40 × $400)	16,000
Order handling costs	(15 × $600)	9,000	(60 × $600)	36,000
		163,000		122,000
Units produced		5,000		7,000
Overhead cost per unit		$32.60		$17.43

These figures suggest that product M absorbs an unrealistic amount of overhead using a direct labour hour basis. Overhead absorption should be based on the activities which drive the costs, in this case machine hours, the number of production run set-ups and the number of orders handled for each product.

3 Merits and criticisms of ABC   6/10

FAST FORWARD

> ABC has both advantages and disadvantages, and tends to be more widely used by larger organisations and the service sector.

As you will have discovered when you attempted the question above, there is nothing difficult about ABC. Once the necessary information has been obtained it is similar to traditional absorption costing. This simplicity is part of its appeal. Further merits of ABC are as follows.

(a) The **complexity of manufacturing has increased**, with wider product ranges, shorter product life cycles and more complex production processes. **ABC recognises this complexity with its multiple cost drivers.**

(b) In a more competitive environment, companies must be able to assess product profitability realistically. **ABC facilitates a good understanding of what drives overhead costs**.

(c) In modern manufacturing systems, overhead functions include a lot of non-factory-floor activities such as product design, quality control, production planning and customer services. **ABC is concerned with all overhead costs** and so it takes management accounting beyond its 'traditional' factory floor boundaries.

3.1 ABC and decision making

Many of ABC's supporters claim that it can assist with decision making in a number of ways.

- Provides accurate and reliable cost information
- Establishes a long-run product cost
- Provides data which can be used to evaluate different ways of delivering business.

It is therefore particularly suited to the following types of decision.

- Pricing
- Promoting or discontinuing products or parts of the business
- Redesigning products and developing new products or new ways to do business

Note, however, that an ABC cost is **not a true cost**, it is **simply an average cost** because some costs such as depreciation are still arbitrarily allocated to products. An ABC cost is therefore **not a relevant cost** for all decisions.

The traditional cost behaviour patterns of fixed cost and variable cost are felt by advocates of ABC to be **unsuitable** for longer-term decisions, when resources are not fixed and changes in the volume or mix of business can be expected to have an impact on the cost of all resources used, not just short-term variable costs.

ABC attempts to **relate the incidence of costs to the level of activities undertaken**. A **hierarchy of activities** has been suggested.

Classification level	Cause of cost	Types of cost	Cost driver
Unit level	Production/acquisition of a single unit of product or delivery of single unit of service	Direct materials Direct labour	Units produced
Batch level	A group of things being made, handled or processed	Purchase orders Set-ups Inspection	Batches produced
Product level	Development, production or acquisition of different items	Equipment maintenance Product development	Product lines produced
Facility sustaining level	Some costs cannot be related to a particular product line, instead they are related to maintaining the buildings and facilities. These costs cannot be related to cost objects with any degree of accuracy and are often excluded from ABC calculations for this reason.	Building depreciation Organisational advertising	None - supports the overall production or service process

3.2 Criticisms of ABC

It has been suggested by critics that **activity based costing has some serious flaws**.

(a) Some measure of (arbitrary) cost apportionment may still be required at the cost pooling stage for items like rent, rates and building depreciation.

(b) Can a single cost driver explain the cost behaviour of all items in its associated pool?

(c) Unless costs are caused by an activity that is measurable in quantitative terms and which can be related to production output, cost drivers will not be usable. What drives the cost of the annual external audit, for example?

(d) ABC is sometimes introduced because it is fashionable, not because it will be used by management to provide meaningful product costs or extra information. If management is not going to use ABC information, an absorption costing system may be simpler to operate.

(e) The cost of implementing and maintaining an ABC system can exceed the benefits of improved accuracy.

(f) **Implementing** ABC is often problematic.

Chapter Roundup

- An alternative to absorption costing is **activity based costing (ABC).**

  ABC involves the identification of the factors **(cost drivers)** which cause the costs of an organisation's major activities. Support overheads are charged to products on the basis of their usage of an activity.

  – For costs that vary with production level in the short term, the cost driver will be volume related (labour or machine hours).

  – Overheads that vary with some other activity (and not volume of production) should be traced to products using transaction-based cost drivers such as production runs or number of orders received

- ABC has both advantages and disadvantages, and tends to be more widely used by larger organisations and the service sector.

Quick Quiz

1   *Choose the correct phrases.*

    Traditional costing systems tend to allocate **too great/too small** a proportion of overheads to high volume products and **too great/too small** a proportion of overheads to low volume products.

2   *Fill in the blanks.*

    The major ideas behind ABC are as follows.

    (a)   Activities cause ....

    (b)   Producing products creates demand for the ....

    (c)   Costs are assigned to a product on the basis of the product's consumption of the

          ....

3   *Match the most appropriate cost driver to each cost.*

	Costs	Cost driver
(a)	Set-up costs	Number of machine hours
(b)	Short-run variable costs	Number of production runs
(c)	Materials handling and despatch	Number of orders executed

4   ABC recognises the complexity of modern manufacturing by the use of multiple cost pools. True or false?

5   The use of direct labour hours or direct machine hours to trace costs to products occurs with the use of absorption costing but not with the use of ABC. True or false?

6   The cost driver for quality inspection is likely to be batch size. **True or false?**

7   ABC is not a system that is suitable for use by service organisations. **True or false?**

Answers to Quick Quiz

1   Too great
    Too small

2   (a)   Costs
    (b)   Activities
    (c)   Activities

3   (a)   Number of production runs
    (b)   Number of machine hours
    (c)   Number of orders executed

4   False. Complexity is recognised by the use of multiple cost drivers.

5   False. The use of volume-related cost drivers should be used for costs that do vary with production volume.

6   False

7   False. It is highly suitable.

Now try the questions below from the Exam Question Bank

Number	Level	Marks	Time
Q2	Introductory	18	32 mins
Q3	Examination	20	36 mins

Target costing

Topic list	Syllabus reference
1 What is target costing?	A2 (a)
2 Implementing target costing	A2 (a)
3 Deriving a target cost	A2 (a)
4 Closing a target cost gap	A2 (c)
5 Target costing in service industries	A2 (b)

Introduction

Target costing is the second specialist cost accounting technique we will
consider. In the modern competitive environment, organisations have to
continually redesign their products or services and it is essential that they try to
achieve a target cost during product and process development.

Target costing is a cost management process which involves setting a target
cost by subtracting a desired profit margin from a competitive market price.

Study guide

		Intellectual level
A2	**Target costing**	
(a)	Derive a target cost in manufacturing and service industries	2
(b)	Explain the difficulties of using target costing in service industries	2
(c)	Suggest how a target cost gap might be closed	2

Exam guide

Target costing may form part of a question comparing its use to other costing techniques or it may form an entire question including calculation of a target cost.

1 What is target costing?   12/07

FAST FORWARD

> **Target costing** involves setting a target cost by subtracting a desired profit margin from a competitive market price.

To compete effectively, organisations must continually redesign their products (or services) in order to shorten **product life cycles** (see Chapter 2c). The **planning, development and design stage** of a product is therefore **critical** to an organisation's cost management process. Considering possible **cost reductions at this stage** of a product's life cycle (rather than during the production process) is now one of the most **important** issues facing management accountants in industry.

Here are some examples of **decisions made at the design stage** which **impact on the cost of a product.**

- The number of different components
- Whether the components are standard or not
- The ease of changing over tools

Japanese companies have developed target costing as a response to the **problem of controlling and reducing costs** over the product life cycle.

Key terms

> **Target costing** involves setting a target cost by subtracting a desired profit margin from a competitive market price.
>
> **Target cost** is an estimate of a product cost which is determined by subtracting a desired profit margin from a competitive market price. This target cost may be less than the planned initial product cost but it is expected to be achieved by the time the product reaches the maturity stage of the product life cycle.

2 Implementing target costing

In 'Product costing/pricing strategy' (*ACCA Students Newsletter*, August 1999),one of the examiners provided a useful summary of the steps in the implementation of the target costing process.

Step 1   Determine a product specification of which an adequate sales volume is estimated.

Step 2   Set a selling price at which the organisation will be able to achieve a desired market share.

Step 3   Estimate the required profit based on return on sales or return on investment.

Step 4   Calculate the target cost = target selling price – target profit.

Step 5   Compile an estimated cost for the product based on the anticipated design specification and current cost levels.

Step 6   Calculate target cost gap = estimated cost – target cost.

Step 7 Make efforts to close the gap. This is more likely to be successful if efforts are made to 'design out' costs prior to production, rather than to 'control out' costs during the production phase.

Step 8 Negotiate with the customer before making the decision about whether to go ahead with the project.

Case Study

Swedish retailer Ikea continues to dominate the home furniture market with more than 300 stores across 35 countries at the end of 2009. The "Ikea concept" as defined on the company website www.ikea.com is "based on offering a wide range of well designed functional home furnishing products at prices so low as many people as possible will be able to afford them."

Ikea is widely known for pricing products at 30-50% below the price charged by competitors. Extracts from the website outline how the company has successfully employed a strategy of target pricing:

"While most retailers use design to justify a higher price, IKEA designers work in exactly the opposite way. Instead they use design to secure the lowest possible price. IKEA designers design every IKEA product starting with a functional need and a price. Then they use their vast knowledge of innovative, low-cost manufacturing processes to create functional products, often co-ordinated in style. Then large volumes are purchased to push prices down even further.

Most IKEA products are also designed to be transported in flat packs and assembled at the customer's home. This lowers the price by minimising transportation and storage costs. In this way, the IKEA Concept uses design to ensure that IKEA products can be purchased and enjoyed by as many people as possible."

3 Deriving a target cost

The target cost is calculated by starting with a market-based price and subtracting a desired profit margin. The target cost is simply the price minus the profit.

3.1 Example: target costing

A car manufacturer wants to calculate a target cost for a new car, the price of which will be set at $17,950. The company requires an 8% profit margin.

Required

What is the target cost?

Solution

Profit required = 8% × $17,950 = $1,436
Target cost = $(17,950 − 1,436) = $16,514

The car manufacturer will then need to carefully compile an estimated cost for the new car. ABC will help to ensure that costs allocated to the new model are more accurate.

3.2 Example: target costing and the target cost gap

Great Games, a manufacturer of computer games, is in the process of introducing a new game to the market and has undertaken market research to find out about customers' views on the value of the product and also to obtain a comparison with competitors' products. The results of this research have been used to establish a target selling price of $60.

Cost estimates have been prepared based on the proposed product specification.

Manufacturing cost	$
Direct material	3.21
Direct Labour	24.03
Direct machinery costs	1.12
Ordering and receiving	0.23
Quality assurance	4.60
Non-manufacturing costs	
Marketing	8.15
Distribution	3.25
After-sales service	1.30

The target profit margin for the game is 30% of the proposed selling price

Required

Calculate the target cost of the new game and the target cost gap.

Solution

	$
Target selling price	60.00
Target profit margin (30% of selling price)	18.00
Target cost (60.00 – 18.00)	42.00
Projected cost	45.89

The projected cost exceeds the target cost by $3.89. This is the target cost gap. Great Games will therefore have to investigate ways to drive the actual cost down to the target cost.

4 Closing a target cost gap   12/07

The **target cost gap** is the estimated cost less the target cost. When a product is first manufactured, its target cost may well be much lower than its currently-attainable cost, which is determined by current technology and processes. Management can then set **benchmarks for improvement** towards the target costs, by improving technologies and processes. Various techniques can be employed.

- Reducing the **number of components**
- Using **standard components** wherever possible
- **Training** staff in more efficient techniques
- Using **different materials**

- Using **cheaper staff**
- Acquiring new, more efficient **technology**
- Cutting out **non-value-added activities** (identified using **activity analysis** etc)

Even if the product can be produced within the target cost the story does not end there. Target costing can be applied throughout the entire life cycle. Once the product goes into production target costs will therefore gradually be reduced. These reductions will be incorporated into the budgeting process. This means that cost savings must be actively sought and made continuously over the life of the product.

Exam focus point

> When answering a question on closing a target cost gap, make sure you refer to the specific circumstances of the business in the question.

5 Target costing in service industries

Target costing is difficult to use in service industries due to the **characteristics** and **information requirements** of service businesses.

5.1 Characteristics of services

FAST FORWARD

Unlike manufacturing companies, services are characterised by **intangibility, inseparability, variability, perishability** and no **transfer of ownership.**

Examples of service businesses include:

(a) **Mass service** eg the banking sector, transportation (rail, air), mass entertainment
(b) **Either / or** eg fast food, teaching, hotels and holidays, psychotherapy
(c) **Personal service** eg pensions and financial advice, car maintenance

Key term

Services are any activity of benefit that one party can offer to another that is essentially intangible and does not result in the ownership of anything. Its production may or may not be tied to a physical product.'

(P Kotler, *Social Marketing*)

There are **five major characteristics** of services that distinguish services from manufacturing.

(a) **Intangibility** refers to the lack of substance which is involved with service delivery. Unlike goods (physical products such as confectionery), there is no substantial material or physical aspects to a service: no taste, feel, visible presence and so on. For example, if you go to the theatre, you cannot take the 'play' with you.

(b) **Inseparability/simultaneity.** Many services are created at the same time as they are consumed. (Think of dental treatment.) No service exists until it is actually being experienced/consumed by the person who has bought it.

(c) **Variability/heterogeneity.** Many services face the problem of maintaining consistency in the standard of output. It may be hard to attain precise standardisation of the service offered, but customers expect it (such as with fast food).

(d) **Perishability.** Services are innately perishable. The services of a beautician are purchased for a period of time.

(e) **No transfer of ownership.** Services do not result in the transfer of property. The purchase of a service only confers on the customer access to or a right to use a facility.

5.2 Information requirements of services

FAST FORWARD

Service businesses need the same aggregate information as manufacturing firms, but also need performance data as to their cost and volume drivers. Operational information is likely to be more qualitative.

A service business needs a mix of **quantitative** and **non-quantitative** information to price its services properly, to optimise capacity utilisation and to monitor performance.

(a) They need to control the **total cost** of providing the **service operation**.
(b) They need positive **cash flow** to **finance activities**.
(c) They need **operating information** to identify how costs are incurred and on what services.

Arguably, small service businesses, whose expenses are mainly overheads, provide a model, in miniature, of the requirements of **activity based costing**.

Are **'mass services'** any different?

(a) Because mass services, such as cheque clearing, are largely automated, there may be a large **fixed cost base**.

(b) Even if a service is heavily automated, each time the service is performed is a 'moment of truth' for the customer. Ensuring consistency and quality is important but this is true for small service businesses too.

Service industries, perhaps more than manufacturing firms, **rely on their staff**. Front-line staff are those who convey the 'service' – and the experience of the brand – to the consumer. They convey the 'moment of truth' with the customer.

For service businesses, **management accounting information** should **incorporate** the **key drivers of service costs**.

- Repeat business
- Churn rate (for subscriptions)*
- Customer satisfaction surveys, complaints
- Opportunity costs of not providing a service
- Avoidable / unavoidable costs

* For any given period of time, the number of participants who discontinue their use of a service divided by the average number of total participants is the churn rate. Churn rate provides insight into the growth or decline of the subscriber base as well as the average length of participation in the service.

Chapter Roundup

- **Target costing** involves setting a target cost by subtracting a desired profit margin from a competitive market price.

- Unlike manufacturing companies, services are characterised by **intangibility, inseparability, variability, perishability** and no **transfer of ownership.**

- **Service businesses need the same aggregate information** as manufacturing firms, but also need performance data as to their cost and volume drivers. Operational information is likely to be more qualitative.

Quick Quiz

1   *Fill in the blanks using words from the list (a) to (h).*

    Target cost   = ... – ....
    Cost gap   = ... – ....

    (a)   target cost   (e)   target selling price
    (b)   cost gap   (f)   estimated cost
    (c)   budgeted selling price   (g)   estimated selling price
    (d)   production cost   (h)   target profit

2   Which of the following are the five major characteristics of services that distinguish services from manufacturing?

    (a)   Intangibility   (e)   Heterogeneity
    (b)   Perishability   (f)   Variability
    (c)   Inseparability   (g)   Simultaneity
    (d)   No transfer of ownership

Answers to Quick Quiz

1   Target cost = estimated selling price – target profit
    Cost gap = estimated cost – target cost

2   This was a bit of a trick question as there are no 'odd ones out'. Inseparability and simultaneity mean the same thing, as do variability and heterogeneity.

Lifecycle costing

Topic list	Syllabus reference
1 What are life cycle costs?	A3 (a)
2 The product life cycle	A3 (c)
3 Life cycle costing in manufacturing and service industries	A3 (b)

Introduction

Life cycle costing is the third specialist cost accounting technique we will consider. It accumulates costs over a **product's life** rather than on a periodic basis and enables the determination of the **total profitability** of any given product.

Study guide

Exam guide

Life cycle costing will probably form part of a question on costing techniques but it has equal weighting in the syllabus as the other management accounting techniques, so could form an entire question.

1 What are life cycle costs?   12/08

FAST FORWARD

Life cycle costing tracks and accumulates costs and revenues attributable to each product over the entire product life cycle.

A product's life cycle costs are incurred **from its design stage through development to market launch, production and sales, and finally to its eventual withdrawal from the market**. The component elements of a product's cost over its life cycle could therefore include the following.

- **Research & development costs**

    - Design
    - Testing
    - Production process and equipment

- The **cost of purchasing any technical data** required

- **Training costs** (including initial operator training and skills updating)

- **Production costs**

- **Distribution costs**. Transportation and handling costs

- **Marketing costs**

    - Customer service
    - Field maintenance
    - Brand promotion

- **Inventory costs** (holding spare parts, warehousing and so on)

- **Retirement and disposal costs**. Costs occurring at the end of a product's life

Life cycle costs can apply to **services**, customers and projects as well as to physical products.

Traditional cost accumulation systems are based on the financial accounting year and tend to dissect a product's life cycle into a series of 12-month periods. This means that traditional management accounting systems **do not accumulate costs over a product's entire life cycle** and **do not** therefore **assess a product's profitability over its entire life**. Instead they do it on a periodic basis.

Life cycle costing, on the other hand, **tracks and accumulates actual costs and revenues** attributable to each product **over the entire product life cycle**. Hence the total profitability of any given product can be determined.

Key term

> **Life cycle costing** is the accumulation of costs over a product's entire life.

2 The product life cycle

A **product life cycle** can be divided into five phases.

- Development
- Introduction
- Growth

- Maturity
- Decline

Every product goes through a life cycle.

(a) **Development.** The product has a research and development stage where costs are incurred but no revenue is generated.

(b) **Introduction**. The product is introduced to the market. Potential customers will be unaware of the product or service, and the organisation may have to spend further on advertising to bring the product or service to the attention of the market.

(c) **Growth**. The product gains a bigger market as demand builds up. Sales revenues increase and the product begins to make a profit.

(d) **Maturity**. Eventually, the growth in demand for the product will slow down and it will enter a period of relative maturity. It will continue to be profitable. The product may be modified or improved, as a means of sustaining its demand.

(e) **Decline**. At some stage, the market will have bought enough of the product and it will therefore reach 'saturation point'. Demand will start to fall. Eventually it will become a loss-maker and this is the time when the organisation should decide to stop selling the product or service.

The level of sales and profits earned over a life cycle can be illustrated diagrammatically as follows.

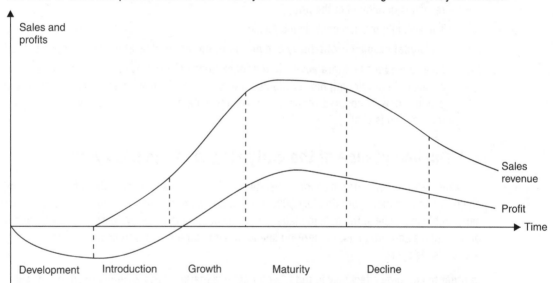

The horizontal axis measures the duration of **the life cycle**, which **can last** from, say, **18 months to several hundred years**. Children's crazes or fad products have very short lives while some products, such as binoculars (invented in the eighteenth century) can last a very long time.

2.1 Problems with traditional cost accumulation systems

Traditional cost accumulation systems do not tend to relate **research and development costs** to the products that caused them. Instead they **write off** these costs on an annual basis **against** the **revenue generated by existing products**. This makes the existing products seem **less profitable** than they really are. If research and development costs are not related to the causal product the true profitability of that product cannot be assessed.

Traditional cost accumulation systems usually **total all non-production costs** and record them as a **period expense**.

2.2 The benefits of life cycle costing

There are a number of benefits associated with life cycle costing.

(a)   The life cycle concept results in earlier actions to generate revenue or to lower costs than otherwise might be considered.

(b)   Better decisions should follow from a more accurate and realistic assessment of revenues and costs, at least within a particular life cycle stage.

(c)   Life cycle thinking can promote long-term rewarding in contrast to short-term profitability rewarding.

(d)   The life cycle concept helps managers to understand acquisition costs vs. operating and support costs. It encourages businesses to find a correct balance between investment costs and operating expenses.

3 Life cycle costing in manufacturing and service industries

Both manufacturing and service industries take similar steps to ensure that returns are maximised over the product/service life cycle.

With life cycle costing, non-production costs are traced to individual products over complete life cycles.

(a)   The total of these costs for each individual product can therefore be reported and compared with revenues generated in the future.

(b)   The visibility of such costs is increased.

(c)   **Individual product profitability can be better understood** by attributing *all* costs to products.

(d)   As a consequence, **more accurate feedback information** is available on the organisation's success or failure in developing new products. In today's competitive environment, where the ability to produce new or updated versions of products is paramount to the survival of an organisation, this information is vital.

3.1 The importance of the early stages of the life cycle

It is reported that some organisations operating within an **advanced manufacturing technology** environment find that approximately 90% of a product's life cycle cost is determined by decisions made early within the cycle at the design stage. Life cycle costing is therefore particularly suited to such organisations and products, monitoring spending and commitments to spend during the early stages of a product's life cycle.

In order to compete effectively in today's competitive market, organisations need to **redesign continually their products** with the result that **product life cycles** have become much **shorter**. The **planning, design and development stages of a product's cycle** are therefore **critical** to an organisation's cost management process. Cost reduction at this stage of a product's life cycle, rather than during the production process, is one of the most important ways of reducing product cost.

Exam focus point

In December 2008, the examiner wanted candidates to realise that a product's performance may look good until initial development costs are included.

3.2 Maximising the return over the product life cycle

3.2.1 Design costs out of products

Between 70% to 90% of a product's life cycle costs are determined by decisions made early in the life cycle, at the design or development stage. Careful design of the product and manufacturing and other processes will keep cost to a minimum over the life cycle.

3.2.2 Minimise the time to market

This is the time from the conception of the product to its launch. More products come onto the market nowadays and development times have been reduced over the years. Competitors watch each other very carefully to determine what types of product their rivals are developing. If an organisation is launching a new product it is vital to get it to the market place as soon as possible. This will give the product as long a period as possible without a rival in the market place and should mean increased market share in the long run. Furthermore, the life span may not proportionally lengthen if the product's launch is delayed and so sales may be permanently lost. It is not unusual for the product's overall profitability to fall by 25% if the launch is delayed by six months. This means that it is usually worthwhile incurring extra costs to keep the launch on schedule or to speed up the launch.

3.2.3 Minimise breakeven time (BET)

A short BET is very important in keeping an organisation liquid. The sooner the product is launched the quicker the research and development costs will be repaid, providing the organisation with funds to develop further products.

3.2.4 Maximise the length of the life span

Product life cycles are not predetermined; they are set by the actions of management and competitors. Once developed, some products lend themselves to a number of different uses; this is especially true of materials, such as plastic, PVC, nylon and other synthetic materials. The life cycle of the material is then a series of individual product curves nesting on top of each other as shown below.

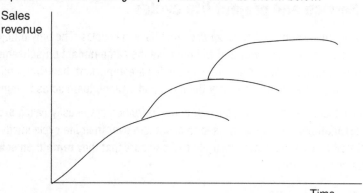

By entering different national or regional markets one after another an organisation may be able to maximise revenue. This allows resources to be better applied, and sales in each market to be maximised. On the other hand, in today's fast moving world, an organisation could lose out to a competitor if it failed to establish an early presence in a particular market.

3.2.5 Minimise product proliferation

If products are updated or superseded too quickly, the life cycle is cut short and the product may just cover its R and D costs before its successor is launched.

3.2.6 Manage the product's cashflows

Hewlett-Packard developed a **return map** to manage the lifecycle of their products. Here is an example.

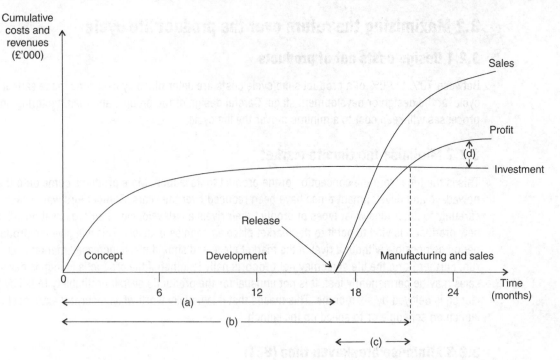

Key time periods are measured by the map:

(a)   Time to market
(b)   Breakeven time
(c)   Breakeven time after product launch
(d)   Return factor (the excess of profit over the investment)

Changes to planned time periods can be incorporated into the map (for example, if the development plan takes longer than expected) and the resulting changes to the return factor at set points after release highlighted.

3.3 Service and project life cycles

A service organisation will have services that have life cycles. The only difference is that the **R & D stages** will not exist in the same way and will not have the same **impact** on subsequent costs. The **different processes** that go to form the complete service are important, however, and consideration should be given in advance as to how to carry them out and arrange them so as to minimise cost.

Products that take years to produce or come to fruition are usually called **projects**, and **discounted cash flow calculations** are invariably used to cost them over their life cycle in advance. The projects need to be **monitored** very carefully over their life to make sure that they **remain on schedule** and that **cost overruns** are not being incurred.

3.4 Customer life cycles

Customers also have life cycles, and an organisation will wish to **maximise the return from a customer over their life cycle**. The aim is to **extend the life cycle of a particular customer** or decrease the 'churn' rate, as the Americans say. This means **encouraging customer loyalty**. For example, some supermarkets and other retail outlets issue **loyalty cards** that offer discounts to loyal customers who return to the shop and spend a certain amount with the organisation. As existing customers tend to be more profitable than new ones they should be retained wherever possible.

Customers become more profitable over their life cycle. The profit can go on increasing for a period of between approximately four and 20 years. For example, if you open a bank account, take out insurance or invest in a pension, the company involved has to set up the account, run checks and so on. The initial cost is high and the company will be keen to retain your business so that it can recoup this cost. Once customers get used to their supplier they tend to use them more frequently, and so there is a double benefit in holding on to customers. For example, you may use the bank to purchase shares on your behalf, or you may take out a second insurance policy with the same company.

The projected cash flows over the full lives of customers or customer segments can be analysed to highlight the worth of customers and the importance of customer retention. It may take a year or more to **recoup the initial costs of winning a customer**, and this could be referred to as the **payback period** of the investment in the customer.

Question   Lifecycle costing

Solaris specialises in the manufacture of solar panels. It is planning to introduce a new slimline solar panel specially designed for small houses. Development of the new panel is to begin shortly and Solaris is in the process of determining the price of the panel. It expects the new product to have the following costs.

	Year 1	Year 2	Year 3	Year 4
Units manufactured and sold	2,000	15,000	20,000	5,000
	$	$	$	$
R&D costs	1,900,000	100,000	-	-
Marketing costs	100,000	75,000	50,000	10,000
Production cost per unit	500	450	400	450
Customer service costs per unit	50	40	40	40
Disposal of specialist equipment				300,000

The Marketing Director believes that customers will be prepared to pay $500 for a solar panel but the Financial Director believes this will not cover all of the costs throughout the lifecycle.

Required

Calculate the cost per unit looking at the whole life cycle and comment on the suggested price.

Answer

Lifecycle costs

	$'000
R&D (1,900 + 100)	2,000
Marketing (100 + 75 + 50 + 10)	235
Production (1,000 + 6,750 + 8,000 + 2,250)	18,000
Customer service (100 + 600 + 800 + 200)	1,700
Disposal	300
Total lifecycle costs	22,235
Total production ('000 units)	42
Cost per unit	529.40

The total lifecycle costs are $529.40 per solar panel which is higher than the price proposed by the marketing director. Solaris will either have to charge a higher price or look at ways to reduce costs.

It may be difficult to increase the price if customers are price sensitive and are not prepared to pay more. Costs could be reduced by analysing each part of the costs throughout the life cycle and actively seeking cost savings. For example, using different materials, using cheaper staff or acquiring more efficient technology.

Chapter Roundup

- **Life cycle costing** tracks and accumulates costs and revenues attributable to each product over the entire product life cycle.

- A **product life cycle** can be divided into five phases.
  - Development   – Maturity
  - Introduction   – Decline
  - Growth

- Both manufacturing and service industries take similar steps to ensure that returns are maximised over the product/service life cycle.

Quick Quiz

1   *Match the following costs to the appropriate life cycle cost classification.*

Costs	Classifications
Design	Inventory costs
Energy costs	Acquisition costs
Warehousing	Maintenance costs
Transportation	Operation costs
Customer service	Product distribution costs

2   Life cycle costing is the profiling of cost over a product's production life.

☐ True   ☐ False

3   Life cycle costing is particularly useful in an AMT environment, where 10% of a product's life cycle costs might be determined by decisions made early within the cycle at the design stage. True or false?

Answers to Quick Quiz

1
Cost	Classification
Design	Acquisition costs
Energy costs	Operation costs
Warehousing	Inventory costs
Transportation	Product distribution costs
Customer service	Maintenance costs

2   False. It also looks at development costs and so on which are incurred prior to production, and any dismantling costs, which are incurred once production ceases.

3   False. The percentage is usually much higher.

Now try the questions below from the Exam Question Bank

Number	Level	Marks	Time
Q4	Introductory	17	31 mins

Throughput accounting

Topic list	Syllabus reference
1 Theory of constraints	A4
2 Throughput accounting	A4
3 Performance measures in throughput accounting	A4 (a), (b)
4 Throughput and decision making	A4 (c)

Introduction

Throughput accounting is the fourth management accounting technique in Section A of the syllabus. It has developed in response to the use of just-in-time and uses the **theory of constraints**. An objective for an organisation is to **maximise throughput** by identifying and eliminating **bottlenecks**.

Study guide

		Intellectual level
A4	**Throughput accounting**	
(a)	Calculate and interpret a throughput accounting ratio (TPAR)	2
(b)	Suggest how a TPAR could be improved	2
(c)	Apply throughput accounting to a multi-product decision-making problem	2

Exam guide

Questions on this topic are likely to be a mixture of calculation and discussion. You may be required to use your knowledge of limiting factors from previous studies.

1 Theory of constraints

FAST FORWARD

Throughput accounting is a product management system which aims to maximise throughput, and therefore cash generation from sales, rather than profit. A **just in time (JIT)** environment is operated, with buffer inventory kept only when there is a **bottleneck resource**.

The theory of constraints (TOC) is an **approach to production management** formulated by Goldratt and Cox in the USA in 1986. Its key financial concept is to turn materials into sales as quickly as possible, thereby maximising the net cash generated from sales. This is achieved by striving for balance in production processes, and so evenness of production flow is also an important aim.

Key terms

Theory of constraints (TOC) is an approach to production management which aims to maximise sales revenue less material and variable overhead cost. It focuses on factors such as bottlenecks which act as constraints to this maximisation.

Bottleneck resource or **binding constraint** – an activity which has a lower capacity than preceding or subsequent activities, thereby limiting throughput.

One process will inevitably act as a **bottleneck** (or limiting factor) and constrain throughput – this is known as the **binding constraint** in TOC terminology. Steps should be taken to remove this by buying more equipment, improving production flow and so on. But ultimately there will always be a binding constraint, unless capacity is far greater than sales demand or all processes are totally in balance, which is unlikely.

Output through the binding constraint should never be delayed or held up otherwise sales will be lost. To avoid this happening a **buffer inventory** should be built up immediately prior to the bottleneck or binding constraint. This is the only inventory that the business should hold, with the exception of possibly a very small amount of finished goods inventory and raw materials that are consistent with the JIT approach.

Operations prior to the binding constraint should operate at the same speed as the binding constraint, otherwise work in progress (other than the buffer inventory) will be built up. According to TOC, inventory costs money in terms of storage space and interest costs, and so **inventory is not desirable**.

Goldratt devised a **five-step approach** to summarise the key stages of **TOC**.

Step 1   **Identify** the constraint.

Step 2   Decide how to **exploit** the constraint.

Step 3   **Subordinate** and **synchronise** everything else to the decisions made in **step 2**.

Step 4   **Elevate** the performance of the constraint.

Step 5   If the **constraint has shifted** during any of the above steps, go back to **step 1**. Do not allow inertia to cause a new constraint.

The overall aim of TOC is to **maximise throughput contribution** (sales revenue – material cost) while keeping **conversion cost** (all operating costs except material costs) and **investment costs** (inventory, equipment and so on) to the **minimum.** A strategy for increasing throughput contribution will only be accepted if conversion and investment costs increase by a lower amount than the increase in contribution.

1.1 Example: An illustration of the theory of constraints

Machine X can process 1,000 kg of raw material per hour, machine Y 800 kg. Of an input of 900 kg, 100 kg of processed material must wait on the bottleneck machine (machine Y) at the end of an hour of processing.

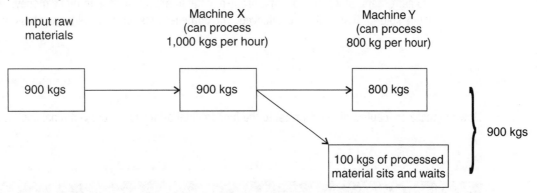

The **traditional view** is that **machines should be working, not sitting idle**. So if the desired output from the above process were 8,100 kgs, **machine X would be kept in continual use** and all 8,100 kgs would be processed through the machine in nine hours. There would be a **backlog** of 900 kgs [8,100 – (9 hrs × 800)] of processed material in front of machine Y, however. All this material **would require handling** and **storage space** and **create the additional costs related to these non-value added activities**. Its **processing would not increase throughput contribution.**

2 Throughput accounting

The concept of throughput accounting has been developed from TOC as an alternative system of cost and management accounting in a **JIT** environment.

Key term

> **Throughput accounting (TA)** is an approach to accounting which is largely in sympathy with the JIT philosophy. In essence, TA assumes that a manager has a given set of resources available. These comprise existing buildings, capital equipment and labour force. Using these resources, purchased materials and parts must be processed to generate sales revenue. Given this scenario the most appropriate financial objective to set for doing this is the maximisation of throughput (Goldratt and Cox, 1984) which is defined as: sales revenue *less* direct material cost.
>
> (Tanaka, Yoshikawa, Innes and Mitchell, *Contemporary Cost Management*)

TA for JIT is said to be based on three concepts.

(a) **Concept 1**

In the short run, most costs in the factory (with the exception of materials costs) are **fixed** (the opposite of ABC, which assumes that all costs are variable). These fixed costs include direct labour. It is useful to group all these costs together and call them **Total Factory Costs (TFC)**.

(b) **Concept 2**

In a JIT environment, all inventory is a 'bad thing' and the **ideal inventory level is zero.** Products should not be made unless a customer has ordered them. When goods are made, the factory effectively operates at the rate of the slowest process, and there will be unavoidable idle capacity in other operations.

Work in progress should be **valued at material cost only** until the output is eventually sold, so that no value will be added and no profit earned until the sale takes place. Working on output just to add to work in progress or finished goods inventory creates no profit, and so should not be encouraged.

(c) **Concept 3**

Profitability is determined by the rate at which 'money comes in at the door' (that is, sales are made) and, in a JIT environment, this depends on **how quickly** goods can be produced to satisfy customer orders. Since the goal of a profit-orientated organisation is to make money, inventory must be sold for that goal to be achieved. The bottleneck resource slows the process of making money.

Question

How are these concepts a direct contrast to the fundamental principles of conventional cost accounting?

Answer

Conventional cost accounting	Throughput accounting
Inventory is an asset.	Inventory is not an asset. It is a result of unsynchronised manufacturing and is a barrier to making profit.
Costs can be classified either as direct or indirect.	Such classifications are no longer useful.
Product profitability can be determined by deducting a product cost from selling price.	Profitability is determined by the rate at which money is earned.
Profit can be increased by reducing cost elements.	Profit is a function of material cost, total factory cost and throughput.

2.1 Bottleneck resources

The aim of modern manufacturing approaches is to match production resources with the demand for them. This implies that there are **no constraints,** termed bottleneck resources in TA, within an organisation. The throughput philosophy entails the identification and elimination of these bottleneck resources by overtime, product changes and process alterations to reduce set-up and waiting times.

Where throughput cannot be eliminated by say prioritising work, and to avoid the build-up of work in progress, **production must be limited to the capacity of the bottleneck resource** but this capacity must be **fully** utilised. If a rearrangement of existing resources or buying-in resources does not alleviate the bottleneck, investment in new equipment may be necessary.

The elimination of one bottleneck is likely to lead to the creation of another at a previously satisfactory location, however. The management of bottlenecks therefore becomes a primary concern of the manager seeking to increase throughput.

There are other factors which might limit throughput other than a lack of production resources (bottlenecks) and these need to be addressed as well.

(a) The existence of an uncompetitive selling price
(b) The need to deliver on time to particular customers
(c) The lack of product quality and reliability
(d) The lack of reliable material suppliers
(e) The shortage of production resources

2.2 Example: Throughput accounting in a service industry

A not-for-profit organisation performs a medical screening service in three sequential stages.

1. Take an X-ray
2. Interpret the result
3. Recall patients who require further investigation / inform others that all is fine.

The 'goal unit' of this organisation will be to progress a patient through all three stages. The number of patients who complete all three stages is the organisation's throughput, and the organisation should seek to maximise its throughput. The duration of each stage and the weekly resource available is as follows.

Process	Time per patient (hours)	Total hours available per week
Take an X-ray (stage 1)	0.50	80
Interpret the result (stage 2)	0.20	40
Recall patients (stage 3)	0.40	60

You can see from the above table that the maximum number of patients (goal units) who can be dealt with in each process is as follows.

X-rays	80/0.5 = 160
Interpret results	40/0.20 = 200
Recall patients	60/0.40 = 150

It is clear that the recall procedure (stage 3) is the bottleneck resource (constraint). Throughput, and therefore the organisation's performance cannot be improved until stage 3 can deal with more patients. There are a number of actions that the organisation could take to improve throughput.

(a) Investigate whether less time could be spent on the bottleneck activity.

(b) Ensure there is no idle time in the bottleneck resource as this will be detrimental to overall performance.

(c) Increase the bottleneck resource available.

There is little point in improving stage 1 and stage 2 if the process grinds to a halt at stage 3. Patients are only helped when the whole process is completed and they are recalled if necessary. Increasing the bottleneck resource, or the efficiency with which it is used may be relatively cheap and easy to do as stage 3 is a relatively simple piece of administration in comparison to the first two stages that use expensive machinery and highly skilled personnel.

2.3 Is it good or bad?

TA is seen by some as **too short term**, as all costs other than direct material are regarded as fixed. Moreover, it **concentrates on direct material costs** and does nothing for the control of other costs such as overheads. These characteristics make throughput accounting a **good complement for ABC**, however, since ABC focuses on labour and overhead costs.

TA attempts to maximise throughput whereas traditional systems attempt to maximise profit. By attempting to maximise throughput an organisation could be producing in excess of the profit-maximising output. **Production scheduling problems** inevitably mean that the throughput-maximising output is never attained, however, and so a **throughput maximising approach** could well **lead to the profit-maximising output** being achieved.

TA helps to direct attention to bottlenecks and focus management on the key elements in making profits, inventory reduction and reducing the response time to customer demand.

3 Performance measures in throughput accounting 6/09

Performance measures in throughput accounting are based around the concept that only **direct materials** are regarded as **variable costs**.

(a) **Return per factory hour**

$$\frac{\text{Sales} - \text{direct material costs}}{\text{Usage of bottleneck resource in hours (factory hours)}}$$

This enables businesses to take short-term decisions when a resource is in scarce supply.

(b) **Throughput accounting ratio**

$$\frac{\text{Return per factory hour}}{\text{Total conversion cost per factory hour}}$$

Again factory hours are measured in terms of use of the bottleneck resource. Businesses should try to maximise the throughput accounting ratio by making process improvements or product specification changes.

This measure has the advantage of including the costs involved in running the factory. The higher the ratio, the more profitable the company. (If a product has a ratio of less than one, the organisation loses money every time it is made.)

Here's an example.

	Product A $ per hour	Product B $ per hour
Sales price	100	150
Material cost	(40)	(50)
Conversion cost	(50)	(50)
Profit	10	50
TA ratio	$\frac{60}{50} = 1.2$	$\frac{100}{50} = 2.0$

Profit will be maximised by manufacturing as much of product B as possible.

| Question | Performance measurement in throughput accounting |

Growler manufactures computer components. Health and safety regulations mean that one of its processes can only be operated 8 hours a day. The hourly capacity of this process is 500 units per hour. The selling price of each component is $100 and the unit material cost is $40. The daily total of all factory costs (conversion costs) is $144,000, excluding materials. Expected production is 3,600 units per day.

Required

Calculate

(a)   Total profit per day
(b)   Return per factory hour
(c)   Throughput accounting ratio

Answer

(a)   Total profit per day   =   Throughput contribution – Conversion costs

                                       = $(3{,}600 \times (100 - 40) - 144{,}000)$

                                       =   \$72,000

(b)   Return per factory hour   = $\dfrac{\text{Sales} - \text{direct material costs}}{\text{Usage of bottleneck resource in hours (factory hours)}}$

                                       = $\dfrac{100 - 40}{1/500}$

                                       =   \$30,000

(c)   Throughput accounting ratio   = $\dfrac{\text{Return per factory hour}}{\text{Total conversion cost per factory hour}}$

                                       = $\dfrac{30{,}000}{144{,}000/8}$

                                       =   1.67

4 Throughput and decision making

FAST FORWARD

In a throughput environment, **production priority** must be given to the products best able to generate throughput, that is those **products that maximise throughput per unit of bottleneck resource.**

The TA ratio can be used to assess the **relative earning capabilities** of different products and hence can help with decision making.

4.1 Example: throughput accounting

Corrie produces three products, X, Y and Z. The capacity of Corrie's plant is restricted by process alpha. Process alpha is expected to be operational for eight hours per day and can produce 1,200 units of X per hour, 1,500 units of Y per hour, and 600 units of Z per hour.

Selling prices and material costs for each product are as follows.

Product	Selling price	Material cost	Throughput contribution
	$ per unit	$ per unit	$ per unit
X	150	80	70
Y	120	40	80
Z	300	100	200

Conversion costs are $720,000 per day.

Required

(a) Calculate the profit per day if daily output achieved is 6,000 units of X, 4,500 units of Y and 1,200 units of Z.

(b) Calculate the TA ratio for each product.

(c) In the absence of demand restrictions for the three products, advise Corrie's management on the optimal production plan.

Solution

(a) Profit per day = throughput contribution − conversion cost

$$= [(\$70 \times 6,000) + (\$80 \times 4,500) + (\$200 \times 1,200)] − \$720,000$$
$$= \$300,000$$

(b) TA ratio = throughput contribution per factory hour/conversion cost per factory hour

Conversion cost per factory hour = $720,000/8 = $90,000

Product	Throughput contribution per factory hour	Cost per factory hour	TA ratio
X	$70 × 1,200 = $84,000	$90,000	0.93
Y	$80 × 1,500 = $120,000	$90,000	1.33
Z	$200 × 600 = $120,000	$90,000	1.33

(c) An attempt should be made to remove the restriction on output caused by process alpha's capacity. This will probably result in another bottleneck emerging elsewhere. The extra capacity required to remove the restriction could be obtained by working overtime, making process improvements or product specification changes. Until the volume of throughput can be increased, output should be concentrated upon products Y and Z (greatest TA ratios), unless there are good marketing reasons for continuing the current production mix.

Product X is losing money every time it is produced so, unless there are good reasons why it is being produced, for example it has only just been introduced and is expected to become more profitable, Corrie should consider ceasing production of X.

4.2 How can a business improve a throughput accounting ratio?

Measures	Consequences
• Increase sales price per unit	• Demand for the product may fall
• Reduce material costs per unit, eg change materials and/or suppliers	• Quality may fall and bulk discounts may be lost
• Reduce operating expenses	• Quality may fall and/or errors increase

4.3 Limitations of the throughput accounting ratio

As we have seen, the TA ratio can be used to decide which products should be produced. However, the huge majority of organisations cannot produce and market products based on short-term profit considerations alone. Strategic-level issues such as market developments, product developments and the stage reached in the product life cycle must also be taken into account.

4.4 Throughput and limiting factor analysis

The throughput approach is very similar to the approach of **maximising contribution per unit of scarce resource**, which you will have covered in your earlier studies.

Limiting factor analysis

- An organisation might be faced with just one limiting factor (other than maximum sales demand) but there might also be several scarce resources, with two or more of them putting an effective limit on the level of activity that can be achieved.

- Examples of limiting factors include sales demand and production constraints.

    - Labour. The limit may be either in terms of total quantity or of particular skills.
    - Materials. There may be insufficient available materials to produce enough units to satisfy sales demand.
    - Manufacturing capacity. There may not be sufficient machine capacity for the production required to meet sales demand.

- It is assumed in limiting factor analysis that management would make a product mix decision or service mix decision based on the option that would maximise profit and that profit is maximised when contribution is maximised (given no change in fixed cost expenditure incurred). In other words, marginal costing ideas are applied.

    - Contribution will be maximised by earning the biggest possible contribution per unit of limiting factor. For example if grade A labour is the limiting factor, contribution will be maximised by earning the biggest contribution per hour of grade A labour worked.
    - The limiting factor decision therefore involves the determination of the contribution earned per unit of limiting factor by each different product.
    - If the sales demand is limited, the profit-maximising decision will be to produce the top-ranked product(s) up to the sales demand limit.

- In limiting factor decisions, we generally assume that fixed costs are the same whatever product or service mix is selected, so that the only relevant costs are variable costs.

- When there is just one limiting factor, the technique for establishing the contribution-maximising product mix or service mix is to rank the products or services in order of contribution-earning ability per unit of limiting factor.

Attention!

Throughput is defined as sales less material costs whereas contribution is defined as sales less **all** variable costs. Throughput assumes that all costs except materials are fixed in the short run.

4.4.1 Example: throughput v limiting factor analysis

A company produces two products, Tatty and Messy, which have the following production costs.

	Tatty	Messy
	$	$
Direct material cost	12	12
Direct labour cost	6	10
Variable overhead	6	10
Fixed overhead	6	10
Total product cost	30	42

Fixed overheads are absorbed on the basis of direct labour cost. Tatty and Messy pass through two processes, blasting and smoothing which incur direct labour time as follows.

	Time taken	
Process	Tatty	Messy
Blasting	15 mins	25 mins
Smoothing	25 mins	20 mins

The current market price for Tatty is $75 and for Messy $60 and, at these prices, customers will buy as many units as are available.

The capacity of the two processes limits the amount of units of products that can be produced. Blasting can be carried out for 8 hours per day but smoothing can only operate for 6 hours per day.

Required

What production plan should the company follow in order to maximise profits?

(a) Using contribution per minute
(b) Using throughput per minute

Solution

The constraint in this situation is the ability to process the product. The total daily processing time for the two processes is as follows.

Maximum blasting time   = 8 × 60 mins = 480 mins
Maximum smoothing time   = 6 × 60 mins = 360 mins

The maximum number of each product that can be produced is therefore:

	Tatty Units	*Messy* Units
Blasting	$\dfrac{480}{15} = 32$	$\dfrac{480}{25} = 19$
Smoothing	$\dfrac{360}{25} = 14$	$\dfrac{360}{20} = 18$

The total number of units that can be processed is greater for blasting so smoothing capacity is the binding constraint or limiting factor.

(a) **Maximising contribution per minute**

Contribution of Tatty   = $(75 − 12 − 6 − 6)   = $51
Contribution of Messy   = $(60 − 12 − 10 − 10)   = $28

Contribution of Tatty per minute in smoothing process $= \dfrac{\$51}{25} = \$2.04$

Contribution of Messy per minute in smoothing process $= \dfrac{\$28}{20} = \$1.40$

The profit maximising solution is therefore to produce the maximum number of units of Tatty, giving a contribution of 14 × $51 = $714

(b) **Maximising throughput per minute**

Contribution of Tatty   = $(75 − 12)   = $63
Contribution of Messy   = $(60 − 12)   = $48

Throughput per minute of Tatty in smoothing process $= \dfrac{\$63}{25} = \$2.52$

Throughput per minute of Messy in smoothing process $= \dfrac{\$48}{20} = \$2.40$

The profit maximising approach is therefore again to produce the maximum number of units of Tatty, but the result is not as clear cut.

Chapter Roundup

- **Throughput accounting** is a product management system which aims to maximise throughput, and therefore cash generation from sales, rather than profit. A **just in time (JIT)** environment is operated, with buffer inventory kept only when there is a **bottleneck resource**.

- Performance measures in throughput accounting are based around the concept that only **direct materials** are regarded as **variable costs**.

- In a throughput environment, **production priority** must be given to the products best able to generate throughput, that is those **products that maximise throughput per unit of bottleneck resource.**

1   Fill in the blanks in the statements below, using the words in the box. Some words may be used twice.

(a)   The theory of constraints is an approach to production management which aims to maximise (1).................................. less (2).. . It focuses on factors such as (3).................................. which act as (4)..

(b)   Throughput contribution = (5)...................................... minus (6) ....

(c)   TA ratio = (7) .... per factory hour ÷ (8) .... per factory hour

• bottlenecks	• throughput contribution
• material costs	• constraints
• sales revenue	• conversion cost

2   Fill in the right hand side of the table below, which looks at the differences between throughput accounting and traditional product costing.

Traditional product costing	Throughput accounting
Labour costs and 'traditional' variable overheads are treated as variable costs.	
Inventory is valued in the income statement and balance sheet at total production cost.	
Variance analysis is employed to determine whether standards were achieved.	
Efficiency is based on labour and machines working to full capacity.	
Value is added when an item is produced.	

3   The following details relate to three services offered by DSF.

	V	A	L
	$ per service	$ per service	$ per service
Selling price of service	120	170	176
Direct labour	20	30	20
Variable overhead	40	56	80
Fixed overhead	20	32	40
	80	118	140
Profit	40	52	36

All three services use the same direct labour, but in different quantities.

In a period when the labour used on these services is in short supply, the most and least profitable use of the labour is:

	Most profitable	Least profitable
A	L	V
B	L	A
C	V	A
D	A	L

1
1   sales revenue
2   material costs
3   bottlenecks
4   constraints
5   sales revenue
6   material costs
7   throughput contribution
8   conversion cost

2

Traditional product costing	Throughput accounting
Labour costs and 'traditional' variable overheads are treated as variable costs.	They are not normally treated as variable costs.
Inventory is valued in the income statement and balance sheet at total production cost.	It is valued at material cost only.
Variance analysis is employed to determine whether standards were achieved.	It is used to determine why the planned product mix was not produced.
Efficiency is based on labour and machines working to full capacity.	Efficiency requires schedule adherence and meeting delivery dates.
Value is added when an item is produced.	It is added when an item is sold.

3   B

	V	A	L
	$	$	$
Selling price per service	120	170	176
Variable cost per service	60	86	100
Contribution per service	60	84	76
Labour cost per service	$20	$30	$20
Contribution per $ of labour	$3	$2.80	$3.80
Ranking	2	3	1

Now try the questions below from the Exam Question Bank

Number	Level	Marks	Time
Q5	Examination	20	36 mins
Q6	Examination	20	36 mins

Environmental accounting

Topic list	Syllabus reference
1 Managing environmental costs	A5 (a)
2 Accounting for environmental costs	A5 (b)

Introduction

Environmental accounting is the last management accounting technique in Section A of the syllabus.

Environmental issues are becoming increasingly important in the business world. Firms have become responsible for the environmental impacts of their operations and therefore they are now more aware of problems such as carbon emissions.

The growth of environmental issues and regulations has also brought greater focus on how businesses **manage** and **account** for environmental costs.

Study guide

		Intellectual level
A5	**Environmental accounting**	
(a)	Discuss the issues businesses face in the management of environmental costs	2
(b)	Describe the different methods a business may use to account for its environmental costs	2

Exam guide

Environmental accounting is becoming increasingly topical in the modern business environment. In the July 2010 edition of *Student Accountant*, there was an **article** on environmental management accounting by the **examiner**. Ensure that you are familiar with the main points in this article.

1 Managing environmental costs

Environmental costs are important to the businesses for a number of reasons.

- Identifying environmental costs associated with individual products and services can assist with **pricing** decisions.
- Ensuring compliance with **regulatory standards.**
- Potential for **cost savings**.

Key term

Environmental management accounting (EMA) is the generation and analysis of both financial and non-financial information in order to support internal environmental management processes.

1.1 Environmental concern and performance

Martin Bennett and Peter James ('The green bottom line: management accounting for environmental improvement and business benefit', *Management Accounting,* November 1998) looked at the **ways in which a company's concern for the environment can impact on its performance.**

(a) **Short-term savings** through waste minimisation and energy efficiency schemes can be substantial.

(b) Companies with poor environmental performance may face **increased cost of capital** because investors and lenders demand a higher risk premium.

(c) There are a number of **energy and environmental taxes**, such as the UK's landfill tax.

(d) **Pressure group campaigns** can cause damage to reputation and/or additional costs.

(e) Environmental legislation may cause the **'sunsetting'** of products and opportunities for **'sunrise' replacements**.

(f) The cost of processing input which becomes **waste** is equivalent to 5-10% of some organisations' revenue.

(g) The phasing out of CFCs has led to markets for alternative products.

 Case Study

On 20 April 2010, multinational oil company BP's Deepwater Horizon rig exploded off the coast of the US state of Louisiana, killing 11 workers. BP chairman, Carl-Henric Svanberg was invited to meet US President Barack Obama amid concerns that the company did not have enough cash to pay for the clean-up operation and compensation for those affected – estimated at $32.2 billion. The reputation of the global BP brand was seriously damaged.

1.1.1 Achieving business and environmental benefits

Bennett and James went on to suggest six main **ways in which business and environmental benefits can be achieved**.

(a) **Integrating the environment into capital expenditure decisions** (by considering environmental opposition to projects which could affect cash flows, for example)

(b) **Understanding and managing environmental costs**. Environmental costs are often 'hidden' in overheads and environmental and energy costs are often not allocated to the relevant budgets.

(c) **Introducing waste minimisation schemes**

(d) **Understanding and managing life cycle costs.** For many products, the greatest environmental impact occurs upstream (such as mining raw materials) or downstream from production (such as energy to operate equipment). This has led to producers being made responsible for dealing with the disposal of products such as cars, and government and third party measures to influence raw material choices. Organisations therefore need to identify, control and make provision for environmental life cycle costs and work with suppliers and customers to identify environmental cost reduction opportunities.

(e) **Measuring environmental performance.** Business is under increasing pressure to measure all aspects of environmental performance, both for statutory disclosure reasons and due to demands for more environmental data from customers.

(f) **Involving management accountants in a strategic approach to environment-related management accounting and performance evaluation.** A 'green accounting team' incorporating the key functions should analyse the strategic picture and identify opportunities for practical initiatives. It should analyse the short-, medium- and long-term impact of possible changes in the following.

    (i) **Government policies**, such as on transport

    (ii) **Legislation and regulation**

    (iii) **Supply conditions**, such as fewer landfill sites

    (iv) **Market conditions**, such as changing customer views

    (v) **Social attitudes**, such as to factory farming

    (vi) **Competitor strategies**

Possible action includes the following.

    (i) Designating an **'environmental champion'** within the strategic planning or accounting function to ensure that environmental considerations are fully considered.

    (ii) Assessing whether **new data sources** are needed to collect more and better data

    (iii) Making **comparisons** between sites/offices to highlight poor performance and generate peer pressure for action

    (iv) Developing **checklists** for internal auditors

Such analysis and action should help organisations to better understand present and future environmental costs and benefits.

1.2 Defining environmental costs

There are many varied definitions of environmental costs. The US Environmental Protection Agency make a distinction between four types of cost.

(a) **Conventional costs** such as raw materials and energy costs that have an impact on the environment.

(b) **Potentially hidden costs** are relevant costs that are captured within accounting systems but may be 'hidden' within 'general overheads'.

(c) **Contingent costs** are costs that will be incurred at a future date as a result of discharging waste into the environment such as **clean-up** costs.

(d) **Image and relationship costs** are costs incurred to preserve the reputation of the business, for example, the costs of preparing environmental reports to ensure compliance with regulatory standards.

1.3 Identifying environmental costs

The majority of environmental costs are already captured within accounting systems. The difficulty lies in **pinpointing** them and **allocating** them to a specific product or service. Typical environmental costs are listed below.

- Consumables and raw materials
- Transport and travel
- Waste and effluent disposal
- Water consumption
- Energy

1.4 Controlling environmental costs

Once a business has **defined**, **identified** and **allocated** environmental costs, it can begin the task of trying to control them through **environmental management systems**.

1.4.1 ISO 14000

ISO 14000 was first published in 1996 and based on earlier quality management standards. It provides a general framework on which a number of specific standards have been based (the ISO family of standards). ISO 14001 prescribes that an environmental management system must comprise:

- An **environmental policy statement**
- An assessment of environmental aspects and legal and voluntary obligations
- A management system
- Internal audits and reports to senior management
- A public declaration that ISO 14001 is being complied with

Critics of ISO 14000 claim that its emphasis on management systems rather than performance is misplaced, and that it does not include rigorous verification and disclosure requirements.

1.4.2 Management systems

In *Accounting for the Environment* Gray and Bebbington listed the functions that environmental management systems should cover.

Function	Description
Environmental review and policy development	A first review of environmental impacts of materials, issues and products and of business issues arising, also the development of a tailored in-house policy or measures to ensure adherence to external standards
Objectives and target development	As with all business objectives and targets, it is preferable that those set be unambiguous and achievable. Targets should be quantified within a specified time period eg reducing carbon dioxide emissions by X% within a specified time period
Life-cycle assessment	This aims to identify all interactions between a product and its environment during its lifetime, including energy and material usage and environmental releases. • Raw materials used have to be traced back to the biosphere and the company recognise impact on habitat, gas balance, the energy used in the extraction and transportation and the energy used to produce the means of extraction • For intermediate stages, emissions, discharges and co-products • At the consumer purchase stage, the impact of manufacture and disposal of packaging, transport to shops and ultimately impacts of consumers using and disposing of the product

Function	Description
Establishment and maintenance of environmental management systems	Key features of environmental management systems (as with other management systems) including information systems, budgeting, forecasting and management accounting systems, structure of responsibilities, establishment of an environmentally-friendly culture, considering impact on human resource issues such as education and performance appraisal
Regulatory compliance	Making sure that current legal requirements are being fulfilled and keeping up-to-date with practical implications of likely changes in legislation
Environmental impact assessment	A regular review of interactions with the environment, the degree of impact and also the impact of forthcoming major investments
Eco-label applications	Eco-labelling allows organisations to identify publicly products and services that meet the highest environmental standards. To be awarded an eco-label requires the product to be the result of a reliable quality management system
Waste minimisation	Whether waste can be minimised (or better still eliminated), possibility of recycling or selling waste
Pollution prevention programmes	Deciding what to target
Research, development and investment in cleaner technologies	How to bring desirable features into product development, bearing in mind product development may take several years, and opinion and legal requirements may change during that period. Desirable features may include minimum resource usage, waste, emissions, packaging and transport, recycling, disassembly and longer product life
Environmental performance and issues reporting	Consideration of the benefits and costs of reporting, how to report and what to include (policies, plans, financial data, activities undertaken, sustainability)

2 Accounting for environmental costs

FAST FORWARD

The UNDSD (2003) idenfitied a number of management accounting techniques to account for environmental costs. They are **input/output analysis**, **flow cost accounting**, **environmental activity-based costing (ABC)** and **life-cycle costing**.

The United Nations Division for Sustainable Development (UNDSD,2003) identified management accounting techniques which are useful for the identification and allocation of environmental costs. They are **input/output analysis**, **flow cost accounting**, **environmental activity-based accounting** and **life-cycle costing**.

2.1 Input/output analysis

Input/output analysis operates on the principal that what comes in must go out. Process flow charts can help to trace inputs and outputs, in particular waste. They effectively demonstrate the details of the processes so that the relevant information can be allocated to the main activities.

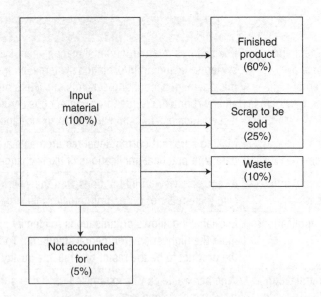

As shown in the diagram above, the input is regarded as 100% and split across the outputs which are **sold and stored goods** and **residual** (regarded as waste).

By accounting for process outputs in this way both in physical quantities and in monetary terms, businesses are forced to focus on environmental costs.

2.2 Flow cost accounting

Under this technique, material flows through an organisation are divided into three categories.

- Material
- System and delivery
- Disposal

The values and costs of each material flow are then calculated. This method of cost accounting focuses on reducing the quantity of materials which, as well as having a positive effect on the environment, should reduce business' total costs in the long-term.

2.3 Environmental activity-based costing

Activity-based costing (ABC) '...represents a method of managerial cost accounting that allocates all internal costs to the cost centres and cost drivers on the basis of the activities that caused the costs,' (UNDSD, 2003).

Under an activity-based system, a distinction is made between **environment-related costs** and **environment-driven costs**. **Environment-driven costs** such as costs relating to a sewage plant or incinerator are attributed to **joint environmental cost centres.**

Environment-related costs such as increased depreciation or a higher cost of staff are allocated to general overheads as they do not relate directly to a joint environmental cost centre.

To decide on the environmental cost drivers, the production processes involved in making a product or providing a service need to be carefully analysed. The **levels** of environmental **hazards** and **costs** need to be **established**. This may mean installing **tracking systems** to track environmental waste.

Schaltegger and Muller (1998) stated 'the choice of an adequate allocation key is crucial for obtaining correct information'. The four main allocations are listed below.

- Volume of emissions or waste
- Toxicity of emissions and waste treated
- Environmental impact added (volume x input per unit of volume)
- The relative costs of treating different kinds of emissions

2.4 Life-cycle costing

Under this method, environmental costs are considered from the **design stage** of a new product right up to the **end-of-life costs** such as decommissioning and removal. This is particularly important in some countries where businesses are held responsible for costs associated with the end of a life of a product.

The consideration of future disposal or remediation costs at the design stage may influence the design of the product itself, saving on future costs.

Chapter Roundup

- **Environmental costs** are important to the businesses for a number of reasons.
    - Identifying environmental costs associated with individual products and services can assist with **pricing** decisions.
    - Ensuring compliance with **regulatory standards.**
    - Potential for **cost savings**.
- The UNDSD (2003) idenfitied a number of management accounting techniques to account for environmental costs. They are **input/output analysis**, **flow cost accounting**, **activity-based costing (ABC)** and **life-cycle costing**.

Quick Quiz

1   What are the main elements of an environmental management system per ISO 14001?

2   *Choose the appropriate words from those highlighted.*

Costs that will be incurred at a future date such as clean up costs are know as **contingent/image and relationship** costs.

Raw materials and energy are examples of **potentially hidden/conventional** costs

3   List the three categories of material flows under a system of flow cost accounting

Answers to Quick Quiz

1
- An environmental policy
- An assessment of environmental aspects and legal and voluntary obligations
- A management system
- Internal audits and reports to senior management
- A public declaration that ISO 14001 is being complied with

2   contingent
    conventional

3
- Material
- System and delivery
- Disposal

P
A
R
T

B

Decision-making techniques

Cost volume profit (CVP) analysis

Topic list	Syllabus reference
1 A recap of basic CVP analysis	A2 (a), (b)
2 Preparing a basic breakeven chart	A2 (a)
3 Breakeven analysis in a multi-product environment	A2 (e)
4 Breakeven point for multiple products	A2 (b)
5 Contribution to sales (C/S) ratio for multiple products	A2 (c)
6 Margin of safety for multiple products	A2 (b)
7 Target profits for multiple products	A2 (d)
8 Multi-product breakeven charts	A2 (e)
9 Further aspects of CVP analysis	A2 (f)

Introduction

You will have **already encountered CVP (or breakeven) analysis** in your earlier studies so you should not be surprised by the terminology or basic techniques that you meet in this chapter. But in case your memory needs refreshing we have included a brief reminder of the material you covered at the beginning of the chapter. You could still be asked to carry out straightforward breakeven analysis in the exam so make sure that you are perfectly happy with the basic stuff before moving on to the higher-level material.

You should remember that one of the **major assumptions** underpinning breakeven analysis is that it can **only be applied to one product or to a constant (fixed proportions) mix of products.**

So far you will only have studied single product breakeven analysis but as most organisations produce and sell a range of products we are going to look at what is known as multi-product breakeven analysis. We will see how to perform calculations you will be familiar with from your earlier studies such as the **contribution to sales (C/S) ratio** and the **margin of safety**, applied to multi-product situations.

Study guide

		Intellectual level
B2	**Cost volume profit analysis**	
(a)	Explain the nature of CVP analysis	2
(b)	Calculate and interpret break even point and margin of safety	2
(c)	Calculate the contribution to sales ratio, in single and multi-product situations, and demonstrate an understanding of its use	2
(d)	Calculate target profit or revenue in single and multi-product situations, and demonstrate an understanding of its use	2
(e)	Prepare break even charts and profit volume charts and interpret the information contained within each, including multi-product situations	2
(f)	Discuss the limitations of CVP analysis for planning and decision making	2

Exam guide

The July 2010 issue of *Student Accountant* contains an **article** on **CVP analysis** written by the **examiner**. Ensure that you are familiar with this article.

1 A recap of basic CVP analysis

1.1 Knowledge brought forward from earlier studies

Cost volume profit (CVP)/breakeven analysis is the study of the interrelationships between costs, volume and profit at various levels of activity.

1.1.1 Breakeven analysis

Key terms

- Contribution per unit = unit selling price − unit variable costs
- Profit = (sales volume × contribution per unit) − fixed costs
- Breakeven point $\quad$ = activity level at which there is neither profit nor loss

$$= \frac{\text{total fixed costs}}{\text{contribution per unit}} = \frac{\text{contribution required to breakeven}}{\text{contribution per unit}}$$

- Contribution/sales (C/S) ratio = profit/volume (P/V) ratio = (contribution/sales) × 100%
- Sales revenue at breakeven point = fixed costs ÷ C/S ratio
- Margin of safety (in units) $\quad$ = budgeted sales units − breakeven sales units
- Margin of safety (as %) $\quad = \dfrac{\text{budgeted sales} - \text{breakeven sales}}{\text{budgeted sales}} \times 100\%$

- Sales volume to achieve a target profit $= \dfrac{\text{fixed cost} + \text{target profit}}{\text{contribution per unit}}$

1.1.2 Assumptions

(a) Can only apply to one product or constant mix
(b) Fixed costs same in total and unit variable costs same at all levels of output
(c) Sales prices constant at all levels of activity
(d) Production = sales

1.1.3 Breakeven, contribution and P/V charts

- Breakeven chart
- Contribution (contribution breakeven) chart

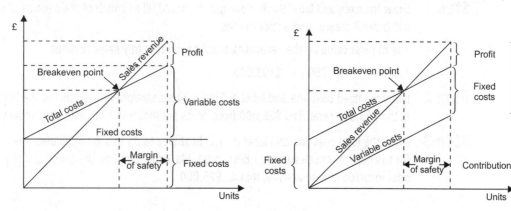

- Profit/volume (P/V) chart

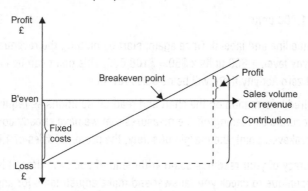

The gradient of the straight line is the contribution per unit (if the horizontal axis is measured in sales value).

2 Preparing a basic breakeven chart

FAST FORWARD

You can prepare a breakeven chart by plotting sales revenue against total cost. The **breakeven point** will be where the **sales revenue** line and **total cost** line intersect.

Key term

Breakeven point is the level of activity at which there is neither profit nor loss.

2.1 Example: Basic breakeven chart

A new product has the following sales and cost data.

Selling price $60 per unit

Variable cost $40 per unit

Fixed costs $25,000 per month

Forecast sales 1,800 units per month

Required

Prepare a breakeven chart using the above data.

Solution

Step 1   Draw the axes and label them. Your graph should fill as much of the page as possible, this will make it clearer and easier to read.

The highest value on the vertical axis will be the monthly sales revenue.

1,800 units   x $60   = $108,000

Step 2   Draw the fixed cost line and label it. This will be a straight line parallel to the horizontal axis at the $25,000 level. The $25,000 fixed costs are incurred even with zero activity.

Step 3   Draw the total cost line and label it. The best way to do this is to calculate the total costs for the maximum sales level (1,800 units). Mark this point on the graph and join it to the cost incurred at zero activity, that is, $25,000.

	$
Variable costs for 1,800 units (1,800 x $40)	72,000
Fixed costs	25,000
Total cost for 1,800 units	97,000

Step 4   Draw the revenue line and label it. Once again, start by plotting the revenue at the maximum activity level. 1,800 units x $60 = $108,000. This point can be joined to the origin, since at zero activity there will be no sales revenue.

Step 5   Mark any required information on the chart and read off solutions as required. Check that your chart is accurate by reading off the measures that we have already covered in this chapter: the breakeven point, the margin of safety, the profit for sales of 1,800 units.

Step 6   Check the accuracy of your readings using arithmetic. If you have time, it is good examination technique to check your answer and make adjustments for any errors in your chart.

The completed graph is shown below.

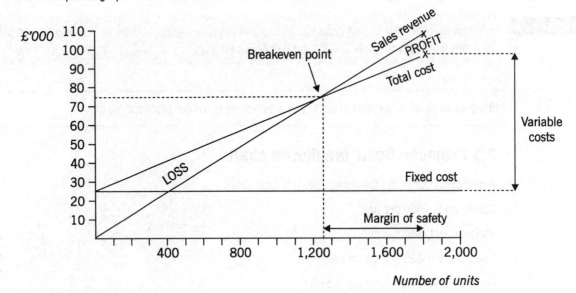

3 Breakeven analysis in a multi-product environment

FAST FORWARD

To perform breakeven analysis in a multi-product organisation, a **constant product sales mix** must be assumed, or all products must have the **same C/S ratio**.

3.1 A major assumption

Organisations typically produce and sell a variety of products and services. To perform breakeven analysis in a multi-product organisation, however, a constant product sales mix must be assumed. In other words, we have to assume that whenever x units of product A are sold, y units of product B and z units of product C are also sold.

Such an assumption allows us to calculate a weighted average contribution per mix, the weighting being on the basis of the quantities of each product in the constant mix. This means that the unit contribution of the product that makes up the largest proportion of the mix has the greatest impact on the average contribution per mix.

The only situation when the mix of products does not affect the analysis is when all of the products have the same ratio of contribution to sales (C/S ratio).

4 Breakeven point for multiple products

FAST FORWARD

The **breakeven point (in number of mixes)** for a standard mix of products is calculated as fixed costs/contribution per mix.

4.1 Example: Breakeven point for multiple products

PL produces and sells two products. The M sells for $7 per unit and has a total variable cost of $2.94 per unit, while the N sells for $15 per unit and has a total variable cost of $4.50 per unit. The marketing department has estimated that for every five units of M sold, one unit of N will be sold. The organisation's fixed costs total $36,000.

Required

Calculate the breakeven point for PL.

Solution

We calculate the breakeven point as follows.

Step 1 Calculate **contribution per unit**

	M	N
	$ per unit	$ per unit
Selling price	7.00	15.00
Variable cost	2.94	4.50
Contribution	4.06	10.50

Step 2 Calculate **contribution per mix**

= ($4.06 × 5) + ($10.50 × 1) = $30.80

Step 3 Calculate the **breakeven point** in terms of the number of mixes

= fixed costs/contribution per mix = $36,000/$30.80

= 1,169 mixes (rounded)

Step 4 Calculate the **breakeven point** in terms of the **number of units of the products**

= (1,169 × 5) 5,845 units of M and (1,169 × 1) 1,169 units of N (rounded)

Step 5 Calculate the **breakeven point** in terms of **revenue**

= (5,845 × $7) + (1,169 × $15)

= $40,915 of M and $17,535 of N = $58,450 in total

It is important to note that the breakeven point is not $58,450 of revenue, whatever the mix of products. The breakeven point is $58,450 provided that the sales mix remains 5:1. Likewise the breakeven point is not at a production/sales level of (5,845 + 1,169) 7,014 units. Rather, it is when 5,845 units of M and 1,169 units of N are sold, assuming a sales mix of 5:1.

Question
Breakeven point for multiple products

Alpha manufactures and sells three products, the beta, the gamma and the delta. Relevant information is as follows.

	Beta $ per unit	Gamma $ per unit	Delta $ per unit
Selling price	135.00	165.00	220.00
Variable cost	73.50	58.90	146.20

Total fixed costs are $950,000.

An analysis of past trading patterns indicates that the products are sold in the ratio 3:4:5.

Required

Fill in the blanks in the sentence below.

Alpha's breakeven point in terms of revenue of the three products is ………….…............... of Beta, ………..…............... of Gamma and ………........…….... of Delta, making …………..…….... in total.

Answer

The correct answer is $393,660 of Beta, $641,520 of Gamma and $1,069,200 of Delta, making $2,104,380 in total.

Step 1 Calculate **contribution per unit**

	Beta $ per unit	Gamma $ per unit	Delta $ per unit
Selling price	135.00	165.00	220.00
Variable cost	73.50	58.90	146.20
	61.50	106.10	73.80

Step 2 Calculate **contribution per mix**

= ($61.50 × 3) + ($106.10 × 4) + ($73.80 × 5)

= $977.90

Step 3 Calculate the **breakeven point** in terms of the **number of mixes**

= fixed costs/contribution per mix

= $950,000/$977.90 = 972 mixes (rounded up)

Step 4   Calculate the **breakeven point** in terms of the **number of units of the products**

= (972 × 3) 2,916 units of Beta, (972 × 4) 3,888 units of Gamma and (972 × 5) 4,860 units of Delta (rounded)

Step 5   Calculate the **breakeven point** in terms of **revenue**

= (2,916 × $135) + (3,888 × $165) + (4,860 × $220)

= $393,660 of Beta, $641,520 of Gamma and $1,069,200 of Delta = $2,104,380 in total

5 Contribution to sales (C/S) ratio for multiple products

FAST FORWARD

The **breakeven point in terms of sales revenue** can be calculated as fixed costs/average C/S ratio.

Any change in the **proportions of products** in the mix will change the **contribution per mix** and the **average C/S ratio** and hence the breakeven point.

Formula to learn

The **breakeven point in terms of sales revenue** can be calculated as fixed costs/average C/S ratio.

5.1 Calculating the ratio

An alternative way of **calculating the breakeven point** is to use the **average contribution to sales (C/S) ratio** for the standard mix.

As you should already know, the C/S ratio is sometimes called the **profit/volume ratio** or **P/V ratio**.

We can calculate the breakeven point of PL (see Section 4.1) as follows.

Step 1   Calculate **revenue per mix**

= (5 × $7) + (1× $15) = $50

Step 2   Calculate **contribution per mix**

= $30.80 (see Section 4.1)

Step 3   Calculate **average C/S ratio**

= ($30.80/$50.00) × 100% = 61.6%

Step 4   Calculate **breakeven point** (total)

= fixed costs ÷ C/S ratio

= $36,000/0.616 = $58,442 (rounded)

Step 5   Calculate **revenue ratio of mix**

= (5 × $7) : (1× $15)

= 35:15, or 7:3

Step 6   **Calculate breakeven sales**

M = $58,442 × 7/10 = $40,909 rounded

N = $58,442 × 3/10 = $17,533 rounded

Question

Required

Calculate the breakeven sales revenue of product Beta, Gamma and Delta (see Question 4.1 above) using the approach shown in Section 5.1.

Answer

Step 1 Calculate revenue per mix
= $(3 \times \$135) + (4 \times \$165) + (5 \times \$220)$
= $2,165

Step 2 Calculate contribution per mix
= $977.90 (from Question: breakeven point for multiple products)

Step 3 Calculate average C/S ratio
= ($977.90/$2,165) × 100%
= 45.17%

Step 4 Calculate breakeven point (total)
= fixed costs ÷ C/S ratio
= $950,000/0.4517
= $2,103,166 (rounded)

Step 5 Calculate revenue ratio of mix
= 405:660:1,100, or 81:132:220

Step 6 Calculate breakeven sales

Breakeven sales of Beta   = 81/433 × $2,103,166 = $393,433

Breakeven sales of Gamma = 132/433 × $2,103,166 = $641,150

Breakeven sales of Delta   = 220/433 × $2,103,166 = $1,068,583

Alternatively you might be provided with the individual C/S ratios of a number of products. For example if an organisation sells two products (A and B) in the ratio 2:5 and if the C/S ratio of A is 10% whereas that of B is 50%, the average C/S ratio is calculated as follows.

$$\text{Average C/S ratio} = \frac{(2 \times 10\%) + (5 \times 50\%)}{2 + 5} = 38.6\%$$

Question

TIM produces and sells two products, the MK and the KL. The organisation expects to sell 1 MK for every 2 KLs and have monthly sales revenue of $150,000. The MK has a C/S ratio of 20% whereas the KL has a C/S ratio of 40%. Budgeted monthly fixed costs are $30,000.

Required

What is the budgeted breakeven sales revenue?

Average C/S ratio = $\dfrac{(20\% \times 1) + (40\% \times 2)}{3}$ = $33^{1}/_{3}\%$

Sales revenue at the breakeven point = $\dfrac{\text{fixed cos ts}}{\text{C / S ratio}}$ = $\dfrac{\$30,000}{0.333}$ = $90,000

The C/S ratio is a measure of how much contribution is earned from each $1 of sales of the standard mix. The C/S ratio of $33^{1}/_{3}\%$ in the question above means that for every $1 of sales of the standard mix of products, a contribution of 33.33c is earned. To earn a total contribution of, say, $20,000, sales revenue from the standard mix must therefore be

$\dfrac{\$1}{33.33c} \times \$20,000 = \$60,006$

Using the C/S ratio

Refer back to the information in the paragraph following Question: C/S ratio for multiple products. Suppose the organisation in question has fixed costs of $100,000, and wishes to earn total contribution of $200,000.

Required

What level of revenue must be achieved?

Sales revenue must be $\dfrac{\$1}{38.6c} \times \$200,000 = \$518,135$

5.2 points to bear in mind

Any change in the proportions of products in the mix will change the contribution per mix and the average C/S ratio and hence the breakeven point.

(a) If the mix shifts towards products with lower contribution margins, the breakeven point (in units) will increase and profits will fall unless there is a corresponding increase in total revenue.

(b) A shift towards products with higher contribution margins without a corresponding decrease in revenues will cause an increase in profits and a lower breakeven point.

(c) If sales are at the specified level but not in the specified mix, there will be either a profit or a loss depending on whether the mix shifts towards products with higher or lower contribution margins.

6 Margin of safety for multiple products

FAST FORWARD

The **margin of safety** for a multi-product organisation is equal to the budgeted sales in the standard mix less the breakeven sales in the standard mix. It may be expressed as a percentage of the budgeted sales.

It should not surprise you to learn that the calculation of the margin of safety for multiple products is exactly the same as for single products, but we use the standard mix. The easiest way to see how it's done is to look at an example which we do in this section.

6.1 Example: Margin of safety for multiple products

BA produces and sells two products. The W sells for $8 per unit and has a total variable cost of $3.80 per unit, while the R sells for $14 per unit and has a total variable cost of $4.20. For every five units of W sold, six units of R are sold. BA's fixed costs are $43,890 per period.

Budgeted sales revenue for next period is $74,400, in the standard mix.

Required

Calculate the margin of safety in terms of sales revenue and also as a percentage of budgeted sales revenue.

Solution

To calculate the margin of safety we must first determine the breakeven point.

Step 1   Calculate **contribution per unit**

	W $ per unit	R $ per unit
Selling price	8.00	14.00
Variable cost	3.80	4.20
Contribution	4.20	9.80

Step 2   Calculate **contribution per mix**

= ($4.20 × 5) + ($9.80 × 6) = $79.80

Step 3   Calculate the **breakeven point** in terms of the **number of mixes**

= fixed costs/contribution per mix = $43,890/$79.80

= 550 mixes

Step 4   Calculate the **breakeven point** in terms of the **number of units of the products**

= (550 × 5) 2,750 units of W and (550 × 6) 3,300 units of R

Step 5   Calculate the **breakeven point** in terms of **revenue**

= (2,750 × $8) + (3,300 × $14)

= $22,000 of W and $46,200 of R = $68,200 in total

Step 6   Calculate the **margin of safety**

= budgeted sales – breakeven sales

= $74,400 – $68,200

= $6,200 sales in total, in the standard mix

Or, as a percentage

= ($74,400 – $68,200)/$74,400 × 100%

= 8.3% of budgeted sales

7 Target profits for multiple products

> The number of mixes of products required to be sold to achieve a **target profit** is calculated as (fixed costs + required profit)/contribution per mix.

You should already be familiar with the problem of target profits for single products in a CVP context from your earlier studies. This section expands the concept to multiple products, illustrating the calculations in several examples.

7.1 A reminder of the formula for target profits

At **breakeven point** there is no profit – that is:

Contribution = Fixed costs

Suppose an organisation wishes to achieve a certain level of profit during a period. To achieve this profit, contribution must cover fixed costs and leave the required profit:

So **total contribution required = fixed costs + required profit**

Once we know the total contribution required we can calculate the sales revenue of each product needed to achieve a target profit. The method is similar to the method used to calculate the breakeven point.

Formula to learn

> The number of mixes of products required to be sold to achieve a **target profit** is calculated as (fixed costs + required profit)/contribution per mix.

7.2 Example: Target profits for multiple products

An organisation makes and sells three products, F, G and H. The products are sold in the proportions F:G:H = 2:1:3. The organisation's fixed costs are $80,000 per month and details of the products are as follows.

Product	Selling price $ per unit	Variable cost $ per unit
F	22	16
G	15	12
H	19	13

The organisation wishes to earn a profit of $52,000 next month. Calculate the required sales value of each product in order to achieve this target profit.

Solution

Step 1   Calculate **contribution per unit**

	F $ per unit	G $ per unit	H $ per unit
Selling price	22	15	19
Variable cost	16	12	13
Contribution	6	3	6

Step 2   Calculate **contribution per mix**

= ($6 × 2) + ($3 × 1) + ($6 × 3) = $33

Step 3 Calculate the **required number of mixes**

= (Fixed costs + required profit)/contribution per mix

= ($80,000 + $52,000)/$33

= 4,000 mixes

Step 4 Calculate the required sales in terms of the number of units of the products and sales revenue of each product

Product	Units	Selling price $ per unit	Sales revenue required $
F	4,000 × 2 = 8,000	22	176,000
G	4,000 × 1 = 4,000	15	60,000
H	4,000 × 3 = 12,000	19	228,000
Total			464,000

The sales revenue of $464,000 will generate a profit of $52,000 if the products are sold in the mix 2:1:3.

Alternatively the C/S ratio could be used to determine the required sales revenue for a profit of $52,000. The method is again similar to that demonstrated earlier when calculating the breakeven point.

7.3 Example: using the C/S ratio to determine the required sales

We'll use the data from the example above.

Step 1 **Calculate revenue per mix**
= (2 × $22) + (1 × $15) + (3 × $19)
= $116

Step 2 **Calculate contribution per mix**
= $33 (from Solution in Section 7.2)

Step 3 **Calculate average C/S ratio**
= ($33/$116) × 100%
= 28.45%

Step 4 **Calculate required total revenue**
= required contribution ÷ C/S ratio
= ($80,000 + $52,000) ÷ 0.2845
= $463,972

Step 5 **Calculate revenue ratio of mix**
= (2 × $22) : (1 × $15) : (3 × $19)
= 44:15:57

Step 6 **Calculate required sales**

Required sales of F = 44/116 × $463,972 = $175,989
Required sales of G = 15/116 × $463,972 = $59,996
Required sales of H = 57/116 × $463,972 = $227,986

Which, allowing for roundings, is the same answer as calculated in the first example.

8 Multi-product breakeven charts

> **FAST FORWARD**
>
> **Breakeven charts** for multiple products can be drawn if a constant product sales mix is assumed.
>
> The **P/V chart** can show information about each product individually.

Exam focus point

> As well as being able to carry out CVP calculations you may be asked to produce a breakeven chart in a multiple product situation. This section focuses on the procedure involved in producing multi-product breakeven charts and profit/volume (P/V) charts.

8.1 Breakeven charts

Key term

> A **breakeven chart** is a chart which indicates approximate profit or loss at different levels of sales volume within a limited range.

A very serious limitation of breakeven charts is that they can show the costs, revenues, profits and margins of safety for a single product only, or at best for a single 'sales mix' of products.

Breakeven charts for multiple products can be drawn if a constant product sales mix is assumed.

For example suppose that FA sells three products, X, Y and Z which have variable unit costs of $3, $4 and $5 respectively. The sales price of X is $8, the price of Y is $6 and the price of Z is $6. Fixed costs per annum are $10,000.

A breakeven chart cannot be drawn, because we do not know the proportions of X, Y and Z in the sales mix.

Exam focus point

> If you are not sure about this point, you should try to draw a breakeven chart with the information given. It should not be possible.

There are a number of ways in which we can overcome this problem, however.

8.1.1 Approach 1: output in $ sales and a constant product mix

Assume that budgeted sales are 2,000 units of X, 4,000 units of Y and 3,000 units of Z. A breakeven chart would make the assumption that output and sales of X, Y and Z are in the proportions 2,000: 4,000: 3,000 at all levels of activity, in other words that the sales mix is 'fixed' in these proportions.

We begin by carrying out some calculations.

Budgeted costs		Costs $		Revenue $
Variable costs of X	(2,000 × $3)	6,000	X (2,000 × $8)	16,000
Variable costs of Y	(4,000 × $4)	16,000	Y (4,000 × $6)	24,000
Variable costs of Z	(3,000 × $5)	15,000	Z (3,000 × $6)	18,000
Total variable costs		37,000	Budgeted revenue	58,000
Fixed costs		10,000		
Total budgeted costs		47,000		

The **breakeven chart** can now be drawn.

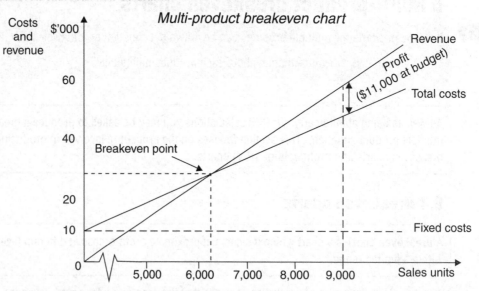

Multi-product breakeven chart

The **breakeven point** is approximately $27,500 of sales revenue. This may either be **read from the chart or computed mathematically**.

(a) The budgeted C/S ratio for all three products together is contribution/sales = $(58,000 − 37,000)/$58,000 = 36.21%.

(b) The required contribution to break even is $10,000, the amount of fixed costs. The breakeven point is $10,000/36.21% = $27,500 (approx) in sales revenue.

The margin of safety is approximately $(58,000 − 27,500) = $30,500.

8.1.2 Approach 2: products in sequence

The products could be plotted in a particular sequence (say X first, then Y, then Z). Using the data from Approach 1, we can calculate cumulative costs and revenues as follows.

Product	Cumulative units	Cumulative costs	Cumulative revenue
		$	$
	Nil	10,000	Nil
X (2,000 units)	2,000	16,000	16,000
Y (4,000 units)	6,000	32,000	40,000
Z (3,000 units)	9,000	47,000	58,000

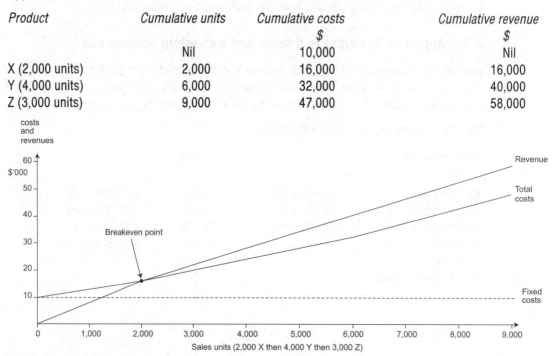

In this case the breakeven point occurs at 2,000 units of sales (2,000 units of product X). The margin of safety is roughly 4,000 units of Y and 3,000 units of Z.

8.1.3 Approach 3: output in terms of % of forecast sales and a constant product mix

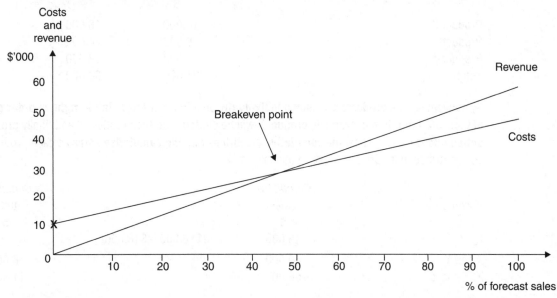

The breakeven point can be read from the graph as approximately 48% of forecast sales ($30,000 of revenue).

Alternatively, with contribution of $(58,000 − 37,000) = $21,000, one percent of forecast sales is associated with $21,000/100 = $210 contribution.

Breakeven point (%)   = fixed costs/contribution per 1%
                                   = $10,000/$210 = 47.62%
∴ Margin of safety   = (100 − 47.62) = 52.38%

Exam focus point

> The general point of setting out these three approaches is to demonstrate that output can be viewed in several different ways .

8.2 Multi-product P/V charts

The same information could be shown on a **P/V chart**, as follows.

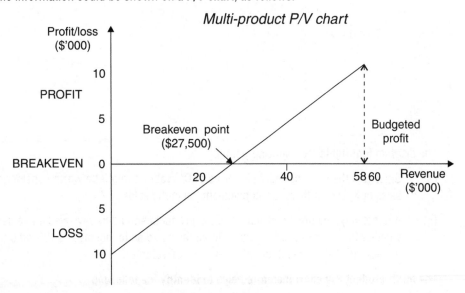

Multi-product P/V chart

An **addition** to the chart would **show further information about the contribution earned by each product individually**, so that their performance and profitability can be compared.

	Contribution $	Sales $	C/S ratio %
Product X	10,000	16,000	62.50
Product Y	8,000	24,000	33.33
Product Z	3,000	18,000	16.67
Total	21,000	58,000	36.21

By convention, the **products are shown individually** on a P/V chart from **left to right**, in **order of the size of their C/S ratio**. In this example, product X will be plotted first, then product Y and finally product Z. A **dotted line** is used to show the **cumulative profit/loss and the cumulative sales** as each product's sales and contribution in turn are added to the sales mix.

Product	Cumulative sales $		Cumulative profit $
X	16,000	($16,000 – $16,000)	–
X and Y	40,000		8,000
X, Y and Z	58,000		11,000

You will see on the graph which follows that these three pairs of data are used to plot the dotted line, to indicate the contribution from each product. The **solid line** which joins the two ends of this dotted line **indicates the average profit** which will be earned from sales of the three products in this mix.

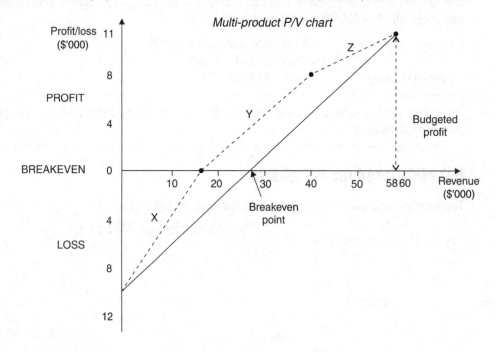

The diagram **highlights** the following points.

(a)   Since X is the most profitable in terms of C/S ratio, it might be worth considering an increase in the sales of X, even if there is a consequent fall in the sales of Z.

(b)   Alternatively, the pricing structure of the products should be reviewed and a decision made as to whether the price of product Z should be raised so as to increase its C/S ratio (although an increase is likely to result in some fall in sales volume).

The **multi-product P/V chart** therefore helps to **identify** the following.

(a)   The overall company breakeven point.

(b)   Which products should be expanded in output and which, if any, should be discontinued.

(c)   What effect changes in selling price and sales volume will have on the company's breakeven point and profit.

Question

A company sells three products, X, Y and Z. Cost and sales data for one period are as follows.

	X	Y	Z
Sales volume	2,000 units	2,000 units	5,000 units
Sales price per unit	$3	$4	$2
Variable cost per unit	$2.25	$3.50	$1.25
Total fixed costs	$3,250		

Required

Construct a multi-product P/V chart based on the above information on the axes below.

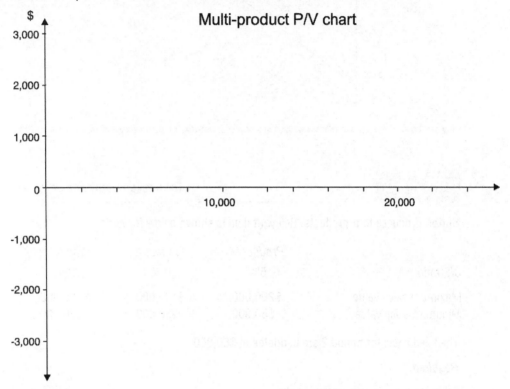

Multi-product P/V chart

Answer

	X	Y	Z	Total
				$
Contribution per unit	$0.75	$0.50	$0.75	
Budgeted contribution (total)	$1,500	$1,000	$3,750	6,250
Fixed costs				3,250
Budgeted profit				3,000

Product	Cumulative sales $		Cumulative profit $
Z	10,000	($3,750 – $3,250)	500
Z and X	16,000		2,000
Z, X and Y	24,000		3,000

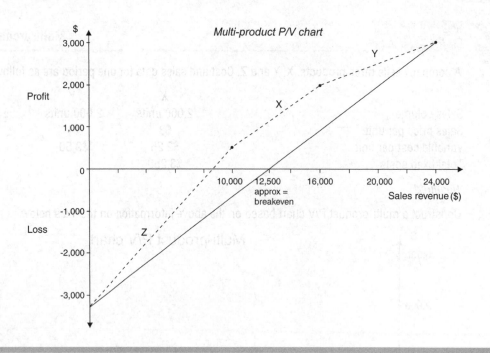

Multi-product P/V chart

Question

Breakeven point and sales value constraints

Sutton produces four products. Relevant data is shown below for period 2.

	Product M	Product A	Product R	Product P
C/S ratio	5%	10%	15%	20%
Maximum sales value	$200,000	$120,000	$200,000	$180,000
Minimum sales value	$50,000	$50,000	$20,000	$10,000

The fixed costs for period 2 are budgeted at $60,000.

Required

Fill in the blank in the sentence below.

The lowest breakeven sales value, subject to meeting the minimum sales value constraints, is $.............

Answer

The correct answer is $390,000

Breakeven point occurs when contribution = fixed costs

∴ Minimum breakeven point occurs when contribution is $60,000.

Contribution achieved from minimum sales value

			$
M	5% × $50,000		2,500
A	10% × $50,000		5,000
R	15% × $20,000		3,000
P	20% × $10,000		2,000
			12,500

Product P has the highest C/S ratio and so should be produced first (as it earns more contribution per $ of revenue than the others).

Contribution from sales of P between minimum and maximum points = $170,000 × 20% = $34,000

∴ Required contribution from Product R (which has the next highest C/S ratio)

    = $(60,000 – 12,500 – 34,000)
    = $13,500

Revenue from Product R of $13,500/0.15 = $90,000 will produce $13,500 of contribution.

∴ Lowest breakeven sales

    = $130,000 (minimum sales) + $170,000 (from P) + $90,000 (from R)
    = $390,000

9 Further aspects of CVP analysis

FAST FORWARD

The usefulness of CVP analysis is restricted by its **unrealistic assumptions**, such as constant sales price at all levels of activity. However CVP has the advantage of being more **easily understood** by non-financial managers due to its graphical depiction of cost and revenue data.

Exam focus point

As well as being able to carry out CVP calculations, you may be asked to criticise the CVP approach to short-term decision-making. This does not only mean giving the limitations of CVP but also being aware of the advantages as well.

9.1 Limitations and advantages

9.1.1 Limitations

(a)   It is assumed that fixed costs are the same in total and variable costs are the same per unit at all levels of output. This assumption is a great simplification.

    (i)   Fixed costs will change if output falls or increases substantially (most fixed costs are step costs).

    (ii)   The variable cost per unit will decrease where economies of scale are made at higher output volumes, but the variable cost per unit will also eventually rise when diseconomies of scale begin to appear at even higher volumes of output (for example the extra cost of labour in overtime working).

    The assumption is only correct within a normal range or relevant range of output. It is generally assumed that both the budgeted output and the breakeven point lie within this relevant range.

(b)   It is assumed that sales prices will be constant at all levels of activity. This may not be true, especially at higher volumes of output, where the price may have to be reduced to win the extra sales.

(c)   Production and sales are assumed to be the same, so that the consequences of any increase in inventory levels or of 'de-stocking' are ignored.

(d)   Uncertainty in the estimates of fixed costs and unit variable costs is often ignored.

9.1.2 Advantages

(a)   Graphical representation of cost and revenue data (breakeven charts) can be more easily understood by non-financial managers.

(b)   A breakeven model enables profit or loss at any level of activity within the range for which the model is valid to be determined, and the C/S ratio can indicate the relative profitability of different products.

(c)   Highlighting the breakeven point and the margin of safety gives managers some indication of the level of risk involved.

Chapter Roundup

- **Cost volume profit (CVP)/breakeven analysis** is the study of the interrelationships between costs, volume and profit at various levels of activity.

- You can prepare a breakeven chart by plotting sales revenue against total cost. The **breakeven point** will be where the **sales revenue** line and **total cost** line intersect.

- To perform breakeven analysis in a multi-product organisation, a **constant product sales** mix must be assumed, or all products must have the **same C/S ratio**.

- The **breakeven point (in number of mixes)** for a standard mix of products is calculated as fixed costs/contribution per mix.

- The **breakeven point in terms of sales revenue** can be calculated as fixed costs/average C/S ratio.

- Any change in the **proportions of products** in the mix will change the **contribution per mix** and the **average C/S ratio** and hence the breakeven point.

- The **margin of safety** for a multi-product organisation is equal to the budgeted sales in the standard mix less the breakeven sales in the standard mix. It may be expressed as a percentage of the budgeted sales.

- The number of mixes of products required to be sold to achieve a **target profit** is calculated as (fixed costs + required profit)/contribution per mix.

- **Breakeven charts** for multiple products can be drawn if a constant product sales mix is assumed.

- The **P/V chart** can show information about each product individually.

- The usefulness of CVP analysis is restricted by its **unrealistic assumptions**, such as constant sales price at all levels of activity. However CVP has the advantage of being more **easily understood** by non-financial managers due to its graphical depiction of cost and revenue data.

Quick Quiz

1   *Fill in the blanks.*

$$\text{Breakeven point} = \frac{}{\text{Contribution per mix}} = \frac{}{\text{Contribution per mix}}$$

2   C/S ratio = P/V ratio × 100. True or false?

3   *Fill in the blanks.*

$$\text{Margin of safety (as \%)} = \left(\frac{\text{........................ sales} - \text{........................ sales}}{\text{........................ sales}} \right) \times 100\%$$

4   Mark the following on the breakeven chart below.

●   Profit   ●   Variable costs
●   Sales revenue   ●   Fixed costs
●   Total costs   ●   Breakeven point
●   Margin of safety

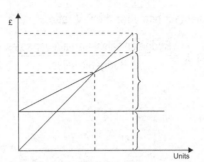

5   Mark the following on the P/V chart below.

●   Breakeven point   ●   Contribution
●   Fixed costs   ●   Profit

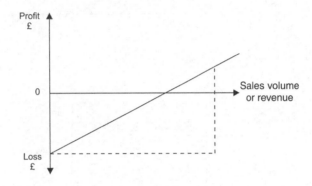

6   Which of the following is not a major assumption of breakeven analysis?

A   It can only apply to one product or a constant mix.
B   Fixed costs are the same in total and unit variable costs are the same at all levels of output.
C   Sales prices vary in line with levels of activity.
D   Production level is equal to sales level.

7   *Choose the appropriate words from those highlighted and fill in the blanks.*

When showing multiple products individually on a P/V chart, the products are shown from **left to right/right to left**, in order of **increasing/decreasing** size of C/S ratio. The line joining the two ends of the dotted line (which shows ....) indicates
....

8   *Choose the appropriate words from those highlighted.*

The assumption in breakeven analysis that variable cost is the same per unit at all levels of output is a great simplification. The variable cost per unit will decrease where (1) **economies/diseconomies** of scale are made at higher volumes of output, but will also eventually rise where (2) **economies/diseconomies** of scale begin to appear at even (3) **higher/lower** volumes of output.

1 $$\text{Breakeven point} = \frac{\text{Total fixed costs}}{\text{Contribution per unit}} = \frac{\text{Contribution required to breakeven}}{\text{Contribution per unit}}$$

2 False. The C/S ratio is another name for the P/V ratio.

3 $$\text{Margin of safety (as \%)} = \left(\frac{\text{Budgeted sales} - \text{breakeven sales}}{\text{Budgeted sales}} \right) \times 100\%$$

4

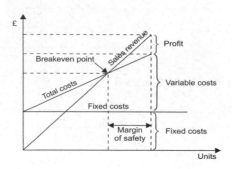

5

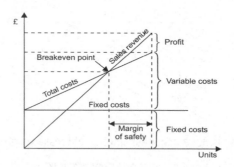

6 C. Sales prices *are constant* at all levels of activity.

7 When showing multiple products individually on a P/V chart, the products are shown from left to right, in order of decreasing size of C/S ratio. The line joining the two ends of the dotted line (which shows the cumulative profit/loss and the cumulative sales) indicates the average profit which will be earned from sales of the products in the mix.

8 (1) economies
  (2) diseconomies
  (3) higher

Now try the questions below from the Exam Question Bank

Number	Level	Marks	Time
7	Examination	20	36 mins

4

Limiting factor analysis

Topic list	Syllabus reference
1 Limiting factors	B3 (a)
2 Limiting factor analysis – make or buy decisions and scarce resources	B3 (b)
3 The principals of linear programming	B3 (a)
4 Formulating the problem	B3 (b),(c)
5 Graphing the model	B3 (c)
6 Finding the best solution	B3 (c)
7 Using simultaneous equations	B3 (c)
8 Slack and surplus	B3 (e)
9 Shadow prices	B3 (d)

Introduction

We have looked at **limiting factor analysis** in connection with throughput accounting in Chapter 2d and you will have encountered it in your earlier studies.

When there is more than one resource constraint, the technique of **linear programming** can be used. A multiple scarce resource problem can be solved using a **graphical method** and **simultaneous equations.**

We also look at the meaning and calculation of **shadow prices** and **slack.**

Study guide

		Intellectual level
B3	**Limiting factors**	
(a)	Identify limiting factors in a scarce resource situation and select an appropriate technique	2
(b)	Determine the optimal production plan where an organisation is restricted by a single limiting factor, including within the context of "make" or "buy" decisions	2
(c)	Formulate and solve a multiple scarce resource problem both graphically and using simultaneous equations as appropriate	2
(d)	Explain and calculate shadow prices (dual prices) and discuss their implications on decision-making and performance management	2
(e)	Calculate slack and explain the implications of the existence of slack for decision-making and performance management (Excluding simplex and sensitivity to changes in objective functions)	2

Exam guide

Linear programming is a popular topic in management accounting exams and is likely to be examined as a mixture of calculations and discussion. There is an article on linear programming in *Student Accountant*, March 2008. Please note that this article was not written by the current examiner.

1 Limiting factors

FAST FORWARD

All companies are limited in their capacity, either for producing goods or providing services. There is always one resource that is most restrictive (the **limiting factor**).

Key terms

A **limiting factor** is any factor that is in scarce supply and that stops the organisation from expanding its activities further, that is, it limits the organisations activities.

Knowledge brought forward from earlier studies

- An organisation might be faced with just one limiting factor (other than maximum sales demand) but there might also be several scarce resources, with two or more of them putting an effective limit on the level of activity that can be achieved.
- Examples of limiting factors include sales demand and production constraints.
  - **Labour**. The limit may be either in terms of total quantity or of particular skills.
  - **Materials**. There may be insufficient available materials to produce enough units to satisfy sales demand.
  - **Manufacturing capacity**. There may not be sufficient machine capacity for the production required to meet sales demand.
- It is assumed in limiting factor analysis that management would make a product mix decision or service mix decision based on the option that would maximise profit and that profit is maximised when contribution is maximised (given no change in fixed cost expenditure incurred). **In other words, marginal costing ideas are applied.**

- Contribution will be maximised by earning the biggest possible contribution per unit of limiting factor. For example if grade A labour is the limiting factor, contribution will be maximised by earning the biggest contribution per hour of grade A labour worked.
  - The limiting factor decision therefore involves the determination of the contribution earned per unit of limiting factor by each different product.
  - If the sales demand is limited, the profit-maximising decision will be to produce the top-ranked product(s) up to the sales demand limit.
- In limiting factor decisions, we generally assume that fixed costs are the same whatever product or service mix is selected, so that the only relevant costs are variable costs.
- When there is just one limiting factor, the technique for establishing the contribution-maximising product mix or service mix is to rank the products or services in order of contribution-earning ability per unit of limiting factor.

Exam focus point

If resources are limiting factors, **contribution** will be **maximised** by earning the biggest possible contribution per unit of limiting factor.

Where there is just one limiting factor, the technique for establishing the contribution-maximising product or service mix is to rank the products or services in order of contribution-earning ability per unit of limiting factor.

1.1 Example: Limiting factor decision

Sausage makes two products, the Mash and the Sauce. Unit variable costs are as follows.

	Mash	Sauce
	$	$
Direct materials	1	3
Direct labour ($3 per hour)	6	3
Variable overhead	1	1
	8	7

The sales price per unit is $14 per Mash and $11 per Sauce. During July the available direct labour is limited to 8,000 hours. Sales demand in July is expected to be as follows.

Mash	3,000 units
Sauce	5,000 units

Required

Determine the production budget that will maximise profit, assuming that fixed costs per month are $20,000 and that there is no opening inventory of finished goods or work in progress.

Solution

Step 1 Confirm that the limiting factor is something other than sales demand.

	Mash	Sauces	Total
Labour hours per unit	2 hrs	1 hr	
Sales demand	3,000 units	5,000 units	
Labour hours needed	6,000 hrs	5,000 hrs	11,000 hrs
Labour hours available			8,000 hrs
Shortfall			3,000 hrs

Labour is the limiting factor on production.

Step 2 Identify the contribution earned by each product per unit of scarce resource, that is, per labour hour worked.

	Mash	Sauce
	$	$
Sales price	14	11
Variable cost	8	7
Unit contribution	6	4
Labour hours per unit	2 hrs	1 hr
Contribution per labour hour (= per unit of limiting factor)	$3	$4

Although Mashes have a higher unit contribution than Sauces, two Sauces can be made in the time it takes to make one Mash. Because labour is in short supply it is more profitable to make Sauces than Mashes.

Step 3 Determine the budgeted production and sales. Sufficient Sauces will be made to meet the full sales demand, and the remaining labour hours available will then be used to make Mashes.

(a)

Product	Demand	Hours required	Hours available	Priority for manufacture
Sauces	5,000	5,000	5,000	1st
Mashes	3,000	6,000	3,000 (bal)	2nd
		11,000	8,000	

(b)

Product	Units	Hours needed	Contribution per unit	Total
			$	$
Sauces	5,000	5,000	4	20,000
Mashes (balance)	1,500	3,000	6	9,000
		8,000		29,000
Less fixed costs				20,000
Profit				9,000

Conclusion

(a) Unit contribution is *not* the correct way to decide priorities.

(b) Labour hours are the scarce resource, therefore **contribution per labour hour** is the correct way to decide priorities.

(c) The Sauce earns $4 contribution per labour hour, and the Mash earns $3 contribution per labour hour. Sauces therefore make more profitable use of the scarce resource, and should be manufactured first.

1.2 Two potentially limiting factors

You may be asked to deal with situations where two limiting factors are potentially limiting (and there are also product/service demand limitations). The approach in these situations is to find out which factor (if any) prevents the business from fulfilling maximum demand.

Exam focus point

Where there is a **maximum potential sales demand** for an organisation's products or services, they should still be ranked in order of contribution-earning ability per unit of the limiting factor. The contribution-maximising decision, however, will be to produce the top-ranked products (or to provide the top-ranked services) up to the sales demand limit.

1.3 Example: Two potentially limiting factors

Lucky manufactures and sells three products, X, Y and Z, for which budgeted sales demand, unit selling prices and unit variable costs are as follows.

	X		Y		Z	
Budgeted sales demand	550 units		500 units		400 units	
	$	$	$	$	$	$
Unit sales price		16		18		14
Variable costs: materials	8		6		2	
labour	4		6		9	
		12		12		11
Unit contribution		4		6		3

The organisation has existing inventory of 250 units of X and 200 units of Z, which it is quite willing to use up to meet sales demand. All three products use the same direct materials and the same type of direct labour. In the next year, the available supply of materials will be restricted to $4,800 (at cost) and the available supply of labour to $6,600 (at cost).

Required

Determine what product mix and sales mix would maximise the organisation's profits in the next year.

Solution

There **appear to be two scarce resources**, direct materials and direct labour. This is not certain, however, and because there is a limited sales demand as well, either of the following might apply.

- There is **no limiting factor at all**, except sales demand.

- There is **only one scarce resource** that prevents the full potential sales demand being achieved.

Step 1 **Establish which of the resources, if any, is scarce.**

	X	Y	Z
	Units	Units	Units
Budgeted sales	550	500	400
Inventory in hand	250	0	200
Minimum production to meet demand	300	500	200

	Minimum production to meet sales demand	Required materials at cost	Required labour at cost
	Units	$	$
X	300	2,400	1,200
Y	500	3,000	3,000
Z	200	400	1,800
Total required		5,800	6,000
Total available		4,800	6,600
(Shortfall)/Surplus		(1,000)	600

Materials are a limiting factor, but labour is not.

Step 2 **Rank** X, Y and Z in order of contribution earned per $1 of direct materials consumed.

	X	Y	Z
	$	$	$
Unit contribution	4	6	3
Cost of materials	8	6	2
Contribution per $1 materials	$0.50	$1.00	$1.50
Ranking	3rd	2nd	1st

Step 3 **Determine a production plan.** Z should be manufactured up to the limit where units produced plus units held in inventory will meet sales demand, then Y second and X third, until all the available materials are used up.

Ranking	Product	Sales demand less units held Units	Production quantity Units		Materials cost $
1st	Z	200	200	(× $2)	400
2nd	Y	500	500	(× $6)	3,000
3rd	X	300	175	(× $8)	*1,400
			Total available		4,800

* Balancing amount using up total available.

Step 4   **Draw up a budget.** The profit-maximising budget is as follows.

	X Units	Y Units	Z Units
Opening inventory	250	0	200
Add production	175	500	200
Sales	425	500	400

	X $	Y $	Z $	Total $
Revenue	6,800	9,000	5,600	21,400
Variable costs	5,100	6,000	4,400	15,500
Contribution	1,700	3,000	1,200	5,900

2 Limiting factor analysis - make or buy decisions and scarce resources

In a situation where a company must **sub-contract work to make up a shortfall in its own in-house capabilities**, its total costs will be minimised if those units bought have the lowest extra variable cost of buying per unit of scarce resource saved by buying.

2.1 Combining internal and external production

An organisation might **want to do more things than it has the resources for**, and so its alternatives would be as follows.

(a)   Make the best use of the available resources and ignore the opportunities to buy help from outside
(b)   Combine internal resources with buying externally so as to do more and increase profitability

Buying help from outside is justifiable if it **adds to profits**. A further decision is then required on how to split the work between **internal** and **external** effort. What parts of the work should be given to suppliers or sub-contractors so as to maximise profitability?

In a situation where a company must **sub-contract work to make up a shortfall in its own in-house capabilities**, its total costs will be minimised if those units bought have the lowest extra variable cost of buying per unit of scarce resource saved by buying.

2.1.1 Example: make or buy decisions with scarce resources

MM manufactures three components, S, A and T using the same machines for each. The budget for the next year calls for the production and assembly of 4,000 of each component. The variable production cost per unit of the final product is as follows.

	Machine hours	Variable cost
		$
1 unit of S	3	20
1 unit of A	2	36
1 unit of T	4	24
Assembly		20
		100

Only 24,000 hours of machine time will be available during the year, and a sub-contractor has quoted the following unit prices for supplying components: S $29; A $40; T $34.

Required

Advise MM.

Solution

The organisation's budget calls for 36,000 hours of machine time, if all the components are to be produced in-house. Only 24,000 hours are available, and so there is a shortfall of 12,000 hours of machine time, which is therefore a limiting factor. The shortage can be overcome by subcontracting the equivalent of 12,000 machine hours' output to the subcontractor.

The assembly costs are not relevant costs because they are unaffected by the decision.

The decision rule is to **minimise the extra variable costs of sub-contracting per unit of scarce resource saved** (that is, per machine hour saved).

	S	A	T
	$	$	$
Variable cost of making	20	36	24
Variable cost of buying	29	40	34
Extra variable cost of buying	9	4	10
Machine hours saved by buying	3 hrs	2 hrs	4 hrs
Extra variable cost of buying per hour saved	$3	$2	$2.50

This analysis shows that it is **cheaper to buy A than to buy T** and it is **most expensive to buy S**. The **priority for making** the components in-house will be in the **reverse order**: S, then T, then A. There are enough machine hours to make all 4,000 units of S (12,000 hours) and to produce 3,000 units of T (another 12,000 hours). 12,000 hours' production of T and A must be sub-contracted.

The cost-minimising and so profit-maximising make and buy schedule is as follows.

Component	Machine hours used/saved	Number of units	Unit variable cost	Total variable cost
			$	$
Make: S	12,000	4,000	20	80,000
T	12,000	3,000	24	72,000
	24,000			152,000
Buy: T	4,000	1,000	34	34,000
A	8,000	4,000	40	160,000
	12,000			346,000

Total variable cost of components, excluding assembly costs

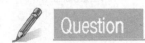

TW manufactures two products, the D and the E, using the same material for each. Annual demand for the D is 9,000 units, while demand for the E is 12,000 units. The variable production cost per unit of the D is $10, that of the E $15. The D requires 3.5 kgs of raw material per unit, the E requires 8 kgs of raw material per unit. Supply of raw material will be limited to 87,500 kgs during the year.

A sub contractor has quoted prices of $17 per unit for the D and $25 per unit for the E to supply the product. How many of each product should TW manufacture in order to maximise profits?

Required

Fill in the blanks in the sentence below.

TW should manufacture .... units of D and .... units of E to maximise profits.

Answer

The correct answer is: TW should manufacture 9,000 units of D and 7,000 units of E.

	D	E
	$ per unit	$ per unit
Variable cost of making	10	15
Variable cost of buying	17	25
Extra variable cost of buying	7	10
Raw material saved by buying	3.5 kgs	8 kgs
Extra variable cost of buying per kg saved	$2	$1.25
Priority for internal manufacture	1	2

Production plan		Material used
		kgs
∴ Make D	(9,000 × 3.5 kgs)	31,500
E	(7,000 × 8 kgs)	56,000
		87,500

The remaining 5,000 units of E should be purchased from the contractor.

3 The principals of linear programming 6/08

FAST FORWARD

Linear programming is a technique for solving problems of profit maximisation or cost minimisation and resource allocation. 'Programming' has nothing to do with computers: the word is simply used to denote a series of events. If a scenario contains **two or more limiting factors**, linear programming must be applied.

A typical business problem is to decide how a company should **divide up its production among the various types of product** it manufactures in order to obtain the **maximum possible profit**. A business cannot simply aim to produce as much as possible because there will be **limitations** or **constraints** within which the production must operate. Such constraints could be one or more of the following.

- Limited quantities of raw materials available
- A fixed number of man-hours per week for each type of worker
- Limited machine hours

Moreover, since the profits generated by different products vary, it may be better not to produce any of a less profitable line, but to concentrate all resources on producing the more profitable ones. On the other hand limitations in market demand could mean that some of the products produced may not be sold.

4 Formulating the problem   6/08

FAST FORWARD

Linear programming, at least at this fairly simple level, is a technique that can be carried out in a fairly 'handle turning' manner once you have got the basic ideas sorted out. The steps involved are as follows.

1	Define variables	5	Establish feasible region
2	Establish constraints	6	Add iso-profit/contribution line
3	Construct objective function	7	Determine optimal solution
4	Graph constraints		

Let us imagine that B Co makes just two models, the Super and the Deluxe, and that the **only constraint** faced by the company is that **monthly machine capacity is restricted to 400 hours**. The Super requires 5 hours of machine time per unit and the Deluxe 1.5 hours. Government restrictions mean that the maximum number of units that can be sold each month is 150, that number being made up of any combination of the Super and the Deluxe.

Let us now work through the steps involved in setting up a linear programming model.

Step 1   Define variables

What are the quantities that the company can vary? Obviously not the number of machine hours or the maximum sales, which are fixed by external circumstances beyond the company's control. The only things which it can determine are the number of each type of unit to manufacture. It is these numbers which have to be determined in such a way as to get the maximum possible profit. Our variables will therefore be as follows.

Let x = the number of units of the Super manufactured.
Let y = the number of units of the Deluxe manufactured.

Step 2   Establish constraints

Having defined these two variables we can now translate the two constraints into inequalities involving the variables.

Let us first consider the machine hours constraint. Each Super requires 5 hours of machine time. Producing five Supers therefore requires $5 \times 5 = 25$ hours of machine time and, more generally, producing x Supers will require $5x$ hours. Likewise producing y Deluxes will require $1.5y$ hours. The total machine hours needed to make x Supers and y Deluxes is $5x + 1.5y$. We know that this cannot be greater than 400 hours so we arrive at the following inequality.

$$5x + 1.5y \leq 400$$

We can obtain the other inequality more easily. The total number of Supers and Deluxes made each month is $x + y$ but this has to be less than 150 due to government restrictions. The sales order constraint is therefore as follows.

$$x + y \leq 150$$

Non-negativity

The variables in linear programming models should usually be non-negative in value. In this example, for instance, you cannot make a negative number of units and so we need the following constraints.

$$x \geq 0; y \geq 0$$

Do not forget these non-negativity constraints when formulating a linear programming model.

Step 3   Construct objective function

We have yet to introduce the question of profits. Let us assume that the profit on each model is as follows.

	$
Super	100
Deluxe	200

The **objective** of B Ltd is to **maximise profit** and so the **function** to be maximised is as follows.

Profit (P) = 100x + 200y

The problem has now been reduced to the following four inequalities and one equation.

$$5x + 1.5y \leq 400$$
$$x + y \leq 150$$
$$x \geq 0$$
$$y \geq 0$$
$$P = 100x + 200y$$

Have you noticed that **the inequalities are all linear expressions**? If plotted on a graph, they would all give **straight lines**. This explains why the technique is called **linear programming** and also gives a hint as to how we should proceed with trying to find the solution to the problem.

Question   Constraints

Patel Co manufactures two products, X and Y, in quantities x and y units per week respectively. The contribution is $60 per X and $70 per Y. For practical reasons, no more than 100 Xs can be produced per week. If Patel Co uses linear programming to determine a profit-maximising production policy and on the basis of this information, which one of the following constraints is correct?

A	$x \leq 60$	C	$x \leq 100$
B	$y \leq 100$	D	$60x + 70y \leq 100$

Answer

The correct answer is C because the question states that the number of Xs produced cannot exceed 100 and so $x \leq 100$.

Option A has no immediate bearing on the number of units of X produced which must be ≤ 100. ($60 represents the contribution per unit of X).

We have no information on the production volume of Product Y and option B is therefore incorrect.

The contribution earned per week is given by 60x + 70y but we have no reason to suppose that this must be less than or equal to 100. Option D is therefore incorrect.

Exam focus point

> Students often have problems with constraints of the style 'the quantity of one type must not exceed twice that of the other'. This can be interpreted as follows: the quantity of one type (say X) must not exceed (must be less than or equal to) twice that of the other (2Y) (ie $X \leq 2Y$).

We have looked at how to **formulate a problem** and in the next section we will look at solving a problem using graphs.

5 Graphing the model

FAST FORWARD A **graphical solution** is only possible when there are **two** variables in the problem. One variable is represented by the x axis and one by the y axis of the graph. Since non-negative values are not usually allowed, the graph shows only zero and positive values of x and y.

A linear equation with one or two variables is shown as a straight line on a graph. Thus y = 6 would be shown as follows.

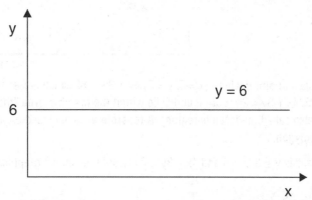

If the problem included a constraint that y could not exceed 6, the **inequality** y ≤ 6 would be represented by the shaded area of the graph below.

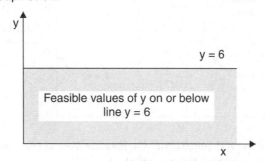

The equation 4x + 3y = 24 is also a straight line on a graph. To draw any straight line, we need only to plot two points and join them up. The easiest points to plot are the following.

(a)   x = 0 (in this example, if x = 0, 3y = 24, y = 8)
(b)   y = 0 (in this example, if y = 0, 4x = 24, x = 6)

By plotting the points, (0, 8) and (6, 0) on a graph, and joining them up, we have the line for 4x + 3y = 24.

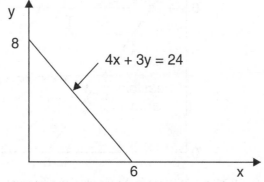

If we had a constraint 4x + 3y ≤ 24, any combined value of x and y within the shaded area below (on or below the line) would satisfy the constraint.

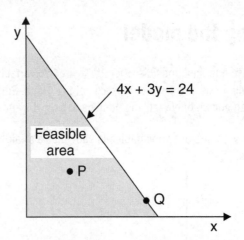

For example, at point P where (x = 2, y = 2) $4x + 3y = 14$ which is less than 24; and at point Q where x = 5.5, y = 2/3, $4x + 3y = 24$. Both P and Q lie within the **feasible area** (the area where the inequality is satisfied, also called the feasible region). A **feasible area** enclosed on all sides may also be called a **feasible polygon**.

The inequalities $y \geq 6$, $x \geq 6$ and $4x + 3y \geq 24$, would be shown graphically as follows.

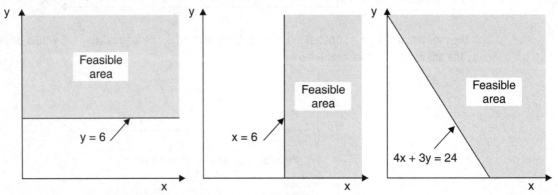

When there are several constraints, the feasible area of combinations of values of x and y must be an area where all the inequalities are satisfied.

Thus, if $y \leq 6$ *and* $4x + 3y \leq 24$ the feasible area would be the shaded area in the graph following

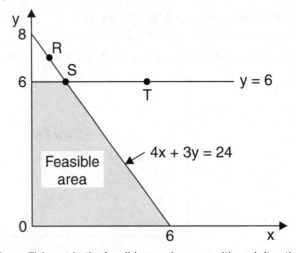

(a)   Point R (x = 0.75, y = 7) is not in the feasible area because although it satisfies the inequality $4x + 3y \leq 24$, it does not satisfy $y \leq 6$.

(b)   Point T (x = 5, y = 6) is not in the feasible area, because although it satisfies the inequality $y \leq 6$, it does not satisfy $4x + 3y \leq 24$.

(c)   Point S (x = 1.5, y = 6) satisfies both inequalities and lies just on the boundary of the feasible area since y = 6 exactly, and $4x + 3y = 24$. Point S is thus at the intersection of the two equation lines.

Similarly, if $y \geq 6$ and $4x + 3y \geq 24$ but $x \leq 6$, the feasible area would be the shaded area in the graph below.

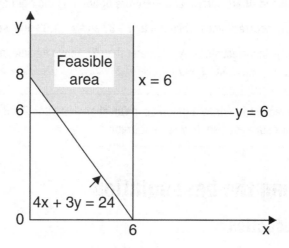

Question

Draw the feasible region which arises from the constraints facing B Co (see Section 2).

Answer

If $5x + 1.5y = 400$, then if $x = 0$, $y = 267$ and if $y = 0$, $x = 80$.
If $x + y = 150$, then if $x = 0$, $y = 150$ and if $y = 0$, $x = 150$

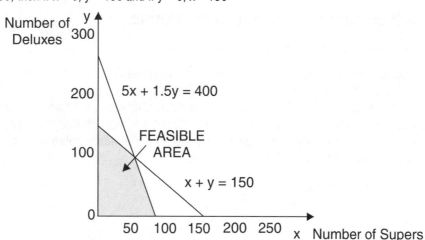

Question
Linear programming problem

In a linear programming problem, one of the constraints is given by $2x \leq 3y$. Which of the following statements about the graphical presentation of this constraint is correct?

I   The constraint line passes through the point $x = 2$, $y = 3$.
II   The constraint line passes through the origin.
III   The constraint line passes through the point $x = 3$, $y = 2$.
IV   The region below the constraint line is part of the feasible area.

A   I and II only   C   II and III only
B   I and III only   D   II, III and IV only

Answer

When $x = 0$ then y must also equal 0, therefore statement II is correct.

LEARNING MEDIA

When x = 3, 6 = 3y and hence y = 2, therefore statement III is correct.

Statements II and III are correct and therefore option C is the right answer.

Statement I is incorrect since when x = 2, 4 = 3y and y = 1.33 and y does not equal 3 when x = 2.

Statement IV is incorrect since 3y is greater than 2x above the line, not below it.

Exam focus point

You may be required to draw a graph as in Question 2 of June 2008. Marks will be available for labels and a title so make sure you can draw a clear graph.

6 Finding the best solution   6/08, 6/10

6.1 Introduction

Having found the **feasible region** (which includes all the possible solutions to the problem) we need to find which of these possible solutions is **'best'** in the sense that it yields the **maximum possible profit**. We could do this by finding out what profit each of the possible solutions would give, and then choosing as our 'best' combination the one for which the profit is greatest.

Consider, however, the feasible region of the problem faced by B Co (see the solution to the question entitled Feasible region). Even in such a simple problem as this, there are a great many possible solution points within the feasible area. Even to write them all down would be a time consuming process and also an unnecessary one, as we shall see.

6.2 Example: Finding the best solution

Let us look again at the graph of B Co's problem.

Consider, for example, the point A at which 40 Supers and 80 Deluxes are being manufactured. This will yield a profit of $((40 \times 100) + (80 \times 200)) = \$20,000$. We would clearly get more profit at point B, where the same number of Deluxes are being manufactured but where the number of Supers being manufactured has increased by five, or from point C where the same number of Supers but 10 more Deluxes are manufactured. This argument suggests that **the 'best' solution is going to be a point on the edge of the feasible area rather than in the middle of it**.

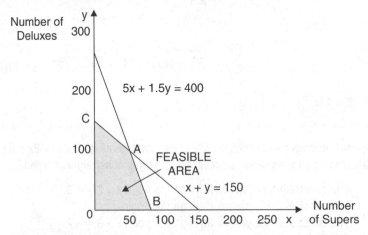

This still leaves us with quite a few points to look at but there is a way we can narrow down the candidates for the best solution still further. Suppose that B Co wish to make a profit of $10,000. The company could sell the following combinations of Supers and Deluxes.

(a)   100 Super, no Deluxe

(b)   No Super, 50 Deluxe

(c)   A proportionate mix of Super and Deluxe, such as 80 Super and 10 Deluxe or 50 Super and 25 Deluxe

The possible combinations of Supers and Deluxes required to earn a profit of $10,000 could be shown by the straight line $100x + 200y = 10{,}000$.

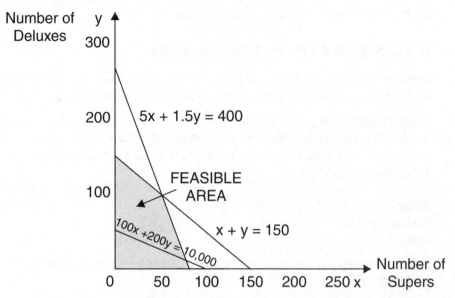

For a total profit of $15,000, a similar line $100x + 200y = 15{,}000$ could be drawn to show the various combinations of Supers and Deluxes which would achieve the total of $15,000.

Similarly a line $100x + 200y = 8{,}000$ would show the various combinations of Supers and Deluxes which would earn a total profit of $8,000.

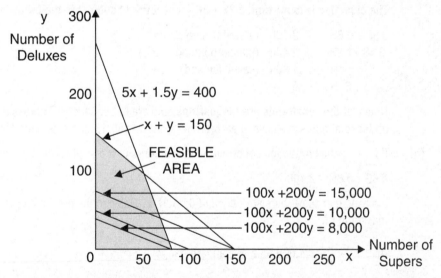

These profit lines are all parallel. (They are called **iso-profit lines**, 'iso' meaning equal.) A similar line drawn for any other total profit would also be parallel to the three lines shown here. This means that if we wish to know the slope or gradient of the profit line, for any value of total profit, we can simply draw one line for any convenient value of profit, and we will know that all the other lines will be parallel to the one drawn: they will have the same slope.

The easiest way to draw an iso-profit line is to multiply the values of x and y together, eg $100x + 200y = 10{,}000$.

Bigger profits are shown by lines further from the origin ($100x + 200y = 15{,}000$), **smaller profits by lines closer to the origin** ($100x + 200y = 8{,}000$). As B Co try to **increase possible profit** we need to **slide the profit line outwards from the origin**, while always keeping it **parallel** to the other profit lines.

As we do this there will come a point at which, if we were to move the profit line out any further, it would cease to lie in the feasible region and therefore larger profits could not be achieved in practice because of the constraints. In our example concerning B Co this will happen, as you should test for yourself, where the profit line is just passing through the intersection of x + y = 150 with the y axis (at (0, 150)). The point (0, 150) will therefore give us the best production combination of the Super and the Deluxe, that is, to produce 150 Deluxe models and no Super models.

6.3 Example: A maximisation problem

Brunel manufactures plastic-covered steel fencing in two qualities, standard and heavy gauge. Both products pass through the same processes, involving steel-forming and plastic bonding.

Standard gauge fencing sells at $18 a roll and heavy gauge fencing at $24 a roll. Variable costs per roll are $16 and $21 respectively. There is an unlimited market for the standard gauge, but demand for the heavy gauge is limited to 1,300 rolls a year. Factory operations are limited to 2,400 hours a year in each of the two production processes.

	Processing hours per roll	
Gauge	Steel-forming	Plastic-bonding
Standard	0.6	0.4
Heavy	0.8	1.2

What is the production mix which will maximise total contribution and what would be the total contribution?

Solution

(a)   Let S be the number of standard gauge rolls per year.

Let H be the number of heavy gauge rolls per year.

The objective is to maximise 2S + 3H (contribution) subject to the following constraints.

$$0.6S + 0.8H \leq 2,400 \quad \text{(steel-forming hours)}$$
$$0.4S + 1.2H \leq 2,400 \quad \text{(plastic-bonding hours)}$$
$$H \leq 1,300 \quad \text{(sales demand)}$$
$$S, H \geq 0$$

Note that **the constraints are inequalities**, and are not equations. There is no requirement to use up the total hours available in each process, nor to satisfy all the demand for heavy gauge rolls.

(b)   If we take the production constraint of 2,400 hours in the steel-forming process

$$0.6S + 0.8H \leq 2,400$$

it means that since there are only 2,400 hours available in the process, output must be limited to a maximum of:

(i) $\dfrac{2,400}{0.6}$ = 4,000 rolls of standard gauge;

(ii) $\dfrac{2,400}{0.8}$ = 3,000 rolls of heavy gauge; or

(iii)   a proportionate combination of each.

This maximum output represents the boundary line of the constraint, where the inequality becomes the equation

$$0.6S + 0.8H = 2,400.$$

(c)   The line for this equation may be drawn on a graph by joining up two points on the line (such as S = 0, H = 3,000; H = 0, S = 4,000).

(d)   The other constraints may be drawn in a similar way with lines for the following equations.

$$0.4S + 1.2H = 2,400 \text{ (plastic-bonding)} \qquad H = 1,300 \text{ (sales demand)}$$

(e)

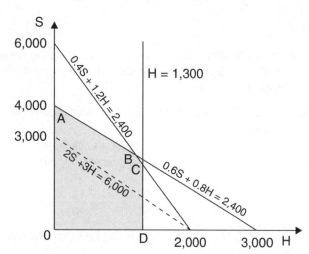

To satisfy all the constraints simultaneously, the values of S and H must lie on or below each constraint line. The outer limits of the **feasible polygon** are the lines, but all combined values of S and H within the shaded area are **feasible solutions**.

(f)   The next step is to find the **optimal solution**, which **maximises the objective function**. Since the objective is to **maximise contribution**, the solution to the problem must involve relatively high values (within the feasible polygon) for S, or H or a combination of both.

If, as is likely, there is only one combination of S and H which provides the optimal solution, this combination will be one of the **outer corners of the feasible polygon**. There are four such corners, A, B, C and D. However, it is possible that any combination of values for S and H on the boundary line between two of these corners might provide solutions with the same total contribution.

(g)   To solve the problem we establish **the slope of the iso-contribution lines**, by drawing a line for any one level of contribution. In our solution, a line 2S + 3H = 6,000 has been drawn. (6,000 was chosen as a convenient multiple of 2 and 3). **This line has no significance except to indicate the slope, or gradient, of every iso-contribution line for 2S + 3H.**

Using a ruler to judge at which corner of the feasible polygon we can draw an **iso-contribution line** which is as far to the right as possible, (away from the origin) but which still touches the **feasible polygon**.

(h)   This occurs at corner B where the constraint line 0.4S + 1.2H = 2,400 crosses with the constraint line 0.6S + 0.8H = 2,400. At this point, there are simultaneous equations, from which the exact values of S and H may be calculated.

0.4S +	1.2H	=	2,400	(1)
0.6S +	0.8H	=	2,400	(2)
1.2S +	3.6H	=	7,200	(3) ((1) × 3)
1.2S +	1.6H	=	4,800	(4) ((2) × 2)
	2H	=	2,400	(5) ((3) − (4))
	H	=	1,200	(6)

Substituting 1,200 for H in either equation, we can calculate that S = 2,400.

The contribution is maximised where H = 1,200, and S = 2,400.

	Units	Contribution per unit $	Total contribution $
Standard gauge	2,400	2	4,800
Heavy gauge	1,200	3	3,600
			8,400

The Dervish Chemical Company operates a small plant. Operating the plant requires two raw materials, A and B, which cost $5 and $8 per litre respectively. The maximum available supply per week is 2,700 litres of A and 2,000 litres of B.

The plant can operate using either of two processes, which have differing contributions and raw materials requirements, as follows.

| Process | Raw materials consumed (litres per processing hour) | | Contribution per hour |
	A	B	$
1	20	10	70
2	30	20	60

The plant can run for 120 hours a week in total, but for safety reasons, process 2 cannot be operated for more than 80 hours a week.

Formulate a linear programming model, and then solve it, to determine how many hours process 1 should be operated each week and how many hours process 2 should be operated each week.

Answer

The decision variables are processing hours in each process. If we let the processing hours per week for process 1 be P_1 and the processing hours per week for process 2 be P_2 we can formulate an objective and constraints as follows.

The objective is to maximise $70P_1 + 60P_2$, subject to the following constraints.

$$20P_1 + 30P_2 \leq 2,700 \quad \text{(material A supply)}$$
$$10P_1 + 20P_2 \leq 2,000 \quad \text{(material B supply)}$$
$$P_2 \leq 80 \quad \text{(maximum time for } P_2\text{)}$$
$$P_1 + P_2 \leq 120 \quad \text{(total maximum time)}$$
$$P_1, P_2 \geq 0 \quad \text{(non-negativity)}$$

The feasible area is ABCDO. The optimal solution, found by moving the iso-contribution line outwards, is at point A, where P_1 = 120 and P_2 = 0. Total contribution would be 120 × 70 = $8,400 a week.

6.4 Multiple solutions

It is possible that the optimum position might lie, not at a particular corner, but **all along the length of one of the sides of the feasibility polygon.** This will occur if the iso-contribution line is **exactly parallel** to one of the constraint lines.

If this happens then there is no one optimum solution but a **range of optimum solutions**. All of these will maximise the objective function at the same level. However, *any* value of the decision variables that happens to satisfy the constraint between the points where the constraint line forms part of the feasibility region would produce this optimum level of contribution.

6.5 Minimisation problems in linear programming

Although decision problems with limiting factors usually involve the maximisation of contribution, there may be a requirement to **minimise costs**. A graphical solution, involving two variables, is very similar to that for a maximisation problem, with the exception that instead of finding a contribution line touching the feasible area as far away from the origin as possible, we look for a **total cost line touching the feasible area as close to the origin as possible**.

6.5.1 Example: A minimisation problem

Claire Speke has undertaken a contract to supply a customer with at least 260 units in total of two products, X and Y, during the next month. At least 50% of the total output must be units of X. The products are each made by two grades of labour, as follows.

	X Hours	Y Hours
Grade A labour	4	6
Grade B labour	4	2
Total	8	8

Although additional labour can be made available at short notice, the company wishes to make use of 1,200 hours of Grade A labour and 800 hours of Grade B labour which has already been assigned to working on the contract next month. The total variable cost per unit is $120 for X and $100 for Y.

Claire Speke wishes to minimise expenditure on the contract next month. How much of X and Y should be supplied in order to meet the terms of the contract?

Solution

(a) Let the number of units of X supplied be x, and the number of units of Y supplied be y.

The objective is to minimise 120x + 100y (costs), subject to the following constraints.

$x + y$	$\geq$	260	(supply total)
x	$\geq$	0.5 (x + y)	(proportion of x in total)
$4x + 6y$	$\geq$	1,200	(Grade A labour)
$4x + 2y$	$\geq$	800	(Grade B labour)
x, y	$\geq$	0	

The constraint $x \geq 0.5\ (x + y)$ needs simplifying further.

$$x \geq 0.5\ (x + y)$$
$$2x \geq x + y$$
$$x \geq y$$

In a graphical solution, the line will be x = y. Check this carefully in the following diagram.

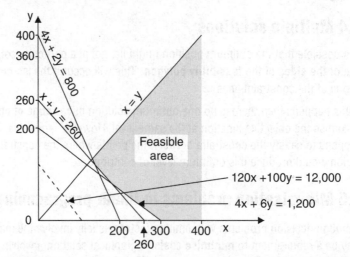

(b) The cost line 120x + 100y = 12,000 has been drawn to show the slope of every cost line 120x + 100y. **Costs are minimised where a cost line touches the feasible area as close as possible to the origin of the graph**. This occurs where the constraint line 4x + 2y = 800 crosses the constraint line x + y = 260. This point is found as follows.

x + y	=	260	(1)
4x + 2y	=	800	(2)
2x + y	=	400	(3) ((2) ÷ 2)
x	=	140	(4) ((3) − (1))
y	=	120	(5)

(c) Costs will be minimised by supplying the following.

	Unit cost	Total cost
	$	$
140 units of X	120	16,800
120 units of Y	100	12,000
		28,800

The proportion of units of X in the total would exceed 50%, and demand for Grade A labour would exceed the 1,200 hours minimum.

6.6 The use of simultaneous equations

You might think that a lot of time could be saved if we started by solving the simultaneous equations in a linear programming problem and did not bother to draw the graph.

Certainly, this procedure may give the right answer, but in general, it is *not* recommended until you have shown graphically which constraints are effective in determining the optimal solution. (In particular, if a question requires 'the graphical method', you *must* draw a graph). To illustrate this point, consider the following graph.

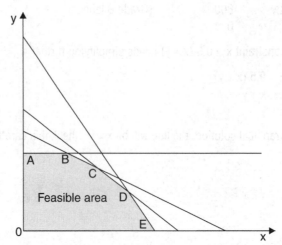

No figures have been given on the graph but the feasible area is OABCDE. When solving this problem, we would know that the optimum solution would be at one of the corners of the feasible area. We need to work out the profit at each of the corners of the feasible area and pick the one where the profit is greatest.

Once the optimum point has been determined graphically, simultaneous equations can be applied to find the exact values of x and y at this point.

7 Using simultaneous equations   6/08

FAST FORWARD

The optimal solution can also be found using **simultaneous equations**.

Instead of a 'sliding the contribution line out' approach, **simultaneous equations** can be used to determine the optimal allocation of resources, as shown in the following example.

7.1 Example: using simultaneous equations

An organisation manufactures plastic-covered steel fencing in two qualities: standard and heavy gauge. Both products pass through the same processes involving steel forming and plastic bonding.

The standard gauge sells at $15 a roll and the heavy gauge at $20 a roll. There is an unlimited market for the standard gauge but outlets for the heavy gauge are limited to 13,000 rolls a year. The factory operations of each process are limited to 2,400 hours a year. Other relevant data is given below.

Variable costs per roll

	Direct material	Direct wages	Direct expense
	$	$	$
Standard	5	7	1
Heavy	7	8	2

Processing hours per 100 rolls

	Steel forming Hours	Plastic bonding Hours
Standard	6	4
Heavy	8	12

Required

Calculate the allocation of resources and hence the production mix which will maximise total contribution.

Solution

Step 1   **Define variables**
Let the number of rolls of standard gauge to be produced be x and the number of rolls of heavy gauge be y.

Step 2   **Establish objective function**
Standard gauge produces a contribution of $2 per roll ($15 − $(5 + 7 + 1)) and heavy gauge a contribution of $3 ($20 − $(7 + 8 + 2)).

Therefore the objective is to maximise contribution (C) = 2x + 3y subject to the constraints below.

Step 3   **Establish constraints**
The constraints are as follows.

$$0.06x + 0.08y \leq 2,400 \quad \text{(steel forming hours)}$$
$$0.04x + 0.12y \leq 2,400 \quad \text{(plastic bonding hours)}$$
$$y \leq 13,000 \quad \text{(demand for heavy gauge)}$$
$$x, y \geq 0 \quad \text{(non-negativity)}$$

Step 4   **Graph problem**

The graph of the problem can now be drawn.

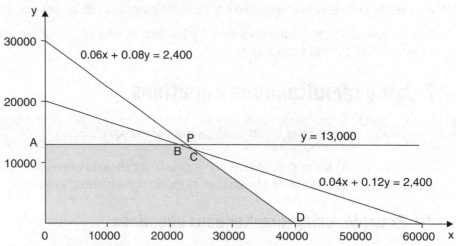

Step 5   **Define feasible area**

The combinations of x and y that satisfy all three constraints are represented by the area OABCD.

Step 6   **Determine optimal solution**

Which combination will maximise contribution? Obviously, the more units of x and y, the bigger the contribution will be, and the optimal solution will be at point B, C or D. It will not be at A, since at A, y = 13,000 and x = 0, whereas at B, y = 13,000 (the same) and x is greater than zero.

Using simultaneous equations to calculate the value of x and y at each of points B, C and D, and then working out total contribution at each point from this, we can establish the contribution-maximising product mix.

Point B

$$
\begin{array}{rcl}
y & = & 13,000 \, (1) \\
0.04x + 0.12y & = & 2,400 \, (2) \\
0.12y & = & 1,560 \, (3) \, ((1) \times 0.12) \\
0.04x & = & 840 \quad (4) \, ((2) - (3)) \\
x & = & 21,000 \, (5)
\end{array}
$$

Total contribution = (21,000 × $2) + (13,000 × $3) = $81,000.

Point C

$$
\begin{array}{rcl}
0.06x + 0.08y & = & 2,400 \, (1) \\
0.04x + 0.12y & = & 2,400 \, (2) \\
0.12x + 0.16y & = & 4,800 \, (3) \, ((1) \times 2) \\
0.12x + 0.36y & = & 7,200 \, (4) \, ((2) \times 3) \\
0.2y & = & 2,400 \, (5) \, ((4) - (3)) \\
y & = & 12,000 \, (6) \\
0.06x + 960 & = & 2,400 \, (7) \, (\text{substitute in } (1)) \\
x & = & 24,000 \, (8)
\end{array}
$$

Total contribution = (24,000 × $2) + (12,000 × $3) = $84,000.

Point D

Total contribution = 40,000 × $2 = $80,000.

Comparing B, C and D, we can see that contribution is maximised at C, by making 24,000 rolls of standard gauge and 12,000 rolls of heavy gauge, to earn a contribution of $84,000.

8 Slack and surplus

Slack occurs when maximum availability of a resource is not used. **Surplus** occurs when more than a minimum requirement is used.

Key term

Slack occurs when maximum availability of a resource is not used.

If, at the optimal solution, the resource used equals the resource available there is **no spare capacity** of a resource and so there is **no slack.**

If a resource which has a **maximum availability** is **not binding** at the optimal solution, there will be **slack**.

For example, a machine shop makes boxes (B) and tins (T). Contribution per box is $5 and per tin is $7. A box requires 3 hours of machine processing time, 16kg of raw materials and 6 labour hours. A tin requires 10 hours of machine processing time, 4kg of raw materials and 6 labour hours. In a given month, 330 hours of machine processing time are available, 400kg of raw material and 240 labour hours. The manufacturing technology used means that at least 12 tins must be made every month. The constraints are:

$3B + 10T \leq 330$
$16B + 4T \leq 400$
$6B + 6T \leq 240$
$\quad\quad T \geq 12$

The optimal solution is found to be to manufacture 10 boxes and 30 tins.

If we substitute these values into the inequalities representing the constraints, we can determine whether the constraints are binding or whether there is slack.

Machine time: $(3 \times 10) + (10 \times 30) = 330 =$ availability
Constraint is **binding**.

Raw materials: $(16 \times 10) + (4 \times 30) = 280 < 400$
There is **slack** of 120kg of raw materials.

Labour: $(6 \times 10) + (6 \times 30) = 240 =$ availability
Constraint is **binding**.

If a minimum quantity of a resource must be used and, at the optimal solution, **more than that quantity is used**, there is a **surplus** on the minimum requirement. This is shown here in the production of tins where the optimal production is 30 tins but $T \geq 12$. There is therefore a **surplus** of 18 tins over the minimum production requirement.

You can see from this that slack is associated with $\leq$ constraints and surplus with $\geq$ constraints. Machine time and labour are **binding constraints** so they have been used to their full capacity. It can be argued that if more machine time and labour could be obtained, more boxes and tins could be produced and contribution increased.

9 Shadow prices

The **shadow price** or **dual price** of a limiting factor is the increase in value which would be created by having one additional unit of the limiting factor at the original cost.

Key term

The **shadow price** is the increase in contribution created by the availability of an extra unit of a limited resource at its original cost.

9.1 Limiting factors and shadow prices

Whenever there are limiting factors, there will be **opportunity costs**. As you know, these are the **benefits forgone** by using a limiting factor in one way instead of in the next most profitable way.

For example, suppose that an organisation provides two services X and Y, which earn a contribution of $24 and $18 per unit respectively. Service X requires 4 labour hours, and service Y 2 hours. Only 5,000 labour hours are available, and potential demand is for 1,000 of each of X and Y.

Labour hours would be a limiting factor, and with X earning $6 per hour and Y earning $9 per hour, the profit-maximising decision would be as follows.

	Services	Hours	Contribution $
Y	1,000	2,000	18,000
X (balance)	750	3,000	18,000
		5,000	36,000

Priority is given to Y because the **opportunity cost** of providing Y instead of more of X is $6 per hour (X's contribution per labour hour), and since Y earns $9 per hour, the incremental benefit of providing Y instead of X would be $3 per hour.

If extra labour hours could be made available, more X (up to 1,000) would be provided, and an extra contribution of $6 per hour could be earned. Similarly, if fewer labour hours were available, the decision would be to provide fewer X and to keep provision of Y at 1,000, and so the loss of labour hours would cost the organisation $6 per hour in lost contribution. This $6 per hour, the **marginal contribution-earning potential of the limiting factor at the profit-maximising output level**, is referred to as the **shadow price** (or **dual price**) of the limiting factor.

Note that the shadow price only applies while the extra unit of resource can be obtained at its normal variable cost. The shadow price also indicates the amount by which contribution could fall if an organisation is deprived of one unit of the resource.

The shadow price of a resource is its **internal opportunity cost.** This is the marginal contribution towards fixed costs and profit that can be earned for each unit of the limiting factor that is available.

Depending on the resource in question, shadow prices enable management to make **better informed decisions** about the payment of overtime premiums, bonuses, premiums on small orders of raw materials and so on.

9.2 Linear programming and shadow prices

In terms of linear programming, the **shadow price** is the **extra contribution or profit that may be earned by relaxing by one unit a binding resource constraint**.

Suppose the availability of materials is a binding constraint. If one extra kilogram becomes available so that an alternative production mix becomes optimal, with a resulting increase over the original production mix contribution of $2, the shadow price of a kilogram of material is $2.

Note, however, that this increase in contribution of $2 per extra kilogram of material made available is calculated on the **assumption** that the **extra kilogram would cost the normal variable amount**.

Note the following points.

(a) The shadow price therefore represents the maximum **premium** above the basic rate that an organisation should be **willing to pay for one extra unit** of a resource.

(b) Since shadow prices indicate the effect of a one unit change in a constraint, they provide a measure of the **sensitivity** of the result.

(c) The **shadow price** of a constraint that is **not binding** at the optimal solution is **zero**.

(d) Shadow prices are **only valid for a small range** before the constraint becomes non-binding or different resources become critical.

9.3 Example: calculating shadow prices

Let us suppose that WX manufactures two products, A and B. Both products pass through two production departments, mixing and shaping. The organisation's objective is to maximise contribution to fixed costs.

Product A is sold for $1.50 whereas product B is priced at $2.00. There is unlimited demand for product A but demand for B is limited to 13,000 units per annum. The machine hours available in each department are restricted to 2,400 per annum. Other relevant data are as follows.

Machine hours required	Mixing	Shaping
	Hrs	Hrs
Product A	0.06	0.04
Product B	0.08	0.12

Variable cost per unit	$
Product A	1.30
Product B	1.70

The constraints are:

$$0.06x + 0.08y \leq 2,400$$
$$0.04x + 0.12y \leq 2,400$$
$$0 \leq y \leq 13,000$$
$$0 \leq x$$

The objective function is:

Contribution (C) = 0.2x + 0.3y

The availability of time in both departments are limiting factors because both are used up fully in the optimal product mix. Let us therefore calculate the effect if **one extra hour of shaping department machine time** was made available so that 2,401 hours were available.

The new optimal product mix would be at the intersection of the two constraint lines 0.06x + 0.08y = 2,400 and 0.04x + 0.12y = 2,401.

Solution by simultaneous equations gives x = 23,980 and y = 12,015.

(You should solve the problem yourself if you are doubtful about the derivation of the solution.)

Product	Units	Contribution per unit $	Total contribution $
A	23,980	0.20	4,796.0
B	12,015	0.30	3,604.5
			8,400.5

Contribution in original problem	
((24,000 × $0.20) + (12,000 × $0.30))	8,400.0
Increase in contribution from one extra hour of shaping time	0.5

The **shadow price** of an hour of machining time in the shaping department is therefore the standard machine cost *plus* $0.50.

This means that extra machine capacity could be rented, for example, provided the cost is less than $0.50 per hour.

This value of machine time only applies as long as shaping machine time is a limiting factor. If more and more machine hours become available, there will eventually be so much machine time that it is no longer a limiting factor.

Question

What is the shadow price of one hour of machine time in the mixing department?

A $3   C $10.50

B $7   D $1,193

Answer

The correct answer is A.

If we assume one more hour of machine time in the mixing department is available, the new optimal solution is at the intersection of $0.06x + 0.08y = 2,401$ and $0.04x + 0.12y = 2,400$

Solution by simultaneous equations gives $x = 24,030$, $y = 11,990$

Product	Units	Contribution per unit $	Total contribution $
A	24,030	0.20	4,806
B	11,990	0.30	3,597
			8,403
Contribution in original problem			8,400
Reduction in contribution			3

∴ Shadow price of one hour of machine time in the mixing department is $3.

Chapter Roundup

- All companies are limited in their capacity, either for producing goods or providing services. There is always one resource that is most restrictive (the **limiting factor**).

- In a situation where a company must **sub-contract work to make up a shortfall in its own in-house capabilities**, its total costs will be minimised if those units bought have the lowest extra variable cost of buying per unit of scarce resource saved by buying.

- **Linear programming** is a technique for solving problems of profit maximisation or cost minimisation and resource allocation. 'Programming' has nothing to do with computers: the word is simply used to denote a series of events. If a scenario contains **two or more limiting factors**, linear programming must be applied.

- **Linear programming**, at least at this fairly simple level, is a technique that can be carried out in a fairly 'handle turning' manner once you have got the basic ideas sorted out. The steps involved are as follows.

1	Define variables	5	Establish feasible region
2	Establish constraints	6	Add iso-profit/contribution line
3	Construct objective function	7	Determine optimal solution
4	Graph constraints		

- A **graphical solution** is only possible when there are two variables in the problem. One variable is represented by the x axis and one by the y axis of the graph. Since non-negative values are not usually allowed, the graph shows only zero and positive values of x and y.

- The optimal solution can also be found using **simultaneous equations**.

- **Slack** occurs when maximum availability of a resource is not used. **Surplus** occurs when more than a minimum requirement is used.

- The **shadow price** or **dual price** of a limiting factor is the increase in value which would be created by having one additional unit of the limiting factor at the original cost.

Quick Quiz

1   *Fill in the blanks.*

The shadow price of a scarce resource indicates the amount by which contribution would
.... if an organisation were deprived of one unit of the resource. The shadow price
only applies while the extra unit of resource can be obtained at its .... cost.

2   *Put the following steps in the graphical approach to linear programming in the correct order.*

Draw a graph of the constraints   Establish constraints
Define variables   Establish objective function
Establish the feasible region   Determine optimal product mix

3   In what circumstances does slack arise?

A   At the optimal solution, when the resource used equals the resource available

B   At the optimal solution, when a minimum quantity of a resource must be used, and more than that
    quantity is used

C   At the optimal solution, when the resource used is less than the resource available

D   At the optimal solution, when a minimum quantity of resource is used

Answers to Quick Quiz

1   fall
    normal variable

2   Define variables   Draw a graph of the constraints
    Establish objective function   Establish the feasible region
    Establish constraints   Determine optimal product mix

3   C. If a resource has a maximum availability and it's not binding at the optimal solution, there will be slack.

Now try the questions below from the Exam Question Bank

Number	Level	Marks	Time
Q8	Examination	20	36 mins

Pricing decisions

Topic list	Syllabus reference
1 Pricing policy and the market	B4 (a)
2 Demand	B4 (b), (c)
3 Decisions to increase production and sales	B4 (e)
4 The profit-maximising price/output level	B4 (d), (f)
5 Price strategies	B4 (g), (h)

Introduction

All profit organisations and many non-profit organisations face the task of setting a price for their products or services. Proper pricing of an organisation's products or services is essential to its profitability and hence its survival.

In this chapter we will begin by looking at the **factors which influence pricing** policy. Perhaps the most important of these is the **level of demand** for an organisation's product and how that demand changes as the price of the product changes (its **elasticity of demand**).

We will then turn our attention to the **profit-maximising price/output level** and a range of different **price strategies.**

Study guide

		Intellectual level
B4	**Pricing decisions**	
(a)	Explain the factors that influence the pricing of a product or service	2
(b)	Explain the price elasticity of demand	1
(c)	Derive and manipulate a straight line demand equation. Derive an equation for the total cost function (including volume-based discounts)	2
(d)	Calculate the optimum selling price and quantity for an organisation, equating marginal cost and marginal revenue	2
(e)	Evaluate a decision to increase production and sales levels, considering incremental costs, incremental revenues and other factors	2
(f)	Determine prices and output levels for profit maximisation using the demand based approach to pricing (both tabular and algebraic methods)	1
(g)	Explain different price strategies, including: (i) All forms of cost-plus (ii) Skimming (iii) Penetration (iv) Complementary product (v) Product-line (vi) Volume discounting (vii) Discrimination (viii) Relevant cost	2
(h)	Calculate a price from a given strategy using cost-plus and relevant cost	2

Exam guide

Exam questions on pricing are likely to be a mixture of calculation and discussion and the examiner will expect a **practical application** of pricing theories.

1 Pricing policy and the market

FAST FORWARD

> In the modern world there are many more **influences on price** than cost (eg competitors, product range, quality).

1.1 Influences on price

Influence	Explanation/Example
Price sensitivity	Sensitivity to price levels will vary amongst purchasers. Those that can pass on the cost of purchases will be the least sensitive and will therefore respond more to other elements of perceived value. For example, a business traveller will be more concerned about the level of service in looking for an hotel than price, provided that it fits the corporate budget. In contrast, a family on holiday are likely to be very price sensitive when choosing an overnight stay.
Price perception	Price perception is the way customers react to prices. For example, customers may react to a price increase by buying more. This could be because they expect further price increases to follow (they are 'stocking up').

Influence	Explanation/Example
Quality	This is an aspect of price perception. In the absence of other information, customers tend to judge quality by price. Thus a price rise may indicate improvements in quality, a price reduction may signal reduced quality.
Intermediaries	If an organisation distributes products or services to the market through independent intermediaries, such intermediaries are likely to deal with a range of suppliers and their aims concern their own profits rather than those of suppliers.
Competitors	In some industries (such as petrol retailing) pricing moves in unison; in others, price changes by one supplier may initiate a price war. Competition is discussed in more detail below.
Suppliers	If an organisation's suppliers notice a price rise for the organisation's products, they may seek a rise in the price for their supplies to the organisation.
Inflation	In periods of inflation the organisation may need to change prices to reflect increases in the prices of supplies, labour, rent and so on.
Newness	When a new product is introduced for the first time there are no existing reference points such as customer or competitor behaviour; pricing decisions are most difficult to make in such circumstances. It may be possible to seek alternative reference points, such as the price in another market where the new product has already been launched, or the price set by a competitor.
Incomes	If incomes are rising, price may be a less important marketing variable than product quality and convenience of access (distribution). When income levels are falling and/or unemployment levels rising, price will be more important.
Product range	Products are often interrelated, being complements to each other or substitutes for one another. The management of the pricing function is likely to focus on the profit from the whole range rather than the profit on each single product. For example, a very low price is charged for a loss leader to make consumers buy additional products in the range which carry higher profit margins (eg selling razors at very low prices whilst selling the blades for them at a higher profit margin).
Ethics	Ethical considerations may be a further factor, for example whether or not to exploit short-term shortages through higher prices.

1.2 Markets

FAST FORWARD

The price that an organisation can charge for its products will be determined to a greater or lesser degree by the **market** in which it operates.

Here are some familiar economic terms that might feature as background for a question or that you might want to use in a written answer.

Key terms

Perfect competition: many buyers and many sellers all dealing in an identical product. Neither producer nor user has any market power and both must accept the prevailing market price.

Monopoly: one seller who dominates many buyers. The monopolist can use his market power to set a profit-maximising price.

Monopolistic competition: a large number of suppliers offer similar, but not identical, products. The similarities ensure elastic demand whereas the slight differences give some monopolistic power to the supplier.

Oligopoly: where relatively few competitive companies dominate the market. Whilst each large firm has the ability to influence market prices, the unpredictable reaction from the other giants makes the final industry price indeterminate. Cartels are often formed.

1.3 Competition

In **established industries** dominated by a few major firms, it is generally accepted that a price initiative by one firm will be countered by a price reaction by competitors. In these circumstances, prices tend to be **fairly stable**, unless pushed upwards by inflation or strong growth in demand.

If a rival **cuts its prices** in the expectation of increasing its market share, a firm has several options.

(a) It will **maintain its existing prices** if the expectation is that only a small market share would be lost, so that it is more profitable to keep prices at their existing level. Eventually, the rival firm may drop out of the market or be forced to raise its prices.

(b) It may maintain its prices but respond with a **non-price counter-attack**. This is a more positive response, because the firm will be securing or justifying its current prices with a product change, advertising, or better back-up services.

(c) It may **reduce its prices**. This should protect the firm's market share so that the main beneficiary from the price reduction will be the consumer.

(d) It may **raise its prices** *and respond with a* **non-price counter-attack**. The extra revenue from the higher prices might be used to finance an advertising campaign or product design changes. A price increase would be based on a campaign to emphasise the quality difference between the firm's and the rival's products.

Question	Pricing in the modern business environment

What technique might be used to relate prices to cost in the modern business environment?

Answer

The answer, of course, is **target costing,** which you met in Chapter 2b. Price is determined by the market. Costs have to come below this price.

2 Demand

FAST FORWARD

Economic theory argues that the **higher the price of a good**, the **lower** will be the **quantity demanded**.

2.1 The economic analysis of demand

You know from your personal experience as a consumer that the theory of demand is essentially true, the higher the price of a good, the less will be demanded. We have already seen that in practice it is by no means as straightforward as this (some goods are bought *because* they are expensive, for example).

There are two extremes in the relationship between price and demand. A supplier can either **sell a certain quantity, Q, at any price** (as in graph (a)). Demand is totally unresponsive to changes in price and is said to be **completely inelastic**. Alternatively, **demand might be limitless at a certain price** P (as in graph (b)), but there would be no demand above price P and there would be little point in dropping the price below P. In such circumstances demand is said to be **completely elastic**.

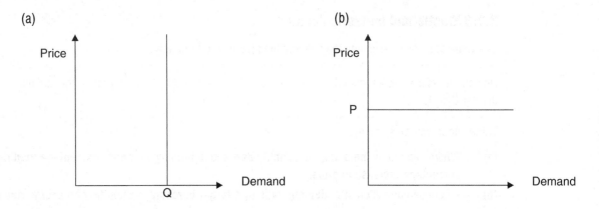

A more **normal situation** is shown below. The **downward-sloping** demand curve shows that demand will increase as prices are lowered. Demand is therefore **elastic**.

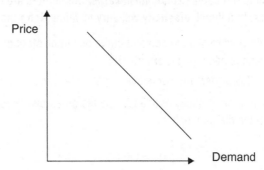

2.1.1 Price elasticity of demand (η)

The **price elasticity of demand (PED)** is a measure of the extent of change in demand for a good in response to a change in its price.

Key term

Price elasticity of demand (η) is a measure of the extent of change in market demand for a good in response to a change in its price. It is measured as:

$$\frac{\text{The change in quantity demanded, as a \% of demand}}{\text{The change in price, as a \% of the price}}$$

Since the demand goes up when the price falls, and goes down when the price rises, the elasticity has a negative value, but it is usual to ignore the minus sign.

2.1.2 Example: price elasticity of demand

The price of a good is $1.20 per unit and annual demand is 800,000 units. Market research indicates that an increase in price of 10 cents per unit will result in a fall in annual demand of 75,000 units. What is the price elasticity of demand?

Solution

Annual demand at $1.20 per unit is 800,000 units.

Annual demand at $1.30 per unit is 725,000 units.

% change in demand	=	(75,000/800,000) × 100% = 9.375%
% change in price	=	(0.10/1.20) × 100% = 8.333%
Price elasticity of demand	=	(−9.375/8.333) = −1.125

Ignoring the minus sign, price elasticity is 1.125.

The demand for this good, at a price of $1.20 per unit, would be referred to as **elastic** because the **price elasticity of demand is greater than 1**.

2.1.3 Elastic and inelastic demand

The value of demand elasticity may be anything from zero to infinity.

Demand is referred to as **inelastic** if the absolute value is less than 1 and **elastic** if the absolute value is greater than 1.

Think about what this means.

(a)   Where demand is **inelastic**, the **quantity demanded falls by a smaller percentage than the percentage increase in price**.

(b)   Where demand is **elastic, demand falls** by a **larger percentage than the percentage rise in price**.

2.1.4 Price elasticity and the slope of the demand curve

Generally, **demand curves slope downwards**. Consumers are willing to buy more at lower prices than at higher prices. In general, **elasticity** will **vary** in value **along the length of a demand curve**.

(a)   If a downward sloping demand curve becomes **steeper** over a particular range of quantity, then demand is becoming **more elastic**.

(b)   A **shallower** demand curve over a particular range indicates **more elastic** demand.

The ranges of price elasticity at different points on a downward sloping straight line demand curve are illustrated in the diagram below.

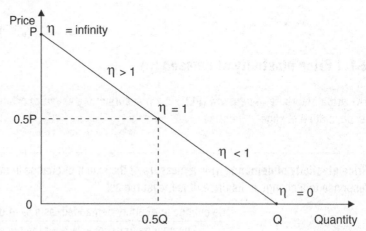

(a)   At **higher prices** on a straight line demand curve (the **top** of the demand curve), **small percentage price reductions** can bring **large percentage increases in the quantity** demanded. This means that **demand is elastic** over these ranges, and **price reductions** bring **increases in total expenditure** by consumers on the commodity in question.

(b)   At **lower prices** on a straight line demand curve (the **bottom** of the demand curve), **large percentage price reductions** can bring **small percentage increases in quantity**. This means that **demand is inelastic** over these price ranges, and **price increases** result in **increases in total expenditure**.

2.1.5 Special values of price elasticity

There are two special values of price elasticity of demand.

(a)   **Demand is perfectly inelastic ($\eta = 0$).** There is **no change in quantity** demanded, **regardless of the change in price**. The demand curve is **a vertical straight line** (as in graph (a) in Section 2.1).

(b)   **Perfectly elastic demand ($\eta = \infty$).** Consumers will want to **buy an infinite amount**, but **only up to a particular price** level. Any price increase above this level will reduce demand to zero. The demand curve is a **horizontal straight line** (as in graph (b) in Section 2.1).

2.1.6 Elasticity and the pricing decision

In practice, organisations will have only a rough idea of the shape of their demand curve: there will only be a limited amount of data about quantities sold at certain prices over a period of time *and,* of course, factors other than price might affect demand. Because any conclusions drawn from such data can only give an indication of likely future behaviour, management skill and expertise are also needed. Despite this limitation, an **awareness of the concept of elasticity can assist management with pricing decisions**.

(a)   (i)   In circumstances of **inelastic demand**, **prices should be increased** because revenues will increase and total costs will reduce (because quantities sold will reduce).

      (ii)   In circumstances of **elastic demand**, increases in prices will bring decreases in revenue and decreases in price will bring increases in revenue. Management therefore have to **decide** whether the **increase/decrease in costs will be less than/greater than the increases/decreases in revenue**.

(b)   In situations of **very elastic demand**, overpricing can lead to a massive drop in quantity sold and hence a massive drop in profits whereas underpricing can lead to costly stock outs and, again, a significant drop in profits. **Elasticity must therefore be reduced by creating a customer preference which is unrelated to price** (through advertising and promotional activities).

(c)   In situations of **very inelastic demand**, customers are **not sensitive to price**. **Quality, service, product mix and location** are therefore **more important** to a firm's pricing strategy.

Question

Elasticity

Read the four statements below. Where the statement is expressed in layman's terms, rephrase it using the appropriate variant of the term *elasticity*. Where it is already phrased in terms of elasticity, translate it into layman's terms.

(a)   We doubled sales of product A by dropping the price from $1.99 to $1.75.
(b)   Price elasticity of product B is low.
(c)   Demand for product C is highly inelastic.
(d)   A large reduction in price will be necessary to stimulate further demand for product D.

Answer

Situation (a) is an example of elastic demand; (b) is a case of *inelasticity* and should be appropriately worded; (c) is the same as (b); (d) is also an example of inelasticity.

2.2 Variables which influence demand

Here are some **variables which determine both the degree of elasticity and the volume of demand for a good in the market as a whole**.

Variable	Detail
Price of other goods	For some goods the market demand is connected to the price of other goods Such goods are of two types. (a) Substitutes, so that an increase in demand for one version of a good is likely to cause a decrease in demand for others. Common examples are rival brands of the same commodity (like Coca-Cola and Pepsi-Cola), bus journeys versus car journeys, or different forms of entertainment. (b) Complements, so that an increase in demand for one is likely to cause an increase in demand for the other. Examples are cups and saucers, cars and components, audits and tax consultancy.

Variable	Detail
Income	A rise in income gives households more to spend and they will want to buy more goods. However this phenomenon does not affect all goods in the same way. (a) Normal goods are those for which a rise in income increases the demand. (b) Inferior goods are those for which demand falls as income rises, such as cheap wine. (c) For some goods demand rises up to a certain point and then remains unchanged, because there is a limit to what consumers can or want to consume. Examples are basic foodstuffs such as salt and bread.
Tastes or fashion	A change in tastes or fashion will alter the demand for a good, or a particular variety of a good. Changes in taste may stem from psychological, social or economic causes. There is an argument that tastes and fashions are created by the producers of products and services. There is undeniably some truth in this, but the modern focus on responding to customers' needs and wants suggests otherwise.
Expectations	If consumers have expectations that prices will rise or that shortages will occur they will attempt to stock up on the product, thereby creating excess demand in the short term.
Obsolescence	Many products and services have to be replaced periodically because of obsolescence. (a) In early 2011 there will be substantial demand for audits for the year ended 31 December 2010. Demand will dry up once the statutory time limit for filing audited accounts is passed. In other words many services need to be bought repeatedly for reasons beyond the control of the consumer. A haircut is another example. (b) Physical goods are literally 'consumed'. Carpets become threadbare, glasses get broken, foodstuffs get eaten, children grow out of clothes. (c) Technological developments render some goods obsolete. Manual office equipment has been replaced by electronic equipment, because it does a better job, more quickly, quietly, efficiently and effectively.

2.3 Demand and the individual firm

We have looked at demand in the market as a whole. We also need to consider **factors that influence demand for one organisation's goods rather than another's.**

2.3.1 Product life cycle

FAST FORWARD

Most products pass through the five stages of the **product life cycle.**

To some extent this is an aspect of general demand and obsolescence: if you like we are talking about **built-in obsolescence** although this a rather cynical point of view. That aside, we can say that most products pass through the phases described in Chapter 2c.

Different versions of the same product may have **different life cycles**, and consumers are often aware of this. For example, the prospective buyer of a new car is more likely to purchase a recently introduced Ford than a Vauxhall that has been on the market for several years, even if there is nothing to choose in terms of quality and price.

2.3.2 Quality

One firm's product may be perceived to be better quality than another's, and may in some cases actually be so, if it uses sturdier materials, goes faster or does whatever it is meant to do in a 'better' way. Other things being equal, the **better quality good** will be **more in demand** than other versions.

2.3.3 Marketing

You may be familiar with the 'four Ps' of the marketing mix, all of which influence demand for a firm's goods.

(a) **Price**

(b) **Product**

(c) **Place** refers to the place **where a good can be purchased**, or is likely to be purchased.

    (i) If potential buyers find that a particular version of a good is difficult to obtain, they will turn to substitutes.

    (ii) Some goods have no more than local appeal.

(d) **Promotion** refers to the various means by which firms draw attention to their products and services.

    (i) A good **brand name** is a strong and relatively permanent influence on demand.

    (ii) Demand can be stimulated by a variety of **promotional tools**, such as free gifts, money off, shop displays, direct mail and media advertising.

In recent years, emphasis has been placed, especially in marketing, on the **importance of non-profit factors** in demand. Thus the roles of product quality, promotion, personal selling and distribution and, in overall terms, brands, have grown. Whilst it can be relatively easy for a competitor to copy a price cut, at least in the short term, it is much **more difficult to copy a successful brand image based on a unique selling proposition.** Successful branding can even imply premium pricing.

2.4 Deriving the demand equation

> **FAST FORWARD**
>
> You need to be able to derive the **demand equation** $P = a - bQ$.

Exam formulae

> When demand is linear the equation for the demand curve is:
>
> $P = a - bQ$
>
> where P = the price
> Q = the quantity demanded
> a = the price at which demand would be nil
> b = $\dfrac{\text{change in price}}{\text{change in quantity}}$
>
> The constant a is calculated as follows.
>
> $a = \$(\text{current price}) + \left(\dfrac{\text{Current quantity at current price}}{\text{Change in quantity when price is changed by \$b}} \times \$b \right)$

Note that 'b' represents the gradient of the demand curve. Since the demand goes up when the price falls, and goes down when the price rises, the elasticity has a negative value, but it is usual to ignore the minus sign.

This looks rather complicated in words, but it is very easy once the numbers are substituted.

2.4.1 Example: deriving the demand equation

The current price of a product is $12. At this price the company sells 60 items a month. One month the company decides to raise the price to $15, but only 45 items are sold at this price. Determine the demand equation.

Solution

Step 1 **Find the price at which demand would be nil**

Assuming demand is linear, each increase of $3 in the price would result in a fall in demand of 15 units. For demand to be nil, the price needs to rise from its current level by as many times as there are 15 units in 60 units (60/15 = 4) ie to $12 + (4 × $3) = $24.

Using the formula above, this can be shown as a = $12 + ((60/15) × $3)= $24

Step 2 **Calculate b**

$$b = \frac{change\ in\ price}{change\ in\ quantity} = \frac{\$15 - \$12}{60 - 45} = \frac{3}{15} = 0.2$$

The demand equation is therefore P = 24 − 0.2Q

Step 3 **Check your equation**

We can check this by finding Q when P is $12.

12 = 24 − (0.2Q)
0.2Q = 24 − 12
0.2Q = 12
$$Q = \frac{12}{0.2} = 60$$

An alternative approach is to find 'b' first, then substitute the known value for 'b' into the demand function.

Step 1 **Calculate b**

$$b = \frac{change\ in\ price}{change\ in\ quantity} = \frac{\$15 - \$12}{60 - 45} = \frac{3}{15} = 0.2$$

Step 2 **Substitute the known value for 'b' into the demand function to find 'a'**

P = a − (0.2Q)

12 = a − (0.2 x 60)

12 = a − 12

a = 24

The demand equation is therefore P = 24 − 0.2Q

Step 3 **Check your equation**

We can check this by finding Q when P is $12.

12 = 24 − (0.2Q)
0.2Q = 24 − 12
0.2Q = 12
$$Q = \frac{12}{0.2} = 60$$

 Question

Deriving the demand equation

The current price of a product is $30 and the producers sell 100 items a week at this price. One week the price is dropped by $3 as a special offer and the producers sell 150 items. Find an expression for the demand curve.

a $= \$30 + (100/50 \times \$3)$ $= \$36$

b $= \dfrac{\$3}{150 - 100} = 0.06$

P $= 36 - 0.06Q$

Check

27 $= 36 - 0.06Q$

0.06Q $= 36 - 27$

Q $= \dfrac{9}{0.06} = 150$

2.5 The total cost function

FAST FORWARD

Cost behaviour can be **modelled** using equations.

Determining the optimum price and output level requires that **cost and revenue behaviour** can be **modelled using equations**. These equations can range from simple to complex, although those you encounter in the exam will tend towards the 'simple' end of the range.

An organisation's total costs (TC) might be modelled by the equation TC = 6,500 + 0.75Q, where Q is the number of units sold.

Here the cost model is a simple linear equation of the form y = a + bx, where a ($6,500) represents the fixed costs and b ($0.75) represents the unit variable cost.

In your earlier studies, you will have covered how this equation can be derived using **linear regression analysis**. As you will remember, 'a' is the intercept of the line on the y axis and 'b' is the slope of the line.

The following graph demonstrates the total cost function.

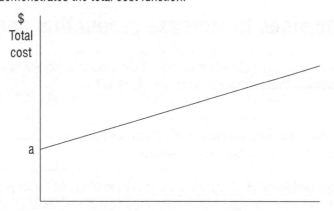

There are a number of **problems** associated with using such models.

(a) The cost model assumes fixed costs remain unchanged over all ranges of output. (Think about the possibility of step costs, say.)

(b) The cost model assumes a constant unit variable cost over all ranges of output (Think about the implications of economies and diseconomies of scale).

2.5.1 Volume based discounts

Key term

A **volume-based discount** is a discount given for buying in bulk.

A volume-based discount will **reduce** the variable cost per unit. The value of b will therefore be lower the more units are purchased.

For example, the price of a unit of material used in production is $5 for the first 1,000 units, $4.50 for 1,001 to 5,000 units and $4 for 5,001 to 10,000 units.

If fixed costs remain at $1,000 up to 10,000 units of production and only material costs vary, there will be three cost equations to consider.

0 →	1,000 units:	y = 1,000 + 5x
1,001 →	5,000 units:	y = 1,000 + 4.5x
5,001 →	10,000 units:	y = 1,000 + 4x

This can be shown on a graph as:

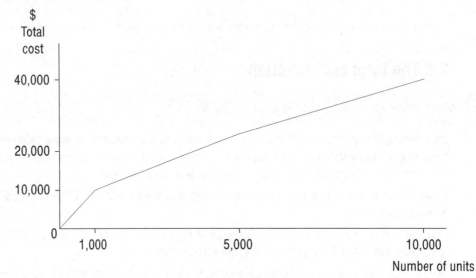

Notice how the slope of the line becomes **less steep** as more units are made and the variable cost per unit **falls**.

3 Decisions to increase production and sales   12/07

If you are required to evaluate a decision to increase production and sales levels, you will need to consider **incremental costs, incremental revenues** and other factors.

Key term

> **Incremental costs and revenues** are the difference between costs and revenues for the corresponding items under each alternative being considered.   *Drury*

The **incremental cost** of increasing production from 500 to 600 units per month is the additional cost of producing an extra 100 units each month. If fixed costs increase as a result of the decision, they are an incremental cost together with the increased variable costs of production.

3.1 Example: a decision to increase production

George manufactures a product which uses two types of material, A and B. Each unit of production currently sells for $10. A local trader has expressed an interest in buying 5,000 units but is only prepared to pay $9 per unit.

Current costs and revenues are as follows.

	$'000	$'000
Sales		350
Less production costs		
Material A – 1 kg per unit	25	
Material B – 1 litre per unit	50	

	$'000	$'000
Labour – 1 hour per unit	75	
Variable overhead	50	
Fixed overhead	25	
Non-production costs	25	
Total cost		250
Budgeted profit		100

The following additional information has also been made available.

(a)   There is minimal inventory of material available and prices for new material are expected to be 5% higher for Material A and 3% higher for Material B.

(b)   George has been having problems with his workforce and is short of labour hours. He currently has the capacity to produce 36,000 units but would have to employ contract labour at $3.50 per hour to make any additional units.

(c)   Included in the fixed production overhead is the salary of the production manager. He is stressed and exhausted and has threatened to leave unless he receives a pay rise of $5,000. George would not be able to fulfil any new orders without him.

Required

Evaluate whether George should accept the new order.

Solution

Workings

Current production = 350,000/10 = 35,000 units

Current cost per unit of Material A $= \dfrac{\$25,000}{35,000} = \$0.71$

Current cost per unit of Material B $= \dfrac{\$50,000}{35,000} = \$1.43$

Current cost of labour $= \dfrac{\$75,000}{35,000} = \$2.14$

	$	$
Incremental revenue (5,000 × $9)		45,000
Incremental costs		
Material A (1.05 × $0.71 × 5,000)	3,728	
Material B (1.03 × $1.43 × 5,000)	7,365	
Labour [(1,000 × $2.14) + (4,000 × $3.50)]	16,140	
Fixed overhead	5,000	
		32,233
Incremental profit		12,767

The new order would produce an additional $12,767 so is probably worthwhile but other factors may need to be considered. For example, the effect of a price cut on existing customer expectations and whether the workforce and production manager will be able to fulfil the new order with the same labour efficiency.

4 The profit-maximising price/output level

Profits are maximised using marginalist theory when **marginal cost (MC) = marginal revenue (MR)**. The **optimal selling price** can be determined using equations (ie when MC = MR). The **optimum selling price** can also be determined using tabulation.

The overall objective of an organisation should be **profit maximisation**. In this section we look at how the profit-maximising price and output levels can be derived. Remember that, in microeconomic theory, profits are maximised when marginal revenue = marginal cost.

4.1 Microeconomic theory and profit maximisation

In economics, **profit maximisation** is the process by which a firm determines the price and output level that returns the greatest profit. There are two common approaches to this problem.

(a)   The **Total revenue (TR) – Total cost (TC)** method is based on the fact that profit equals revenue minus cost.

(b)   The **Marginal revenue (MR) – Marginal cost (MC)** method is based on the fact that total profit in a perfect market reaches its maximum point where marginal revenue equals marginal cost.

To obtain the profit maximising output quantity under the TR – TC method, we start by recognising that profit is equal to total revenue minus total cost.

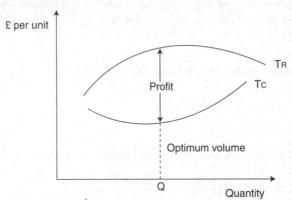

From the graph above it is evident that the difference between **total costs** and **total revenue** is greatest at point Q. This is the profit maximising output quantity.

4.2 MC = MR

Microeconomic theory suggests that as output increases, the marginal cost per unit might rise (due to the law of diminishing returns) and whenever the firm is faced with a downward sloping demand curve, the **marginal revenue per unit will decline**.

Eventually, a level of output will be reached where the **extra cost** of making one extra unit of output is greater than the **extra revenue** obtained from its sale. It would then be unprofitable to make and sell that extra unit.

Profits will continue to be maximised only up to the output level where marginal cost has risen to be exactly equal to the marginal revenue.

Profits are maximised using marginalist theory when **marginal cost (MC) = marginal revenue (MR)**.

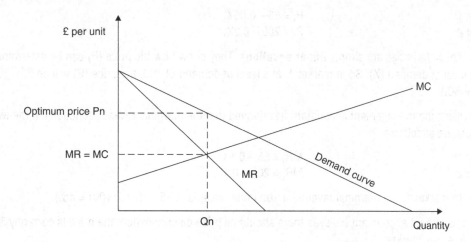

Profits are **maximised** at the point where **MC = MR**, ie at a volume of Qn units. If we add a demand curve to the graph, we can see that at an output level of Qn, the sales price per unit would be Pn.

It is important to make a clear distinction in your mind between the **sales price** and **marginal revenue**. In this example, the optimum price is Pn, but the marginal revenue is much less. This is because the 'additional' sales unit to reach output Qn has only been achieved by reducing the unit sales **price** from an amount higher than Pn for all the units to be sold, not just the marginal extra one. The increase in sales volume is therefore partly offset by a reduction in unit price; hence MR is lower than Pn.

4.3 Determining the profit-maximising selling price: using equations

The **optimal selling price** can be determined using equations (ie when **MC = MR**).

You could be **provided with equations for marginal cost and marginal revenue** and/or have to **devise them from information** in the question. By **equating the two equations** you can determine the optimal price. Remember, **marginal cost** is the **extra cost of producing one extra unit**, **marginal revenue** is the **extra revenue from producing one extra unit**. **Marginal revenue may not be the same as** the **price** charged for all units up to that demand level, as to increase volumes the price may have to be reduced.

Section 2.4 outlined the demand curve equation. The **marginal revenue equation** can be found by doubling the value of *b*. The **marginal cost** is the variable cost of production

Exam formulae

$$MR = a - 2bQ$$

where   P   = the price
              Q   = the quantity demanded
              a   = the price at which demand would be nil
              b $= \dfrac{\text{change in price}}{\text{change in quantity}}$

The constant a is calculated as follows.

$$a = \$(\text{current price}) + \left(\frac{\text{Current quantity at current price}}{\text{Change in quantity when price is changed by \$b}} \times \$b \right)$$

You will need to be able to solve simple examples like those that follow.

4.3.1 Example: MC = MR

MOC makes and sells a copyrighted, executive game for two distinct markets, in which it has a monopoly. The fixed costs of production per month are $20,000 and variable costs per unit produced, and sold, are $40. (The monthly sales can be thought of as X, where $X = X_1 + X_2$, with X_1 and X_2 denoting monthly sales in their respective markets.) Detailed market research has revealed the demand functions in the markets to be as follows, with prices shown as P_1, P_2.

Market 1: $P_1 = 55 - 0.05X_1$
Market 2: $P_2 = 200 - 0.2X_2$

(Note. These formulae are simply **linear equations**. They show how the price (P) can be determined for a given level of demand (X). So in market 1, at a level of demand of 100, the price (P) will be $55 - (0.05 \times 100) = 50$.)

From these, the management accountant has derived that the marginal revenue functions in the two markets are as follows.

Market 1: $MR_1 = 55 - 0.1X_1$
Market 2: $MR_2 = 200 - 0.4X_2$

(Note. In market 1, the marginal revenue if 100 units are sold is $55 - (0.1 \times 100) = 45$.)

The management accountant believes there should be price discrimination; the price is currently $50 per game in either market.

Required

Analyse the information for the executive game and, given the management accountant's belief, do the following.

(a)   Calculate the price to charge in each market, and the quantity to produce (and sell) each month, to maximise profit.

(b)   Determine the revenue function for each market and the maximum monthly profit in total.

(c)   Calculate and comment on the change in total profitability and prices.

Solution

(a)   In both markets, **marginal cost = variable cost per unit** = $40

Profit is maximised when **marginal revenue = marginal cost**.

Market 1
$55 - 0.1X_1$ $= 40$
$0.1X_1$ $= 15$
X_1 $= 15/0.1 = 150$

and price $P_1 = 55 - (0.05 \times 150) = \$47.5$.

Hence the price in market 1 should be $47.50 per unit and 150 units should be produced.

Market 2
$200 - 0.4X_2$ $= 40$
$0.4X_2$ $= 160$
X_2 $= 160/0.4 = 400$

and price $P_2 = 200 - (0.2 \times 400) = \$120$.

Hence the price in market 2 should be $120 per unit and 400 units should be produced.

Total number of items to be produced per month is 550.

(b)   **Revenue = unit price × number of units sold**

Market 1

Revenue $= P_1X_1 = 55X_1 - 0.05X_1^2$

Market 2

Revenue $= P_2X_2 = 200X_2 - 0.2X_2^2$

From (a), profit is maximised when

$X_1 = 150$ and $X_2 = 400$

$P_1 = 47.5$ and $P_2 = 120$

At maximum profit:

Total revenue = (47.5 × 150) + (120 × 400) = $55,125

Total costs = 20,000 + (40 × 550) = $42,000

Total maximum monthly profit = $13,125

(c) Currently the price is $50 in both markets.

Market 1	$50 = 55 - 0.05X_1$
	$0.05X_1 = 55 - 50 = 5$
	$X_1 = 5/0.05 = 100$
Market 2	$50 = 200 - 0.2X_2$
	$0.2X_2 = 200 - 50 = 150$
	$X_2 = 150/0.2 = 750$

Therefore the **total number of units** = 100 + 750 = 850.

Total revenue = $50 × 850 = $42,500.

Total cost = 20,000 + (40 × 850) = $54,000.

So the game **currently makes a loss** of $11,500.

Hence, if the prices are changed to $47.50 in market 1 and $120 in market 2, the company can expect to turn a monthly loss of $11,500 into a profit of $13,125.

You will be provided with equations representing MC and MR if they are needed. Note, however, that if a question states that the extra cost of producing one extra item is $20, say, you will be expected to realise that the MC is $20. Likewise, if you are told that **100 units are sold for $10 each**, but **101 can only be sold for $9.99**, the **MR of the 101st item is (101 × $9.99) – (100 × $10) = $8.99**.

Question
Deriving a MR equation from the demand curve

AB has used market research to determine that if a price of $250 is charged for product G, demand will be 12,000 units. It has also been established that demand will rise or fall by 5 units for every $1 fall/rise in the selling price. The marginal cost of product G is $80.

Required

If marginal revenue = a –2bQ when the selling price (P) = a – bQ, calculate the profit-maximising selling price for product G.

Answer

$$b = \frac{\text{change in price}}{\text{change in quantity}} = \frac{\$1}{5} = 0.2$$

$a = \$250 + ((12,000/5) \times \$1) = \$2,650$

$MR = 2,650 - (2 \times 0.2)Q \quad = 2,650 - 0.4Q$

Profits are maximised when MC = MR, ie when $80 = 2,650 - 0.4Q$

$$2,650 - 80 = 2,570 \times \frac{10}{4} = 6,425$$

Profit-maximising demand = 6,425

Now, substitute the values into the demand curve equation to find the profit-maximising selling price

$P = a - bQ$

$P = 2,650 - (0.2 \times 6,425)$

$\therefore$ Profit-maximising price $= \$(2,650 - 1,285)$

$\qquad\qquad\qquad\qquad\quad = \$1,365$

4.4 Determining the profit-maximising selling price: visual inspection of a tabulation of data

The **optimum selling price** can also be determined using tabulation.

To determine the profit-maximising selling price:

(a) Work out the **demand curve** and hence the **price** and the **total revenue** (PQ) at various levels of demand.

(b) Calculate **total cost** and hence **marginal cost** at each level of demand.

(c) Finally calculate **profit** at each level of demand, thereby determining the price and level of demand at which profits are maximised.

Question | Tabulation approach to find profit-maximising price

An organisation operates in a market where there is imperfect competition, so that to sell more units of output, it must reduce the sales price of all the units it sells. The following data is available for prices and costs.

Total output Units	Sales price per unit (AR) $	Average cost of output (AC) $ per unit
0	–	–
1	504	720
2	471	402
3	439	288
4	407	231
5	377	201
6	346	189
7	317	182
8	288	180
9	259	186
10	232	198

The total cost of zero output is $600.

Required

Complete the table below to determine the output level and price at which the organisation would maximise its profits, assuming that fractions of units cannot be made.

Units	Price $	Total revenue $	Marginal revenue $	Total cost $	Marginal cost $	Profit $
0						
1						
2						
3						
4						
5						
6						
7						

Units	Price	Total revenue	Marginal revenue	Total cost	Marginal cost	Profit
8						
9						
10						

Answer

The correct answer is that profit is maximised at seven units of output and a price of $317, when MR is most nearly equal to MC.

Units	Price	Total revenue	Marginal revenue	Total cost	Marginal cost	Profit
	$	$	$	$	$	$
0	0	0	0	600	-	(600)
1	504	504	504	720	120	(216)
2	471	942	438	804	84	138
3	439	1,317	375	864	60	453
4	407	1,628	311	924	60	704
5	377	1,885	257	1,005	81	880
6	346	2,076	191	1,134	129	942
7	317	2,219	143	1,274	140	945
8	288	2,304	85	1,440	166	864
9	259	2,331	27	1,674	234	657
10	232	2,320	(11)	1,980	306	340

5 Price strategies   6/10

> **FAST FORWARD**
>
> The price to be charged for a product or service is often one of the most important decisions made by managers. There are a number of alternative pricing strategies.

5.1 Cost-plus pricing

> **FAST FORWARD**
>
> **Full cost-plus pricing** is a method of determining the sales price by calculating the full cost of the product and adding a percentage mark-up for profit.

In practice cost is one of the most important influences on price. Many firms base price on simple **cost-plus rules** (costs are estimated and then a profit margin is added in order to set the price).

The 'full cost' may be a fully absorbed production cost only, or it may include some absorbed administration, selling and distribution overhead.

A business might have an idea of the percentage profit margin it would like to earn, and so might **decide on an average profit mark-up** as a general guideline for pricing decisions.

Businesses that carry out a large amount of **contract work or jobbing work**, for which individual job or contract prices must be quoted regularly would find this a useful method to adopt. The percentage profit **mark-up**, however, **does not have to be rigid and fixed**, but can be varied to suit different circumstances.

5.1.1 Example: Full cost-plus pricing

Markup has begun to produce a new product, Product X, for which the following cost estimates have been made.

	$
Direct materials	27
Direct labour: 4 hrs at $5 per hour	20
Variable production overheads: machining, ½ hr at $6 per hour	3
	50

Production fixed overheads are budgeted at $300,000 per month and because of the shortage of available machining capacity, the company will be restricted to 10,000 hours of machine time per month. The absorption rate will be a direct labour rate, however, and budgeted direct labour hours are 25,000 per month. It is estimated that the company could obtain a minimum contribution of $10 per machine hour on producing items other than product X.

The direct cost estimates are not certain as to material usage rates and direct labour productivity, and it is recognised that the estimates of direct materials and direct labour costs may be subject to an error of ± 15%. Machine time estimates are similarly subject to an error of ± 10%.

The company wishes to make a profit of 20% on full production cost from product X.

Required

Ascertain the full cost-plus based price.

Solution

Even for a relatively 'simple' cost-plus pricing estimate, some problems can arise, and certain assumptions must be made and stated. In this example, we can identify two problems.

- Should the opportunity cost of machine time be included in cost or not?
- What allowance, if any, should be made for the possible errors in cost estimates?

Different assumptions could be made.

(a) **Exclude machine time opportunity costs: ignore possible costing errors**

	$
Direct materials	27.00
Direct labour (4 hours)	20.00
Variable production overheads	3.00
Fixed production overheads	48.00
(at $\dfrac{\$300,000}{25,000}$ = $12 per direct labour hour)	
Full production cost	98.00
Profit mark-up (20%)	19.60
Selling price per unit of product X	117.60

(b) **Include machine time opportunity costs: ignore possible costing errors**

	$
Full production cost as in (a)	98.00
Opportunity cost of machine time:	
contribution forgone (½ hr × $10)	5.00
Adjusted full cost	103.00
Profit mark-up (20%)	20.60
Selling price per unit of product X	123.60

(c) **Exclude machine time opportunity costs but make full allowance for possible under-estimates of cost**

	$	$
Direct materials	27.00	
Direct labour	20.00	
	47.00	
Possible error (15%)	7.05	
		54.05
Variable production overheads	3.00	
Possible error (10%)	0.30	
		3.30
Fixed production overheads (4 hrs × $12)	48.00	
Possible error (labour time) (15%)	7.20	
		55.20
Potential full production cost		112.55
Profit mark-up (20%)		22.51
Selling price per unit of product X		135.06

(d) **Include machine time opportunity costs and make a full allowance for possible under-estimates of cost**

	$
Potential full production cost as in (c)	112.55
Opportunity cost of machine time:	
Potential contribution forgone (½ hr × $10 × 110%)	5.50
Adjusted potential full cost	118.05
Profit mark-up (20%)	23.61
Selling price per unit of product X	141.66

Using different assumptions, we could arrive at any of four different unit prices in the range $117.60 to $141.66.

5.1.2 Disadvantages of full cost-plus pricing

(a) It fails to recognise that since demand may be determining price, there will be a profit-maximising combination of price and demand.

(b) There may be a need to **adjust prices to market and demand conditions**.

(c) **Budgeted output volume** needs to be established. Output volume is a key factor in the overhead absorption rate.

(d) A **suitable basis for overhead absorption** must be selected, especially where a business produces more than one product.

5.1.3 Advantages of full cost-plus pricing

(a) It is a **quick, simple and cheap** method of pricing which can be delegated to junior managers.

(b) Since the size of the profit margin can be varied, a decision based on a price in excess of full cost should ensure that a company working at normal capacity will **cover all of its fixed costs and make a profit.**

Question   Full cost-plus method

A company budgets to make 20,000 units which have a variable cost of production of $4 per unit. Fixed production costs are $60,000 per annum. If the selling price is to be 40% higher than full cost, what is the selling price of the product using the full cost-plus method?

Full cost per unit = variable cost + fixed cost

Variable cost = $4 per unit

Fixed cost = $\dfrac{\$60,000}{20,000}$ = $3 per unit

Full cost per unit = $(4 + 3) = $7

∴ Selling price using full cost-plus pricing method = $7.00 × $\dfrac{140\%}{100}$

$\hspace{11cm}$ = $9.80

5.2 Marginal cost-plus pricing

5.2.1 Introduction

FAST FORWARD

Marginal cost-plus pricing/mark-up pricing involves adding a profit margin to the marginal cost of production/sales.

Whereas a full cost-plus approach to pricing draws attention to net profit and the net profit margin, a variable cost-plus approach to pricing **draws attention to gross profit** and the **gross profit margin**, or **contribution**.

Question

$\hspace{10cm}$ **Profit margin**

A product has the following costs.

	$
Direct materials	5
Direct labour	3
Variable overheads	7

Fixed overheads are $10,000 per month. Budgeted sales per month are 400 units to allow the product to break even.

Required

Determine the profit margin which needs to be added to *marginal* cost to allow the product to break even.

Answer

Breakeven point is when total contribution equals fixed costs.

At breakeven point, $10,000 = 400 (price – $15)

∴ $25 = price – $15
∴ $40 = price
∴ Profit margin = $(40 – 15 / 15) × 100\% = 166\%$

5.2.2 Advantages of marginal cost-plus pricing

(a)   It is a **simple and easy** method to use.

(b)   The **mark-up percentage can be varied**, and so mark-up pricing can be adjusted to reflect demand conditions.

(c)   It **draws management attention to contribution**, and the effects of higher or lower sales volumes on profit. For example, if a product costs $10 per unit and a mark-up of 150% ($15) is added to reach a price of $25 per unit, management should be clearly aware that every additional $1 of sales revenue would add 60 cents to contribution and profit ($15 ÷ $25 = $0.60).

(d)   In practice, mark-up pricing is **used** in businesses **where there is a readily-identifiable basic variable cost**. Retail industries are the most obvious example, and it is quite common for the prices of goods in shops to be fixed by adding a mark-up (20% or 33.3%, say) to the purchase cost.

5.2.3 Disadvantages of marginal cost-plus pricing

(a)   Although the size of the mark-up can be varied in accordance with demand conditions, it does not ensure that sufficient attention is paid to demand conditions, competitors' prices and profit maximisation.

(b)   It **ignores fixed overheads** in the pricing decision, but the sales price must be sufficiently high to ensure that a profit is made after covering fixed costs.

5.3 Full cost pricing versus marginal cost pricing

Perhaps the most important **criticism** of full cost pricing is that it **fails to recognise** that since sales demand may be determined by the sales price, there will be a **profit-maximising combination** of price and demand. A full cost based approach to pricing will be most unlikely, except by coincidence or 'luck', to arrive at the profit-maximising price. In contrast, a marginal costing approach to looking at costs and prices would be more likely to help with identifying a profit-maximising price.

5.3.1 Example: full cost versus profit-maximising prices

Tigger has budgeted to make 50,000 units of its product, timm. The variable cost of a timm is $5 and annual fixed costs are expected to be $150,000.

The financial director of Tigger has suggested that a profit margin of 25% on full cost should be charged for every product sold.

The marketing director has challenged the wisdom of this suggestion, and has produced the following estimates of sales demand for timms.

Price per unit	Demand
$	Units
9	42,000
10	38,000
11	35,000
12	32,000
13	27,000

Required

(a)   Calculate the profit for the year if a full cost price is charged.
(b)   Calculate the profit-maximising price.

Assume in both (a) and (b) that 50,000 units of timm are produced regardless of sales volume.

Solution

(a) (i) The full cost per unit is $5 variable cost plus $3 fixed costs, ie $8 in total. A 25% mark-up on this cost gives a selling price of $10 per unit so that sales demand would be 38,000 units. (Production is given as 50,000 units.)

	$	$
Profit (absorption costing)		
Sales		380,000
Costs of production (50,000 units)		
Variable (50,000 × $5)	250,000	
Fixed (50,000 × $3)	150,000	
	400,000	
Less increase in inventory (12,000 units × 8)	(96,000)	
Cost of sales		304,000
Profit		76,000

(ii) **Profit using marginal costing** instead of absorption costing, so that fixed overhead costs are written off in the period they occur, would be as follows. (The 38,000 unit demand level is chosen for comparison.)

	$
Contribution (38,000 × $(10 – 5))	190,000
Fixed costs	150,000
Profit	40,000

Since the company cannot go on indefinitely producing an output volume in excess of sales volume, this profit figure is more indicative of the profitability of timms in the longer term.

(b) A **profit-maximising price** is one which gives the greatest net (relevant) cash flow, which in this case is the **contribution-maximising price**.

Price	Unit contribution	Demand	
$	$	Units	$
9	4	42,000	168,000
10	5	38,000	190,000
11	6	35,000	210,000
12	7	32,000	224,000
13	8	27,000	216,000

The profit maximising price is $12, with annual sales demand of 32,000 units.

This example shows that a **cost based price** is **unlikely to be the profit-maximising** price, and that a **marginal costing approach**, calculating the total contribution at a variety of different selling prices, will be **more helpful** for establishing what the profit-maximising price ought to be.

5.3.2 Cost plus pricing versus target costing

As you should remember from Chapter 2b, **target prices** are set in order to achieve a desired market share. Deduction of a desired profit margin produces the cost that has to be achieved. Design specifications and production methods are examined to establish ways in which the target cost can be met without reducing the value of the product to the customer.

Such an approach is likely to **offer greater competitive advantage** than cost plus pricing, being far more **strategically orientated** as it **takes account of the external environment**.

5.4 Market skimming pricing

New product pricing strategies include **market skimming** and **market penetration pricing.**

Key term

> **Price skimming** involves charging high prices when a product is first launched in order to maximise short-term profitability. Initially there is heavy spending on advertising and sales promotion to obtain sales. As the product moves into the later stages of its life cycle (growth, maturity and decline) progressively lower prices are charged. The profitable 'cream' is thus skimmed off in stages until sales can only be sustained at lower prices.

The aim of market skimming is to gain **high unit profits** early in the product's life. High unit prices make it more likely that **competitors** will enter the market than if lower prices were to be charged.

Such a policy may be appropriate in the cases below.

(a) The product is **new and different**, so that customers are prepared to pay high prices so as to be one up on other people who do not own it.

(b) The strength of **demand** and the sensitivity of demand to price are **unknown**. It is better from the point of view of marketing to start by charging high prices and then reduce them if the demand for the product turns out to be price elastic than to start by charging low prices and then attempt to raise them substantially if demand appears to be insensitive to higher prices.

(c) High prices in the early stages of a product's life might generate **high initial cash flows**. A firm with liquidity problems may prefer market-skimming for this reason.

(d) The firm can identify **different market segments** for the product, each prepared to pay progressively lower prices. It may therefore be possible to continue to sell at higher prices to some market segments when lower prices are charged in others. This is discussed further below.

(e) Products may have a **short life cycle**, and so need to recover their development costs and make a profit relatively quickly.

Products to which the policy has been applied include:

- Calculators
- Video recorders
- Desktop computers

5.5 Market penetration pricing

Key term

> **Penetration pricing** is a policy of low prices when a product is first launched in order to obtain sufficient penetration into the market.

A penetration policy may be appropriate in the cases below.

(a) The firm wishes to **discourage new entrants** into the market.

(b) The firm wishes to **shorten the initial period** of the product's life cycle in order to enter the growth and maturity stages as quickly as possible.

(c) There are significant **economies of scale** to be achieved from a high volume of output.

(d) Demand is **highly elastic** and so would respond well to low prices.

Penetration prices are prices which aim to secure a substantial share in a substantial total market. A firm might therefore deliberately build **excess production capacity** and set its prices very low. As demand builds up the spare capacity will be used up gradually and unit costs will fall; the firm might even reduce prices further as unit costs fall. In this way, early losses will enable the firm to dominate the market and have the lowest costs.

5.6 Complementary product pricing

Complementary products are goods that tend to be bought and used together.

Complementary products are sold separately but are **connected** and dependant on each other for sales, for example, an electric toothbrush and replacement toothbrush heads. The electric toothbrush may be priced competitively to attract demand but the replacement heads can be relatively expensive.

A **loss leader** is when a company sets a very low price for one product intending to make consumers buy other products in the range which carry higher profit margins. Another example is selling razors at very low prices whilst selling the blades for them at a higher profit margin. People will buy many of the high profit items but only one of the low profit items – yet they are 'locked in' to the former by the latter. This can also be described as **captive product pricing**.

5.7 Product-line pricing

A **product line** is a group of products that are related to one another.

A **product line** is the marketing strategy of offering for sale several related products. A line can comprise related products of various sizes, types, colours, qualities, or prices. Demand for and costs of the products are likely to be **interrelated.**

There is a range of product line pricing strategies.

(a) Set prices proportional to full or marginal cost with the same percentage profit margin for all products. This means that prices are dependent on cost and ignore demand.

(b) Set prices reflecting the demand relationships between the products so that an overall required rate of return is achieved.

5.8 Volume discounting

A **volume discount** is a reduction in price given for larger than average purchases.

The aim of a volume discount is to increase sales from large customers. The discount acts as a form of **differentiation** between types of customer (wholesale, retail and so on).

The reduced costs of a large order will hopefully compensate for the loss of revenue from offering the discount.

5.9 Price discrimination

The use of **price discrimination** means that the same product can be sold at different prices to different customers. This can be very difficult to implement in practice because it relies for success upon the continued existence of certain market conditions.

In certain circumstances the **same product** can be sold at different prices to **different customers**.

Price discrimination is the practice of charging different prices for the same product to different groups of buyers when these prices are not reflective of cost differences.

There are a number of bases on which such discriminating prices can be set.

(a) **By market segment**. A cross-channel ferry company would market its services at different prices in England and France, for example. Services such as cinemas and hairdressers are often available at lower prices to old age pensioners and/or juveniles.

(b) **By product version**. Many car models have 'add on' extras which enable one brand to appeal to a wider cross-section of customers. The final price need not reflect the cost price of the add on extras directly: usually the top of the range model would carry a price much in excess of the cost of provision of the extras, as a prestige appeal.

(c) **By place**. Theatre seats are usually sold according to their location so that patrons pay different prices for the same performance according to the seat type they occupy.

(d) **By time**. This is perhaps the most popular type of price discrimination. Off-peak travel bargains, hotel prices and telephone charges are all attempts to increase sales revenue by covering variable but not necessarily average cost of provision. Railway companies are successful price discriminators, charging more to rush hour rail commuters whose demand is inelastic at certain times of the day.

Price discrimination can only be effective if a number of **conditions** hold.

(a) The market must be **segmentable** in price terms, and different sectors must show different intensities of demand. Each of the sectors must be identifiable, distinct and separate from the others, and be accessible to the firm's marketing communications.

(b) There must be little or **no** chance of a **black market** developing (this would allow those in the lower priced segment to resell to those in the higher priced segment).

(c) There must be little or **no** chance that **competitors** can and will undercut the firm's prices in the higher priced (and/or most profitable) market segments.

(d) The cost of segmenting and **administering** the arrangements should not exceed the extra revenue derived from the price discrimination strategy.

Try the following question which, although it has a few 'tricks', **looks more daunting than it is** if you keep your head and take care.

 Question   **Differential pricing**

Curltown Cinemas operates a chain of 30 cinemas. Standard admission price is $7 per person, but this is subject to certain discounts. Average attendance at a cinema per month on normal price days is 5,000 people, but this is expected to be subject to seasonal variation, as follows.

Month	J	F	M	A	M	J	J	A	S	O	N	D
%	+10	−2	0	+5	−5	−5	+10	+7	−4	−4	0	+12

In December, January, July and August audiences are made up of 60% under-14s, who pay half-price admission. For the rest of the year under 14s represent only 10% of the audience. One day per month all tickets are sold at a special offer price of $1, irrespective of the age of the customer. This invariably guarantees a full house of 200 customers.

Required

(a) What is Curltown Cinemas' total revenue from cinema admissions for a year?

(b) If Curltown puts up prices for over-14s (other than the $1 special offer price) to $8 what will its total revenue from cinema admissions be for the year?

(c) Should the special offer be continued?

Answer

(a) This is simply a matter of reading the question carefully and patiently tabulating the data using a **different layout** to the one given in the question. Note that you save yourself potential error if you convert percentages into decimals as you transfer the question information into your own table. Don't forget that there are 30 cinemas.

Month	Variation	Average no	Adjusted no	Full price	Revenue @ $7.00 $	Half price	Revenue @ $3.50 $
Jan	+0.10	5,000	5,500	0.4	15,400.00	0.6	11,550.00
Feb	-0.02	5,000	4,900	0.9	30,870.00	0.1	1,715.00
Mar	+0.00	5,000	5,000	0.9	31,500.00	0.1	1,750.00
Apr	+0.05	5,000	5,250	0.9	33,075.00	0.1	1,837.50
May	-0.05	5,000	4,750	0.9	29,925.00	0.1	1,662.50
Jun	-0.05	5,000	4,750	0.9	29,925.00	0.1	1,662.50
Jul	+0.10	5,000	5,500	0.4	15,400.00	0.6	11,550.00
Aug	+0.07	5,000	5,350	0.4	14,980.00	0.6	11,235.00
Sept	-0.04	5,000	4,800	0.9	30,240.00	0.1	1,680.00
Oct	-0.04	5,000	4,800	0.9	30,240.00	0.1	1,680.00
Nov	0.00	5,000	5,000	0.9	31,500.00	0.1	1,750.00
Dec	+0.12	5,000	5,600	0.4	15,680.00	0.6	11,760.00
					308,735.00		59,832.50

	$
Total normal price ($308,735.00 + $59,832.50)	368,567.50
Special offer (12 × $1 × 200)	2,400.00
Total per cinema	370,967.50
Total per 30 cinemas	11,129,025.00

(b) **There is no need to work out all the numbers again at the new prices.**

	$
Total as calculated above	11,129,025.00
Less: current adult normal price ($308,735 × 30)	(9,262,050.00)
Add: revised adult normal price ($308,735 × 30 × 8/7)	10,585,200.00
	12,452,175.00

(c) If the income of $200 per cinema on the twelve special offer days is compared with an average of, say, $368,567.50/(365 – 12 days) = over $1,000, then it is clearly not worthwhile. The cinemas get average attendances of (5000 × 12)/365 = about 164 people in any case, even without special offers. (You could do **rough calculations** to estimate the overall loss of revenue per annum. Try it, making any **assumptions** you need, if you haven't done so, but not at the expense of written comments.)

However, the offer is a **loss-leader** which probably has other benefits. It will be liked by customers, and if the film they see is a good one they will recommend it to their friends. It may help to encourage the cinema-going habit amongst potential new regular customers. You may have thought of other relevant comments, either in favour of the policy or against it.

Exam focus point

An exam question on this topic would have less calculations and more interpretation so make sure you really think about the implications of continuing the special offer.

5.10 Relevant cost pricing

FAST FORWARD

Special orders require a **relevant cost** approach to the calculation of the price.

A special order is a **one-off** revenue earning opportunity. These may arise in the following situations.

(a) When a business has a regular source of income but also has some **spare capacity** allowing it to take on extra work if demanded. For example a brewery might have a capacity of 500,000 barrels per month but only be producing and selling 300,000 barrels per month. It could therefore consider special orders to use up some of its spare capacity.

(b)   When a business has **no regular source of income** and relies exclusively on its ability to respond to demand. A building firm is a typical example as are many types of sub-contractors. In the service sector consultants often work on this basis.

The reason for making the distinction is that in the case of (a), a firm would normally attempt to cover its longer-term running costs in its prices for its regular product. Pricing for special orders need therefore take no account of unavoidable fixed costs. This is clearly not the case for a firm in (b)'s position, where special orders are the only source of income for the foreseeable future.

5.10.1 Minimum pricing

The basic approach in both situations is to determine the price at which the firm would break even if it undertook the work, that is, the **minimum price** that it could afford to charge.

A minimum price is the minimum price that would have to be charged so as to cover the following two groups of cost.

(a)   The **incremental costs** of producing and selling the item
(b)   The **opportunity costs** of the resources consumed in making and selling the item

A minimum price would leave the business no better or worse off than if it did not sell the item.

Two essential points to understand immediately about a minimum price are as follows.

(a)   It is based on **relevant** costs, that is the incremental costs plus the opportunity costs of making and selling the product or providing the service. You have covered this in your earlier studies and we will look at this aspect again in Chapter 6.

(b)   It is **unlikely that a minimum price would actually be charged**, because if it were it would not provide the business with any incremental profit. However, the minimum price for an item shows the following.

(i)   An **absolute minimum** below which the price should not be set.
(ii)   The **incremental profit** that would be obtained from any price that is actually charged in excess of the minimum. For example, if the minimum price is $200 and the actual price charged is $240, the incremental profit on the sale would be $40.

If there are no **scarce resources**, and a company has **spare capacity**, the **minimum price** of a product would be an amount which equals the **incremental cost of making it**. Any price in excess of this minimum would provide an incremental contribution towards profit.

If there are scarce resources and a company makes more than one product, minimum prices would include an allowance for the **opportunity cost** of using the scarce resources to make and sell the product (instead of using the resources on the next most profitable product).

Where a firm also has to consider its **long-term costs** in the decision because it has no other way of recovering them it would have to **add a proportion of estimated unattributable costs to the price of each order**. This could be calculated on a time basis (if the job is expected to take one month, $1/12$ of unavoidable costs would be included), but this might lead to inconsistencies if, say, the unavoidable costs were all borne by one customer in one month and shared between several customers in another month.

Question   **Relevant cost pricing**

Ennerdale has been asked to quote a price for a one-off contract. The following information is available:

Materials

The contract requires 3,000 kg of material K, which is a material used regularly by the company in other production. The company has 2,000 kg of material K currently in stock which had been purchased last month for a total cost of $19,600. Since then the price per kilogram for material K has increased by 5%.

The contract also requires 200 kg of material L. There are 250 kg of material L in stock which are not required for normal production. This material originally cost a total of $3,125. If not used on this contract, the stock of material L would be sold for $11 per kg.

Labour

The contract requires 800 hours of skilled labour. Skilled labour is paid $9.50 per hour. There is a shortage of skilled labour and all the available skilled labour is fully employed in the company in the manufacture of product P. The following information relates to product P:

	$ per unit	$ per unit
Selling price		100
Less:		
Skilled labour	38	
Other variable costs	22	
		(60)
		40

Required

Prepare on a relevant cost basis, the lowest cost estimate that could be used as the basis for a quotation.

Answer

Relevant cost – Material K

Since the material is regularly used by the company, the relevant cost of material K is the current price of the material.

$$\text{Cost last month} = \frac{\$19,600}{2,000 \text{ kg}}$$

= $9.80

Revised cost (+5%) = $9.80 × 1.05

= $10.29

∴ Relevant cost of Material K = 3,000 kg × $10.29 per kg

= $30,870

Relevant cost – Material L

Since the material is not required for normal production, the relevant cost of this material is its net realisable value if it were sold.

∴ Relevant cost of Material L = 200 kg × $11 per kg

= $2,200

Relevant cost – Skilled labour

Skilled labour is in short supply and therefore the relevant cost of this labour will include both the actual cost and the opportunity cost of the labour employed.

	$
Cost of skilled labour (800 hours × $9.50)	7,600
Opportunity cost of skilled labour (see working)	8,000
Relevant cost – skilled labour	15,600

Working

Skilled labour cost per unit of Product P = $38

Cost per skilled labour hour = $9.50

∴ Number of hours required per unit of Product P $= \dfrac{\$38}{\$9.50}$

= 4 hours

Contribution per unit of Product P = $40

∴ Contribution per skilled labour hour $= \dfrac{\$40}{4\,\text{hours}}$

= $10 per hour

∴ Opportunity cost of skilled labour = 800 hours × $10 per hour

= $8,000

The total relevant costs of this contract are therefore $(30,870 + 2,200 + 15,600) = $48,670

Chapter Roundup

- In the modern world there are many more **influences on price** than cost (eg competitors, product range, quality).

- The price that an organisation can charge for its products will be determined to a greater or lesser degree by the **market** in which it operates

- **Economic theory** argues that the **higher the price of a good**, the **lower** will be the **quantity demanded**.

- The **price elasticity of demand (PED)** is a measure of the extent of change in demand for a good in response to a change in its price.

- Most products pass through the five stages of the **product life cycle.**

- You need to be able to derive the **demand equation** $P = a - bQ$.

- Cost behaviour can be **modelled** using equations.

- If you are required to evaluate a decision to increase production and sales levels, you will need to consider **incremental costs, incremental revenues** and other factors.

- **Profits are maximised** using marginalist theory when **marginal cost (MC) = marginal revenue (MR)**.

- The **optimal selling price** can be determined using equations (ie when MC = MR).

- The **optimum selling price** can also be determined using tabulation.

- The price to be charged for a product or service is often one of the most important decisions made by managers. There are a number of alternative pricing strategies.

- **Full cost-plus pricing** is a method of determining the sales price by calculating the full cost of the product and adding a percentage mark-up for profit.

- Marginal cost-plus pricing/mark-up pricing involves adding a profit margin to the marginal cost of production/sales.

- New product pricing strategies include market skimming and market penetration pricing.

- The use of **price discrimination** means that the same product can be sold at different prices to different customers. This can be very difficult to implement in practice because it relies for success upon the continued existence of certain market conditions.

- Special orders require a **relevant cost** approach to the calculation of the price.

1   *Fill in the blanks.*

Demand is said to be elastic when a .... change in price produces a ....
change in quantity demanded. PED is .... than 1.

Demand is said to be inelastic when a .... change in price produces a ....
change in quantity demanded. PED is .... than 1.

2   Fill in the blanks in the formula below for the variable 'a' in the equation for a demand curve.

$$a = \$(............\,...............) + \left(\frac{\text{..}}{\text{..}} \times \$...... \right)$$

3   Cost-based approaches to pricing take more account of the external environment than target costing. *True or false?*

4   *Fill in the blanks.*

(a)   One of the problems with relying on a full cost-plus approach to pricing is that it fails to recognise that since price may be determining demand, there will be a .... combination of .... and ....

(b)   An advantage of the full cost-plus approach is that, because the size of the profit margin can be varied, a decision based on a price in excess of full cost should ensure that a company working at .... capacity will cover .... and make a ....

5   Pricing based on mark-up per unit of limiting factor is particularly useful if an organisation is not working to full capacity. *True or false?*

6   *Fill in the blank.*

The .... price is the price at which an organisation will break even if it undertakes particular work.

7   *Choose the correct word from those highlighted.*

Market **skimming/penetration** pricing should be used if an organisation wishes to discourage new entrants into a market.

1   (a)   Demand is said to be elastic when a **small change** in the price produces a **large change** in the quantity demanded. PED is **greater** than 1.

     (b)   Demand is said to be **inelastic** when a small change in the price produces only a **small change in the quantity** demanded. **PED is less than 1**.

2    $$a = (\text{current price}) + \left(\frac{\text{Current quantity at current price}}{\text{Change in quantity when price is changed by \$b}} \times \$b \right)$$

3   False

4   (a)   profit-maximising combination of price and demand

     (b)   working at normal capacity will cover all of its fixed costs and make a profit

5   False. It is useful if the organisation is working at full capacity.

6   Minimum

7   Market penetration

Now try the question below from the Exam Question Bank

Number	Level	Marks	Time
Q9	Examination	20	36 mins

Short-term decisions

Topic list	Syllabus reference
1 Identifying relevant costs	B1 (a), (b), (c)
2 Make or buy decisions	B5 (a), (b), (c)
3 Outsourcing	B5 (a), (b), (c)
4 Further processing decisions	B5 (d)
5 Shut down decisions	B5 (d)

Introduction

The concept of **relevant costs** has already been revisited in this study text and their use in one-off contracts was examined in the last chapter.

In this chapter we look in greater depth at relevant costs and at how they should be applied in **decision-making situations**.

We look at a variety of common short-run business decisions and consider how they can be dealt with using relevant costs as appropriate.

Study guide

		Intellectual level
B1	**Relevant cost analysis**	
(a)	Explain the concept of relevant costing	2
(b)	Identify and calculate relevant costs for specific decision situations from given data	2
(c)	Explain and apply the concept of opportunity costs	2
B5	**Make-or-buy and other short-term decisions**	
(a)	Explain the issues surrounding make vs buy and outsourcing decisions	2
(b)	Calculate and compare 'make' costs with 'buy-in' costs	2
(c)	Compare in-house costs and outsource costs of completing tasks and consider other issues surrounding this decision	2
(d)	Apply relevant costing principles in situations involving shut down, one-off contracts and the further processing of joint products	2

Exam guide

The ability to recognise relevant costs and revenues is a key skill for the F5 exam and is highly examinable. Questions will be based on practical scenarios.

One of the competencies you require to fulfil performance objective 12 of the PER is the ability to prepare management information to assist in decision making. You can apply the knowledge you obtain from this section of the text to help to demonstrate this competence.

1 Identifying relevant costs

FAST FORWARD

Relevant costs are future cash flows arising as a direct consequence of a decision.

- Relevant costs are **future costs**
- Relevant costs are **cash flows**
- Relevant costs are **incremental costs**

In this section we provide a fairly gentle introduction to the sort of thought processes that you will have to go through when you encounter a decision-making question. First some general points about machinery, labour, and particularly materials, that often catch people out.

1.1 Machinery user costs

Once a machine has been bought its cost is a **sunk** cost. **Depreciation** is not a relevant cost, because it is not a cash flow. However, **using** machinery may involve some incremental costs. These costs might be referred to as **user costs** and they include hire charges and any fall in resale value of owned assets, through use.

1.1.1 Example: machine user costs

Bronty Co is considering whether to undertake some contract work for a customer. The machinery required for the contract would be as follows.

(a)   A special cutting machine will have to be hired for three months for the work (the length of the contract). Hire charges for this machine are $75 per month, with a minimum hire charge of $300.

(b)   All other machinery required in the production for the contract has already been purchased by the organisation on hire purchase terms. The monthly hire purchase payments for this machinery are $500. This consists of $450 for capital repayment and $50 as an interest charge. The last hire purchase payment is to be made in two months time. The cash price of this machinery was $9,000 two years ago. It is being depreciated on a straight line basis at the rate of $200 per month. However, it still has a useful life which will enable it to be operated for another 36 months.

The machinery is highly specialised and is unlikely to be required for other, more profitable jobs over the period during which the contract work would be carried out. Although there is no immediate market for selling this machine, it is expected that a customer might be found in the future. It is further estimated that the machine would lose $200 in its eventual sale value if it is used for the contract work.

What is the relevant cost of machinery for the contract?

Solution

(a)   The **cutting machine** will incur an incremental cost of $300, the minimum hire charge.

(b)   The historical cost of the **other machinery** is irrelevant as a past cost; depreciation is irrelevant as a non-cash cost; and future hire purchase repayments are irrelevant because they are committed costs. The only relevant cost is the loss of resale value of the machinery, estimated at $200 through use. This 'user cost' will not arise until the machinery is eventually resold and the $200 should be discounted to allow for the time value of money. However, discounting is ignored here, and will be discussed in a later chapter.

(c)   **Summary of relevant costs**

	$
Incremental hire costs	300
User cost of other machinery	200
	500

1.2 Labour

Often the labour force will be paid irrespective of the decision made and the costs are therefore **not incremental**. Take care, however, if the labour force could be put to an **alternative use**, in which case the relevant costs are the **variable costs** of the labour and associated variable overheads **plus** the **contribution forgone** from not being able to put it to its alternative use.

1.3 Materials

The relevant cost of raw materials is generally their current **replacement** cost, unless the materials have already been purchased and would not be replaced once used.

If materials have already been purchased but will not be replaced, then the relevant cost of using them is **either** (a) their current **resale** value **or** (b) the value they would obtain if they were put to an **alternative use**, if this is greater than their current resale value.

The **higher** of (a) or (b) is then the opportunity cost of the materials. If the materials have no resale value and no other possible use, then the relevant cost of using them for the opportunity under consideration would be nil.

The flowchart below shows how the relevant costs of materials can be identified, **provided that** the materials are **not in short supply**, and so have **no internal opportunity cost**.

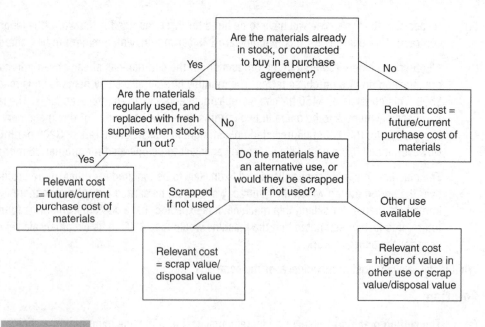

 Question

O'Reilly Co has been approached by a customer who would like a special job to be done for him, and who is willing to pay $22,000 for it. The job would require the following materials:

Material	Total units required	Units already in inventory	Book value of units in inventory $/unit	Realisable value $/unit	Replacement cost $/unit
A	1,000	0	–	–	6
B	1,000	600	2	2.5	5
C	1,000	700	3	2.5	4
D	200	200	4	6.0	9

(a) Material B is used regularly by O'Reilly Ltd, and if units of B are required for this job, they would need to be replaced to meet other production demand.

(b) Materials C and D are in inventory as the result of previous over-buying, and they have a restricted use. No other use could be found for material C, but the units of material D could be used in another job as substitute for 300 units of material E, which currently costs $5 per unit (of which the company has no units in inventory at the moment).

What are the relevant costs of material, in deciding whether or not to accept the contract?

Answer

(a) **Material A** is not owned and would have to be bought in full at the replacement cost of $6 per unit.

(b) **Material B** is used regularly by the company. There is existing inventory (600 units) but if these are used on the contract under review a further 600 units would be bought to replace them. Relevant costs are therefore 1,000 units at the replacement cost of $5 per unit.

(c) **Material C:** 1,000 units are needed and 700 are already in inventory. If used for the contract, a further 300 units must be bought at $4 each. The existing inventory of 700 will not be replaced. If they are used for the contract, they could not be sold at $2.50 each. The realisable value of these 700 units is an opportunity cost of sales revenue forgone.

(d) **Material D:** these are already in inventory and will not be replaced. There is an opportunity cost of using D in the contract because there are alternative opportunities either to sell the existing inventory for $6 per unit ($1,200 in total) or avoid other purchases (of material E), which would cost 300 × $5 = $1,500. Since substitution for E is more beneficial, $1,500 is the opportunity cost.

(e)   **Summary of relevant costs**

	$
Material A (1,000 × $6)	6,000
Material B (1,000 × $5)	5,000
Material C (300 × $4) plus (700 × $2.50)	2,950
Material D	1,500
Total	15,450

1.4 Opportunity costs

Other potential relevant costs include **opportunity costs**.

Opportunity cost is the **benefit sacrificed** by choosing one opportunity rather than the next best alternative. You will often encounter opportunity costs when there are several possible uses for a scarce resource.

For example, if a material is in short supply, it may be transferred from the production of one product to that of another product. The opportunity cost is the **contribution lost** from ceasing production of the original product.

Key term

> **Opportunity cost** is the value of a benefit sacrificed when one course of action is chosen, in preference to an alternative. The opportunity cost is represented by the forgone potential benefit from the best rejected course of action.

Question   Opportunity costs

An information technology consultancy firm has been asked to do an urgent job by a client, for which a price of $2,500 has been offered. The job would require the following.

(a)   30 hours' work from one member of staff, who is paid on an hourly basis, at a rate of $20 per hour, but who would normally be employed on work for clients where the charge-out rate is $45 per hour. No other member of staff is able to do the member of staff in question's work.

(b)   The use of 5 hours of mainframe computer time, which the firm normally charges out to external users at a rate of $50 per hour. Mainframe computer time is currently used 24 hours a day, 7 days a week.

(c)   Supplies and incidental expenses of $200.

Required

Fill in the blank in the sentence below.

The relevant cost or opportunity cost of the job is $........

Answer

The correct answer is $1,800.

The relevant cost or opportunity cost of the job would be calculated as follows.

	$
Labour (30 hours × $45)	1,350
Computer time opportunity cost (5 hours × $50)	250
Supplies and expenses	200
	1,800

2 Make or buy decisions

In a **make or buy decision** with no limiting factors, the relevant costs are the differential costs between the two options.

A make or buy problem involves a decision by an organisation about **whether it should make a product or whether it should pay another organisation to do so**. Here are some examples of make or buy decisions.

(a) Whether a company should manufacture its own components, or else buy the components from an outside supplier

(b) Whether a construction company should do some work with its own employees, or whether it should sub-contract the work to another company

(c) Whether a service should be carried out by an internal department or whether an external organisation should be employed (discussed more fully later in this chapter)

The **'make'** option should give **management more direct control** over the work, but the **'buy'** option often has the benefit that the **external organisation** has a **specialist skill** and expertise in the work. Make or buy decisions should certainly **not be based exclusively on cost considerations.**

If an organisation has the freedom of choice about whether to make internally or buy externally and has no scarce resources that put a restriction on what it can do itself, the **relevant costs** for the decision will be the **differential costs** between the two options.

2.1 Example: make or buy decision

Shellfish Co makes four components, W, X, Y and Z, for which costs in the forthcoming year are expected to be as follows.

	W	X	Y	Z
Production (units)	1,000	2,000	4,000	3,000
Unit marginal costs	$	$	$	$
Direct materials	4	5	2	4
Direct labour	8	9	4	6
Variable production overheads	2	3	1	2
	14	17	7	12

Directly attributable fixed costs per annum and committed fixed costs:

	$
Incurred as a direct consequence of making W	1,000
Incurred as a direct consequence of making X	5,000
Incurred as a direct consequence of making Y	6,000
Incurred as a direct consequence of making Z	8,000
Other fixed costs (committed)	30,000
	50,000

A sub-contractor has offered to supply units of W, X, Y and Z for $12, $21, $10 and $14 respectively. Should Shellfish make or buy the components?

Solution

(a) The **relevant costs** are the differential costs between making and buying, and they consist of **differences in unit variable costs plus differences in directly attributable fixed costs**. Sub-contracting will result in some **fixed cost savings.**

	W	X	Y	Z
	$	$	$	$
Unit variable cost of making	14	17	7	12
Unit variable cost of buying	12	21	10	14
	(2)	4	3	2
Annual requirements (units)	1,000	2,000	4,000	3,000
	$	$	$	$
Extra variable cost of buying (per annum)	(2,000)	8,000	12,000	6,000
Fixed costs saved by buying	(1,000)	(5,000)	(6,000)	(8,000)
Extra total cost of buying	(3,000)	3,000	6,000	(2,000)

(b) The company would save $3,000 pa by sub-contracting component W (where the purchase cost would be less than the marginal cost per unit to make internally) and would save $2,000 pa by sub-contracting component Z (because of the saving in fixed costs of $8,000).

(c) In this example, relevant costs are the variable costs of in-house manufacture, the variable costs of sub-contracted units, and the saving in fixed costs.

(d) **Further considerations**

 (i) If components W and Z are sub-contracted, the company will have **spare capacity**. How should that spare capacity be profitably used? Are there hidden benefits to be obtained from sub-contracting? Would the company's workforce resent the loss of work to an outside sub-contractor, and might such a decision cause an industrial dispute?

 (ii) Would the sub-contractor be **reliable** with delivery times, and would he supply components of the same **quality** as those manufactured internally?

 (iii) Does the company wish to be **flexible** and maintain better **control** over operations by making everything itself?

 (iv) Are the **estimates** of fixed cost savings reliable? In the case of Product W, buying is clearly cheaper than making in-house. In the case of product Z, the decision to buy rather than make would only be financially beneficial if it is feasible that the fixed cost savings of $8,000 will really be 'delivered' by management. All too often in practice, promised savings fail to materialise!

3 Outsourcing 12/07

FAST FORWARD

The relevant costs/revenues in decisions relating to the **operating of internal service departments or the use of external services** are the differential costs between the two options.

3.1 The trend in outsourcing

A significant trend in the 1990s was for companies and government bodies to **concentrate on their core competences** – what they are really good at (or set up to achieve) – and turn other functions over to **specialist contractors.** A company that earns its profits from, say, manufacturing bicycles, does not also need to have expertise in, say, mass catering or office cleaning. **Facilities management** companies such as Rentokil have grown in response to this.

Key term

> **Outsourcing** is the use of external suppliers for finished products, components or services. This is also known as **contract manufacturing** or **sub-contracting.**

Reasons for this trend include:

(a) Frequently the decision is made on the grounds that **specialist contractors** can offer **superior quality** and **efficiency**. If a contractor's main business is making a specific component it can invest in the specialist machinery and labour and knowledge skills needed to make that component.

However, this component may be only one of many needed by the contractor's customer, and the complexity of components is now such that attempting to keep internal facilities up to the standard of specialists detracts from the main business of the customer.

(b)   Contracting out manufacturing **frees capital** that can then be invested in core activities such as market research, product definition, product planning, marketing and sales.

(c)   **Contractors** have the **capacity** and **flexibility** to start production very quickly to meet sudden **variations in demand**. In-house facilities may not be able to respond as quickly, because of the need to redirect resources from elsewhere.

3.2 Internal and external services

In administrative and support functions, too, companies are increasingly likely to use specialist companies. Decisions such as the following are now common.

(a)   Whether the **design and development of a new computer system** should be entrusted to in-house data processing staff or whether an external software house should be hired to do the work.

(b)   Whether **maintenance and repairs** of certain items of equipment should be dealt with by in-house engineers, or whether a maintenance contract should be made with a specialist organisation.

Even if you are not aware of specialist 'facilities management' companies such as Securicor, you will be familiar with the idea of office cleaning being done by contractors.

The costs **relevant** to such decisions are little different to those that are taken into account in a 'conventional' make or buy situation: they will be the **differential costs** between performing the service internally or using an external provider.

Exam focus point

> The major problem in examination questions is likely to be identifying whether existing staff will be made redundant or whether they will be redeployed, and whether there are alternative uses for the other resources made available by ceasing to perform the service internally. These, it hardly needs stating, are also likely to be the major problems in practice.

3.3 Performance of outsourcers

Once a decision has been made to outsource, it is essential that the **performance** of the outsourcer is monitored and **measured**.

Measures could include cost savings, service improvement and employee satisfaction. It is important to have **realistic goals** and expectations and to have **objective ways** to measure success.

The performance of the outsourcer, whether good or bad, can interfere with the performance assessment of an **internal function**. For example:

- Maintenance of equipment could be carried out badly by an outsourcer and this may result in increased breakdowns and reduced labour efficiency of a production team
- If information arrives late or is incorrect, the wrong decision may be made

3.4 Example: outsourcing

Stunnaz is considering a proposal to use the services of a press cuttings agency. At the moment, press cuttings are collected by a junior member of the marketing department, who is also responsible for office administration (including filing), travel bookings, a small amount of proof reading and making the tea. The total annual cost of employing this person is $15,000 pa.

There is concern that the ability of this person to produce a comprehensive file of cuttings is limited by the time available. She has calculated that she needs to spend about two hours of her seven and a half hour day simply reading the national and trade press, but usually only has about five hours a week for this job.

Press subscriptions currently cost $850 pa and are paid annually in advance.

The assistant makes use of a small micro-fiche device for storing cuttings. The cuttings are sent to a specialist firm once a month to be put onto fiche. Stunnaz pays $45 each month for this service. The micro-fiche reader is leased at a cost of $76 per calendar month. This lease has another 27 months to run.

The cuttings service bureau has proposed an annual contract at a cost of $1,250. Several existing users have confirmed their satisfaction with the service they receive.

Should Stunnaz outsource its press cuttings work?

Solution

Current annual costs amount to:

	$
Micro fiche service	$45 x 12 = 540
Subscriptions	850
	1,390

The monthly leasing charge is a **committed cost** that must be paid whatever the decision. It is not therefore a decision-relevant cost.

Engaging the services of the press cuttings agency therefore has the *potential* to save Stunnaz $140 pa. However, this is not the final word: there are other considerations.

(a)   The **'in-house' option** should give management **more direct control** over the work, but the **'outsource' option** often has the benefit that the external organisation has a **specialist skill and expertise** in the work. Decisions should certainly not be based exclusively on cost considerations.

(b)   Will outsourcing create **spare capacity**? How should that spare capacity be profitably used?

(c)   Are there **hidden benefits** to be obtained from subcontracting?

(d)   Would the company's workforce resent the loss of work to an outside subcontractor, and might such a decision cause an **industrial dispute**?

(e)   Would the subcontractor be **reliable with delivery times** and **quality**?

(f)   Does the company wish to be **flexible** and **maintain better control** over operations by doing everything itself?

4 Further processing decisions   12/07

FAST FORWARD

A joint product should be **processed further** past the split-off point if sales value minus post-separation (further processing) costs is greater than sales value at split-off point.

4.1 Joint products

You will have covered joint products in your earlier studies and the following will act as a brief reminder.

Knowledge brought forward from earlier studies

- **Joint products** are two or more products which are output from the same processing operation, but which are indistinguishable from each other up to their point of separation.

- Joint products have a **substantial sales value**. Often they require further processing before they are ready for sale. Joint products arise, for example, in the oil refining industry where diesel fuel, petrol, paraffin and lubricants are all produced from the same process.

- A joint product is regarded as an important saleable item, and so it should be **separately costed**. The profitability of each joint product should be assessed in the cost accounts.

- The point at which joint products become separately identifiable is known as the **split-off point** or **separation point**.

- Costs incurred prior to this point of separation are **common** or **joint costs**, and these need to be allocated (apportioned) in some manner to each of the joint products.

- Problems in **accounting** for joint products are basically of two different sorts.

    (a)   How common costs should be apportioned between products, in order to put a value to closing inventory and to the cost of sale (and profit) for each product.

    (b)   Whether it is more profitable to sell a joint product at one stage of processing, or to process the product further and sell it at a later stage.

Suppose a manufacturing company carries out process operations in which two or more joint products are made from a common process. If the joint products can be sold either in their existing condition at the 'split-off' point at the end of common processing or after further separate processing, **a decision should be taken about whether to sell each joint product at the split-off point or after further processing.**

Attention!

Note that **joint (pre-separation) costs** are incurred regardless of the decision and are therefore **irrelevant**.

4.2 Example: further processing

The Poison Chemical Company produces two joint products, Alash and Pottum from the same process. Joint processing costs of $150,000 are incurred up to split-off point, when 100,000 units of Alash and 50,000 units of Pottum are produced. The selling prices at split-off point are $1.25 per unit for Alash and $2.00 per unit for Pottum.

The units of Alash could be processed further to produce 60,000 units of a new chemical, Alashplus, but at an extra fixed cost of $20,000 and variable cost of 30c per unit of input. The selling price of Alashplus would be $3.25 per unit. Should the company sell Alash or Alashplus?

Solution

The only relevant costs/incomes are those which compare selling Alash against selling Alashplus. Every other cost is irrelevant: they will be incurred regardless of what the decision is.

	Alash			Alashplus
Selling price per unit	$1.25			$3.25
	$		$	$
Total sales	125,000			195,000
Post-separation processing costs	–	Fixed	20,000	
	–	Variable	30,000	50,000
Sales minus post-separation (further processing) costs	125,000			145,000

It is $20,000 more profitable to convert Alash into Alashplus.

Question

Further processing decision

A company manufactures four products from an input of a raw material to Process 1. Following this process, product A is processed in Process 2, product B in Process 3, product C in Process 4 and product D in Process 5.

The normal loss in Process 1 is 10% of input, and there are no expected losses in the other processes. Scrap value in Process 1 is $0.50 per litre. The costs incurred in Process 1 are apportioned to each product according to the volume of output of each product. Production overhead is absorbed as a percentage of direct wages.

Data in respect of the month of October

	Process					
	1	2	3	4	5	Total
	$'000	$'000	$'000	$'000	$'000	$'000
Direct materials at $1.25 per litre	100					100
Direct wages	48	12	8	4	16	88
Production overhead						66

	Product			
	A	B	C	D
	litres	litres	litres	litres
Output	22,000	20,000	10,000	18,000
	$	$	$	$
Selling price	4.00	3.00	2.00	5.00
Estimated sales value at end of Process 1	2.50	2.80	1.20	3.00

Required

Suggest and evaluate an alternative production strategy which would optimise profit for the month. It should not be assumed that the output of Process 1 can be changed.

Answer

During the month, the quantity of input to Process 1 was 80,000 litres. Normal loss is 10% = 8,000 litres, and so total output should have been 72,000 litres of A, B, C and D. Instead, it was only 70,000 litres. In an 'average' month, output would have been higher, and this might have some bearing on the optimal production and selling strategy.

The **central question** is whether or not the output from Process 1 should be **processed further** in processes 2, 3, 4 and 5, or whether it should be **sold at the 'split-off' point**, at the end of Process 1. Each joint product can be looked at **individually**.

A further question is whether the **wages costs** in process 2, 3, 4 and 5 would be avoided if the joint products were sold at the end of process 1 and not processed further. It will be assumed that all the wages costs would be **avoidable**, but none of the **production overhead** costs would be. This assumption can be challenged, and in practice would have to be investigated.

	A	B	C	D
	$	$	$	$
Selling price, per litre	4.00	3.00	2.00	5.00
Selling price at end of process 1	2.50	2.80	1.20	3.00
Incremental selling price, per litre	1.50	0.20	0.80	2.00
Litres output	22,000	20,000	10,000	18,000
	$'000	$'000	$'000	$'000
Total incremental revenue from further processing	33	4	8	36
Avoidable costs from selling at split-off point (wages saved)	12	8	4	16
Incremental benefit/(cost) of further processing	21	(4)	4	20

This analysis would seem to indicate that **products A, C and D should be further processed** in processes 2, 4 and 5 respectively, but that **product B should be sold at the end of process 1**, without further processing in process 3. The saving would be at least $4,000 per month.

If **some production overhead** (which is 75% of direct wages) were also **avoidable**, this would mean that:

(a)   Selling product B at the end of process 1 would offer further savings of up to (75% of $8,000) $6,000 in overheads, and so $10,000 in total.

(b)   The incremental benefit from further processing product C might fall by up to (75% of $4,000) $3,000 to $1,000, meaning that it is only just profitable to process C beyond the split-off point.

5 Shut down decisions

> **Shutdown/discontinuance problems** can be simplified into short-run relevant cost decisions.

5.1 Simplifying decisions

Discontinuance or shutdown problems involve the following decisions.

(a) **Whether or not to close down** a product line, department or other activity, either because it is making losses or because it is too expensive to run

(b) If the decision is to shut down, **whether the closure should be permanent or temporary**

In practice, shutdown decisions may often involve **longer-term considerations,** and **capital expenditures and revenues.**

(a) A shutdown should result in savings in **annual operating costs** for a number of years into the future.

(b) Closure will probably release **unwanted non-current assets for sale**. Some assets might have a small scrap value, but other assets, in particular property, might have a substantial sale value.

(c) **Employees** affected by the closure must be made redundant or relocated, perhaps after retraining, or else offered early retirement. There will be lump sum payments involved which must be taken into account in the financial arithmetic. For example, suppose that the closure of a regional office would result in annual savings of $100,000, non-current assets could be sold off to earn income of $2 million, but redundancy payments would be $3 million. The shutdown decision would involve an assessment of the net capital cost of closure ($1 million) against the annual benefits ($100,000 pa).

It is possible, however, for shutdown problems to be **simplified into short-run decisions**, by making one of the following assumptions.

(a) Non-current asset sales and redundancy costs would be negligible.

(b) Income from non-current asset sales would match redundancy costs and so these capital items would be self-cancelling.

In such circumstances the financial aspect of shutdown decisions would be based on **short-run relevant costs.**

5.2 Example: adding or deleting products (or departments)

A company manufactures three products, Pawns, Rooks and Bishops. The present net annual income from these is as follows.

	Pawns	Rooks	Bishops	Total
	$	$	$	$
Sales	50,000	40,000	60,000	150,000
Variable costs	30,000	25,000	35,000	90,000
Contribution	20,000	15,000	25,000	60,000
Fixed costs	17,000	18,000	20,000	55,000
Profit/loss	3,000	(3,000)	5,000	5,000

The company is concerned about its poor profit performance, and is considering whether or not to cease selling Rooks. It is felt that selling prices cannot be raised or lowered without adversely affecting net income. $5,000 of the fixed costs of Rooks are direct fixed costs which would be saved if production ceased (ie there are some attributable fixed costs). All other fixed costs, it is considered, would remain the same.

By **stopping production of Rooks**, the **consequences** would be a $10,000 fall in profits.

	$
Loss of contribution	(15,000)
Savings in fixed costs	5,000
Incremental loss	(10,000)

Suppose, however, it were possible to use the resources realised by stopping production of Rooks and **switch to producing a new item**, Crowners, which would sell for $50,000 and incur variable costs of $30,000 and extra direct fixed costs of $6,000. A new decision is now required.

	Rooks $	Crowners $
Sales	40,000	50,000
Less variable costs	25,000	30,000
	15,000	20,000
Less direct fixed costs	5,000	6,000
Contribution to shared fixed costs and profit	10,000	14,000

It would be **more profitable to shut down production of Rooks and switch** resources to making Crowners, in order to boost profits by $4,000 to $9,000.

5.3 Timing of shutdown

An organisation may also need to consider the most appropriate **timing** for a shutdown. Some costs may be avoidable in the long run but not in the short run. For example, office space may have been rented and three months notice is required. This cost is therefore **unavoidable** for three months. In the same way supply contracts may require notice of cancellation. A month by month analysis of when notice should be given and savings will be made will help the decision making process.

5.4 Qualitative factors

As usual the decision is not merely a matter of choosing the best financial option. **Qualitative** factors must once more be considered.

(a)   What impact will a shutdown decision have on employee morale?

(b)   What signal will the decision give to competitors? How will they react?

(c)   How will customers react? Will they lose confidence in the company's products?

(d)   How will suppliers be affected? If one supplier suffers disproportionately there may be a loss of goodwill and damage to future relations.

Question   Shutdown decisions

How would the above decision change if Pawns, Rooks and Bishops were manufactured in different departments, variable costs could be split down into the costs of direct materials, labour and overheads, and fixed costs could be analysed into the costs of administrative staff and equipment and premises costs?

Answer

The decision would not change at all – unless perhaps activity based analysis of overheads were undertaken and unexpected cost patterns were revealed. The point of this exercise is to make you realise that problems that look complicated are sometimes very simple in essence even if the volume of calculations seems daunting.

5.5 Judging relative profitability

A common approach to judging the relative profitability of products is to calculate **C/S ratios**. The most profitable option is to concentrate on the product(s) with the highest C/S ratios.

Chapter Roundup

- **Relevant costs** are future cash flows arising as a direct consequence of a decision.

  - Relevant costs are **future costs**   – Relevant costs are **incremental costs**

  - Relevant costs are **cash flows**

- In a **make or buy decision** with no limiting factors, the relevant costs are the differential costs between the two options.

- The relevant costs/revenues in decisions relating to the **operating of internal service departments or the use of external services** are the differential costs between the two options.

- A joint product should be **processed further** past the split-off point if sales value minus post-separation (further processing) costs is greater than sales value at split-off point.

- **Shutdown/discontinuance problems** can be simplified into short-run relevant cost decisions.

1 *Fill in the relevant costs in the four boxes in the diagram below.*

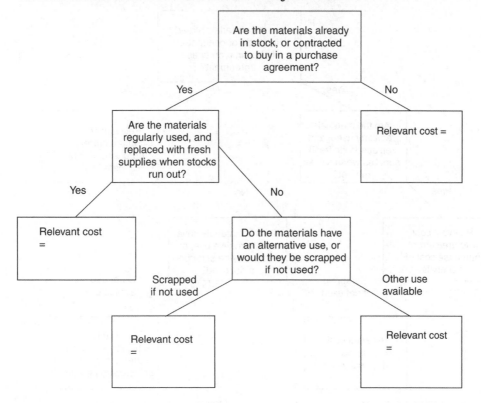

2 *Choose the correct word(s) from those highlighted.*

In a situation where a company must subcontract work to make up a shortfall in its own in-house capabilities, its total cost will be minimised if those units **bought out from a sub-contractor/made in-house** have the **lowest/highest** extra **variable/fixed** cost of **buying out/making in-house** per unit of **scarce resource/material.**

3 In a decision about whether or not to sell a joint product at the split-off point or after further processing, joint costs are relevant. True or false?

4 *Fill in the blanks.*

Most of the decisions considered in this chapter involve calculating .... obtained from

various options after identifying .... They always involve ....

issues, which depend upon the precise situation described.

1

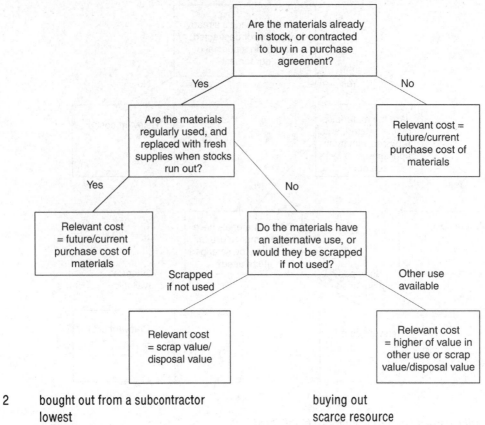

2   bought out from a subcontractor   buying out
     lowest   scarce resource
     variable

3   False

4   contribution

     relevant costs

     qualitative

Now try the question below from the Exam Question Bank

Number	Level	Marks	Time
Q10	Examination	20	36 mins

7

Risk and uncertainty

Topic list	Syllabus reference
1 Risk and uncertainty	B6 (a)
2 Allowing for uncertainty	B6 (a)
3 Probabilities and expected values	B6 (b), (c)
4 Decision rules	B6 (d)
5 Decision trees	B6 (e)
6 The value of information	B6 (f)
7 Sensitivity analysis	B6 (b), (c)
8 Simulation models	B6 (b)

Introduction

Decision making involves making decisions now about what will happen in the future. Obviously, decisions can turn out badly, or actual results can prove to be very different from the estimates on which the original decision was made. **Ideally** the decision maker would **know with certainty** what the future consequences would be for each choice facing him. But the real world is not normally so helpful, and decisions must be made in the knowledge that their **consequences**, although probable perhaps, are **rarely 100% certain**.

Various **methods of bringing uncertainty and risk analysis** into the evaluation of decisions will be described in this chapter. You may well think that some methods are more sensible or practical than others but you should **judge** each method on its merits, and be able to **apply** it if necessary in an examination.

Study guide

		Intellectual level
B6	**Dealing with risk and uncertainty in decision-making**	
(a)	Suggest research techniques to reduce uncertainty eg Focus groups, market research	2
(b)	Explain the use of simulation, expected values and sensitivity	1
(c)	Apply expected values and sensitivity to decision-making problems	2
(d)	Apply the techniques of maximum, minimin, and minimax regret to decision-making problems including the production of profit tables	2
(e)	Draw a decision tree and use it to solve a multi-stage decision problem	1
(f)	Calculate the value of perfect information	2

Exam guide

Management accounting exams have increasingly expected candidates to have a good understanding of risk. Questions are likely to be a mixture of calculations and explanation.

1 Risk and uncertainty

FAST FORWARD

An example of a **risky situation** is one in which we can say that there is a 70% probability that returns from a project will be in excess of $100,000 but a 30% probability that returns will be less than $100,000. If we cannot predict an outcome or assign probabilities, we are faced with an **uncertain** situation.

Key terms

Risk involves situations or events which may or may not occur, but whose probability of occurrence can be calculated statistically and the frequency of their occurrence predicted from past records. Thus insurance deals with risk.

Uncertain events are those whose outcome cannot be predicted with statistical confidence.

In everyday usage the terms risk and uncertainty are not clearly distinguished. If you are asked for a definition, do not make the mistake of believing that the latter is a more extreme version of the former. It is not a question of degree, it is a question of whether or not sufficient information is available to allow the lack of certainty to be quantified. As a rule, however, the terms are used interchangeably.

1.1 Risk preference

FAST FORWARD

People may be **risk seekers**, **risk neutral** or **risk averse**.

Key terms

A **risk seeker** is a decision maker who is interested in the best outcomes no matter how small the chance that they may occur.

A decision maker is **risk neutral** if he is concerned with what will be the most likely outcome.

A **risk averse** decision maker acts on the assumption that the worst outcome might occur.

This has clear implications for managers and organisations. A **risk seeking manager** working for an **organisation** that is characteristically **risk averse** is likely to make decisions that are **not congruent with the goals of the organisation**. There may be a role for the management accountant here, who could be instructed to present decision-making information in such a way as to ensure that the manager considers *all* the possibilities, including the worst.

2 Allowing for uncertainty

Management accounting directs its attention towards the **future** and the future is **uncertain**. For this reason a number of methods of taking **uncertainty** into consideration have evolved.

2.1 Research techniques to reduce uncertainty

Market research can be used to reduce uncertainty.

Key term

> **Market research** is the systematic process of gathering, analysing and reporting data about markets to investigate, describe, measure, understand or explain a situation or problem facing a company or organisation.

Market research involves **tackling problems**. The assumption is that these problems can be solved, no matter how complex the issues are, if the researcher follows a line of enquiry in a **systematic** way, without losing sight of the main objectives. Gathering and analysing all the facts will ultimately lead to **better decision making**.

2.1.1 The role of market research

In the last 20 years or so market research has become a much more widespread activity. Organisations – in the private sector, the public sector and the not-for-profit sector – rely on research to inform and improve their **planning and decision making**.

Market research enables organisations to understand the needs and opinions of their customers and other stakeholders. Armed with this knowledge they are able to make better quality decisions and provide better products and better services.

Thus, research influences what is provided and the way it is provided. It **reduces uncertainty and monitors performance.** A management team which possesses accurate information relating to the marketplace will be in a strong position to make the best decisions in an increasingly competitive world.

Decision-makers need data to reduce **uncertainty** and **risk** when planning for the future and to monitor business performance. Market researchers provide the data that helps them to do this.

2.1.2 Types of data collected

Data can be either **primary** (collected at first hand from a sample of respondents), or **secondary** (collected from previous surveys, other published facts and opinions, or from experts). Secondary research is also known as **desk research**, because it can be carried out from one's desk.

More importantly for research practice and analysis, data can be either quantitative or qualitative.

Quantitative data usually deals with numbers and typically provides the decision maker with information about **how many** customers, competitors etc act in a certain way. Quantitative data can, for example, tell the researcher **what** people need or consume, or **where**, **when** and **how** people buy goods or consumer services.

Qualitative data tells us **why** consumers think/buy or act the way they do. Qualitative data is used in **consumer insight** (eg understanding what makes consumers prefer one brand to another), **media awareness** (eg how much of an advertisement is noticed by the public), **new product development** studies and for many other reasons.

Qualitative research has as its specific purpose the uncovering and understanding of thought and opinion. It is carried out on relatively small samples and unstructured or semi-structured techniques, such as individual in depth interviews and group discussions (also known as **focus groups**), are used.

2.2 Conservatism

This approach simply involves estimating outcomes in a conservative manner in order to provide a built-in safety factor.

However, the method fails to consider explicitly a **range** of outcomes and, by concentrating only on conservative figures, may also fail to consider the **expected** or most likely outcomes.

Conservatism is associated with **risk aversion** and prudence (in the general sense of the word). In spite of its shortcomings it is probably the **most widely used** method in practice.

2.3 Worst/most likely/best outcome estimates

A more scientific version of conservatism is to measure the most likely outcome from a decision, and the worst and best possible outcomes. This will show the **full range of possible outcomes** from a decision, and might help managers to reject certain alternatives because the worst possible outcome might involve an unacceptable amount of loss. This requires the preparation of **pay-off tables**.

2.3.1 Pay-off tables

Pay-off tables **identify and record all possible outcomes (or pay-offs)** in situations where the action taken affects the outcomes.

2.3.2 Example: worst/best possible outcomes

Omelette Co is trying to set the sales price for one of its products. Three prices are under consideration, and expected sales volumes and costs are as follows.

Price per unit	$4	$4.30	$4.40
Expected sales volume (units)			
Best possible	16,000	14,000	12,500
Most likely	14,000	12,500	12,000
Worst possible	10,000	8,000	6,000

Fixed costs are $20,000 and variable costs of sales are $2 per unit.

Which price should be chosen?

Solution

Here we need to prepare a pay-off table showing **pay-offs** (contribution) **dependent on different levels of demand and different selling prices.**

Price per unit	$4	$4.30	$4.40
Contribution per unit	$2	$2.30	$2.40
Total contribution towards fixed costs	$	$	$
Best possible	32,000	32,200	30,000
Most likely	28,000	28,750	28,800
Worst possible	20,000	18,400	14,400

(a)   The highest contribution based on **most likely** sales volume would be at a price of $4.40 but arguably a price of $4.30 would be much better than $4.40, since the most likely profit is almost as good, the worst possible profit is not as bad, and the best possible profit is better.

(b)   However, only a price of $4 guarantees that the company would **not make a loss,** even if the worst possible outcome occurs. (Fixed costs of $20,000 would just be covered.) A risk averse management might therefore prefer a price of $4 to either of the other two prices.

We consider pay-off tables and expected values in paragraph 3.1.2 below.

3 Probabilities and expected values

Expected values indicate what an outcome is likely to be in the long term with repetition. Fortunately, many business transactions do occur over and over again.

Although the outcome of a decision may not be certain, there is some likelihood that probabilities could be assigned to the various possible outcomes from an analysis of previous experience.

3.1 Expected values

Where probabilities are assigned to different outcomes we can evaluate the worth of a decision as the **expected value**, or weighted average, of these outcomes. The principle is that when there are a number of alternative decisions, each with a range of possible outcomes, the optimum decision will be the one which gives the highest expected value.

3.1.1 Example: expected values

Suppose a manager has to choose between mutually exclusive options A and B, and the probable outcomes of each option are as follows.

Option A		Option B	
	Profit	Probability	Profit
Probability			
	$		$
0.8	5,000	0.1	(2,000)
0.2	6,000	0.2	5,000
		0.6	7,000
		0.1	8,000

The expected value (EV) of profit of each option would be measured as follows.

	Option A				Option B		
Prob		Profit $		EV of profit $	Prob	Profit $		EV of profit $

Prob		Profit $		EV of profit $	Prob		Profit $		EV of profit $
0.8	×	5,000	=	4,000	0.1	×	(2,000)	=	(200)
0.2	×	6,000	=	1,200	0.2	×	5,000	=	1,000
		EV	=	5,200	0.6	×	7,000	=	4,200
					0.1	×	8,000	=	800
							EV	=	5,800

In this example, since it offers a higher EV of profit, option B would be selected in preference to A, unless further risk analysis is carried out.

3.1.2 Example: expected values and pay-off tables

IB Newsagents stocks a weekly lifestyle magazine. The owner buys the magazines for $0.30 each and sells them at the retail price of $0.50 each.

At the end of the week unsold magazines are obsolete and have no value. The estimated probability distribution for weekly demand is shown below.

Weekly demand in units	Probability
20	0.20
30	0.55
40	0.25
	1.00

Requirement

What is the expected value of demand?

If the owner is to order a fixed quantity of magazines per week how many should that be?

Assume no seasonal variations in demand.

Solution

EV of demand (units per week) = (20 x 0.20) + (30 x 0.55) + (40 x 0.25) = 30.5 units per week

The next step is to set up a decision matrix of possible strategies (numbers bought) and possible demand.

The 'pay-off' from each combination of action and outcome is then computed.

No sale = cost of $0.30 per magazine

Sale = profit of $0.20 per magazine ($0.50 - $0.30)

Probability	Outcome (number demanded)	Decision (number bought)		
		20	30	40
		$	$	$
0.20	20	4.00	1.00*	(2.00)
0.55	30	4.00	6.00	3.00
0.25	40	4.00	6.00	8.00
1	EV	4.00	5.00**	3.25

* Buy 30 and sell only 20 gives a profit of (20 x $0.5) – (30 x $0.3) = $1

** (0.2 x 0.1) + (0.55 x 6) + (0.25 x 6) = 5

The strategy which gives the highest expected pay-off is to stock 30 magazines each week.

Question

EVs

A manager has to choose between mutually exclusive options C and D and the probable outcomes of each option are as follows.

Option C		Option D	
Probability	Cost	Probability	Cost
	$		$
0.29	15,000	0.03	14,000
0.54	20,000	0.30	17,000
0.17	30,000	0.35	21,000
		0.32	24,000

Both options will produce an income of $30,000. Which should be chosen?

Answer

Option C. Do the workings yourself in the way illustrated above. Note that the probabilities are for *costs* not profits.

3.1.3 Limitations of expected values

The preference for B over A on the basis of expected value is marred by the fact that A's **worst possible** outcome is a profit of $5,000, whereas B might incur a loss of $2,000 (although there is a 70% chance that profits would be $7,000 or more, which would be more than the best profits from option A).

Since the decision must be made **once only** between A and B, the expected value of profit (which is **merely a weighted average** of all possible outcomes) has severe limitations as a decision rule by which to judge preference. The expected value will **never actually occur**.

Expected values are used to support a **risk-neutral attitude**. A risk-neutral decision maker will ignore any variability in the range of possible outcomes and be concerned only with the expected value of outcomes.

Expected values are more valuable as a guide to decision making where they refer to outcomes which will occur **many times over**. Examples would include the probability that so many customers per day will buy a can of baked beans, the probability that a customer services assistant will receive so many phone calls per hour, and so on.

4 Decision rules

12/08

The 'play it safe' basis for decision making is referred to as the **maximin basis**. This is short for 'maximise the minimum achievable profit'.

A basis for making decisions by looking for the best outcome is known as the **maximax basis**, short for 'maximise the maximum achievable profit'.

The 'opportunity loss' basis for decision making is known as **minimax regret**.

4.1 The maximin decision rule

Key term

The **maximin decision rule** suggests that a decision maker should select the alternative that offers the least unattractive worst outcome. This would mean choosing the alternative that *maximises* the *minimum* profits.

Suppose a businessman is trying to decide which of three mutually exclusive projects to undertake. Each of the projects could lead to varying net profit under three possible scenarios.

		Profits Project		
		D	E	F
	I	100	80	60
Scenarios	II	90	120	85
	III	(20)	10	85

The maximin decision rule suggests that he should select the 'smallest worst result' that could happen. This is the decision criterion that managers should 'play safe' and either minimise their losses or costs, or else go for the decision which gives the higher minimum profits. If he selects project D the worst result is a loss of 20. The worst results for E and F are profits of 10 and 60 respectively. The best worst outcome is 60 and project F would therefore be selected (because this is a better 'worst possible' than either D or E).

4.1.1 Criticisms of maximin

(a) It is **defensive** and **conservative**, being a safety first principle of avoiding the worst outcomes without taking into account opportunities for maximising profits.

(b) It ignores the **probability** of each different outcome taking place.

4.2 Maximax

Key term

The **maximax criterion** looks at the best possible results. Maximax means 'maximise the maximum profit'.

Using the information in Section 4.1 above, the maximum profit for D is 100, for E is 120 and for F is 85.

Project E would be chosen if the maximax rule is followed.

4.2.1 Criticisms of maximax

(a)   It ignores probabilities.
(b)   It is **over-optimistic**.

A company is considering which one of three alternative courses of action, A, B and C to take. The profit or loss from each choice depends on which one of four economic circumstances, I, II, III or IV will apply. The possible profits and losses, in thousands of pounds, are given in the following payoff table. Losses are shown as negative figures.

		A	*B*	*C*
			Action	
Circumstance	I	70	60	70
	II	−10	20	−5
	III	80	0	50
	IV	60	100	115

Required

State which action would be selected using each of the maximax and maximin criteria.

Answer

(a)   The **best possible outcomes** are as follows.

  A (circumstance III):   80
  B (circumstance IV):   100
  C (circumstance IV):   115

  As 115 is the highest of these three figures, action C would be chosen using the maximax criterion.

(b)   The **worst possible outcomes** are as follows.

  A (circumstance II):   −10
  B (circumstance III):   0
  C (circumstance II):   −5

  The best of these figures is 0 (neither a profit nor a loss), so action B would be chosen using the maximin criterion.

4.3 Minimax regret rule

Key term

> The **minimax regret rule** aims to minimise the regret from making the wrong decision. **Regret** is the opportunity lost through making the wrong decision.

We first consider the extreme to which we might come to regret an action we had chosen.

Regret for any combination of action and circumstances	=	Profit for best action in those circumstances	−	Profit for the action actually chosen in those circumstances

The minimax regret decision rule is that the decision option selected should be the one which **minimises the maximum potential regret** for any of the possible outcomes.

Using the example in Section 4.1, a table of regrets can be compiled as follows.

	Project		
	D	E	F
Scenario I	0	20*	40**
Scenario II	30***	0	35
Scenario III	105	75	0
Maximum regret	105	75	40

* 100 – 80 ** 100 – 60 *** 120 – 90

The **lowest** of maximum regrets is 40 with project F so project F would be selected if the minimax regret rule is used.

4.4 Contribution tables

Questions requiring application of the decision rules often incorporate a **number of variables, each with a range of possible values**. For example these variables might be:

- Unit price and associated level of demand
- Unit variable cost

Each variable might have, for example, three possible values.

Before being asked to use the decision rules, exam questions could ask you to **work out contribution** for each of the possible outcomes. (Alternatively profit figures could be required if you are given information about fixed costs.)

The **number of possible outcomes** = number of values of variable 1 × number of values of variable 2 × number of values of variable 3 etc

So, for example, if there are **two** variables, each with **three** possible values, there are **3 × 3 = 9 outcomes**.

Perhaps the easiest way to see how to draw up contribution tables is to look at an example.

4.4.1 Example: contribution tables and the decision rules

Suppose the budgeted demand for product X will be 11,500 units if the price is $10, 8,500 units if the price is $12 and 5,000 units if the price is $14. Variable costs are estimated at either $4, $5, or $6 per unit. A decision needs to be made on the **price** to be charged.

Here is a contribution table showing the budgeted contribution for each of the nine possible outcomes.

Demand	Price $	Variable cost $	Unit contribution $	Total contribution $'000
11,500	10	4	6	69.0
11,500	10	5	5	57.5
11,500	10	6	4	46.0
8,500	12	4	8	68.0
8,500	12	5	7	59.5
8,500	12	6	6	51.0
5,000	14	4	10	50.0
5,000	14	5	9	45.0
5,000	14	6	8	40.0

Once the table has been drawn up, the decision rules can be applied.

Solution

Maximin

We need to maximise the minimum contribution.

Demand/price	Minimum contribution
11,500/$10	$46,000
8,500/$12	$51,000
5,000/$14	$40,000

Set a price of $12.

Maximax

We need to maximise the maximum contribution.

Demand/price	Maximum contribution
11,500/$10	$69,000
8,000/$12	$68,000
5,000/$14	$50,000

Set a price of $10.

Minimax regret

We need to minimise the maximum regret (lost contribution) of making the wrong decision.

Variable cost		Price	
$	*$10*	*$12*	*$14*
4	–	$1,000	$19,000
5	$2,000	–	$14,500
6	$5,000	–	$11,000
Minimax regret	$5,000	$1,000	$19,000

Minimax regret strategy (**price of $12**) is that which minimises the maximum regret ($1,000).

Sample working

At a variable cost of $4, the best strategy would be a price of $10. Choosing a price of $12 would mean lost contribution of $69,000 – $68,000, while choosing a price of $14 would mean lost contribution of $69,000 – $50,000.

Exam focus point

Decision rules were examined in December 2008 and the examiner commented that candidates struggled to apply their knowledge to the scenario.

5 Decision trees

FAST FORWARD

Decision trees are diagrams which illustrate the choices and possible outcomes of a decision.

Rollback analysis evaluates the EV of each decision option. You have to work from right to left and calculate EVs at each outcome point.

A probability problem such as 'what is the probability of throwing a six with one throw of a die?' is fairly straightforward and can be solved using the basic principles of probability.

More complex probability questions, although solvable using the basic principles, require a clear logical approach to ensure that all possible choices and outcomes of a decision are taken into consideration. **Decision trees** are a useful means of interpreting such probability problems.

Key term

A **decision tree** is a pictorial method of showing a sequence of interrelated decisions and their expected outcomes. Decision trees can incorporate both the probabilities of, and values of, expected outcomes, and are used in decision-making.

Exactly how does the use of a decision tree permit a clear and logical approach?

- All the possible **choices** that can be made are shown as **branches** on the tree.
- All the possible **outcomes** of each choice are shown as **subsidiary branches** on the tree.

5.1 Constructing a decision tree

There are two stages in preparing a decision tree.

- Drawing the tree itself to show all the choices and outcomes
- Putting in the numbers (the probabilities, outcome values and EVs)

Every **decision tree starts** from a **decision point** with the **decision options** that are currently being considered.

(a)   It helps to identify the **decision point**, and any subsequent decision points in the tree, with a symbol. Here, we shall use a **square shape**.

(b)   There should be a **line**, or **branch**, for each **option** or **alternative**.

It is conventional to draw decision trees from left to right, and so a decision tree will start as follows.

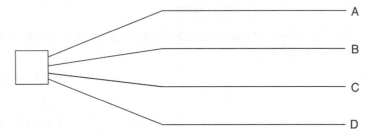

The **square** is the **decision point**, and A, B, C and D represent **four alternatives** from which a choice must be made (such as buy a new machine with cash, hire a machine, continue to use existing machine, raise a loan to buy a machine).

If the outcome from any choice is certain, the branch of the decision tree for that alternative is complete.

If the outcome of a particular choice is uncertain, the various possible outcomes must be shown.

We show the various possible outcomes on a decision tree by inserting an **outcome point** on the **branch** of the tree. Each possible outcome is then shown as a **subsidiary branch**, coming out from the outcome point. The probability of each outcome occurring should be written on to the branch of the tree which represents that outcome.

To distinguish decision points from outcome points, **a circle will be used as the symbol for an outcome point**.

In the example above, there are two choices facing the decision-maker, A and B. The outcome if A is chosen is known with certainty, but if B is chosen, there are two possible outcomes, high sales (0.6 probability) or low sales (0.4 probability).

When several outcomes are possible, it is usually simpler to show two or more stages of outcome points on the decision tree.

5.2 Example: several possible outcomes

A company can choose to launch a new product XYZ or not. If the product is launched, expected sales and expected unit costs might be as follows.

Sales		Unit costs	
Units	Probability	£	Probability
10,000	0.8	6	0.7
15,000	0.2	8	0.3

(a)   The decision tree could be drawn as follows.

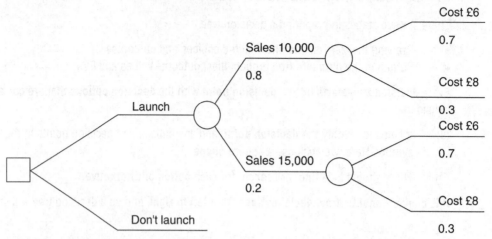

(b)   The layout shown above will usually be easier to use than the alternative way of drawing the tree, which is as follows.

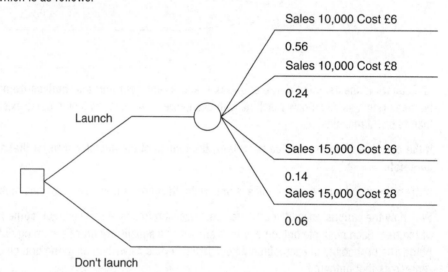

Sometimes, a **decision taken now** will lead to **other decisions to be taken in the future**. When this situation arises, the decision tree can be drawn as a **two-stage tree**, as follows.

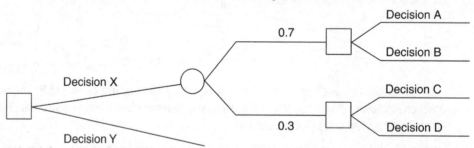

In this tree, either a choice between A and B or else a choice between C and D will be made, depending on the outcome which occurs after choosing X.

The decision tree should be in **chronological order** from **left to right**. When there are two-stage decision trees, the first decision in time should be drawn on the left.

5.3 Example: a decision tree

Beethoven has a new wonder product, the vylin, of which it expects great things. At the moment the company has two courses of action open to it, to test market the product or abandon it.

If the company test markets it, the cost will be $100,000 and the market response could be positive or negative with probabilities of 0.60 and 0.40.

If the response is positive the company could either abandon the product or market it full scale.

If it markets the vylin full scale, the outcome might be low, medium or high demand, and the respective net gains/(losses) would be (200), 200 or 1,000 in units of $1,000 (the result could range from a net loss of $200,000 to a gain of $1,000,000). These outcomes have probabilities of 0.20, 0.50 and 0.30 respectively.

If the result of the test marketing is negative and the company goes ahead and markets the product, estimated losses would be $600,000.

If, at any point, the company abandons the product, there would be a net gain of $50,000 from the sale of scrap. All the financial values have been discounted to the present.

Required

(a)   Draw a decision tree.
(b)   Include figures for cost, loss or profit on the appropriate branches of the tree.

Solution

The starting point for the tree is to **establish what decision has to be made now**. What are the options?

(a)   To test market
(b)   To abandon

The outcome of the 'abandon' option is known with certainty. There are two possible outcomes of the option to test market, positive response and negative response.

Depending on the outcome of the test marketing, another decision will then be made, to abandon the product or to go ahead.

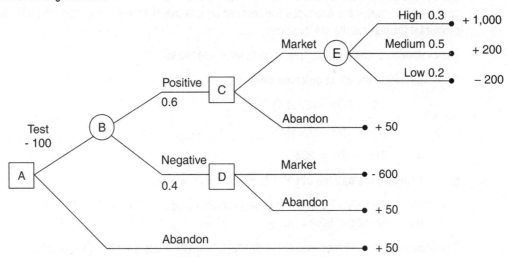

5.4 Evaluating the decision with a decision tree

Rollback analysis evaluates the EV of each decision option. You have to work from right to left and calculate EVs at each outcome point.

The EV of each decision option can be evaluated, using the decision tree to help with keeping the logic on track. The basic rules are as follows.

(a)   We start on the **right hand side** of the tree and **work back** towards the left hand side and the current decision under consideration. This is sometimes known as the **'rollback' technique** or 'rollback analysis'.

(b)   Working from **right to left**, we calculate the **EV of revenue, cost, contribution or profit** at each outcome point on the tree.

In the above example, the right-hand-most outcome point is point E, and the EV is as follows.

	Profit	Probability	
	x	p	px
	$'000		$'000
High	1,000	0.3	300
Medium	200	0.5	100
Low	(200)	0.2	(40)
		EV	360

This is the EV of the decision to market the product if the test shows positive response. It may help you to write the EV on the decision tree itself, at the appropriate outcome point (point E).

(a)   **At decision point C**, the **choice** is as follows.

> (i)   Market, EV = + 360 (the EV at point E)
> (ii)   Abandon, value = + 50

The choice would be to market the product, and so the EV at decision point C is +360.

(b)   **At decision point D**, the **choice** is as follows.

> (i)   Market, value = – 600
> (ii)   Abandon, value = +50

The choice would be to abandon, and so the EV at decision point D is +50.

The second stage decisions have therefore been made. If the original decision is to test market, the company will market the product if the test shows positive customer response, and will abandon the product if the test results are negative.

The evaluation of the decision tree is completed as follows.

(a)   **Calculate the EV at outcome point B.**

> 0.6 × 360   (EV at C)
>
> +   0.4 × 50   (EV at D)
>
> =   216 + 20 = 236.

(b)   **Compare the options at point A**, which are as follows.

> (i)   Test: EV = EV at B minus test marketing cost = 236 – 100 = 136
> (ii)   Abandon: Value = 50

The choice would be to test market the product, because it has a **higher EV of profit**.

Consider the following diagram.

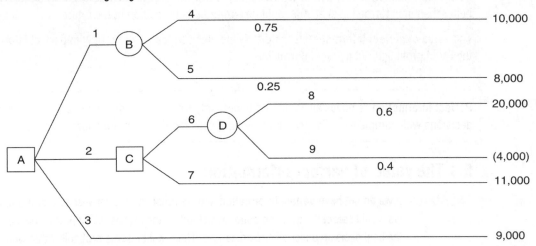

If a decision maker wished to maximise the value of the outcome, which options should be selected?

A   Option 2 and option 7

B   Option 3

C·   Option 1 and option 4

D   Option 2, option 6 and option 8

Answer

The correct answer is A.

The various outcomes must be evaluated using expected values.

EV at point B: $(0.75 \times 10,000) + (0.25 \times 8,000) = 9,500$

EV at point D: $(0.6 \times 20,000) + (0.4 \times (4,000)) = 10,400$

EV at point C: Choice between 10,400 and 11,000

EV at point A: Choice between B (9,500), C (10,400 or 11,000) and choice 3 (9,000).

If we are trying to maximise the figure, option 2 and then option 7 are chosen to give 11,000.

Evaluating decisions by using **decision trees has a number of limitations**.

(a)   The time value of money may not be taken into account.

(b)   Decision trees are not very suitable for use in complex situations.

(c)   The outcome with the highest EV may have the greatest risks attached to it. Managers may be reluctant to take risks which may lead to losses.

(d)   The probabilities associated with different branches of the 'tree' are likely to be estimates, and possibly unreliable or inaccurate.

6 The value of information

FAST FORWARD

Perfect information is guaranteed to predict the future with 100% accuracy. **Imperfect information** is better than no information at all but could be wrong in its prediction of the future.

The **value of perfect information** is the difference between the EV of profit with perfect information and the EV of profit without perfect information.

Key term

Perfect information removes all doubt and uncertainty from a decision, and enables managers to make decisions with complete confidence that they have selected the optimum course of action.

6.1 The value of perfect information

Step 1 If we **do not have perfect information** and we must choose between two or more decision options, we would **select** the decision option which offers the **highest EV** of profit. This option will not be the best decision under all circumstances. There will be some probability that what was really the best option will not have been selected, given the way actual events turn out.

Step 2 With **perfect information**, the **best decision option will always be selected**. The profits from the decision will depend on the future circumstances which are predicted by the information; nevertheless, the EV of profit with perfect information should be higher than the EV of profit without the information.

Step 3 The **value of perfect information** is **the difference between these two EVs**.

6.2 Example: the value of perfect information

The management of Ivor Ore must choose whether to go ahead with either of two mutually exclusive projects, A and B. The expected profits are as follows.

	Profit if there is strong demand	Profit/(loss) if there is weak demand
Option A	$4,000	$(1,000)
Option B	$1,500	$500
Probability of demand	0.3	0.7

Required

(a) Ascertain what the decision would be, based on expected values, if no information about demand were available.

(b) Calculate the value of perfect information about demand.

Solution

Step 1 If there were **no information** to help with the decision, the project with the higher EV of profit would be selected.

Probability	Project A		Project B	
	Profit	EV	Profit	EV
	$	$	$	$
0.3	4,000	1,200	1,500	450
0.7	(1,000)	(700)	500	350
		500		800

Project B would be selected.

This is clearly the better option if demand turns out to be weak. However, if demand were to turn out to be strong, project A would be more profitable. There is a 30% chance that this could happen.

Step 2 **Perfect information** will indicate for certain whether demand will be weak or strong. If demand is forecast 'weak' project B would be selected. If demand is forecast as 'strong', project A would be selected, and perfect information would improve the profit from $1,500, which would have been earned by selecting B, to $4,000.

Forecast demand	Probability	Project chosen	Profit $	EV of profit $
Weak	0.7	B	500	350
Strong	0.3	A	4,000	1,200
		EV of profit with perfect information		1,550

Step 3

	$
EV of profit without perfect information (ie if project B is always chosen)	800
EV of profit with perfect information	1,550
Value of perfect information	750

Provided that the information does not cost more than $750 to collect, it would be worth having.

Question   Decision based on EV of profit

WL must decide at what level to market a new product, the urk. The urk can be sold nationally, within a single sales region (where demand is likely to be relatively strong) or within a single area. The decision is complicated by uncertainty about the general strength of consumer demand for the product, and the following conditional profit table has been constructed.

		Demand		
		Weak $	Moderate $	Strong $
Market	nationally (A)	(4,000)	2,000	10,000
	in one region (B)	0	3,500	4,000
	in one area (C)	1,000	1,500	2,000
Probability		0.3	0.5	0.2

Required

Option B should be selected, based on EVs of profit. *True or false?*

Answer

The correct answer is option B and so the statement is true.

Without perfect information, the option with the highest EV of profit will be chosen.

	Option A (National)		Option B (Regional)		Option C (Area)	
Probability	Profit $	EV $	Profit $	EV $	Profit $	EV $
0.3	(4,000)	(1,200)	0	0	1,000	300
0.5	2,000	1,000	3,500	1,750	1,500	750
0.2	10,000	2,000	4,000	800	2,000	400
		1,800		2,550		1,450

Marketing regionally (option B) has the highest EV of profit, and would be selected.

Use the information in your answer to the question above (Decision based on EV of profit).

Required

Calculate the value of perfect information about the state of demand.

Answer

The correct answer is $1,500.

If perfect information about the state of consumer demand were available, option A would be preferred if the forecast demand is strong and option C would be preferred if the forecast demand is weak.

Demand	Probability	Choice	Profit $	EV of profit $
Weak	0.3	C	1,000	300
Moderate	0.5	B	3,500	1,750
Strong	0.2	A	10,000	2,000
EV of profit with perfect information				4,050
EV of profit, selecting option B				2,550
Value of perfect information				1,500

6.3 Perfect information and decision trees

When the option exists to obtain information, the decision can be shown, like any other decision, in the form of a decision tree, as follows. We will suppose, for illustration, that the cost of obtaining perfect information is $400.

			Profit
	Demand strong	0.2	Choose A	10,000

EV 4,050 → ①

Obtain information (400)

	Demand strong	0.2	Choose A	10,000
	Demand moderate	0.5	Choose B	3,500
	Demand weak	0.3	Choose C	1,000

No information
Choose A ②
EV 1,800

Demand strong	0.2	10,000
Demand moderate	0.5	2,000
Demand weak	0.3	(4,000)

No information
Choose B ③
EV 2,550

Demand strong	0.2	4,000
Demand moderate	0.5	3,500
Demand weak	0.3	0

No information
Choose C ④
EV 1,450

Demand strong	0.2	2,000
Demand moderate	0.5	1,500
Demand weak	0.3	1,000

The decision would be to obtain perfect information, since the EV of profit is $4,050 – $400 = $3,650.

You should check carefully that you understand the logic of this decision tree and that you can identify how the EVs at outcome boxes 1, 2, 3 and 4 have been calculated.

7 Sensitivity analysis

FAST FORWARD

> **Sensitivity analysis** can be used in any situation so long as the relationships between the key variables can be established. Typically this involves changing the value of a variable and seeing how the results are affected.

7.1 Approaches to sensitivity analysis

Key term

> **Sensitivity analysis** is a term used to describe any technique whereby decision options are tested for their vulnerability to changes in any 'variable' such as expected sales volume, sales price per unit, material costs, or labour costs.

Here are three useful approaches to sensitivity analysis.

(a)   To estimate by **how much costs and revenues would need to differ** from their estimated values before the decision would change.

(b)   To estimate whether a decision would change if estimated costs were **x% higher** than estimated, or estimated revenues **y% lower** than estimated.

(c)   To estimate by how much costs and/or revenues would need to differ from their estimated values before the decision maker would be **indifferent** between two options.

The essence of the approach, therefore, is to carry out the calculations with one set of values for the variables and then substitute other possible values for the variables to see how this affects the overall outcome.

(a)   From your studies of information technology you may recognise this as **what if analysis** that can be carried out using a **spreadsheet**.

(b)   From your studies of **linear programming** you may remember that sensitivity analysis can be carried out to determine over which ranges the various constraints have an impact on the optimum solution.

(c)   **Flexible budgeting** can also be a form of sensitivity analysis.

7.2 Example: sensitivity analysis

Sensivite has estimated the following sales and profits for a new product which it may launch on to the market.

		$	$
Sales	(2,000 units)		4,000
Variable costs:	materials	2,000	
	labour	1,000	
			3,000
Contribution			1,000
Less incremental fixed costs			800
Profit			200

Required

Analyse the sensitivity of the project.

Solution

(a)   If incremental **fixed costs** are more than 25% above estimate, the project would make a loss.

(b)   If **unit costs of materials** are more than 10% above estimate, the project would make a loss.

(c)   Similarly, the project would be sensitive to an **increase in unit labour costs** of more than $200, which is 20% above estimate, or else to a drop in the **unit selling price** of more than 5%.

(d)   The **margin of safety**, given a breakeven point of 1,600 units, is (400/2,000) × 100% = 20%.

Management would then be able to judge more clearly whether the product is likely to be profitable. The items to which profitability is most sensitive in this example are the selling price (5%) and material costs (10%). Sensitivity analysis can help to **concentrate management attention** on the most important factors.

8 Simulation models   12/08

FAST FORWARD

Simulation models can be used to deal with decision problems involving a number of uncertain variables. **Random numbers** are used to assign values to the variables.

One of the chief problems encountered in decision making is the uncertainty of the future. Where only a few factors are involved, probability analysis and expected value calculations can be used to find the most likely outcome of a decision. Often, however, in real life, there are so **many uncertain variables** that this approach does not give a true impression of possible variations in outcome.

To get an idea of what will happen in real life one possibility is to use a **simulation model** in which the **values and the variables are selected at random**. Obviously this is a situation **ideally suited to a computer** (large volume of data, random number generation).

The term 'simulation' model is often used more specifically to refer to modelling which **makes use of random numbers**. This is the **'Monte Carlo'** method of simulation. In the business environment it can, for example, be used to examine inventory, queuing, scheduling and forecasting problems.

Random numbers are allocated to each possible value of the uncertain variable in proportion to the probabilities, so that a probability of 0.1 gets 10% of the total numbers to be assigned. These random numbers are used to assign values to the variables.

Exam focus
point

You will **not** be required to develop a simulation model in your exam. The following example is provided so that you can **understand** how simulation models are developed.

8.1 Example: simulation and spreadsheets

A supermarket sells a product for which the daily demand varies. An analysis of daily demand over a period of about a year shows the following probability distribution.

Demand per day Units	Probability
35	0.10
36	0.20
37	0.25
38	0.30
39	0.08
40	0.07
	1.00

To develop a simulation model in which one of the variables is daily demand, we would **assign a group of numbers to each value for daily demand**. The probabilities are stated to two decimal places, and so there must be 100 random numbers in total, 00 – 99 (we use 00-99 rather than 1-100 so that we can use two-digit random numbers.) Random numbers are assigned in proportion to the **probabilities**, so that a probability of 0.1 gets 10% of the total numbers to be assigned, that is 10 numbers: 0, 1, 2, 3, 4, 5, 6, 7, 8 and 9.

The assignments would therefore be as follows.

Demand per day	Probability	Numbers assigned
Units		
35	0.10	00 – 09
36	0.20	10 – 29
37	0.25	30 – 54
38	0.30	55 – 84
39	0.08	85 – 92
40	0.07	93 – 99

When the simulation model is run, random numbers will be generated to derive values for daily demand. For example, if the model is used to simulate demand over a ten day period, the random numbers generated might be as follows.

19007174604721296802

The model would then **assign values** to the demand per day as follows.

Day	Random number	Demand
		Units
1	19	36
2	00	35
3	71	38
4	74	38
5	60	38
6	47	37
7	21	36
8	29	36
9	68	38
10	02	35

You might notice that on none of the ten days is the demand 39 or 40 units, because the random numbers generated did not include any value in the range 85 – 99. When a simulation model is used, there must be a long enough run to give a good representation of the system and all its potential variations.

8.2 Uses of simulation

In the supermarket example above, the supermarket would use the information to minimise inventory holding without risking running out of the product. This will reduce costs but avoid lost sales and profit.

A supermarket can also use this technique to estimate queues with predicted length of waiting time determining the number of staff required.

Chapter Roundup

- An example of a **risky situation** is one in which we can say that there is a 70% probability that returns from a project will be in excess of $100,000 but a 30% probability that returns will be less than $100,000. If we cannot predict an outcome or assign probabilities, we are faced with an **uncertain** situation.

- People may be **risk seekers**, **risk neutral** or **risk averse**.

- Management accounting directs its attention towards the **future** and the future is **uncertain**. For this reason a number of methods of taking **uncertainty** into consideration have evolved.

- **Market research** can be used to reduce uncertainty.

- **Expected values** indicate what an outcome is likely to be in the long term with repetition. Fortunately, many business transactions do occur over and over again.

- The 'play it safe' basis for decision making is referred to as the **maximin basis**. This is short for '**maximise the minimum achievable profit**'.

- A basis for making decisions by looking for the best outcome is known as the **maximax basis**, short for '**maximise the maximum achievable profit**'.

- The 'opportunity loss' basis for decision making is known as **minimax regret**.

- **Decision trees** are diagrams which illustrate the choices and possible outcomes of a decision.

- **Rollback analysis** evaluates the EV of each decision option. You have to work from right to left and calculate EVs at each outcome point.

- **Perfect information** is guaranteed to predict the future with 100% accuracy. **Imperfect information** is better than no information at all but could be wrong in its prediction of the future.

- The **value of perfect information** is the difference between the EV of profit with perfect information and the EV of profit without perfect information.

- **Sensitivity analysis** can be used in any situation so long as the relationships between the key variables can be established. Typically this involves changing the value of a variable and seeing how the results are affected.

- **Simulation models** can be used to deal with decision problems involving a number of uncertain variables. **Random numbers** are used to assign values to the variables.

1   *Match the terms to the correct definitions.*

Terms

(a)   Risk seeker   (c)   Risk averse
(b)   Risk neutral

Definitions

1   A decision maker concerned with what will be the most likely outcome

2   A decision maker interested in the best outcomes no matter how small the chance that they may occur

3   A decision maker who acts on the assumption that the worst outcome might occur

2   *Fill in the blanks.*

(a)   Maximin decision rule: choosing the alternative that .... the ....

(b)   Minimax decision rule: choosing the alternative that .... the ....

(c)   Maximax decision rule: choosing the alternative that .... the...........................

(d)   Minimin decision rule: choosing the alternative that .... the...........................

3   How is expected value calculated?

A   Σpx   C   eΣpx
B   pΣx   D   xΣp

4   *Tick the correct boxes to indicate the usefulness of expected values as a guide to decision making in the following decisions.*

		Most useful	Not as useful
(a)	Whether to change the logo painted on the window of 700 retail outlets		
(b)	Whether to purchase machine X or machine Y		
(c)	Whether to launch product A		
(d)	Deciding on the optimum daily purchases of a perishable item		

5   If the decision maker is trying to maximise the figure, what figure would the decision maker choose at point B in the diagram below?

A   40,000   C   13,900

B   11,800   D   22,000

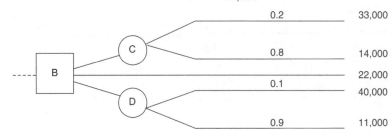

Answers to Quick Quiz

1   (a) 2; (b) 1; (c) 3

2   (a)   Maximise, minimum profits   (c)   Maximise, maximum profits
    (b)   Minimise, maximum costs/losses   (d)   Minimise, minimum costs/losses

3   A

4   Expected values would be useful for decisions (a) and (d) because they are repeated several times.

5   D   Choice between $((0.2 \times 33{,}000) + (0.8 \times 14{,}000)) = 17{,}800$ at C, 22,000, and $((0.1 \times 40{,}000) + (0.9 \times 11{,}000)) = 13{,}900$ at D.

Now try the question below from the Exam Question Bank

Number	Level	Marks	Time
Q11	Examination	20	36 mins

P
A
R
T

C

Budgeting

Objectives of
budgetary control

Topic list	Syllabus reference
1 Objectives	C1 (b), (c)
2 The planning and control cycle	C2 (a)
3 Planning and control in the performance hierarchy	C2 (a)
4 Objectives of budgetary systems	C1 (a)
5 Behavioural implications of budgeting	C5 (a)
6 Setting the difficulty level of a budget	C5 (b)
7 Participation in budgeting	C5 (c)

Introduction

This chapter serves as an introduction to Part C of the Study Text and looks at
the **objectives** of budgetary control.

We look at what is meant by objectives and how they relate to budgetary
control.

We look at the various stages in the planning process, and where the annual
budget fits in to this. We also see how the budget is used in the control
process. Finally, we consider the **behavioural aspects** of budgeting, identifying
and explaining the factors which influence behaviour and budgets.

In the next chapter we go on to consider different types of budgetary systems.

Study guide

		Intellectual level
C1	**Objectives**	
(a)	Outline the objectives of a budgetary control system	2
(b)	Explain how corporate and divisional objectives may differ and can be reconciled	2
(c)	Identify and resolve conflicting objectives and explain implications	2
C2	**Budgetary systems**	
(a)	Explain how budgetary systems fit within the performance hierarchy	2
C5	**Behavioural aspects of budgeting**	
(a)	Identify the factors which influence behaviour	2
(b)	Discuss the issues surrounding setting the difficulty level for a budget	2
(c)	Explain the benefits and difficulties of the participation of employees in the negotiation of targets	2

Exam guide

The topics covered in this chapter may form the discussion part of a budget question or may form an entire narrative question. Much of the material is common sense and you should always try to relate it to your own experience.

1 Objectives

 FAST FORWARD

Corporate objectives concern the firm as a whole. **Unit objectives** are specific to individual units, divisions or functions of an organisation.

Corporate objectives are set as part of the **corporate planning process** which is concerned with the selection of **strategies** which will achieve the corporate objectives of the organisation.

1.1 Corporate objectives versus unit objectives

Corporate objectives should relate to the **key factors for business success.**

- Profitability
- Market share
- Growth
- Cash flow
- Return on capital employed
- Risk

- Customer satisfaction
- Quality
- Industrial relations
- Added value
- Earnings per share

Unit objectives, on the other hand, **are specific to individual business units, divisions or functions of an organisation**.

Types	Examples
Commercial	• Increase the number of customers by x% (an objective of a sales department) • Reduce the number of rejects by 50% (an objective of a production department) • Produce monthly reports more quickly, within 5 working days of the end of each month (an objective of the management accounting department)
Public sector	• Introduce x% more places at nursery schools (an objective of a borough education department) • Respond more quickly to calls (an objective of a local police station, fire department or hospital ambulance service)
General	• Resources (eg cheaper raw materials, lower borrowing costs, 'top-quality college graduates') • Market (eg market share, market standing) • Employee development (eg training, promotion, safety) • Innovation in products or processes • Productivity (the amount of output from resource inputs) • Technology

1.2 Primary and secondary objectives

FAST FORWARD

Primary corporate objectives are supported by **secondary objectives**, for example for product development or market share. In practice there may be a trade off between different objectives.

An organisation has many objectives. It has been argued that there is a **limit** to the **number of objectives** that a manager can **pursue effectively**. Too many and the manager cannot give adequate attention to each and/or the focus may inadvertently be placed on minor ones. Some objectives are more important than others. It has therefore been suggested that there should be one **primary corporate objective** (restricted by certain constraints on corporate activity) and other **secondary objectives**. These are **strategic objectives** which should **combine to ensure the achievement of the primary corporate objective**.

(a)   For example, if a company sets itself a **primary objective** of **growth in profits**, it will then have to develop strategies by which this primary objective can be achieved.

(b)   **Secondary objectives** might then be concerned with sales growth, continual technological innovation, customer service, product quality, efficient resource management (eg labour productivity) or reducing the company's reliance on debt capital.

1.3 Conflicting objectives

Corporate objectives may **conflict** with divisional objectives in large organisations. A danger is that the organisation will divide into a number of **self-interested** segments, each acting at times against the wishes and interests of other segments. Decisions might be taken by a divisional manager in the best interests of his **own part** of the business, but possibly against the interests of the organisation as a whole. The **setting** of objectives is very much a **political process**: objectives are formulated following **bargaining** by the various interested parties whose requirements may conflict. Such conflict may be resolved via **prioritisation**, **compromise**, **negotiation** and **satisficing**.

(a)   **Prioritisation** is where certain goals get priority over others. This is usually determined by senior managers but there can be quite complicated systems to rank goals and strategies according to certain criteria.

(b)   **Negotiation** is the bargaining process that occurs at each stage of the budgeting process. This allows full participation to take place by all budgetees. Any revisions to the budget must be after giving full consideration to arguments for including any of the budgeted items.

(c) **Compromise** is the central aspect of any process of negotiation where there is disagreement. It can be seen as positive where both parties win something but also negative where both parties lose something.

(d) **Satisficing** occurs when a satisfactory rather than an optimal solution is found. Organisations may not aim to maximise performance in one area if this leads to poor performance elsewhere. Rather they will accept satisfactory, if not excellent performance in a number of areas.

Goal congruence exists when managers working in their best interests also act in harmony with the goals of the organisation as a whole. This is not easy to achieve and a budgetary control system needs to be designed to evoke the required behaviour.

2 The planning and control cycle

FAST FORWARD

The **planning and control cycle** has seven steps.

- *Step 1.* Identify **objectives**
- *Step 2.* Identify potential **strategies**
- *Step 3.* Evaluate strategies
- *Step 4.* Choose alternative courses of action
- *Step 5.* Implement the long-term plan
- *Step 6.* Measure actual results and compare with the plan
- *Step 7.* Respond to divergences from the plan

The diagram below represents the planning and control cycle. The first five steps cover the planning process. **Planning** involves making choices between alternatives and is primarily a decision-making activity. The last two steps cover the **control** process, which involves measuring and correcting actual performance to ensure that the alternatives that are chosen and the plans for implementing them are carried out.

The planning and control cycle

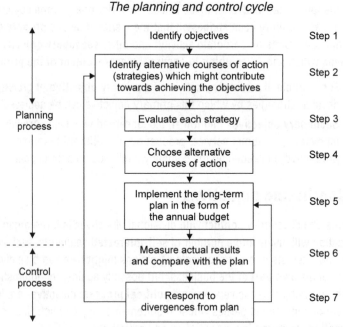

Step 1   Identify objectives

Objectives establish the direction in which the management of the organisation wish it to be heading. They answer the question: 'where do we want to be?'

Step 2   Identify potential strategies

Once an organisation has decided 'where it wants to be', the next step is to identify a range of possible courses of action or **strategies** that might enable the organisation to get there. The organisation must therefore carry out an **information-gathering exercise** to ensure that it has a full **understanding of where it is now.** This is known as a **'position audit'** or **'strategic analysis'** and involves looking both inwards and outwards.

(a) The organisation must **gather information from all of its internal parts** to find out what resources it possesses: what its manufacturing capacity and capability is, what is the state of its technical know-how, how well it is able to market itself, how much cash it has in the bank and so on.

(b) It must also **gather information externally** so that it can assess its position in the environment. Just as it has assessed its **own strengths and weaknesses**, it must do likewise for its competitors (**threats**). Current and potential markets must be analysed to identify possible new **opportunities**. The 'state of the world' must be considered. Is it in recession or is it booming? What is likely to happen in the future?

Having carried out a strategic analysis, alternative strategies can be identified. An organisation might decide to be the lowest cost producer in the industry, perhaps by withdrawing from some markets or developing new products for sale in existing markets. This may involve internal development or a joint venture.

Step 3   **Evaluate strategies**

The strategies must then be evaluated **in terms of suitability, feasibility and acceptability**. Management should select those strategies that have the greatest potential for achieving the organisation's objectives.

Step 4   **Choose alternative courses of action**

The next step in the process is to collect the **chosen strategies** together and **co-ordinate them into a long-term financial plan.** Typically this would show the following.

- Projected cash flows
- Projected long-term profits
- A description of the long-term objectives and strategies in words

- Capital expenditure plans
- Balance sheet forecasts

Step 5   **Implement the long-term plan**

The **long-term plan** should then be **broken down into smaller parts**. It is unlikely that the different parts will fall conveniently into successive time periods. Strategy A may take two and a half years, while Strategy B may take five months, but not start until year three of the plan. It is usual, however, to break down the plan as a whole into equal time periods (usually one year). The resulting **short-term plan** is called a **budget**.

Step 6   **Measure actual results and compare with plan**

Actual results are recorded and analysed and information about actual results is fed back to the management concerned, often in the form of accounting reports. This reported information is **feedback** (see section 3.2.1 below).

Step 7   **Respond to divergences from plan**

By comparing actual and planned results, management can then do one of three things, depending on how they see the situation.

(a) They can take control action. By identifying what has gone wrong, and then finding out why, corrective measures can be taken.

(b) They can decide to do nothing. This could be the decision when actual results are going better than planned, or when poor results were caused by something which is unlikely to happen again in the future.

(c) They can alter the plan or target if actual results are different from the plan or target, and there is nothing that management can do (or nothing, perhaps, that they want to do) to correct the situation.

Is your organisation's planning and control cycle similar to the one described here? If it differs, how does it differ? Why does it differ? Try to find out your organisation's objectives and the strategies being adopted to attain these objectives.

Answers to this question could be usefully employed in the exam.

3 Planning and control in the performance hierarchy

Planning and control occurs at all levels of the performance hierarchy to different degrees.

3.1 Planning

Although it implies a 'top down' approach to management, we could describe **a cascade of goals, objectives and plans** down through the layers of the organisation. The **plans** made at the **higher levels** of the performance hierarchy provide a **framework** within which the plans at the lower levels must be achieved. The **plans** at the **lower levels** are the **means** by which the plans at the higher levels are achieved.

It could therefore be argued that without the plans allied directly to the vision and corporate objective the operational-level and departmental plans have little meaning. **Planning** could therefore be deemed as **more significant** at the **higher levels** of the performance hierarchy than the lower levels.

This is not to say that planning at an operational level is not important. It is just that the two types of planning are different.

Level	Detail
Corporate plans	• Focused on overall performance • Environmental influence • Set plans and targets for units and departments • Sometimes qualitative (eg a programme to change the culture of the organisation) • Aggregate
Operational plans	• Based on objectives about 'what' to achieve • Specific (eg acceptable number of 'rings' before a phone is answered) • Little immediate environmental influence • Likely to be quantitative • Detailed specifications • Based on 'how' something is achieved • Short time horizons

3.2 Control

Consider how the activities of **planning** and **control** are **inter-related**.

(a) **Plans** set the targets.

(b) **Control** involves two main processes.

    (i) **Measure** actual results against the plan.

    (ii) **Take action** to adjust actual performance to achieve the plan or to change the plan altogether.

Control is therefore **impossible without planning**.

The essence of control is the **measurement of results** and **comparing** them with the original **plan**. Any deviation from plan indicates that **control action** is required to make the results conform more closely with plan.

3.2.1 Feedback

Key term

> **Feedback** occurs when the results (outputs) of a system are used to control it, by adjusting the input or behaviour of the system.

A business organisation uses feedback for control.

(a) **Negative feedback** indicates that results or activities must be brought back on course, as they are deviating from the plan.

(b) **Positive feedback** results in control action continuing the current course. You would normally assume that positive feedback means that results are going according to plan and that no corrective action is necessary: but it is best to be sure that the control system itself is not picking up the wrong information.

(c) **Feedforward control** is control based on **forecast** results: in other words if the forecast is bad, control action is taken well in advance of actual results.

There are two types of feedback.

(a) **Single loop feedback** is control, like a thermostat, which regulates the output of a system. For example, if sales targets are not reached, control action will be taken to ensure that targets will be reached soon. The plan or target itself is not changed, even though the resources needed to achieve it might have to be reviewed.

(b) **Double loop feedback** is of a different order. It is information used to **change the plan itself**. For example, if sales targets are not reached, the company may need to change the plan.

3.2.2 Control at different levels

> **Budgetary control** occurs at the **lower** levels of the performance hierarchy.

Control at **the lower-levels** of the performance hierarchy, such as standard costing, and budgetary control has the following features.

- Exercised externally by management or, in the case of empowered teams, by the staff themselves
- Immediate or rapid feedback
- Single loop feedback (ie little authority to change plans or targets)

Control does also occur at the **higher-levels of the hierarchy**, however, and has the following characteristics.

- Exercised by external stakeholders (eg shareholders)
- Exercised by the market
- Double loop feedback (ie relatively free to change targets)
- Often feedforward elements

4 Objectives of budgetary systems

> Here are the objectives of a budgetary planning and control system.
>
> - Ensure the achievement of the organisation's objectives
> - Compel planning
> - Communicate ideas and plans
> - Coordinate activities
> - Provide a framework for responsibility accounting
> - Establish a system of control
> - Motivate employees to improve their performance

A budgetary planning and control system is essentially a system for ensuring **communication**, **coordination** and **control** within an organisation. Communication, coordination and control are general objectives: more information is provided by an inspection of the specific objectives of a budgetary planning and control system.

Objective	Comment
Ensure the achievement of the organisation's objectives	Objectives are set for the organisation as a whole, and for individual departments and operations within the organisation. Quantified expressions of these objectives are then drawn up as targets to be achieved within the timescale of the budget plan.
Compel planning	This is probably the most important feature of a budgetary planning and control system. Planning forces management to **look ahead**, to set out **detailed plans** for achieving the targets for each department, operation and (ideally) each manager and to anticipate problems. It thus prevents management from relying on ad hoc or uncoordinated planning which may be detrimental to the performance of the organisation.
Communicate ideas and plans	A formal system is necessary to ensure that each person affected by the plans is aware of what he or she is **supposed to be doing**. Communication might be one-way, with managers giving **orders to subordinates**, or there might be a two-way dialogue and exchange of ideas.
Coordinate activities	The activities of different departments or sub-units of the organisation need to be coordinated to ensure **maximum integration** of effort towards common goals. This concept of coordination implies, for example, that the purchasing department should base its budget on production requirements and that the production budget should in turn be based on sales expectations. Although straightforward in concept, coordination is remarkably difficult to achieve, and there is often **'sub-optimality'** and conflict between departmental plans in the budget so that the efforts of each department are not fully integrated into a combined plan to achieve the company's best targets.
Provide a framework for responsibility accounting	Budgetary planning and control systems require that managers of **budget centres** are made responsible for the achievement of budget targets for the operations under their personal control.
Establish a system of control	A budget is a **yardstick** against which actual performance is measured and assessed. Control over actual performance is provided by the comparisons of actual results against the budget plan. Departures from budget can then be investigated and the reasons for the departures can be divided into **controllable** and **uncontrollable** factors.
Motivate employees to improve their performance	The interest and commitment of employees can be retained via a system of **feedback of actual results**, which lets them know how well or badly they are performing. The identification of controllable reasons for departures from budget with managers responsible provides an incentive for improving future performance.

Exam focus point

An exam question could well ask you to explain a number of these objectives in the context of a particular scenario such as a not-for-profit organisation.

FAST FORWARD

> Used correctly, a budgetary control system can **motivate** but it can also produce undesirable **negative reactions**.

The purpose of a budgetary control system is to assist management in planning and controlling the resources of their organisation by providing appropriate control information. The information will only be valuable, however, if it is interpreted correctly and used purposefully by managers *and* employees.

The correct use of control information therefore depends not only on the content of the information itself, but also on the behaviour of its recipients. This is because control in business is exercised by people. Their attitude to control information will colour their views on what they should do with it and a number of behavioural problems can arise.

(a)   The **managers who set the budget** or standards are **often not the managers** who are then made **responsible for achieving budget targets.**

(b)   The **goals of the organisation as a whole**, as expressed in a budget, **may not coincide with the personal aspirations of individual managers**.

(c)   **Control is applied at different stages by different people**. A supervisor might get weekly control reports, and act on them; his superior might get monthly control reports, and decide to take different control action. Different managers can get in each others' way, and resent the interference from others.

5.1 Motivation

Motivation is what makes people behave in the way that they do. It comes from individual attitudes, or group attitudes. Individuals will be motivated by personal desires and interests. These may be in line with the objectives of the organisation, and some people 'live for their jobs'. Other individuals see their job as a chore, and their motivations will be unrelated to the objectives of the organisation they work for.

It is therefore vital that the goals of management and the employees harmonise with the goals of the organisation as a whole. This is known as goal congruence. Although obtaining goal congruence is essentially a behavioural problem, **it is possible to design and run a budgetary control system which will go some way towards ensuring that goal congruence is achieved**. Managers and employees must therefore be favourably disposed towards the budgetary control system so that it can operate efficiently.

The management accountant should therefore try to ensure that employees have positive attitudes towards **setting budgets, implementing budgets** (that is, putting the organisation's plans into practice) and feedback of results (**control information**).

5.2 Poor attitudes when setting budgets

Poor attitudes or hostile behaviour towards the budgetary control system can begin at the **planning stage. If managers are involved in preparing a budget** the following may happen.

(a)   Managers may **complain that they are too busy** to spend much time on budgeting.

(b)   They may **build 'slack' into their expenditure estimates**.

(c)   They may argue that **formalising a budget plan on paper is too restricting** and that managers should be allowed flexibility in the decisions they take.

(d)   They may set budgets for their budget centre and **not coordinate** their own plans with those of other budget centres.

(e)   They may **base future plans on past results**, instead of using the opportunity for formalised planning to look at alternative options and new ideas.

On the other hand, **managers may not be involved in the budgeting process**. Organisational goals may not be communicated to them and they might have their budget decided for them by senior management or administrative decision. It is **hard for people to be motivated to achieve targets set by someone else.**

5.2.1 Poor attitudes when putting plans into action

Poor attitudes also arise **when a budget is implemented**.

(a) Managers might **put in only just enough effort** to achieve budget targets, without trying to beat targets.

(b) A formal budget might **encourage rigidity and discourage flexibility**.

(c) **Short-term planning** in a budget **can draw attention away from the longer-term consequences** of decisions.

(d) There might be **minimal cooperation and communication** between managers.

(e) Managers will often try to make sure that they **spend up to their full budget allowance, and do not overspend**, so that they will not be accused of having asked for too much spending allowance in the first place.

5.2.2 Poor attitudes and the use of control information

The **attitude of managers towards the accounting control information** they receive **might reduce the information's effectiveness**.

(a) Management accounting control reports could well be seen as having a relatively **low priority** in the list of management tasks. Managers might take the view that they have more pressing jobs on hand than looking at routine control reports.

(b) Managers might **resent control information**; they may see it as **part of a system of trying to find fault with their work**. This resentment is likely to be particularly strong when budgets or standards are imposed on managers without allowing them to participate in the budget-setting process.

(c) If budgets are seen as **pressure devices** to push managers into doing better, control reports will be resented.

(d) Managers **may not understand the information** in the control reports, because they are unfamiliar with accounting terminology or principles.

(e) Managers might have a **false sense of what their objectives should be**. A production manager might consider it more important to maintain quality standards regardless of cost. He would then dismiss adverse expenditure variances as inevitable and unavoidable.

(f) **If there are flaws in the system of recording actual costs**, managers will dismiss control information as unreliable.

(g) **Control information** might be **received weeks after the end of the** period to which it relates, in which case managers might regard it as out-of-date and no longer useful.

(h) Managers might be **held responsible for variances outside their control**.

It is therefore obvious that accountants and senior management should try to implement systems that are acceptable to budget holders and which produce positive effects.

5.2.3 Pay as a motivator

Many researchers agree that **pay can be an important motivator**, when there is a formal link between higher pay (or other rewards, such as promotion) and achieving budget targets. Individuals are likely to work harder to achieve budget if they know that they will be rewarded for their successful efforts. There are, however, problems with using pay as an incentive.

(a) A serious problem that can arise is that **formal reward and performance evaluation systems can encourage dysfunctional behaviour**. Many investigations have noted the tendency of managers to pad their budgets either in anticipation of cuts by superiors or to make the subsequent variances more favourable. And there are numerous examples of managers making decisions in response to performance indices, even though the decisions are contrary to the wider purposes of the organisation.

(b) The targets must be challenging but fair, otherwise individuals will become dissatisfied. **Pay can be a demotivator as well as a motivator!**

6 Setting the difficulty level of a budget

'Aspirations' budgets can be used as **targets** to motivate higher levels of performance but a budget for **planning and decision making** should be based on **reasonable expectations.**

Budgets can motivate managers to achieve a high level of performance. But **how difficult** should targets be? And how might people react to targets of differing degrees of difficulty in achievement?

(a) There is likely to be a **demotivating** effect where an **ideal standard** of performance is set, because adverse efficiency variances will always be reported.

(b) A **low standard** of efficiency is also **demotivating**, because there is no sense of achievement in attaining the required standards. If the budgeted level of attainment is too 'loose', targets will be achieved easily, and there will be no impetus for employees to try harder to do better than this.

(c) A budgeted level of attainment could be the **same** as the level that has been achieved in the past. Arguably, this level will be too low. It might encourage **budgetary slack**.

Academics have argued that each individual has a **personal 'aspiration level'.** This is a level of performance, in a task with which the individual is familiar, which the individual undertakes for himself to reach.

Individual aspirations might be much higher or much lower than the organisation's aspirations, however. The solution might therefore be to have **two budgets**.

(a) A budget for **planning and decision making** based on **reasonable expectations**
(b) A budget for **motivational purposes**, with more **difficult targets of performance**

These two budgets might be called an '**expectations budget**' and an '**aspirations budget**' respectively.

7 Participation in budgeting

A budget can be set from the **top down** (**imposed** budget) or from the **bottom up** (**participatory** budget). Many writers refer to a third style, the negotiated budget.

7.1 Participation

It has been argued that **participation** in the budgeting process **will improve motivation** and so will improve the quality of budget decisions and the efforts of individuals to achieve their budget targets (although obviously this will depend on the personality of the individual, the nature of the task (narrowly defined or flexible) and the organisational culture).

There are basically two ways in which a budget can be set: from the **top down** (imposed budget) or from the **bottom up** (participatory budget).

7.2 Imposed style of budgeting (top-down budgeting)

In this approach to budgeting, **top management prepare a budget with little or no input from operating personnel** which is then imposed upon the employees who have to work to the budgeted figures.

The times when imposed budgets are effective are as follows.

- In newly-formed organisations
- In very small businesses
- During periods of economic hardship
- When operational managers lack budgeting skills
- When the organisation's different units require precise coordination

They are, of course, advantages and disadvantages to this style of setting budgets.

Advantages

- **Strategic plans** are likely to be incorporated into planned activities
- They **enhance** the **coordination** between the plans and objectives of divisions
- They use **senior management's awareness** of total resource availability
- They **decrease the input from inexperienced or uninformed lower-level employees**
- They **decrease the period of time taken** to draw up the budgets

Disadvantages

- **Dissatisfaction**, **defensiveness** and **low morale** amongst employees
- The **feeling of team spirit** may disappear
- The **acceptance of organisational goals** and **objectives** could be limited
- The feeling of the budget as a **punitive device** could arise
- **Unachievable budgets** for overseas divisions could result if consideration is not given to local operating and political environments
- **Lower-level management initiative** may be **stifled**

7.3 Participative style of budgeting (bottom-up budgeting)

In this approach to budgeting, **budgets are developed by lower-level managers who then submit the budgets to their superiors**. The budgets are based on the lower-level managers' perceptions of what is achievable and the associated necessary resources.

Participative budgets are effective in the following circumstances.

- In **well-established organisations**
- In **very large businesses**
- During periods of **economic affluence**
- When operational managers have **strong budgeting skills**
- When the organisation's different units act **autonomously**

The **advantages** of participative budgets are as follows.

- They are based on **information from employees** most familiar with the department
- **Knowledge spread** among several levels of management is pulled **together**
- **Morale** and **motivation** is improved
- They **increase operational managers' commitment** to organisational objectives
- In general they are **more realistic**
- **Co-ordination** between units is **improved**
- **Specific resource requirements** are **included**
- **Senior managers' overview** is mixed with operational level details

There are, on the other hand, a number of **disadvantages** of participative budgets.

- They **consume more time**
- **Changes implemented** by senior management may **cause dissatisfaction**
- Budgets may be **unachievable** if managers' are not qualified to participate
- They may cause managers to introduce **budgetary slack**
- They can support **'empire building'** by subordinates
- An **earlier start** to the budgeting process could be required

7.4 Negotiated style of budgeting

At the two extremes, budgets can be dictated from above or simply emerge from below but, in practice, different levels of management often agree budgets by a process of negotiation. In the imposed budget approach, operational managers will try to negotiate with senior managers the budget targets which they consider to be unreasonable or unrealistic. Likewise senior management usually review and revise budgets presented to them under a participative approach through a process of negotiation with lower level managers. **Final budgets are therefore most likely to lie between what top management would really like and what junior managers believe is feasible.** The budgeting process is hence a **bargaining process** and it is this bargaining which is of vital importance, **determining whether the budget is an effective management tool or simply a clerical device.**

Chapter Roundup

- **Corporate objectives** concern the firm as a whole. **Unit objectives** are specific to individual units , divisions or functions of an organisation.

- **Primary corporate objectives** are supported by **secondary objectives**, for example for product development or market share. In practice there may be a trade off between different objectives.

- The **planning and control cycle** has seven steps.

  - *Step 1.* Identify **objectives**
  - *Step 2.* Identify potential **strategies**
  - *Step 3.* Evaluate strategies
  - *Step 4.* Choose alternative courses of action
  - *Step 5.* Implement the long-term plan
  - *Step 6.* Measure actual results and compare with the plan
  - *Step 7.* Respond to divergences from the plan

- **Planning** and **control** occurs at all levels of the **performance hierarchy** to different degrees.

- **Budgetary control** occurs at the **lower** levels of the performance hierarchy.

- Here are the objectives of a budgetary planning and control system.

  - Ensure the achievement of the organisation's objectives
  - Compel planning
  - Communicate ideas and plans
  - Coordinate activities
  - Provide a framework for responsibility accounting
  - Establish a system of control
  - Motivate employees to improve their performance

- Used correctly, a budgetary control system can **motivate** but it can also produce undesirable **negative reactions**.

- **'Aspirations'** budgets can be used as **targets** to motivate higher levels of performance but a budget for **planning and decision making** should be based on **reasonable expectations.**

- A budget can be set from the **top down** (**imposed** budget) or from the **bottom up** (**participatory** budget). Many writers refer to a third style, the negotiated budget.

1   *Put the following steps in the planning cycle in the correct order.*

- Evaluate strategies
- Implement the long-term plan
- Identify objectives

- Choose alternative courses of action
- Identify potential strategies

2   What question does an objective answer?

3   *Complete the following steps in the control cycle.*

Step 6..

Step 7..

(a)   ....

(b)   ....

(c)   ....

4   Here are four characteristics of long-term planning information. List the corresponding characteristics of short-term planning information.

(a)   Used by top management   (c)   External
(b)   Broad in scope rather than deep in detail   (d)   Looks to the future and lacks certainty

5   List the ten purposes of using budgets.

6   Which of the following is **not** a use of budgetary control?

A   To define the objectives of the organisation as a whole
B   To ensure that resources are used as efficiently as possible
C   To provide some central control when activities are centralised
D   To provide the basis for the preparation of future budgets

7   What three factors are said to determine the effectiveness of participation?

A   Nature of the task, organisation structure, personality
B   Personality, technology, organisation structure
C   Nature of the task, production processes, personality
D   Personality, leadership style, aspirations

8   A budget for motivational purposes, with fairly difficult targets of performance, is an aspirations budget. *True or false?*

9   Provide four reasons why poor attitudes could arise when a budget is implemented.

10   *Match the description to the correct term.*

	Term		Description
(a)	Motivation	1	Exists where managers working in their own interests also act in harmony with the interests of the organisation as a whole
(b)	Goal congruence	2	Comes from individual or group attitudes
(c)	Incentive	3	Concerned with getting subordinates to run rather than walk towards desired goals

1   Identify objectives
     Identify potential strategies
     Evaluate strategies
     Choose alternative courses of action
     Implement the long-term plan

2   'Where do we want to be?'

3   *Step 6.* Management uses the feedback to compare actual results and targets.

     Step 7. The comparison leads management to do one of three things.

     (a)   Take control action
     (b)   Decide to do nothing
     (c)   Alter the plan or target

4   (a)   Used at a lower level by those who implement plans   (c)   Internal
     (b)   Detailed   (d)   Definite

5   Ensure the achievement of the organisation's objectives
     Compel planning
     Communicate ideas and plans
     Co-ordinate activities
     Allocate resources
     Authorisation
     Provide a framework for responsibility accounting
     Establish a system of control
     Provide a means of performance evaluation
     Motivate employees to improve their performance

6   C   It should provide some central control when activities are decentralised.

7   A

8   True

9   (a)   Managers might put in only just enough effort to achieve budget targets, without trying to beat targets.

     (b)   A formal budget might encourage rigidity and discourage flexibility in operational decision making.

     (c)   Short-term planning in a budget can draw attention away from the longer-term consequences of decisions.

     (d)   Cooperation and communication between managers might be minimal.

     (e)   Managers will often try to make sure that they spend up to their full budget allowance, and do not overspend, so that they will not be accused of having asked for too much spending allowance in the first place.

10   (a) 2; (b) 1; (c) 3

Now try the questions below from the Exam Question Bank

Number	Level	Marks	Time
Q12	Introductory	12	22 mins

Budgetary systems

Introduction

This chapter starts by looking at the **traditional approach** to budgeting and the preparation of budgets. **Incremental budgeting** bases next year's budget on this year's, with increases for inflation and changes in activity levels. However, this may not always be appropriate for certain organisations or for certain types of cost and revenue. **Zero based budgeting** and **rolling budgets** are alternative budget systems which can be applied in certain circumstances and situations. **Activity based budgets** may use bases other than volume of output for flexing budgets. This chapter looks in detail at these systems.

In the next chapter we will look at quantitative aids to budgeting, in other words, different ways of forecasting future figures for use in budgets.

Study guide

		Intellectual level
C2	**Budgetary systems**	
(b)	Select and explain appropriate budgetary systems for an organisation, including top-down, bottom-up, rolling, zero base, activity-base, incremental and feed-forward control	2
(c)	Describe the information used in budget systems and the sources of the information needed	2
(d)	Explain the difficulties of changing a budgetary system	2
(e)	Explain how budget systems can deal with uncertainty in the environment	2
C3	**Types of budget**	
(a)	Indicate the usefulness and problems with different budget types (zero-base, activity-based, incremental, master, functional and flexible)	2
(b)	Explain the difficulties of changing the type of budget used	2

Exam guide

The examiner expects you to be aware of the problems of traditional budget systems and why organisations may be reluctant to change to more appropriate systems.

One of the competencies you require to fulfil performance objective 13 is the ability to contribute to budget planning and production. You can apply the knowledge you obtain from this chapter to help to demonstrate this competence.

1 Traditional budgetary systems

FAST FORWARD

A budget is a **quantified plan of action** for a forthcoming accounting period.
A budget can be set from the **top down** (**imposed** budget) or from the **bottom up** (**participatory** budget).

1.1 Budget preparation

You will have covered budget preparation in your earlier studies and will not be required to prepare sales, production, materials etc budgets in this exam.

The following are the key points of budget preparation to remind you.

Point	Detail
Long-term plan	The **starting point**, this will show **what the budget has to achieve** (the introduction of new production, the required return, and so on) and outline **how it is to be done**. It will also contain **general guidelines** on allowable price increases like wage rates. The **long-term policy** needs to be **communicated** to all managers responsible for preparing budgets so that they are aware of the context within which they are budgeting and how their area of responsibility is expected to contribute.
Limiting factor	The factor that **limits the scale of operations**, this is usually sales demand, but it may be production capacity where demand is high. Budgeting cannot proceed until the budget for the limiting factor has been prepared, since this affects all the other budgets.

Point	Detail
Budget manual	Prepared to **assist functional managers**, this will show how figures and forecasts are to be arrived at and give any other information that is to apply across the organisation. It is likely to include **proformas** showing how the information is to be presented. If budgeting is done with spreadsheets, layouts and computations may be pre-programmed, requiring only the entry of the figures. It may include a **flow diagram** showing how individual budgets are interlinked and specify deadlines by which first drafts must be prepared.
Sales budget	This contains **information on the expected volume of sales** (based on estimates or market research), the **sales mix, and selling prices.** The total revenues indicated will be used to compile the cash budget, although this information needs to be adjusted to allow for the expected timing of receipts. The volume of sales indicates the level of production required and the extent of spending on distribution and administration.
Production capacity	The level of sales anticipated is matched against opening inventory and desired closing inventory to establish the level of production. From this can be calculated the need for materials (again allowing for opening and closing inventory), labour and machine hours. In other words production budgeting is **done in terms of physical resources initially and costed afterwards**. At this stage, too, it is likely that needs for new capital expenditure will be identified. This information will be used in preparing the capital budget.
Functional budgets	Budgets **for other areas of the organisation** like distribution and administration take the anticipated sales level as their point of reference. Vehicle costs, carriage costs, stationery and communication costs, and above all staff costs feature in these budgets.
Discretionary costs	**Training and R&D** are known as 'discretionary costs' and have special features.
Consolidation and coordination	This can begin once all parts of the organisation have submitted their individual budgets. It is most **unlikely** that **all of the budgets will be in line with each other** at the first attempt. Areas of **incompatibility** must be identified and the **budgets modified** in consultation with individual managers. **Spreadsheets** are invaluable at this stage, both for the consolidation itself and to allow changes to be made quickly and accurately.
Cash budget	This can only be prepared at this stage because it **needs to take account of all of the plans of the organisation** and translate them into expected cash flows. Cash must be available when it is needed to enable the plans to be carried out. Overdraft facilities may need to be negotiated in advance, or some activities may need to be deferred until cash has been collected.
Master budget	The final stage, once all of the necessary modifications have been made, is to prepare a **summary** of all of the budgets in the form of a master budget, which generally comprises a **budgeted income statement, a budgeted balance sheet and a budgeted cash flow statement.**

1.2 Incremental budgeting   12/08

FAST FORWARD

The traditional approach to budgeting, known as **incremental budgeting**, bases the budget on the current year's results plus an extra amount for estimated growth or inflation next year. It encourages slack and wasteful spending to creep into budgets.

Key term

Incremental budgeting is so called because it is concerned mainly with the increments in costs and revenues which will occur in the coming period.

Incremental budgeting is a reasonable procedure if current operations are as effective, efficient and economical as they can be. It is also appropriate for budgeting for costs such as staff salaries, which may be estimated on the basis of current salaries plus an increment for inflation and are hence administratively fairly easy to prepare.

In general, however, it is an **inefficient form of budgeting** as it **encourages slack** and **wasteful spending** to creep into budgets. Past inefficiencies are perpetuated because cost levels are rarely subjected to close scrutiny.

Advantages of incremental budgets	Disadvantages of incremental budgets
• Considered to be the quickest and easiest method of budgeting	• Builds in previous problems and inefficiencies
• Suitable for organisations that operate in a stable environment where historic figures are reliable and are not expected to change significantly	• Managers may spend for the sake of spending in order to use up their budget for the year and thus ensure that they get the same (or larger) budget next year
	• Uneconomic activities may be continued. For example, a car manufacturer may continue to make parts in-house when it may be cheaper to outsource

Question

Incremental budgeting

Can incremental budgeting be used to budget for rent? What about for advertising expenditure?

Answer

Incremental budgeting is appropriate for budgeting for rent, which may be estimated on the basis of current rent plus an increment for the annual rent increase. Advertising expenditure, on the other hand, is not so easily quantifiable and is more discretionary in nature. Using incremental budgeting for advertising expenditure could allow slack and wasteful spending to creep into the budget.

1.2.1 Incremental budgeting in the public sector

The traditional approach to budgeting in the public sector has been incremental and this has resulted in existing patterns of public expenditure being locked in. The public spending round in the UK established an annual cycle of year-on-year incremental bids by departments rather than an analysis of outputs and efficiency.

We will look at public sector objectives and performance measurement in more detail in Chapter 16.

2 Fixed and flexible budgets

FAST FORWARD

Fixed budgets remain unchanged regardless of the level of activity; **flexible budgets** are designed to flex with the level of activity.

PER alert

One of the competencies you require to fulfil performance objective 13 is the ability to amend budgets to reflect changes in circumstances. You can apply the knowledge you obtain from this chapter to help to demonstrate this competence.

2.1 Fixed budgets

Key term

> A **fixed budget** is a budget which is designed to remain unchanged regardless of the volume of output or sales achieved.

The master budget prepared before the beginning of the budget period is known as the **fixed budget**. The term 'fixed' means the following.

(a)   The budget is **prepared on the basis of an estimated volume of production** and an **estimated volume of sales**, but no plans are made for the event that actual volumes of production and sales may differ from budgeted volumes.

(b)   When actual volumes of production and sales during a control period (month or four weeks or quarter) are achieved, a fixed budget is **not adjusted (in retrospect) to the new levels of activity.**

The major purpose of a fixed budget is at the planning stage, when it seeks to define the broad objectives of the organisation.

2.2 Flexible budgets

Key term

> A **flexible budget** is a budget which, by recognising different cost behaviour patterns, is designed to change as volumes of output change.

Flexible budgets may be used in one of two ways.

(a)   **At the planning stage.** For example, suppose that a company expects to sell 10,000 units of output during the next year. A master budget (the fixed budget) would be prepared on the basis of these expected volumes. However, if the company thinks that output and sales might be as low as 8,000 units or as high as 12,000 units, it may prepare **contingency flexible budgets**, at volumes of, say 8,000, 9,000, 11,000 and 12,000 units and then assess the possible outcomes.

(b)   **Retrospectively.** At the end of each month (control period) or year, the results that should have been achieved given the actual circumstances (the flexible budget) can be compared with the actual results. As we shall see, flexible budgets are an essential factor in **budgetary control**.

The preparation and use of flexible budgets will be looked at in more detail in Chapter 10.

3 Zero based budgetary systems   6/09

FAST FORWARD

> The principle behind **zero based budgeting (ZBB)** is that the budget for each cost centre should be made from 'scratch' or zero. Every item of expenditure must be justified in its entirety in order to be included in the next year's budget.

ZBB rejects the assumption inherent in **incremental budgeting** that this year's activities will continue at the same level or volume next year, and that next year's budget can be based on this year's costs plus an extra amount, perhaps for expansion and inflation.

Key term

> **Zero based budgeting** involves preparing a budget for each cost centre from a zero base. Every item of expenditure has then to be justified in its entirety in order to be included in the next year's budget.

In reality, however, managers do not have to budget from zero, but can **start from their current level of expenditure and work downwards**, asking what would happen if any particular aspect of current expenditure and current operations were removed from the budget. In this way, every aspect of the budget is examined in terms of its cost and the benefits it provides and the selection of better alternatives is encouraged.

3.1 Implementing zero based budgeting

There is a three-step approach to ZBB.

- Define decision units
- Evaluate and rank packages
- Allocate resources

The implementation of ZBB involves a number of steps but of greater importance is the **development of a questioning attitude** by all those involved in the budgetary process. Existing practices and expenditures must be challenged and searching questions asked.

- Does the activity need to be carried out?
- What would be the consequences if the activity was not carried out?
- Is the current level of provision sufficient?
- Are there alternative ways of providing the function?
- How much should the activity cost?
- Is the expenditure worth the benefits achieved?

The basic approach of ZBB has three steps.

Step 1 **Define decision packages**, comprehensive descriptions of specific organisational activities which management can use to evaluate the activities and **rank** them in order of priority against other activities. There are two types.

(a) **Mutually exclusive packages** contain alternative methods of getting the same job done. The best option among the packages must be selected by comparing costs and benefits and the other packages are then discarded.

(b) **Incremental packages** divide one aspect of an activity into different levels of effort. The 'base' package will describe the minimum amount of work that must be done to carry out the activity and the other packages describe what additional work could be done, at what cost and for what benefits.

Suppose that a cost centre manager is preparing a budget for maintenance costs. He might first consider two mutually exclusive packages.

- Package A might be to keep a maintenance team of two men per shift for two shifts each day at a cost of $60,000 per annum
- Package B might be to obtain a maintenance service from an outside contractor at a cost of $50,000

A **cost-benefit analysis** will be conducted because the quicker repairs obtainable from an in-house maintenance service might justify its extra cost. If we now suppose that package A is preferred, the budget analysis must be completed by describing the incremental variations in this chosen alternative.

(a) The 'base' package would describe the minimum requirement for the maintenance work. This might be to pay for one man per shift for two shifts each day at a cost of $30,000.

(b) Incremental package 1 might be to pay for two men on the early shift and one man on the late shift, at a cost of $45,000. The extra cost of $15,000 would need to be justified, for example by savings in lost production time, or by more efficient machinery.

(c) Incremental package 2 might be the original preference, for two men on each shift at a cost of $60,000. The cost-benefit analysis would compare its advantages, if any, over incremental package 1; and so on.

Step 2 **Evaluate and rank each activity (decision package)** on the basis of its benefit to the organisation. This can be a lengthy process. Minimum work requirements (those that are essential to get a job done) will be given high priority and so too will work which meets legal obligations. In the accounting department these would be minimum requirements to operate the payroll, purchase ledger and sales ledger systems, and to maintain and publish a set of accounts. Common problems that can occur at the ranking stage are discussed in the next section.

Step 3 **Allocate resources** in the budget according to the funds available and the evaluation and ranking of the competing packages. For example, a car manufacturer may choose to allocate significantly more funds to production processes than service and admin functions, based on the ranking of each activity in step 2.

Question   Base and incremental packages

What might the base and incremental packages for a personnel department cover?

Answer

The base package might cover the recruitment and dismissal of staff. Incremental packages might cover training, pension administration, trade union liaison, staff welfare and so on.

Case Study

In July 2010, South Carolina Treasurer Converse Chellis commenced a study on the implementation of zero-based budgeting for all state departments and agencies, as put forward by the General Assembly.

The General Assembly believes, if implemented correctly, a system of zero-based budgeting will cut down on efficiency and waste in government.

Chellis will examine how other US states have implemented zero-based budgeting and says he hopes to save the state of South Carolina millions of dollars.

'It's time to hold every agency in state government accountable for every dollar it spends. With the implementation of zero-based budgeting, agencies and departments will have to justify every tax dollar they spend each and every year. We've seen how agencies have incrementally increased their budgets. During these remarkably tough economic times, having government examine and explain how it spends money each and every year is just common sense'.

The Treasurer will make his recommendation on whether to implement zero-based budgeting to state lawmakers before the beginning of its 2011 session.

3.2 The advantages and limitations of implementing ZBB

The **advantages** of zero based budgeting are as follows.

- It is possible to identify and **remove inefficient or obsolete operations**.
- It forces employees to **avoid wasteful expenditure**.
- It can **increase motivation**.
- It **responds to changes** in the business environment.
- **ZBB documentation provides** an in-depth **appraisal of an organisation's operations**.
- It **challenges the status quo**.
- In summary, ZBB should result in a **more efficient allocation of resources**.

The major **disadvantage** of zero based budgeting is the **volume of extra paperwork** created. The assumptions about costs and benefits in each package must be continually updated and new packages developed as soon as new activities emerge. The following problems might also occur.

(a) **Short-term benefits** might be **emphasised** to the detriment of long-term benefits.

(b) It might give the impression **that all decisions have to be made in the budget**. Management must be able to meet unforeseen opportunities and threats at all times, however, and must not feel restricted from carrying out new ideas simply because they were not approved by a decision package, cost benefit analysis and the ranking process.

(c) It may **call for management skills** both in constructing decision packages and in the ranking process **which the organisation does not possess**. Managers may have to be trained in ZBB techniques.

(d) The organisation's **information systems may not be capable of providing suitable information**.

(e) **The ranking process can be difficult**. Managers face three common problems.

   (i) A large number of packages may have to be ranked.
   (ii) It can be difficult to rank packages which appear to be equally vital, for legal or operational reasons.
   (iii) It is difficult to rank activities which have qualitative rather than quantitative benefits – such as spending on staff welfare and working conditions.

In summary, perhaps the **most serious drawback to ZBB is that it requires a lot of management time and paperwork**. One way of obtaining the benefits of ZBB but of overcoming the drawbacks is to apply it selectively on a rolling basis throughout the organisation. This year finance, next year marketing, the year after personnel and so on. In this way all activities will be thoroughly scrutinised over a period of time.

3.3 Using zero based budgeting

ZBB is particularly useful for budgeting for discretionary costs and for rationalisation purposes.

ZBB is not particularly suitable for direct manufacturing costs, which are usually budgeted using standard costing, work study and other management planning and control techniques. It is best applied to **support expenses**, that is expenditure incurred in departments which exist to support the essential production function. These support areas include marketing, finance, quality control, personnel, data processing, sales and distribution. In many organisations, these expenses make up a large proportion of the total expenditure. These activities are less easily quantifiable by conventional methods and are more **discretionary** in nature.

ZBB can also be successfully applied to **service industries** and **non-profit-making organisations** such as local and central government departments, educational establishments, hospitals and so on, and in any organisation where alternative levels of provision for each activity are possible and where the costs and benefits are separately identifiable.

ZBB can also be used to make **rationalisation decisions**. 'Rationalisation' is a euphemism for cutting back on production and activity levels, and cutting costs. The need for service departments to operate above a minimum service level or the need for having a particular department at all can be questioned, and ZBB can be used to make rationalisation decisions when an organisation is forced to make spending cuts.

4 Activity based budgeting

At its simplest, **activity based budgeting (ABB)** is merely the use of costs determined using ABC as a basis for preparing budgets.

Key term

Activity based budgeting involves defining the activities that underlie the financial figures in each function and using the level of activity to decide how much resource should be allocated, how well it is being managed and to explain variances from budget.

Implementing ABC (see Chapter 2) leads to the realisation that the **business as a whole** needs to be managed with far more reference to the **behaviour of activities and cost drivers** identified. For example, traditional budgeting may make managers 'responsible' for activities which are driven by factors beyond their control: the personnel department cost of setting up new employee records is driven by the number of new employees required by managers other than the personnel manager.

4.1 Principles of ABB

ABB involves defining the activities that underlie the financial figures in each function and using the **level of activity** to decide how much resource should be **allocated**, how well it is being **managed** and to **explain variances** from budget.

ABB is therefore based on the following **principles**.

(a)   It is **activities which drive costs** and the aim is to **control the causes** (drivers) of costs rather than the costs themselves, with the result that in the long term, costs will be better managed and better understood.

(b)   **Not all activities are value adding** and so activities must be examined and split up according to their ability to add value.

(c)   Most departmental activities are driven by demands and decisions **beyond the immediate control** of the manager responsible for the department's budget.

(d)   Traditional financial measures of performance are unable to fulfil the objective of **continuous improvement**. Additional measures which focus on drivers of costs, the quality of activities undertaken, the responsiveness to change and so on are needed.

4.2 Example: ABB

A stores department has two main activities, receiving deliveries of raw materials from suppliers into stores and issuing raw materials to production departments. Two major cost drivers, the number of deliveries of raw materials and the number of production runs, have been identified. Although the majority of the costs of the department can be attributed to the activities, there is a small balance, termed 'department running costs', which includes general administration costs, part of the department manager's salary and so on.

Based on activity levels expected in the next control period, the following cost driver volumes have been budgeted.

250 deliveries of raw materials
120 production runs

On the basis of budgeted departmental costs and the cost analysis, the following budget has been drawn up for the next control period.

Cost	Total	Costs attributable to receiving deliveries	Costs attributable to issuing materials	Dept running costs
	$'000	$'000	$'000	$'000
Salaries – management	25	8	12	5
Salaries – store workers	27	13	12	2
Salaries – administration	15	4	5	6
Consumables	11	3	5	3
Information technology costs	14	5	8	1
Other costs	19	10	6	3
	111	43	48	20
Activity volumes		250	120	
Cost per unit of cost driver		$172	$400	$20,000

Points to note

(a) The apportionment of cost will be subjective to a certain extent. The objective of the exercise is that the resource has to be justified as supporting one or more of the activities. Costs cannot be hidden.

(b) The cost driver rates of $172 and $400 can be used to calculate product costs using ABC.

(c) Identifying activities and their costs helps to focus attention on those activities which add value and those that do not.

(d) The budget has highlighted the cost of the two activities.

4.3 Benefits of ABB

Some writers treat ABB as a complete philosophy in itself and attribute to it all the good features of strategic management accounting, zero base budgeting, total quality management, and other ideas. For example, the following claims have been made.

(a) Different **activity levels** will provide a foundation for the 'base' package and incremental packages of **ZBB**.

(b) It will ensure that the organisation's overall **strategy** and any actual or likely changes in that strategy will be taken into account, because it attempts to manage the business as the **sum of its interrelated parts**.

(c) **Critical success factors** will be identified and performance measures devised to monitor progress towards them. (A critical success factor is an activity in which a business **must** perform well if it is to succeed).

(d) Because concentration is focused on the **whole of an activity**, not just its separate parts, there is more likelihood of **getting it right first time**. For example what is the use of being able to **produce** goods in time for their despatch date if the budget provides insufficient resources for the distribution manager who has to **deliver** them?

5 Rolling budgets

FAST FORWARD

> **Rolling budgets (continuous budgets)** are budgets which are continuously updated by adding a further period (say a month or a quarter) and deducting the earliest period.

5.1 Dynamic conditions

Actual conditions may differ from those anticipated when the budget was drawn up for a number of reasons.

(a) **Organisational changes** may occur.

  (i)   A change in structure, from a functional basis, say, to a process-based one

  (ii)   New agreements with the workforce about flexible working or safety procedures

  (iii) The reallocation of responsibilities following, say, the removal of tiers of middle management and the 'empowerment' of workers further down the line

(b) Action may be needed to **combat an initiative by a competitor.**

(c) **New technology** may be introduced to improve productivity, reduce labour requirements or enhance quality.

(d) **Environmental conditions** may change: there may be a general boom or a recession, an event affecting supply or demand, or a change in government or government policy.

(e) The level of **inflation** may be higher or lower than that anticipated.

(f) The **level of activities** may be different from the levels planned.

Any of these changes **may make the original budget quite inappropriate**, either in terms of the numbers expected, or the way in which responsibility for achieving them is divided, or both.

If management need the chance to revise their plans, they may decide to introduce a system of **rolling budgets**.

Key term

> A **rolling budget** is a budget which is continuously updated by adding a further accounting period (a month or quarter) when the earlier accounting period has expired.

Rolling budgets are an attempt to prepare targets and plans which are **more realistic and certain**, particularly with a regard to price levels, by **shortening the period between preparing budgets.**

Instead of preparing a **periodic budget** annually for the full budget period, there would be **budgets every one, two, three or four months** (three to six, or even twelve budgets each year). **Each of these budgets would plan for the next twelve months** so that the current budget is extended by an extra period as the current period ends: hence the name rolling budgets.

Suppose, for example, that a rolling budget is prepared every three months. The first three months of the budget period would be planned in great detail, and the remaining nine months in lesser detail, because of the greater uncertainty about the longer-term future. If a first continuous budget is prepared for January to March in detail and April to December in less detail, a new budget will be prepared towards the end of March, planning April to June in detail and July to March in less detail. Four rolling budgets would be prepared every 12 months on this 3 and 9 month basis, requiring, inevitably, greater administrative effort.

5.2 The advantages and disadvantages of rolling budgets

The **advantages** are as follows.

(a) They **reduce the element of uncertainty** in budgeting because they concentrate detailed planning and control on short-term prospects where the degree of uncertainty is much smaller.

(b) They force managers to reassess the budget regularly, and to produce budgets which are **up to date** in the light of current events and expectations.

(c) **Planning and control will be based on a recent plan** which is likely to be far more realistic than a fixed annual budget made many months ago.

(d) Realistic budgets are likely to have a **better motivational influence** on managers.

(e) There is **always a budget which extends for several months ahead**. For example, if rolling budgets are prepared quarterly there will always be a budget extending for the next 9 to 12 months. This is not the case when fixed annual budgets are used.

The **disadvantages** of rolling budgets can be a deterrent to using them.

(a) They involve **more time, effort and money** in budget preparation.

(b) Frequent budgeting might have an **off-putting effect on managers** who doubt the value of preparing one budget after another at regular intervals.

(c) Revisions to the budget might involve revisions to standard costs too, which in turn would involve revisions to stock valuations. This could replace a large **administrative effort** from the accounts department every time a rolling budget is prepared.

5.3 Continuous budgets or updated annual budgets

If the expected changes are not likely to be continuous there is a strong argument that routine updating of the budget is unnecessary. **Instead the annual budget could be updated whenever changes become foreseeable,** so that a budget might be updated once or twice, and perhaps more often, during the course of the year.

When a fixed budget is updated, a 'rolling' budget would probably not be prepared. If a budget is updated in month 8 of the year, the updated budget would relate to months 8 – 12. It would not be extended to month 7 of the following year.

6 Beyond Budgeting

Beyond Budgeting is a model that proposes that traditional budgeting should be abandoned. **Adaptive management processes** should be used rather than fixed annual budgets.

6.1 Criticisms of budgeting

In our discussion of the budgetary planning process we have come across many difficulties with budgets and criticisms of how they are used in organisations.

The Beyond Budgeting Round Table (BBRT), an independent research collaborative, propose that budgeting, as most organisations practise it, should be abandoned. Their website at www.bbrt.org lists the following ten criticisms of budgeting as put forward by Hope and Fraser *Beyond Budgeting*, 1st edition, Harvard Business School Press, 2003.

(a)   **Budgets are time consuming and expensive**. Even with the support of computer models it is estimated that the budgeting process uses up to 20 to 30 per cent of senior executives' and financial managers' time.

(b)   **Budgets provide poor value to users**. Although surveys have shown that some managers feel that budgets give them control, a large majority of financial directors wish to reform the budgetary process because they feel that finance staff spend too much time on 'lower value added activities'.

(c)   **Budgets fail to focus on shareholder value**. Most budgets are set on an incremental basis as an acceptable target agreed between the manager and the manager's superior. Managers may be rewarded for achieving their short term budgets and will not look to the longer term or take risks, for fear of affecting their own short term results.

(d)   **Budgets are too rigid and prevent fast response**. Although most organisations do update and revise their budgets at regular intervals as the budget period proceeds the process is often too slow compared with the pace at which the external environment is changing.

(e)   **Budgets protect rather than reduce costs**. Once a manager has an authorised budget he can spend that amount of resource without further authorisation. A 'use it or lose it' mentality often develops so that managers will incur cost unnecessarily. This happens especially towards the end of the budget period in the expectation that managers will not be permitted to carry forward any unused resource into the budget for next period.

(f)   **Budgets stifle product and strategy innovation**. The focus on achieving the budget discourages managers from taking risks in case this has adverse effects on their short term performance. Managers do not have the freedom to respond to changing customer needs in a fast changing market because the activity they would need to undertake is not authorised in their budget.

(g)   **Budgets focus on sales targets rather than customer satisfaction**. The achievement of short term sales forecasts becomes the focus of most organisations. However this does not necessarily result in customer satisfaction. The customer may be sold something **inappropriate to their needs**, as in recent years in the UK financial services industry. Alternatively if a manager has already met the sales target for a particular period they might try to **delay sales to the next period**, in order to give themselves a 'head start' towards achieving the target for the next period. Furthermore, there is an incentive towards the end of a period, if a manager feels that the sales target is not going to be achieved for the period, to **delay sales until the next period**, and thus again have a head start towards achieving the target for the next period. All of these actions, focusing on sales targets rather than customer satisfaction, will have a detrimental effect on the organisation in the longer term.

(h)   **Budgets are divorced from strategy**. Most organisations monitor the monthly results against the short term budget for the month. What is needed instead is a system of monitoring the longer term progress against the organisation's strategy.

(i)   **Budgets reinforce a dependency culture**. The process of planning and budgeting within a framework devolved from senior management perpetuates a culture of dependency. Traditional budgeting systems, operated on a centralised basis, do not encourage a culture of **personal responsibility**.

(j)   **Budgets lead to unethical behaviour**. For example building **slack** into the budget in order to create an easier target for achievement.

6.2 Beyond Budgeting concepts

Two fundamental concepts underlie the Beyond Budgeting approach.

(a)   **Use adaptive management processes rather than the more rigid annual budget**. Traditional annual plans tie managers to predetermined actions which are not responsive to current situations. Managers should instead be planning on a **more adaptive**, rolling basis but with the focus on cash forecasting rather than purely on cost control. Performance is monitored against world-class benchmarks, competitors and previous periods.

(b)   **Move towards devolved networks rather than centralised hierarchies**. The emphasis is on encouraging a culture of personal responsibility by delegating decision making and performance accountability to line managers.

7 Information used in budget systems

Information used in budget systems will come from a wide variety of sources.

Past data may be used as a starting point for the preparation of budgets but other information from a wide variety of sources will also be used. Each **function** of the organisation will be required to estimate revenue and expenditure for the budget period. For example, marketing, personnel and research and development.

7.1 Sales budget information

As we have seen, for many organisations, the principal budget factor is sales volume. The sales budget is therefore often the primary budget from which the majority of the other budgets are derived. Before the sales budget can be prepared a **sales forecast** has to be made. Sales forecasting is complex and difficult and involves the use of information from a variety of sources.

- Past sales patterns
- The economic environment
- Results of market research
- Anticipated advertising
- Competition
- Changing consumer taste

- New legislation
- Distribution
- Pricing policies and discounts offered
- Legislation
- Environmental factors

7.2 Production budget information

Sources of information for the production budget will include:

(a)   **Labour costs** including idle time, overtime and standard output rates per hour.
(b)   **Raw material costs** including allowances for losses during production.
(c)   **Machine hours** including expected idle time and expected output rates per machine hour.

This information will come from the production department and a large part of the traditional work of **cost accounting** involves ascribing costs to the physical information produced.

8 Changing budgetary systems

An organisation which decides to **change** its budgetary practices will face a number of difficulties.

The business environment has become increasingly complex, uncertain and dynamic and organisations need to be able to adapt quickly to changing conditions. It has been argued that traditional budgets are too rigid and prevent fast response to changing conditions.

However, an organisation which decides to **change** its type of budget used, or budgetary system, will face a number of **difficulties**.

(a) **Resistance by employees.** Employees will be familiar with the current system and may have built in slack so will not easily accept new targets. New control systems that threaten to alter existing power relationships may be thwarted by those affected.

(b) **Loss of control.** Senior management may take time to adapt to the new system and understand the implications of results.

(c) **Training.** In order for the new budget to operate effectively, everyone within the organisation will need to be fully trained. This is time-consuming and expensive.

(d) **Costs of implementation.** Any new system or process requires careful implementation which will have cost implications.

(e) **Lack of accounting information**. The organisation may not have the **systems** in place to obtain and analyse the necessary information.

9 Budget systems and uncertainty

Uncertainty can be allowed for in budgeting by means of **flexible budgeting, rolling budgets, probabilistic budgeting** and **sensitivity analysis**.

Causes of uncertainty in the budgeting process include:

(a) **Customers.** They may decide to buy less than forecast, or they may buy more.

(b) **Products/services**. In the modern business environment, organisations need to respond to customers' rapidly changing requirements.

(c) **Inflation** and movements in **interest and exchange rates.**

(d) **Volatility** in the **cost of materials.**

(e) **Competitors.** They may steal some of an organisation's expected customers, or some competitors' customers may change their buying allegiance.

(f) **Employees.** They may not work as hard as was hoped, or they may work harder.

(g) **Machines.** They may break down unexpectedly.

(h) There may be **political unrest** (terrorist activity), **social unrest** (public transport strikes) or minor or major **natural disasters** (storms, floods).

Rolling budgets are a way of trying to **reduce the element of uncertainty** in the plan. There are **other planning methods** which try to **analyse the uncertainty** such as **probabilistic budgeting** (where probabilities are assigned to different conditions – see Chapter 9) and **sensitivity analysis**. These methods are suitable when the **degree of uncertainty is quantifiable** from the start of the budget period and actual results are not expected to go outside the range of these expectations.

Chapter Roundup

- A budget is a **quantified plan of action** for a forthcoming accounting period.

- A budget can be set from the **top down** (**imposed** budget) or from the **bottom up** (**participatory** budget).

- The traditional approach to budgeting, known as **incremental budgeting**, bases the budget on the current year's results plus an extra amount for estimated growth or inflation next year. It encourages slack and wasteful spending to creep into budgets.

- **Fixed budgets** remain unchanged regardless of the level of activity; **flexible budgets** are designed to flex with the level of activity

- The principle behind **zero based budgeting (ZBB)** is that the budget for each cost centre should be made from 'scratch' or zero. Every item of expenditure must be justified in its entirety in order to be included in the next year's budget.

- There is a three-step approach to ZBB.
    - Define decision units
    - Evaluate and rank packages
    - Allocate resources

- ZBB is particularly useful for budgeting for discretionary costs and for rationalisation purposes.

- At its simplest, **activity based budgeting (ABB)** is merely the use of costs determined using ABC as a basis for preparing budgets.

- **Rolling budgets** (**continuous budgets**) are budgets which are continuously updated by adding a further period (say a month or a quarter) and deducting the earliest period.

- **Beyond Budgeting** is a model that proposes that traditional budgeting should be abandoned. **Adaptive management processes** should be used rather than fixed annual budgets.

- **Information** used in budget systems will come from a wide variety of sources.

- An organisation which decides to **change** its budgetary practices will face a number of difficulties.

- Uncertainty can be allowed for in budgeting by means of **flexible budgeting, rolling budgets, probabilistic budgeting** and **sensitivity analysis**.

Quick Quiz

1   Which of the following could not be a principal budget factor?

   (a)   Cash   (b)   Machine capacity
   (c)   Sales demand   (d)   Selling price
   (e)   Labour   (f)   Premises

2   *Fill in the gaps.*

   A flexible budget is a budget which, by recognising ………………………………, is designed to ……………………………… as the level of activity changes.

3   *Match the descriptions to the budgeting style.*

   Description

   (a)   Budget allowances are set without the involvement of the budget holder
   (b)   All budget holders are involved in setting their own budgets

   Budgeting style

   Bottom-up budgeting
   Top-down budgeting

4   Incremental budgeting is widely used and is a particularly efficient form of budgeting.

   ☐   True   ☐   False

5   What are the three steps of ZBB?

   Step 1 ……………………………………………………………………………

   Step 2 ……………………………………………………………………………

   Step 3 ……………………………………………………………………………

6   To which of the following can ZBB be usefully applied?

	Use ZBB	Do not use ZBB
Personnel		
Social services department of local government		
Direct material costs		
Sales department		
Schools		
An inefficient production department		
An efficient production department		

7   *Choose the appropriate word from those highlighted.*

   A rolling budget is also known as a **periodic/continuous** budget.

8   If a system of a ABB is in use, how might the cost of scheduling production be flexed?

   A   Number of items produced
   B   Number of set-ups
   C   Number of direct labour hours
   D   Number of parts used in production

9   A system of zero-based budgeting forces employees to remove wasteful expenditure.

   ☐ True   ☐ False

10   Use of zero-based budgeting implies flexing budgets on the basis of differences between budgeted and actual cost-driving activities.

   ☐ True   ☐ False

Answers to Quick Quiz

1   (d)

2   cost behaviour patterns
     flex or change

3   (a)   Top-down budgeting
     (b)   Bottom-up budgeting

4   False. Incremental budgeting is inefficient.

5   Step 1. Define decision packages
     Step 2. Evaluate and rank activities (decision package)
     Step 3. Allocate resources

6

	Use ZBB	Do not use ZBB
Personnel	✓	
Social services department of local government	✓	
Direct material costs		✓
Sales department	✓	
Schools	✓	
An inefficient production department	✓	
An efficient production department		✓

7   It is also known as a continuous budget.

8   B   Number of set-ups

9   True

10   False. This is a common feature of **activity-based** budgeting.

Now try the questions below from the Exam Question Bank

Number	Level	Marks	Time
Q13	Introductory	15	27 mins

10

Quantitative analysis in budgeting

Topic list	Syllabus reference
1 Analysing fixed and variable costs	C4 (a)
2 Forecasting techniques	C4 (b)
3 Time series	C4 (b)
4 Learning curves	C4 (c), (d)
5 Applying expected values	C4 (e)
6 Using spreadsheets in budgeting	C4 (f)

Introduction

In this chapter we will look at where the figures which go into the budgets come from. To produce a budget calls for the **preparation of forecasts of costs and revenues**. Various quantitative techniques can assist with these **'number-crunching' aspects of budgeting.** This chapter aims to provide an understanding of those techniques within their budgetary context.

There is a certain amount of truth in the comment that **budgeting is more a test of forecasting skill than anything else** and forecasts need to be made of sales volumes and prices, wage rates, material availability and prices, rates of inflation, the cost of bought-in services and overheads such as power. It is not sufficient to simply add a percentage to last year's budget in the hope of achieving a realistic forecast.

A **forecast** is a **best estimate** of what might happen in the future, based on certain assumptions about the conditions that are expected to apply. A **budget**, in contrast, is a **plan** of what the organisation is aiming to achieve and what it has set as a target. A budget should be **realistic** and so it will be based to some extent on forecasts prepared. In formulating a budget, management will try to establish some control over the conditions that will apply in the future.

Study guide

		Intellectual level
C4	Quantitative analysis in budgeting	
(a)	Analyse fixed and variable cost elements from total cost data using high/low and regression methods	2
(b)	Explain the use of forecasting techniques, including time series, simple average growth models and estimates based on judgement and experience. Predict a future value from provided time series analysis data using both additive and proportional data	2
(c)	Estimate the learning effect and apply the learning curve to a budgetary problem, including calculations on steady states	2
(d)	Discuss the reservations with the learning curve	2
(e)	Apply expected values and explain the problems and benefits	2
(f)	Explain the benefits and dangers inherent in using spreadsheets in budgeting	1

Exam guide

The quantitative techniques covered in this chapter are likely to form the calculation part of a budgeting question. Learning curves will probably be the hardest calculation you will need to tackle in this exam.

One of the competencies you require to fulfil performance objective 13 of the PER is the ability to prepare forecasts. You can apply the knowledge you obtain from this chapter of the text to help to demonstrate this competence.

1 Analysing fixed and variable costs

FAST FORWARD

Two important quantitative methods the management accountant can use to analyse fixed and variable cost elements from total cost data are the **high-low** and **regression methods**.

1.1 The high-low method   12/07, 12/08

You will have encountered the high-low method in your earlier studies. It is used to identify the fixed and variable elements of costs that are **semi-variable**. Read through the knowledge brought forward and do the question below to jog your memory.

Follow the steps below.

Step 1 Review records of costs in previous periods.

- Select the period with the **highest** activity level
- Select the period with the **lowest** activity level

Step 2 If inflation makes it difficult to compare costs, adjust by indexing up or down.

Step 3 Determine the following.

- Total cost at high activity level
- Total costs at low activity level
- Total units at high activity level
- Total units at low activity level

Step 4 Calculate the following.

$$\frac{\text{Total cost at high activity level} - \text{total cost at low activity level}}{\text{Total units at high activity level} - \text{total units at low activity level}}$$

= variable cost per unit (v)

Step 5 The fixed costs can be determined as follows. (Total cost at high activity level) – (total units at high activity level × variable cost per unit)

Question

High-low method

A department in a large organisation wishes to develop a method of predicting its total costs in a period. The following data have been recorded.

Month	Activity level (X) units	Cost $
January	1,600	28,200
February	2,300	29,600
March	1,900	28,800
April	1,800	28,600
May	1,500	28,000
June	1,700	28,400

The total cost model for a period could be represented by what equation?

Answer

The highest activity level is in February and the lowest in May.

Total cost at highest activity level	= $29,600
Total cost at lowest activity level	= $28,000
Total units at highest activity level	= 2,300
Total units at lowest activity level	= 1,500

$$\text{Variable cost per unit} = \frac{29,600 - 28,000}{2,300 - 1,500} = \frac{1,600}{800} = \$2$$

Fixed costs = 29,600 – (2,300 × 2) = $25,000
Total costs = 25,000 + 2x

1.2 The usefulness of the high-low method

The high-low method is a simple and easy to use method of estimating fixed and variable costs. However there are a number of problems with it.

(a) The method **ignores** all cost information apart from at the highest and lowest volumes of activity and these may not be **representative** of costs at all levels of activity.

(b) **Inaccurate** cost estimates may be produced as a result of the assumption of a constant relationship between costs and volume of activity.

(c) Estimates are based on **historical** information and conditions may have changed.

Exam focus point

> The examiner has stated that she will use the high-low method to provide overhead data within a question.

1.3 Linear regression analysis

Knowledge brought forward from earlier studies

Linear relationships

- A **linear relationship** can be expressed in the form of an equation which has the general form $y = a + bx$

  where y   is the **dependent** variable, depending for its value on the value of x

  x   is the **independent** variable, whose value helps to determine the value of y

  a   is a **constant**, a fixed amount

  b   is a constant, being the **coefficient of x** (that is, the number by which the value of x should be multiplied to derive the value of y)

- If there is a linear relationship between total costs and level of activity, y = total costs, x = level of activity, a = fixed cost (the cost when there is no activity level) and b = variable cost per unit.

- The graph of a linear equation is a **straight line** and is determined by two things, the **gradient** (or slope) of the straight line and the point at which the straight line crosses the y axis (the **intercept**).

  - Gradient = b in the equation $y = a + bx = (y_2 - y_1)/(x_2 - x_1)$ where (x_1, y_1), (x_2, y_2) are two points on the straight line

  - Intercept = a in the equation $y = a + bx$

- **Linear regression analysis**, also known as the **'least squares technique'**, is a **statistical method** of estimating costs using historical data from a number of previous accounting periods.

Exam formula

If $y = a + bx$, $b = \dfrac{n\Sigma xy - \Sigma x\Sigma y}{n\Sigma x^2 - (\Sigma x)^2}$ and $a = \dfrac{\Sigma y}{n} - \dfrac{b\Sigma x}{n}$

where n is the number of pair of data for x and y.

Exam focus point

> Note that you don't need to learn these formulae, as they are provided in the exam, but it would be very easy to make a mistake when copying them down so always double check back to the exam paper. Make sure you are confident using these formulae quickly and accurately.

1.3.1 Example: linear regression analysis

The transport department of Norwest Council operates a large fleet of vehicles. These vehicles are used by the various departments of the Council. Each month a statement is prepared for the transport department comparing actual results with budget. One of the items in the transport department's monthly statement is the cost of vehicle maintenance. This maintenance is carried out by the employees of the department.

To facilitate control, the transport manager has asked that future statements should show vehicle maintenance costs analysed into fixed and variable costs.

Data from the six months from January to June inclusive are given below.

	Vehicle maintenance cost	Vehicle running hours
	$	
January	13,600	2,100
February	15,800	2,800
March	14,500	2,200
April	16,200	3,000
May	14,900	2,600
June	15,000	2,500

Required

Analyse the vehicle maintenance costs into fixed and variable costs, based on the data given, utilising the least squares method.

Solution

If $y = a + bx$, where y represents costs and x represents running hours (since costs depend on running hours) then $b = (n\Sigma xy - \Sigma x\Sigma y)/(n\Sigma x^2 - (\Sigma x)^2)$, when n is the number of pairs of data, which is 6 in this problem.

x	y	xy	x^2
'000 hrs	$'000		
2.1	13.6	28.56	4.41
2.8	15.8	44.24	7.84
2.2	14.5	31.90	4.84
3.0	16.2	48.60	9.00
2.6	14.9	38.74	6.76
2.5	15.0	37.50	6.25
15.2	90.0	229.54	39.10

Variable cost per hour, b $= \dfrac{(6\times229.54)-(15.2\times90.0)}{(6\times39.10)-15.2^2}$

$= (1,377.24 - 1,368)/(234.6 - 231.04) = 9.24/3.56 = \$2.60$

Fixed costs (in $'000), a $= (\Sigma y/n) - (b\Sigma x/n) = (90/6) - (2.6(15.2)/6) = 8.41$ approx, say $8,400

Question   **Cost levels**

You are given the following data for output at a factory and costs of production over the past five months.

Month	Output	Costs
	'000 units	$'000
	x	y
1	20	82
2	16	70
3	24	90
4	22	85
5	18	73

Required

(a) Calculate an equation to determine the expected cost level for any given output volume.

(b) Prepare a budget for total costs if output is 22,000 units.

(a) *Workings*

x	y	xy	x^2	y^2
20	82	1,640	400	6,724
16	70	1,120	256	4,900
24	90	2,160	576	8,100
22	85	1,870	484	7,225
18	73	1,314	324	5,329
$\Sigma x = 100$	$\Sigma y = 400$	$\Sigma xy = 8,104$	$\Sigma x^2 = 2,040$	$\Sigma y^2 = 32,278$

n = 5 (There are five pairs of data for x and y values)

b = $(n\Sigma xy - \Sigma x\Sigma y)/(n\Sigma x^2 - (\Sigma x)^2)$ = $((5 \times 8,104) - (100 \times 400))/ ((5 \times 2,040) - 100^2)$

= (40,520 – 40,000)/(10,200 – 10,000) = 520/200 = 2.6

a = $\dfrac{\Sigma y}{n} - \dfrac{b\Sigma x}{n}$ = (400/5) – (2.6 × (100/5)) = 28

y = 28 + 2.6x

where y = total cost, in thousands of dollars and x = output, in thousands of units.

(b) If the output is 22,000 units, we would expect costs to be 28 + 2.6 × 22 = 85.2 = $85,200.

1.3.2 The conditions suited to the use of linear regression analysis

The conditions which should apply if linear regression analysis is to be used to estimate costs are as follows.

(a) A **linear cost function should be assumed**. This assumption can be tested by measures of reliability, such as the correlation coefficient and the coefficient of determination (which ought to be reasonably close to 1).

(b) When calculating a line of best fit, there will be a range of values for x. In Question 1, the line y = 28 + 2.6x was predicted from data with output values ranging from x = 16 to x = 24. Depending on the degree of correlation between x and y, we might safely use the estimated line of best fit to forecast values for y, provided that the value of x remains within the range 16 to 24. We would be on less safe ground if we used the equation to predict a value for y when x = 10, or 30, or any other value outside the range 16 to 24, because we would **have to assume that costs behave in the same way outside the range of x values used to establish the line in the first place.**

Key terms

> **Interpolation** means using a line of best fit to predict a value within the two extreme points of the observed range.
>
> **Extrapolation** means using a line of best fit to predict a value outside the two extreme points.

(c) The **historical data** for cost and output should be **adjusted to a common price level** (to overcome cost differences caused by inflation) and the historical data should also be **representative of current technology, current efficiency levels and current operations** (products made).

(d) As far as possible, **historical data should be accurately recorded** so that variable costs are properly matched against the items produced or sold, and fixed costs are properly matched against the time period to which they relate. For example, if a factory rental is $120,000 per annum, and if data is gathered monthly, these costs should be charged $10,000 to each month instead of $120,000 in full to a single month.

(e) Management should either be **confident that conditions** which have existed in the past **will continue into the future or amend the estimates** of cost produced by the linear regression analysis to **allow for expected changes** in the future.

(f)   As with any forecasting process, the **amount of data available is very important**. Even if correlation is high, if we have fewer than about ten pairs of data, we must regard any forecast as being somewhat unreliable.

(g)   It must be assumed that the **value of one variable, y, can be predicted or estimated from the value of one other variable, x.**

| Question | Linear regression model |

The relationship between total operating cost and quantity produced (in a manufacturing company) is given by the linear regression model TC = 5,000 + 500Q, where   TC = total operating cost (in $) per annum and   Q = quantity produced per annum (kg).

What reservations might you have about relying on the above model for decision-making purposes?

Answer

(a)   The reliability of the model is unknown if we do **not know the correlation coefficient**. A low correlation would suggest that the model may be unreliable.

(b)   The model is probably **valid only over a certain range** of quantity produced. Outside this range, the relationship between the two variables may be very different.

(c)   The model is **based on past data**, and assumes that what has happened in the past will happen in the future.

(d)   The model **assumes that a linear relationship exists** between the quantity produced per annum and the total operating costs per annum. It is possible that a non-linear relationship may exist.

(e)   The **fixed costs** of $5,000 per annum may be **misleading** if they include an element of allocated costs.

1.4 Scatter diagrams

FAST FORWARD

Scatter diagrams can be used to estimate the fixed and variable components of costs.

By this method of cost estimation, cost and activity data are plotted on a graph. A **'line of best fit'** is then drawn. This line should be drawn through the middle of the plotted points as closely as possible so that the distance of points above the line are equal to distances below the line. Where necessary costs should be adjusted to the same indexed price level to allow for inflation.

Scatter diagram method of estimating costs

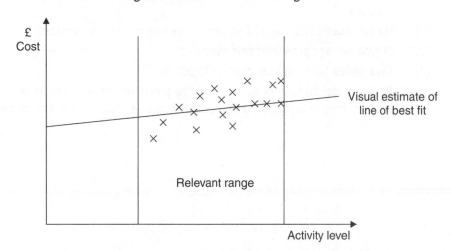

The fixed cost is the intercept of the line of best fit on the vertical axis. Suppose the fixed cost is $500 and that one of the plotted points (which is very close to the line or actually on it) represents output of 100

units and total cost of $550. The variable cost of 100 units is therefore calculated as $(550 − 500) = $50 and so the variable cost per unit is $0.50. The equation of the line of best fit is therefore *approximately*

y = 500 + 0.5x.

If the company to which this data relate wanted to forecast total costs when output is 90 units, a forecast based on the equation would be 500 + (0.5 × 90) = $545. Alternatively the **forecast could be read directly from the graph using the line of best fit.**

The disadvantage of the scatter diagram method is that the cost line is drawn by visual judgement and so is a **subjective approximation**.

2 Forecasting techniques

Forecasting techniques include estimates based on **judgement and experience,** simple **average growth models** and **time series.**

Numerous techniques have been developed for using past data as the basis for forecasting future values. These techniques range from simple arithmetic and visual methods to advanced computer-based statistical systems. With all techniques, however, there is the **presumption that the past will provide guidance to the future**. Before using any extrapolation techniques, the **past data** must therefore be critically examined to **assess their appropriateness for the intended purpose**. The following checks should be made.

(a)   The **time period** should be long enough to include any periodically paid costs but short enough to ensure that averaging of variations in the level of activity has not occurred.

(b)   The **data** should be examined to ensure that any non-activity level factors affecting costs were roughly the same in the past as those forecast for the future. Such factors might include changes in technology, changes in efficiency, changes in production methods, changes in resource costs, strikes, weather conditions and so on. Changes to the past data are frequently necessary.

(c)   The **methods of data collection** and the accounting policies used should not introduce bias. Examples might include depreciation policies and the treatment of by-products.

(d)   Appropriate choices of **dependent** and **independent variables** must be made.

The sales budget is frequently the first budget prepared since **sales is usually the principal budget factor,** but before the sales budget can be prepared a sales forecast has to be made. Sales forecasting is complex *and* difficult and involves the consideration of a number of factors.

Management can use a number of forecasting methods, often combining them to reduce the level of uncertainty.

(a)   **Sales personnel** can be asked to provide estimates. Such estimates are based on **judgement and experience.**

(b)   **Market research** can be used (especially for new products or services).

(c)   **Simple average growth models** can be used.

(d)   **Time series** can be used to produce forecasts.

(e)   **Mathematical** models can be set up so that repetitive computer simulations can be run which permit managers to review the results that would be obtained in various circumstances.

2.1 Simple average growth models

A **growth rate** can be estimated from an analysis of the growth in, for example sales, over the past few years.

Year	Sales revenue
	$
20X1	150,000
20X2	192,000
20X3	206,000
20X4	245,000
20X5	262,350

Sales have risen from $150,000 in 20X1 to $262,350 in 20X5. The increase represents four years growth. (Check that you can see that there are four years growth, and not five years growth, in the table.) The average growth rate, g, may be calculated as follows.

$$\text{Sales in 20X1} \times (1+g)^4 = \text{Sales in 20X5}$$

$$(1+g)^4 = \frac{\text{Sales in 20X5}}{\text{Sales in 20X1}}$$

$$= \frac{\$262,350}{\$150,000}$$

$$= 1.749$$

$$1 + g = \sqrt[4]{1.749} = 1.15$$

$$g = 0.15, \text{ ie } 15\%$$

3 Time series

12/09

FAST FORWARD

A **time series** is a series of figures or values recorded over time.

The following are examples of time series.

- Output at a factory each day for the last month
- Monthly sales over the last two years
- The Retail Prices Index each month for the last ten years

Key term

A graph of a time series is called a **historigram**.

(Note the letters 'ri'; this is not the same as a histogram.) For example, consider the following time series.

Year	20X0	20X1	20X2	20X3	20X4	20X5	20X6
Sales ($'000)	20	21	24	23	27	30	28

The historigram is as follows.

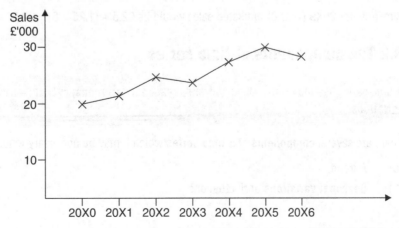

The horizontal axis is always chosen to represent time, and the vertical axis represents the values of the data recorded.

3.1 Regression and forecasting

> **FAST FORWARD**
>
> Regression can be used to find a **trend line**, such as the trend in sales over a number of periods.

The same regression techniques as those considered earlier in the chapter can be used to **calculate a regression line (a trend line) for a time series**. A time series is simply a series of figures or values recorded over time (such as total annual costs for the last ten years). The determination of a trend line is particularly useful in forecasting.

The **years (or days or months) become the x variables in the regression formulae** by **numbering them from 0 upwards.**

3.1.1 Example: Regression and forecasting

Sales of product B over the seven year period from 20X1 to 20X7 were as follows.

Year	20X1	20X2	20X3	20X4	20X5	20X6	20X7
Sales of B ('000 units)	22	25	24	26	29	28	30

There is high correlation between time and the volume of sales.

Required

Calculate the trend line of sales, and forecast sales in 20X8 and 20X9.

Solution

Workings

Year	x	y	xy	x^2
20X1	0	22	0	0
20X2	1	25	25	1
20X3	2	24	48	4
20X4	3	26	78	9
20X5	4	29	116	16
20X6	5	28	140	25
20X7	6	30	180	36
	$\Sigma x = 21$	$\Sigma y = 184$	$\Sigma xy = 587$	$\Sigma x^2 = 91$

n   = 7

Where y = a + bx

b $= ((7 \times 587) - (21 \times 184))/((7 \times 91) - (21 \times 21)) = 245/196 = 1.25$
a $= (184/7) - ((1.25 \times 21)/7) = 22.5357$, say 22.5
y   = 22.5 + 1.25x where x = 0 in 20X1, x = 1 in 20X2 and so on.

Using this trend line, predicted sales in 20X8 (year 7) would be $22.5 + (1.25 \times 7) = 31.25 = 31,250$ units.

Similarly, for 20X9 (year 8) predicted sales would be $22.5 + (1.25 \times 8) = 32.50 = 32,500$ units.

3.2 The components of time series

> **FAST FORWARD**
>
> A time series has four components: a **trend**, **seasonal variations**, **cyclical variations** and **random variations**.

There are several **components of a time series** which it may be necessary to identify.

(a) **A trend**

(b) **Seasonal variations** or fluctuations

(c)   Cycles, or **cyclical variations**

(d)   Non-recurring, **random variations**. These may be caused by unforeseen circumstances such as a change in government, a war, technological change or a fire.

3.2.1 The trend

> The **trend** is the underlying long-term movement over time in values of data recorded.

In the following examples of time series, there are three types of trend.

	Output per labour hour Units	Cost per unit $	Number of employees
20X4	30	1.00	100
20X5	24	1.08	103
20X6	26	1.20	96
20X7	22	1.15	102
20X8	21	1.18	103
20X9	17	1.25	98
	(A)	(B)	(C)

(a)   In time series **(A)** there is a **downward trend** in the output per labour hour. Output per labour hour did not fall every year, because it went up between 20X5 and 20X6, but the long-term movement is clearly a downward one.

(b)   In time series **(B)** there is an **upward trend** in the cost per unit. Although unit costs went down in 20X7 from a higher level in 20X6, the basic movement over time is one of rising costs.

(c)   In time series **(C)** there is **no clear movement** up or down, and the number of employees remained fairly constant. The trend is therefore a static, or level one.

3.2.2 Seasonal variations

> **Seasonal variations** are short-term fluctuations in recorded values, due to different circumstances which affect results at different times of the year, on different days of the week, at different times of day, or whatever.

Here are two examples of seasonal variations.

(a)   Sales of ice cream will be higher in summer than in winter.

(b)   The telephone network may be heavily used at certain times of the day (such as mid-morning and mid-afternoon) and much less used at other times (such as in the middle of the night).

'Seasonal' is a term which may appear to refer to the seasons of the year, but its meaning in time series analysis is somewhat broader, as the examples given above show.

3.2.3 Example: A trend and seasonal variations

The number of customers served by a company of travel agents over the past four years is shown in the following historigram.

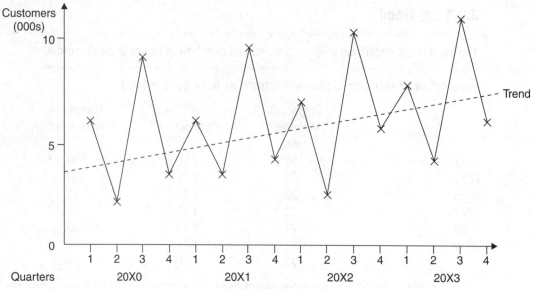

In this example, there would appear to be large seasonal fluctuations in demand, but there is also a basic upward trend.

3.2.4 Cyclical variations

Cyclical variations are **medium-term changes in results caused by circumstances which repeat in cycles**. In business, cyclical variations are commonly associated with economic cycles, successive booms and slumps in the economy. Economic cycles may last a few years. Cyclical variations are longer term than seasonal variations.

3.2.5 Summarising the components

In practice a time series could incorporate all of the four features we have been looking at and, to make reasonably accurate forecasts, the four features often have to be isolated. We can begin the process of isolating each feature by summarising the components of a time series as follows.

The **actual time series, Y= T + S + C + R**

where			
Y	= **the actual time series**	**C**	= **the cyclical component**
T	= **the trend series**	**R**	= **the random component**
S	= **the seasonal component**		

Though you should be aware of the cyclical component, it is unlikely that you will be expected to carry out any calculation connected with isolating it. The mathematical models which we will use therefore excludes any reference to C.

We will begin by looking at how to find the trend in a time series.

3.3 Moving averages

> **Trend** values can be determined by a process of **moving averages**.

Look at these monthly sales figures.

	August	September	October	November	December
Sales ($'000)	0.02	0.04	0.04	3.20	14.60

It looks as though the business is expanding rapidly – and so it is, in a way. But when you know that the business is a Christmas card manufacturer, then you see immediately that the January sales will no doubt slump right back down again.

It is obvious that the business will do better in the Christmas season than at any other time – that is the seasonal variation. Using the monthly figures, how can we tell whether or not the business is doing well overall – whether there is a rising sales trend over time other than the short-term rise over Christmas?

One possibility is to compare figures with the equivalent figures of a year ago. However, many things can happen over a year to make such a comparison misleading – new products might now be manufactured and prices will probably have changed.

In fact, there are a number of ways of overcoming this problem of distinguishing trend from seasonal variations. One such method is called **moving averages**. This method attempts to **remove seasonal (or cyclical) variations from a time series by a process of averaging so as to leave a set of figures representing the trend**.

A moving average is an average of the results of a fixed number of periods. Since it is an average of several time periods, it is **related to the mid-point of the overall period**.

Exam focus point

> Whilst it is unlikely that you will be required to carry out a time series analysis from raw data, you do need to be able to explain the approach and discuss its use.

3.3.1 Example: Moving averages

Year	Sales Units
20X0	390
20X1	380
20X2	460
20X3	450
20X4	470
20X5	440
20X6	500

Required

Take a moving average of the annual sales over a period of three years.

Solution

(a) Average sales in the three year period 20X0 – 20X2 were (390 + 380 + 460)/3 = 1,230/3 = 410. This average relates to the middle year of the period, 20X1.

(b) Similarly, average sales in the three year period 20X1 – 20X3 were (380 + 460 + 450)/3 = 1,290/3 = 430. This average relates to the middle year of the period, 20X2.

(c) The average sales can also be found for the periods 20X2 – 20X4, 20X3 – 20X5 and 20X4 – 20X6, to give the following.

Year	Sales	Moving total of 3 years sales	Moving average of 3 years sales ($\div$ 3)
20X0	390		
20X1	380	1,230	410
20X2	460	1,290	430
20X3	450	1,380	460
20X4	470	1,360	453
20X5	440	1,410	470
20X6	500		

Note the following points.

(i) The moving average series has five figures relating to the years 20X1 to 20X5. The original series had seven figures for the years from 20X0 to 20X6.

(ii) There is an upward trend in sales, which is more noticeable from the series of moving averages than from the original series of actual sales each year.

3.3.2 Moving averages of an even number of results

In the previous example, moving averages were taken of the results in an **odd** number of time periods, and the average then related to the **mid-point** of the overall period.

If a moving average of results was taken in an **even** number of time periods, the basic technique would be the same, but the mid-point of the overall period would not relate to a single period. For example, suppose an average were taken of the following four results.

Spring	120	
Summer	90	Average = 115
Autumn	180	
Winter	70	

The average would relate to the mid-point of the period, between summer and autumn.

The trend line average figures need to relate to a particular time period; otherwise, seasonal variations cannot be calculated. To overcome this difficulty, we take a **moving average of the moving average**. An example will illustrate this technique.

3.3.3 Example: Moving averages over an even number of periods

Calculate a moving average trend line of the following results.

Year	Quarter	Volume of sales '000 units
20X5	1	600
	2	840
	3	420
	4	720
20X6	1	640
	2	860
	3	420
	4	740

Solution

A moving average of **four** will be used, since the volume of sales would appear to depend on the season of the year, and each year has four **quarterly** results. The moving average of four does not relate to any specific period of time; therefore a second moving average of two will be calculated on the first moving averages.

Year	Quarter	Actual volume of sales '000 units (A)	Moving total of 4 quarters' sales '000 units (B)	Moving average of 4 quarters' sales '000 units (B ÷ 4)	Mid-point of 2 moving averages Trend line '000 units (C)
20X5	1	600			
	2	840			
	3	420	2,580	645.0	650.00
	4	720	2,620	655.0	657.50
20X6	1	640	2,640	660.0	660.00
	2	860	2,640	660.0	662.50
	3	420	2,660	665.0	
	4	740			

By taking a mid point (a moving average of two) of the original moving averages, we can relate the results to specific quarters (from the third quarter of 20X5 to the second quarter of 20X6).

3.4 Finding the seasonal variations

> **Seasonal variations** can be estimated using the **additive** model or the **proportional (multiplicative)** model.

Once a trend has been established we can find the seasonal variations.

3.4.1 The additive model

Key term

The **additive model** for time series analysis is Y = T + S + R.

We can therefore write Y – T = S + R. In other words, if we deduct the trend series from the actual series, we will be left with the seasonal and random components of the time series. If we assume that the random component is relatively small, and hence negligible, the **seasonal component can be found as S = Y – T,** the **de-trended series.**

The actual and trend sales for the example above are set out below. The **difference** between the **actual** results for any one quarter (Y) and the **trend** figure for that quarter (T) will be the **seasonal variation** for that quarter.

Year	Quarter	Actual	Trend	Seasonal variation
20X5	1	600		
	2	840		
	3	420	650.00	–230.00
	4	720	657.50	62.50
20X6	1	640	660.00	–20.00
	2	860	662.50	197.50
	3	420		
	4	740		

Suppose that seasonal variations for the third and fourth quarters of 20X6 and the first and second quarters of 20X7 are –248.75, 62.50, –13.75 and 212.50 respectively. The variation between the actual result for a particular quarter and the trend line average is not the same from year to year, but an **average of these variations can be taken**.

	Q_1	Q_2	Q_3	Q_4
20X5			–230.00	62.50
20X6	–20.00	197.50	–248.75	62.50
20X7	–13.75	212.50		
Total	–33.75	410.00	–478.75	125.00
Average (÷ 2)	–16.875	205.00	–239.375	62.50

Variations around the basic trend line should cancel each other out, and add up to zero. At the moment, they do not. We therefore **spread** the total of the variations (11.25) across the four quarters (11.25 ÷ 4) so that the final total of the variations **sum to zero.**

	Q_1	Q_2	Q_3	Q_4	Total
Estimated quarterly variations	– 16.8750	205.0000	–239.3750	62.5000	11.250
Adjustment to reduce variations to 0	–2.8125	–2.8125	–2.8125	–2.8125	–11.250
Final estimates of quarterly variations	–19.6875	202.1875	–242.1875	59.6875	0

These might be rounded as follows   QI: –20,   Q2: 202,   Q3:-242,   Q4: 60,   Total: 0

3.4.2 The proportional model

The method of estimating the seasonal variations in the above example was to use the differences between the trend and actual data. This model **assumes that the components of the series are independent** of each other, so that an increasing trend does not affect the seasonal variations and make them increase as well, for example.

The alternative is to use the **proportional model** whereby each actual figure is expressed as a proportion of the trend. Sometimes this method is called the **multiplicative model**.

Key term

> The **proportional (multiplicative) model** summarises a time series as $Y = T \times S \times R$.

The **trend component** will be the **same whichever model is used** but the values of the **seasonal and random components** will **vary** according to the model being applied.

The example above can be reworked on this alternative basis. The trend is calculated in exactly the same way as before but we need a different approach for the seasonal variations. The proportional model is $Y = T \times S \times R$ and, just as we calculated $S = Y - T$ for the additive model above we can calculate **$S = Y/T$** for the proportional model.

Year	Quarter	Actual (Y)	Trend (T)	Seasonal percentage (Y/T)
20X5	1	600		
	2	840		
	3	420	650.00	0.646
	4	720	657.50	1.095
20X6	1	640	660.00	0.970
	2	860	662.50	1.298
	3	420		
	4	740		

Suppose that seasonal variations for the next four quarters are 0.628, 1.092, 0.980 and 1.309 respectively. The summary of the seasonal variations expressed in proportional terms is therefore as follows.

	Q_1 %	Q_2 %	Q_3 %	Q_4 %
20X5			0.646	1.095
20X6	0.970	1.298	0.628	1.092
20X7	0.980	1.309		
Total	1.950	2.607	1.274	2.187
Average	0.975	1.3035	0.637	1.0935

Instead of summing to zero, as with the additive approach, the **averages should sum** (in this case) **to 4.0, 1.0 for each of the four quarters.** They actually sum to 4.009 so 0.00225 has to be deducted from each one.

	Q_1	Q_2	Q_3	Q_4
Average	0.97500	1.30350	0.63700	1.09350
Adjustment	−0.00225	−0.00225	−0.00225	−0.00225
Final estimate	0.97275	1.30125	0.63475	1.09125
Rounded	0.97	1.30	0.64	1.09

Note that the **proportional model is better than the additive model when the trend is increasing or decreasing over time**. In such circumstances, seasonal variations are likely to be increasing or decreasing too. The additive model simply adds absolute and unchanging seasonal variations to the trend figures whereas the proportional model, by multiplying increasing or decreasing trend values by a constant seasonal variation factor, takes account of changing seasonal variations.

3.5 Time series analysis and forecasting

FAST FORWARD

> **Forecasts** can be made by calculating a **trend line** (using moving averages or linear regression), using the trend line to forecast future trend line values, and adjusting these values by the **average seasonal variation** applicable to the future period.

By extrapolating a trend and then adjusting for seasonal variations, forecasts of future values can be made.

Forecasts of future values should be made as follows.

(a) Find a trend line using moving averages or using linear regression analysis

(b) Use the trend line to forecast future trend line values.

(c) Adjust these values by the average seasonal variation applicable to the future period, to determine the forecast for that period. With the additive model, **add** (or subtract for negative variations) the variation. With the multiplicative model, **multiply** the trend value by the variation proportion.

Extending a trend line outside the range of known data, in this case forecasting the future from a trend line based on historical data, is known as **extrapolation**.

3.5.1 Example: Forecasting

The sales (in $'000) of swimwear by a large department store for each period of three months and trend values found using moving averages are as follows.

Quarter	20X4		20X5		20X6		20X7	
	Actual	Trend	Actual	Trend	Actual	Trend	Actual	Trend
	$'000	$'000	$'000	$'000	$'000	$'000	$'000	$'000
First			8		20	40	40	57
Second			30	30	50	45	62	
Third			60	31	80	50	92	
Fourth	24		20	35	40	54		

Using the additive model, seasonal variations have been determined as follows.

Quarter 1	Quarter 2	Quarter 3	Quarter 4
–$18,250	+$2,750	+$29,750	–$14,250

Required

Predict sales for the last quarter of 20X7 and the first quarter of 20X8, stating any assumptions.

Solution

We might guess that the trend line is rising steadily, by $(57 - 40)/4 = 4.25$ per quarter in the period 1st quarter 20X6 to 1st quarter 20X7 (57 being the prediction in 1st quarter 20X7 and 40 the prediction in 1st quarter 20X6). Since the trend may be levelling off a little, a quarterly increase of +4 in the trend will be assumed.

		Trend	Seasonal variation	Forecast
1st quarter	20X7	57		
4th quarter	20X7 (+ (3 × 4))	69	–14.25	54.75
1st quarter	20X8 (+ (4 × 4))	73	–18.25	54.75

Rounding to the nearest thousand pounds, the forecast sales are $55,000 for each of the two quarters.

Note that you could actually plot the trend line figures on a graph, extrapolate the trend line into the future and read off forecasts from the graph using the extrapolated trend line.

If we had been using the proportional model, with an average variation for (for example) quarter 4 of 0.8, our prediction for the fourth quarter of 20X7 would have been 69 × 0.8 = 55.2, say $55,000.

Question   Sales forecast

The trend in a company's sales figures can be described by the linear regression equation $y = 780 + 4x$, where x is the month number (with January 20X3 as month 0) and y is sales in thousands of pounds. The average seasonal variation for March is 106%.

Required

Forecast the sales for March 20X5.

x = 26

Forecast = 1.06 × [780 + (4 × 26)] = 937.04 = $937,040 or about $937,000.

3.6 Forecasting problems

Errors can be expected in forecasting due to unforeseen changes. This is more likely to happen the further into the future the forecast is for, and the smaller the quantity of data on which the forecast is based.

All forecasts are subject to error, but the likely errors vary from case to case.

- The **further into the future** the forecast is for, the **more unreliable** it is likely to be
- The **less data** available on which to base the forecast, the **less reliable** the forecast
- The historic **pattern** of trend and seasonal variations **may not continue** in the future
- **Random variations** may upset the pattern of trend and seasonal variation
- **Extrapolation** of the **trend line** is done by judgment and can introduce errors

There are a number of changes that also may make it difficult to forecast future events.

Type of change	Examples
Political and economic changes	Changes in interest rates, exchange rates or inflation can mean that future sales and costs are difficult to forecast.
Environmental changes	The opening of high-speed rail links might have a considerable impact on some companies' markets.
Technological changes	These may mean that the past is not a reliable indication of likely future events. For example new faster machinery may make it difficult to use current output levels as the basis for forecasting future production output.
Technological advances	Advanced manufacturing technology is changing the cost structure of many firms. Direct labour costs are reducing in significance and fixed manufacturing costs are increasing. This causes forecasting difficulties because of the resulting changes in cost behaviour patterns, breakeven points and so on.
Social changes	Alterations in taste, fashion and the social acceptability of products can cause forecasting difficulties.

Management should have reasonable **confidence** in their estimates and forecasts. The assumptions on which the forecasts/estimates are based should be properly understood and the methods used to make a forecast or estimate should be in keeping with the nature, quantity and reliability of the data on which the forecast or estimate will be based. There is no point in using a 'sophisticated' technique with unreliable data; on the other hand, if there is a lot of accurate data about historical costs, it would be a waste of the data to use the scatter diagram method for cost estimating.

4 Learning curves   12/08, 12/09

Learning curve theory may be useful for forecasting production time and labour costs in certain circumstances, although the method has many limitations.

Whenever an individual starts a job which is **fairly repetitive** in nature, and provided that his speed of working is not dictated to him by the speed of machinery (as it would be on a production line), he is likely to become **more confident and knowledgeable** about the work as he gains experience, to become **more efficient**, and to do the work **more quickly**.

Eventually, however, when he has acquired enough experience, there will be nothing more for him to learn, and so **the learning process will stop**.

Key term

> **Learning curve theory** applies to situations where the work force as a whole improves in efficiency with experience. The **learning effect** or **learning curve effect** describes the speeding up of a job with repeated performance.

4.1 Where does learning curve theory apply?

Labour time should be expected to get shorter, with experience, in the production of items which exhibit any or all of the following features.

- Made largely **by labour effort** (rather than by a **highly mechanised** process)
- Brand **new** or relatively **short-lived** (learning process does not continue indefinitely)
- **Complex** and made in **small quantities** for **special orders**

4.2 The 3 approaches to learning curve problems

There are 3 methods that can be used to address learning curve scenarios.

- **Method 1**. The tabular approach
- **Method 2**. The graphical approach
- **Method 3**. The algebraic approach

4.3 Method 1 – The tabular approach: cumulative average time and the learning rate

The **tabular approach** is only effective in scenarios where output is doubling.

Under this approach, a table is set up to show levels of output, cumulative average time required per unit and incremental time for additional units. The **cumulative average time per unit** produced is assumed to **decrease** by a **constant percentage** every time **total output** of the product **doubles**.

For instance, where an 80% learning effect occurs, the cumulative average time required per unit of output is reduced to 80% of the previous cumulative average time when output is doubled.

(a) By **cumulative average time**, we mean the average time per unit for all units produced so far, back to and including the first unit made.

(b) The **doubling** of output is an important feature of the learning curve measurement.

Don't worry if this sounds quite hard to grasp in words, because it is hard to grasp (until you've learned it!). It is best explained by a numerical example.

4.4 Example: an 80% learning curve

The first unit of output of a new product requires 100 hours. An 80% learning curve applies. The production times would be as follows.

Number of units produced	Cumulative avg time required per unit		Total time required		Incremental time for additional units	
1		100.0	(× 1)	100.0		
2*	(80%)	80.0	(× 2)	160.0	60.0	(for 1 extra unit)
4*	(80%)	64.0	(× 4)	256.0	96.0	(for 2 extra units)
8*	(80%)	51.2	(× 8)	409.6	153.6	(for 4 extra units)

* Output is being **doubled** each time.

4.5 Method 2 – The graphical approach

The learning effect from the above example can also be shown on a **graph**, as a learning curve either for **unit times** or **cumulative total times or costs**.

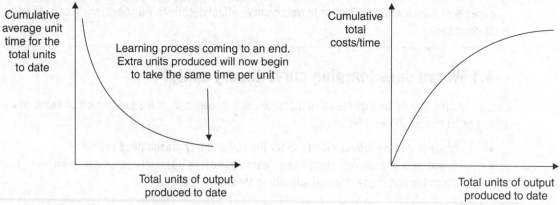

Whilst this approach is useful in scenarios where output is not doubling, in reality it is not as accurate as methods 1 and 3.

4.6 Example: the learning curve

Captain Kitts has designed a new type of sailing boat, for which the cost of the first boat to be produced has been estimated as follows:

	$
Materials	5,000
Labour (800 hrs × $5 per hr)	4,000
Overhead (150% of labour cost)	6,000
	15,000
Profit mark-up (20%)	3,000
Sales price	18,000

It is planned to sell all the yachts at full cost plus 20%. An 80% learning curve is expected to apply to the production work. The management accountant has been asked to provide cost information so that decisions can be made on what price to charge.

(a) What is the separate cost of a second yacht?

(b) What would be the cost per unit for a third and a fourth yacht, if they are ordered separately later on?

(c) If they were all ordered now, could Captain Kitts quote a single unit price for four yachts and eight yachts?

Solution

Number of yachts		Cumulative average time per yacht		Total time for all yachts to date		Incremental time for additional yachts
		Hours		Hours		Hours
1				800.0		800.0
2	(× 80%)	640.0	(× 2)	1,280.0	(1,280 – 800)	480.0
4	(× 80%)	512.0	(× 4)	2,048.0	(2,048 – 1,280)	768.0
8	(× 80%)	409.6	(× 8)	3,276.8	(3,276.8 – 2,048)	1,228.8

(a) **Separate cost of a second yacht**

	$
Materials	5,000
Labour (480 hrs × $5)	2,400
Overhead (150% of labour cost)	3,600
Total cost	11,000

(b) **Cost of the third and fourth yachts**

	$
Materials cost for two yachts	10,000
Labour (768 hours × $5)	3,840
Overhead (150% of labour cost)	5,760
Total cost	19,600
Cost per yacht (÷2)	9,800

(c) **A price for the first four yachts together and for the first eight yachts together**

		First four yachts		First eight yachts
		$		$
Materials		20,000		40,000
Labour	(2,048 hrs)	10,240	(3,276.8 hrs)	16,384
Overhead (150% of labour cost)		15,360		24,576
Total cost		45,600		80,960
Profit (20%)		9,120		16,192
Total sales price		54,720		97,152
Price per yacht	(÷4)	13,680	(÷8)	12,144

This assumes that Captain Kitts is happy to pass on the efficiency savings to the customer in the form of a lower price.

Question
Learning curve theory

Bortamord anticipates that a 90% learning curve will apply to the production of a new item. The first item will cost $2,000 in materials, and will take 500 labour hours. The cost per hour for labour and variable overhead is $5.

You are required to calculate the total cost for the first unit and for the first 8 units.

Answer

	Units		Cumulative average time per unit Hours		Total time for all units produced to date Hours
	1		500.0		500
(double)	2	(90%)	450.0	(× 2)	900
(double)	4	(90%)	405.0	(× 4)	1,620
(double)	8	(90%)	364.5	(× 8)	2,916

	Cost of 1st unit		Cost of 1st 8 units
	$		$
Materials	2,000		16,000
Labour and variable o/hd (500 hrs)	2,500	(2,916 hours)	14,580
	4,500		30,580
Average cost/unit	4,500		3,822.50

4.7 Method 3 – The algebraic approach

FAST FORWARD

The formula for the learning curve is $Y = ax^b$, where b, the learning coefficient or learning index, is defined as (log of the learning rate/log of 2). The learning curve formula can be used to solve all learning curve scenarios.

Exam formula

The formula for the learning curve is $Y = ax^b$

where   **Y** is the cumulative average time per unit to produce x units
           x is the cumulative number of units
           a is the time taken for the first unit of output
           b is the index of learning (logLR/log2)
           LR is the learning rate as a decimal

Exam focus point

This is the formula that is provided in the pilot paper which refers to labour cost rather than time. The formula can also be used to calculate the labour hours per unit. The labour **times** are calculated using the curve formula and then converted to cost.

4.7.1 Logarithms and the value of b

When $y = ax^b$ in learning curve theory, the value of **b = log of the learning rate/log of 2**. The learning rate is expressed as a proportion, so that for an 80% learning curve, the learning rate is 0.8, and for a 90% learning curve it is 0.9, and so on.

For an 80% learning curve, b = log 0.8/log 2.

Using the button on your calculator marked 'log'

$$b = \frac{-0.0969}{0.3010} = -0.322$$

4.7.2 Example: using the formula

Suppose, for example, that an 80% learning curve applies to production of item ABC. To date (the end of June) 230 units of ABC have been produced. Budgeted production for July is 55 units.

The cost of the very first unit of ABC, in January, was $120.

Required

Calculate the budgeted total labour cost for July.

Solution

To solve this problem, we need to calculate three things.

(a)   The cumulative total labour cost so far to produce 230 units of ABC.
(b)   The cumulative total labour cost to produce 285 units of ABC, that is adding on the extra 55 units for July.
(c)   The extra cost of production of 55 units of ABC in July, as the difference between (b) and (a).

Calculation (a)

$y = ax^b$ and we know that for 230 cumulative units, a = $120 (cost of first unit), x = 230 (cumulative units) and b = –0.322 (80% learning curve) and so y = 120 × $(230^{-0.322})$ = $20.83.

So when x = 230 units, the cumulative average cost per unit is $20.83.

Calculation (b)

Now we do the same sort of calculation for x = 285.

If x = 285, y = 120 × ($285^{-0.322}$) = $19.44

So when X = 285 units, the cumulative average cost per unit is $19.44.

Calculation (c)

Cumulative units	Average cost per unit	Total cost
	$	$
230	20.83	4,790.90
285	19.44	5,540.40
Incremental cost for 55 units		749.50

Average cost per unit, between 230 and 285 units = 749.50/55 = $13.63 per unit approx.

4.8 Example: Learning curves and standard costs

A company needs to calculate a new standard cost for one of its products. When the product was introduced, the standard variable cost of the first unit was as follows.

		Cost per unit
		$
Direct material	10 kg @ $3 per kg	30
Direct labour	10 hours @ $9 per hour	90
Variable overhead	10 hours @ $5 per hour	50
Total		170

During the following year, a 90% learning curve was observed. The cumulative production at the end of the third quarter was 50 units and the budgeted production for the fourth quarter is 10 units.

Required

(a) What is the standard cost per unit for the fourth quarter assuming that the 90% learning curve still applies?

(b) What is the standard cost per unit for the fourth quarter assuming the learning curve had reached a **steady state** ie peak efficiency was reached after the 50th unit was produced?

Solution

on calc $60 / xy / -0.152$ =
$y / 0 = 5.37$

(a) $y = ax^b$ and for 60 cumulative units a = 10 hours (time for first unit), x = 60 (cumulative units) and b = -0.152 (90% learning curve) and so y = 10 x ($60^{-0.152}$) = 5.37 hours.

For 50 cumulative units y = 10 x ($50^{-0.152}$) = 5.52 hours.

Cumulative units	Average time per unit	Total time
50	5.52	276.0
60	5.37	322.2
Incremental time for 10 units		46.2

The standard time per unit is therefore 46.2/10 = 4.62 hours
The standard cost per unit is:

		Cost per unit
		$
Direct material	10 kg @ $3 per kg	30.00
Direct labour	4.62 hours @ $9 per hour	41.58
Variable overhead	4.62 hours @ $5 per hour	23.10
Total		94.68

(b) A steady state is reached after the 50th unit so we need the time taken to produce the 50th unit.

For 49 cumulative units a = 10 hours (time for first unit), x = 49 (cumulative units) and b = -0.152 (90% learning curve) and so y = 10 x ($49^{-0.152}$) = 5.535 hours.

Cumulative units	Average time per unit	Total time
49	5.535	271.2
50	5.520	276.0
Incremental time for 50th unit		4.8

The standard cost per unit is:

		Cost per unit $
Direct material	10 kg @ $3 per kg	30.00
Direct labour	4.8 hours @ $9 per hour	43.20
Variable overhead	4.8 hours @ $5 per hour	24.00
Total		97.20

4.9 The practical application of learning curve theory

What costs are affected by the learning curve?

(a) Direct labour time and costs

(b) Variable overhead costs, if they vary with direct labour hours worked.

(c) **Materials costs** are usually **unaffected** by learning among the workforce, although it is conceivable that materials handling might improve, and so wastage costs be reduced.

(d) **Fixed overhead expenditure** should be **unaffected** by the learning curve (although in an organisation that uses absorption costing, if fewer hours are worked in producing a unit of output, and the factory operates at full capacity, the **fixed overheads recovered or absorbed per unit** in the cost of the output **will decline** as more and more units are made).

4.10 The relevance of learning curve effects in management accounting

Learning curve theory can be used to:

(a) Calculate the marginal (incremental) cost of making extra units of a product.

(b) **Quote selling prices for a contract**, where prices are calculated at cost plus a percentage mark-up for profit. An awareness of the learning curve can make all the difference between winning contracts and losing them, or between making profits and selling at a loss-making price.

(c) **Prepare realistic production budgets** and more **efficient production schedules**.

(d) **Prepare realistic standard costs** for cost control purposes.

Considerations to bear in mind include:

(a) **Sales projections, advertising expenditure and delivery date commitments.** Identifying a learning curve effect should allow an organisation to plan its advertising and delivery schedules to coincide with expected production schedules. Production capacity obviously affects sales capacity and sales projections.

(b) **Budgeting with standard costs.** Companies that use standard costing for much of their production output cannot apply standard times to output where a learning effect is taking place. This problem can be overcome in practice by:

   (i) Establishing **standard times** for output, once the learning effect has worn off or become insignificant, and

   (ii) Introducing a **'launch cost'** budget for the product for the duration of the learning period.

(c) **Budgetary control.** When learning is still taking place, it would be unreasonable to compare actual times with the standard times that ought eventually to be achieved when the learning effect wears off. **Allowance should be made** accordingly when interpreting labour efficiency variances.

(d) **Cash budgets.** Since the learning effect reduces unit variable costs as more units are produced, it should be allowed for in **cash flow projections**.

(e) **Work scheduling and overtime decisions**. To take full advantage of the learning effect, **idle production time** should be avoided and work scheduling/overtime decisions should pay regard to the expected learning effect.

(f) **Pay**. Where the workforce is paid a **productivity bonus**, the time needed to learn a new production process should be allowed for in calculating the bonus for a period.

(g) **Recruiting new labour**. When a company plans to take on new labour to help with increasing production, the learning curve assumption will have to be reviewed.

(h) **Market share**. The significance of the learning curve is that by increasing its share of the market, a company can benefit from shop-floor, managerial and technological 'learning' to achieve **economies of scale**.

4.11 Limitations of learning curve theory

(a) The learning curve phenomenon is **not always present**.

(b) It assumes **stable conditions** at work which will **enable learning to take place**. This is not always practicable, for example because of **labour turnover**.

(c) It must also assume a certain degree of **motivation** amongst employees.

(d) Breaks between repeating production of an item must not be too long, or workers will **'forget'** and the learning process will have to begin all over again.

(e) It might be difficult to **obtain accurate data** to decide what the learning curve is.

(f) **Workers might not agree** to a gradual reduction in production times per unit.

(g) **Production techniques might change**, or product design alterations might be made, so that it takes a long time for a **'standard'** production method to emerge, to which a learning effect will apply.

5 Applying expected values

Expected values can be used in budgeting to determine the best combination of expected profit and risk.

Key term

> **Probabilistic budgeting** assigns probabilities to different conditions (most likely, worst possible, best possible) to derive an EV of profit.

A company, for example might make the following estimates of profitability for a given budget strategy under consideration.

	Profit/(loss) $'000	Probability
Worst possible outcome	(220)	0.3
Most likely outcome	300	0.6
Best possible outcome	770	0.1

The EV of profit would be calculated as follows.

	Probability	Profit $'000	Expected $'000
Worst possible	0.3	(220)	(66)
Most likely	0.6	300	180
Best possible	0.1	770	77
Expected value of profits			191

5.1 Example: a probabilistic budget

PIB has recently developed a new product, and is planning a marketing strategy for it. A choice must be made between selling the product at a unit price of either $15 or $17.

Estimated sales volumes are as follows.

At price of $15 per unit		At price of $17 per unit	
Sales volume	Probability	Sales volume	Probability
Units		Units	
20,000	0.1	8,000	0.1
30,000	0.6	16,000	0.3
40,000	0.3	20,000	0.3
		24,000	0.3

(a)   Sales promotion costs would be $5,000 at a price of $15 and $12,000 at a price of $17.

(b)   Material costs are $8 per unit.

(c)   Labour and variable production overhead costs will be $5 per unit up to 30,000 units and $5.50 per unit for additional units.

(d)   Fixed production costs will be $38,000.

The management of PIB wish to allow for the risk of each pricing decision before choosing $15 or $17 as the selling price.

Required

Determine which sales price would be preferred if the management selected the alternative which did the following.

(a)   Minimised the worst possible outcome of profit

(b)   Maximised the best possible outcome of profit

Solution

The unit contribution will be as follows.

	Price per unit	
	$15	$17
Up to 30,000 units	$2	$4
Above 30,000 units	$1.50	N/A

Sales price $15

Units of sale '000	Unit contb'n $	Total contb'n $'000	Fixed costs $'000	Profit $'000	Probability	EV of profit $'000
20	2	40	43	(3)	0.1	(0.3)
30	2	60	43	17	0.6	10.2
40	30 @ $2 10 @ $1.50	75	43	32	0.3	9.6
						19.5

Sales price $17

Units of sale '000	Unit contb'n $	Total contb'n $'000	Fixed costs $'000	Profit $'000	Probability	EV of profit $'000
8	4	32	50	(18)	0.1	(1.8)
16	4	64	50	14	0.3	4.2
20	4	80	50	30	0.3	9.0
24	4	96	50	46	0.3	13.8
						25.2

(a)   The price which minimises the worst possible outcome is $15 (with a worst-possible loss of $3,000).

(b)   The price which maximises the best possible outcome is $17 (with a best-possible profit of $46,000).

6 Using spreadsheets in budgeting

> **Spreadsheet packages** can be used to build business **models** to assist the forecasting and planning process. They are particularly useful for 'what if?' analysis.

A spreadsheet is a type of general purpose software package with **many business applications**, not just accounting ones. It **can be used to build a model**, in which data is presented in these **rows and columns**, and it is up to the model builder to determine what data or information should be presented in it, how it should be presented and how the data should be manipulated by the spreadsheet program. The most widely used spreadsheet packages are Lotus 1-2-3 and Excel.

The idea behind a spreadsheet is that the model builder should **construct a model as follows**.

(a) Identify what data goes into each row and column and by **inserting text** (for example, column headings and row identifications).

(b) **Specify how the numerical data in the model should be derived**. Numerical data might be derived using one of the following methods.

- **Insertion into the model via keyboard input**.

- **Calculation from other data in the model** by means of a formula specified within the model itself. The model builder must insert these formulae into the spreadsheet model when it is first constructed.

- **Retrieval from data on a disk file** from another computer application program or module.

6.1 The advantages of spreadsheets

The uses of spreadsheets are really only limited by your imagination, and by the number of rows and columns in the spreadsheet, but some of the more **common accounting applications** are listed below.

- Balance sheets
- Cash flow analysis/forecasting
- General ledger
- Inventory records
- Job cost estimates
- Market share analysis and planning

- Profit projections
- Profit statements
- Project budgeting and control
- Sales projections and records
- Tax estimation

The great value of spreadsheets derives from their **simple format** of rows, columns and worksheets of data, and the ability of the data **users to have direct access themselves** to their spreadsheet model via their own PC. For example, an accountant can construct a cash flow model with a spreadsheet package on the PC on his desk: he can **create** the model, **input** the data, **manipulate** the data and **read or print the output** direct. He will also have fairly **instant access** to the model whenever it is needed, in just the time it takes to load the model into his PC. Spreadsheets therefore bring computer modelling within the everyday reach of data users.

6.2 The disadvantages of spreadsheets

Spreadsheets have disadvantages if they are not properly used.

(a) A **minor error in the design** of a model at any point can **affect the validity of data** throughout the spreadsheet. Such errors can be very difficult to trace.

(b) Even if it is properly designed in the first place, it is very **easy to corrupt** a model by accidentally changing a cell or inputting data in the wrong place.

(c) It is possible to **become over-dependent on them**, so that simple one-off tasks that can be done in seconds with a pen and paper are done on a spreadsheet instead.

(d) The possibility for experimentation with data is so great that it is possible to **lose sight of the original intention** of the spreadsheet.

(e)   Spreadsheets **cannot take account of qualitative factors** since they are invariably difficult to quantify. Decisions should not be made on the basis of quantitative information alone.

In summary, spreadsheets should be seen as a **tool in planning and decision making**. The user must make the decision.

6.3 'What if' analysis

Once a model has been constructed the consequences of changes in any of the variables may be tested by asking **'what if' questions, a form of sensitivity analysis**. For example, a spreadsheet may be used to develop a cash flow model, such as that shown below.

	A	B	C	D
		Month 1	Month 2	Month 3
1				
2	Sales	1,000	1,200	1,440
3	Cost of sales	(650)	(780)	(936)
4	Gross profit	350	420	504
5				
6	Receipts:			
7	Current month	600	720	864
8	Previous month		400	480
9		–	–	–
10		600	1,120	1,344
11	Payments	(650)	(780)	(936)
12		(50)	340	408
13	Balance b/f	–	(50)	290
14	Balance c/f	(50)	290	698

Typical 'what if' questions for sensitivity analysis

(a)   What if the cost of sales is 68% of sales revenue, not 65%?

(b)   What if payment from debtors is received 40% in the month of sale, 50% one month in arrears and 10% two months in arrears, instead of 60% in the month of sale and 40% one month in arrears?

(c)   What if sales growth is only 15% per month, instead of 20% per month?

Using the spreadsheet model, the answers to such questions can be obtained simply and quickly, using the editing facility in the program. The information obtained should provide management with a **better understanding** of what the cash flow position in the future might be, and what **factors are critical** to ensuring that the cash position remains reasonable. For example, it might be found that the cost of sales must remain less than 67% of sales value to achieve a satisfactory cash position.

Chapter Roundup

- Two important quantitative methods the management accountant can use to analyse fixed and variable cost elements from total cost data are the **high-low** and **regression methods.**

- **Scatter diagrams** can be used to estimate the fixed and variable components of costs.

- Forecasting techniques include estimates based on **judgement and experience,** simple **average growth models** and **time series.**

- A **time series** is a series of figures or values recorded over time.

- Regression can be used to find a **trend line,** such as the trend in sales over a number of periods.

- A time series has four components: a **trend, seasonal variations, cyclical variations** and **random variations.**

- **Trend** values can be determined by a process of **moving averages.**

- **Seasonal variations** can be estimated using the **additive** model or the **proportional (multiplicative)** model.

- **Forecasts** can be made by calculating a **trend line** (using moving averages or linear regression), using the trend line to forecast future trend line values, and adjusting these values by the **average seasonal variation** applicable to the future period.

- Errors can be expected in forecasting due to unforeseen changes. This is more likely to happen the further into the future the forecast is for, and the smaller the quantity of data on which the forecast is based.

- **Learning curve theory** may be useful for forecasting production time and labour costs in certain circumstances, although the method has many limitations.

- The formula for the learning curve is $y = ax^b$, where b, the learning coefficient or learning index, is defined as (log of the learning rate/log of 2). The learning curve formula can be used to solve all learning curve scenarios.

- **Expected values** can be used in budgeting to determine the best combination of expected profit and risk.

- **Spreadsheet packages** can be used to build business **models** to assist the forecasting and planning process. They are particularly useful for 'what if?' analysis.

1   If the relationship between production costs and output is connected by the linear relationship y = 75x + 47,000, what is 47,000?

    A   The number of units produced
    B   Total production costs
    C   The production cost if 75 units are produced
    D   The fixed production costs

2   The costs of production runs consist of a mix of fixed and variable elements. The lowest number of production runs during the year was 120 during February, the highest number 150 during October. If the total costs of production runs in February were $80,000 and in October were $95,000, calculate the fixed and variable cost elements.

3   *Fill in the missing words.*

Extrapolation involves using a .... of best .... to predict a value .... the two extreme points of the observed range.

4   What variable is used to signify 'time' in the regression equation y = a + bx when regression analysis is used for forecasting?

    A   x   C   b
    B   a   D   Y

5   Which of the four components of a time series is missing from the list below?

Trend
Seasonal variations
Random variations

6   *Fill in the gaps with the appropriate mathematical symbols.*

Additive model of time series   Y = T .... S .... R
  Seasonal component, S   S = Y .... T
Proportional model of time series   Y = T .... S .... R
  Seasonal component, S   S = Y .... T

7   List five limitations of learning curve theory.

8   *Calculate the EV of revenue using the following information.*

Sales volume	Probability	Selling price	Probability
		$	
10,000	0.2	3.00	0.1
12,000	0.7	3.50	0.1
13,000	0.1	4.50	0.8

1   D   The fixed production costs

2

	Number of runs	Total costs
		$
High	150	95,000
Low	120	80,000
Difference	30	15,000

Variable costs per run = $\dfrac{15,000}{30}$ = $500

Fixed costs = 95,000 − (500 × 150) = $20,000

3   line
    fit
    outside

4   A   The correct answer is x.

5   Cyclical variations

6

Additive model of time series	=	T + S + R
Seasonal component, S	=	Y − T
Proportional model of time series	=	T x S x R
Seasonal component, S	=	Y ÷ T

7   (i)   The learning curve phenomenon is **not always present**.

   (ii)   It assumes **stable conditions** at work which will **enable learning to take place**. This is not always practicable, for example because of **labour turnover**.

   (iii) It must also assume a certain degree of **motivation** amongst employees.

   (iv)   Breaks between repeating production of an item must not be too long, or workers will **'forget'** and the learning process will have to begin all over again.

   (v)   It might be difficult to **obtain accurate data** to decide what the learning curve is.

   (vi)   **Workers might not agree** to a gradual reduction in production times per unit.

   (vii) **Production techniques might change**, or product design alterations might be made, so that it takes a long time for a **'standard'** production method to emerge, to which a learning effect will apply.

8   EV   = ((10,000 × 0.2) + (12,000 × 0.7) + (13,000 × 0.1)) × ((3 × 0.1) + (3.5 × 0.1) + (4.5 × 0.8))
         = 11,700 × $4.25
         = $49,725

Now try the questions below from the Exam Question Bank

Number	Level	Marks	Time
Q14	Introductory	18	32 mins
Q15	Introductory	12	22 mins

Standard costing and variance analysis

11

Budgeting and standard costing

Topic list	Syllabus reference
1 The use of standard costs	D1 (a)
2 Deriving standards	D1 (b)
3 Budgets and standards compared	D1 (d)
4 Allowing for waste and idle time	D1 (d), D2(e)
5 Flexible budgets	D1 (c), (f)
6 The principle of controllability	D1 (e)

Introduction

In this chapter we will be looking at **standard costs** and **standard costing.**

You will have studied standard costing before and have learned about the principles of standard costing and how to calculate a number of cost and sales variances. We obviously look at the topic in more depth for your studies of this syllabus.

We begin this chapter by reviewing the **main principles of standard costing** as well as looking in some detail at the **way in which standard costs are set.**

Flexible budgets are vital for both planning and control and we will look at how they are constructed and their use in the overall budgetary control process.

Study guide

		Intellectual level
D1	**Budgeting and standard costing**	
(a)	Explain the use of standard costs	2
(b)	Outline the methods used to derive standard costs and discuss the different types of cost possible	2
(c)	Explain the importance of flexing budgets in performance management	2
(d)	Prepare budgets and standards that allow for waste and idle time	2
(e)	Explain and apply the principle of controllability in the performance management system	2
(f)	Prepare a flexed budget and comment on its usefulness	2
D2	**Basic variances and operating statements**	
(e)	Explain the possible causes of idle time and waste and suggest methods of control	2

Exam guide

The contents of this chapter are likely to be examined in conjunction with variance analysis, covered in the next chapter.

1 The use of standard costs   12/08

A **standard cost** is an estimated unit cost built up of standards for each cost element (standard resource price and standard resource usage).

Standard costing is principally used to value inventories and cost production and to act as a control device.

1.1 What is a standard cost?

Key term

A **standard cost** is an estimated unit cost.

The standard cost of product 12345 is set out below on a **standard cost card.**

STANDARD COST CARD

Product: the Splodget, No 12345

	Cost	Requirement	$	$
Direct materials				
A	$2.00 per kg	6 kgs	12.00	
B	$3.00 per kg	2 kgs	6.00	
C	$4.00 per litre	1 litre	4.00	
Others			2.00	
				24.00
Direct labour				
Grade I	$4.00 per hour	3 hrs	12.00	
Grade II	$5.40 per hour	5 hrs	27.00	
				39.00
Variable production overheads	$1.00 per hour	8 hrs	8.00	
Fixed production overheads	$3.00 per hour	8 hrs	24.00	
Standard full cost of production				95.00

Notice how it is **built up from standards for each cost element:** standard quantities of materials at standard prices, standard quantities of labour time at standard rates and so on. It is therefore determined by management's estimates of the following.

- The expected prices of materials, labour and expenses
- Efficiency levels in the use of materials and labour
- Budgeted overhead costs and budgeted volumes of activity

We will see how management arrives at these estimates later in the chapter.

But why should management want to prepare standard costs? Obviously to assist with standard costing, but what is the point of standard costing?

1.2 The uses of standard costing

Standard costing has two principal **uses**.

- **To value inventories and cost production** for cost accounting purposes. It is an alternative method of valuation to methods like FIFO and LIFO which you will have covered in your earlier studies.
- **To act as a control device** by establishing standards (expected costs) and comparing actual costs with the expected costs, thus highlighting areas of the organisation which may be out of control.

It can also be used in the following circumstances.

(a) To assist in setting **budgets** and **evaluating managerial performance**.

(b) To enable the principle of **'management by exception'** to be practised. A standard cost, when established, is an average expected unit cost. Because it is only an average, actual results will vary to some extent above and below the average. Only significant differences between actual and standard should be reported.

(c) To provide a prediction of future costs to be used in **decision-making** situations.

(d) To **motivate** staff and management by the provision of challenging targets.

(e) To provide guidance on possible ways of **improving efficiency**.

Although the various uses of standard costing should not be overlooked, we will be concentrating on the control aspect.

1.3 Standard costing as a control technique

Key terms

> **Standard costing** involves the establishment of predetermined estimates of the costs of products or services, the collection of actual costs and the comparison of the actual costs with the predetermined estimates. The predetermined costs are known as standard costs and the difference between standard and actual cost is known as a **variance**. The process by which the total difference between standard and actual results is analysed in known as **variance analysis**.

Question
Standard costing

What are the possible advantages for the control function of an organisation of having a standard costing system?

Answer

(a) Carefully planned standards are an aid to more accurate **budgeting**.

(b) Standard costs provide a **yardstick** against which actual costs can be measured.

(c) The setting of standards involves determining the **best** materials and methods which may lead to economies.

(d) A **target of efficiency** is set for employees to reach and **cost-consciousness** is stimulated.

(e)   Variances can be calculated which enable the principle of **'management by exception'** to be operated. Only the variances which exceed acceptable tolerance limits need to be investigated by management with a view to control action.

(f)   Standard costs and variance analysis can provide a way of **motivation** to managers to achieve better performance. However, care must be taken to distinguish between controllable and non-controllable costs in variance reporting.

1.4 Where standard costing should be used

Standard costing is most suited to mass production and repetitive assembly work.

Although standard costing can be used in a variety of costing situations (batch and mass production, process manufacture, jobbing manufacture (where there is standardisation of parts) and service industries (if a realistic cost unit can be established)), the **greatest benefit** from its use can be gained if there is a **degree of repetition** in the production process so that average or expected usage of resources can be determined. It is therefore most suited to **mass production** and **repetitive assembly work** and less suited to organisations which produce to customer demand and requirements.

Question   Standard service costing

Can you think of a service organisation that could apply standard costing?

Answer

One example could be restaurants which deal with standard recipes for meals. If a large number of meals are produced, say, for conference delegates, mass production systems will apply. Standards may not be calculated with the same accuracy as in manufacturing environments, but the principles are still relevant. Other examples are equally valid.

Exam focus point

The examiner is interested in whether a standard is 'meaningful'. Standards can be set for everything but not all would have meaning.

2 Deriving standards

The **responsibility for deriving standard costs** should be shared between **managers able to provide the necessary information** about levels of expected efficiency, prices and overhead costs.

2.1 Setting standards for materials costs

Direct materials costs per unit of raw material will be estimated by the purchasing department from their knowledge of the following.

- Purchase contracts already agreed
- Pricing discussions with regular suppliers
- The forecast movement of prices in the market
- The availability of bulk purchase discounts
- The quality of material required by the production departments

The standard cost ought to include an allowance for **bulk purchase discounts**, if these are available on all or some of the purchases, and it may have to be a weighted average price of the differing prices charged for the same product by alternative suppliers.

A decision must also be taken as to how to deal with price **inflation**. Suppose that a material costs $10 per kilogram at the moment, and during the course of the next 12 months, it is expected to go up in price by 20% to $12 per kilogram. What standard price should be selected?

(a)   If the **current price** of $10 per kilogram **were used in the standard**, the reported price variance would become adverse as soon as prices go up, which might be very early in the year. If prices go up gradually rather than in one big jump, it would be difficult to select an appropriate time for revising the standard.

(b)   If an **estimated mid-year price** of, say, $11 per kilogram **were used**, price variances should be favourable in the first half of the year and adverse in the second half, again assuming that prices go up gradually. Management could only really check that in any month, the price variance did not become excessively adverse (or favourable) and that the price variance switched from being favourable to adverse around month six or seven and not sooner.

Standard costing is therefore more **difficult in times of inflation but it is still worthwhile.**

*   Usage and efficiency variances will still be meaningful
*   Inflation is measurable: there is no reason why its effects cannot be removed
*   Standard costs can be revised, so long as this is not done too frequently

2.2 Setting standards for labour costs

Direct labour rates per hour will be set by reference to the payroll and to any agreements on pay rises with trade union representatives of the employees. A separate hourly rate or weekly wage will be set for each different labour grade/type of employee and an average hourly rate will be applied for each grade (even though individual rates of pay may vary according to age and experience).

Similar problems to those which arise when setting material standards in times of high inflation can be met when setting labour standards.

2.3 Setting standards for material usage and labour efficiency

To estimate the materials required to make each product (material usage) and also the labour hours required (labour efficiency), technical specifications must be prepared for each product by production experts (either in the production department or the work study department).

2.4 Setting standards for overheads

When standard costs are fully absorbed costs (standard costs can be used in both marginal and absorption costing systems), the **absorption rate** of fixed production overheads will be **predetermined** and **based on budgeted** fixed production **overhead** and planned **production volume**.

Production volume will depend on two factors.

(a)   **Production capacity** (or 'volume capacity') measured perhaps in standard hours of output (a standard hour being the amount of work achievable at standard efficiency levels in an hour), which in turn reflects direct production labour hours.

(b)   **Efficiency of working**, by labour or machines, allowing for rest time and contingency allowances.

Suppose that a department has a work force of ten men, each of whom works a 36 hour week to make standard units, and each unit has a standard time of two hours to make. The expected efficiency of the work-force is 125%.

(a)   Budgeted capacity, in direct labour hours, would be 10 × 36 = 360 production hours per week.

(b)   Budgeted efficiency is 125% so that the work-force should take only 1 hour of actual production time to produce 1.25 standard hours of output.

(c)   This means in our example that budgeted output is 360 production hours × 125% = 450 standard hours of output per week. At 2 standard hours per unit, this represents production activity or volume of 225 units of output per week.

Question   Budgeted output

ABC carries out routine office work in a sales order processing department, and all tasks in the department have been given standard times. There are 40 clerks in the department who work on average 140 hours per month each. The efficiency ratio of the department is 110%.

Required

Calculate the budgeted output in the department.

Answer

Capacity	= 40 × 140 = 5,600 hours per month
Efficiency	= 110%
Budgeted output	= 5,600 × 110% = 6,160 standard hours of work per month.

2.5 Setting standards for sales price and margin

The **standard selling price** will depend on a number of factors including the following.

- Anticipated market demand
- Competing products
- Manufacturing costs
- Inflation estimates

The **standard sales margin** is the difference between the standard cost and the standard selling price.

Question   Standard setting

What problems do you think could occur when standards are being set?

Answer

The following problems can occur when setting standards.

(a)   Deciding how to incorporate **inflation** into planned unit costs

(b)   Agreeing on a **performance standard** (attainable or ideal)

(c)   Deciding on the **quality** of materials to be used (a better quality of material will cost more, but perhaps reduce material wastage)

(d)   Estimating materials prices where **seasonal price variations** or **bulk purchase discounts** may be significant

(e)   Finding sufficient **time** to construct standards as standard setting can be time consuming

(f)   Incurring the **cost** of setting up and maintaining a system for establishing standards

2.6 Types of standard

FAST FORWARD

> There are four **types of standard: ideal, attainable, current** and **basic**. These can have an impact on employee motivation.

How demanding should a standard be? Should the standard represent perfect performance or easily attainable performance? There are four types of standard.

An **ideal standard** is a standard which can be attained under perfect operating conditions: no wastage, no inefficiencies, no idle time, no breakdowns

An **attainable standard** is a standard which can be attained if production is carried out efficiently, machines are properly operated and/or materials are properly used. Some allowance is made for wastage and inefficiencies

A **current standard** is standard based on current working conditions (current wastage, current inefficiencies)

A **basic standard** is a long-term standard which remains unchanged over the years and is used to show trends

The **different types of standard have a number of advantages and disadvantages.**

(a) **Ideal standards** can be seen as **long-term targets** but are not very useful for day-to-day control purposes.

(b) **Ideal standards cannot be achieved**. If such standards are used for budgeting, an allowance will have to be included to make the budget realistic and attainable.

(c) **Attainable standards** can be used for **product costing**, cost control, inventory valuation, estimating and as a basis for budgeting.

(d) **Current standards** or attainable standards provide the **best basis for budgeting**, because they represent an achievable level of productivity.

(e) Current standards **do not attempt to improve** on current levels of efficiency.

(f) **Current standards** are useful during **periods when inflation is high**. They can be set on a month by month basis.

(g) **Basic standards** are used to show **changes in efficiency or performance** over a long period of time. They are perhaps the least useful and least common type of standard in use.

2.6.1 The impact on employee behaviour of the type of standard set

The type of standard set can have an impact on the behaviour of the employees trying to achieve those standards.

Type of standard	Impact
Ideal	Some say that they provide employees with an **incentive to be more efficient** even though it is highly unlikely that the standard will be achieved. Others argue that they are likely to have an unfavourable effect on employee motivation because the differences between standards and actual results will always be adverse. The **employees may feel that the goals are unattainable** and so **they will not work so hard**.
Attainable	Might be an **incentive to work harder** as they provide a **realistic but challenging target of efficiency**.
Current	**Will not motivate employees to do anything more than they are currently doing**.
Basic	May have an **unfavourable impact** on the motivation of employees. Over time they will discover that they are easily able to achieve the standards. They may become bored and lose interest in what they are doing if they have nothing to aim for.

3 Budgets and standards compared

Budgets and standards are very similar and interrelated, but there are important differences between them.

You will recall from previous chapters that a **budget** is a **quantified monetary plan** for a future period, which managers will try to achieve. Its major function lies in **communicating plans** and **coordinating activities** within an organisation.

On the other hand, a **standard** is a **carefully predetermined quantity target** which can be **achieved in certain conditions**.

Budgets and standards are **similar** in the following ways.

(a) They both involve looking to the future and **forecasting** what is likely to happen given a certain set of circumstances.

(b) They are both **used for control purposes**. A budget aids control by setting financial targets or limits for a forthcoming period. Actual achievements or expenditures are then compared with the budgets and action is taken to correct any variances where necessary. A standard also achieves control by comparison of actual results against a predetermined target.

As well as being similar, **budgets and standards are interrelated**. For example, a standard unit production cost can act as the basis for a production cost budget. The unit cost is multiplied by the budgeted activity level to arrive at the budgeted expenditure on production costs.

There are, however, **important differences between budgets and standards**.

Budgets	Standards
Gives planned total aggregate costs for a function or cost centre	Shows the unit resource usage for a single task, for example the standard labour hours for a single unit of production
Can be prepared for all functions, even where output cannot be measured	Limited to situations where repetitive actions are performed and output can be measured
Expressed in money terms	Need not be expressed in money terms. For example a standard rate of output does not need a financial value put on it

4 Allowing for waste and idle time

In the exam you may be asked to deal with a situation in which not all resources are actually used to make saleable products.

4.1 Wastage

The amount of raw material used to meet the budgeted production level might be **less** than the amount of raw material contained in the finished products for a number of reasons.

- Evaporation
- Spillage
- Natural wastage (such as the skin of fruit used to make fruit juice)

This wastage can be built into an **attainable materials standard** and adjustments can be made to **materials budgets**.

If the wastage occurs **before** production commences, the **materials purchases budget** must be adjusted. If the wastage occurs **during** production, the **materials usage budget** must be adjusted.

4.1.1 Example: wastage in budgets

The production quantities required for each of the first four periods of the year are as follows.

Production budget – units

Period 1	Period 2	Period 3	Period 4
10,204	13,010	14,796	12,755

From the standard cost card it is determined that each unit of production requires 2 kg of raw material X. However we also know that the production process has a normal loss of 20% of the materials input into the process.

This means that although each unit of product requires 2 kg of material X, this represents only 80% of the actual amount required. 25% (100/80) more than 2 kg per unit must be input into the process. The amount of material X required for each unit is therefore:

2 kg × 100/80 = 2.5 kg

The amount of normal loss can be calculated separately as:

2 kg × 20/80 = 0.5 kg

The materials usage budget can now be prepared.

Materials usage budget

	Period 1	Period 2	Period 3	Period 4
Quantity of production	10,204	13,010	14,796	12,755
Materials usage (quantity × 2.5 kg)	25,510 kg	32,525 kg	36,990 kg	31,888 kg

Question

A business requires 15,400 units of production in a period and each unit uses 5 kg of raw materials. The production process has a normal loss of 10% during the production process. What is the total amount of the raw material required for the period?

Answer

		Kg
Kg required for production	5 × 15,400	77,000
Additional for normal loss	77,000 × 10/90	8,556
Required usage	15,400 × 5 × 100/90	85,556

4.2 Idle time

A workforce that is expected to work at a particular level of efficiency may not always be able to achieve this. **Idle time** may be caused by machine breakdowns or not having enough work to give to employees, perhaps because of bottlenecks in production or a shortage of orders for customers.

Idle time can again be built into an **attainable labour hours standard** and adjustments can be made to the **labour budget**.

4.2.1 Example: idle time and standards

A machine has running costs of $60 per hour and typically incurs 5% non-productive time. To get 60 minutes of output (a standard hour) would take 60 ÷ (100 − 5)% = 63.16 minutes. The **standard cost of production** or **cost of idle time** is therefore $63.16 per hour.

4.2.2 Example: idle time and the labour usage budget

The standard cost card for the Stephenson shows that the standard time for production of one unit is 1 grade A labour hour. However due to necessary break times only 80% of the time paid is productive, that is there is 20% idle time.

To calculate the number of hours of labour required, again the starting point will be the production budget showing the number of units to be produced in each period. However the number of hours that must be paid in total in order to produce one unit is:

1 hour × 100/80 = 1.25 hours

The idle time per product can be calculated as 1 hour $\times \dfrac{20}{80} = 0.25$ hours.

Production budget

	Period 1	Period 2	Period 3	Period 4
Quantity of production	10,204	13,010	14,796	12,755

Labour usage budget – hours

	Period 1	Period 2	Period 3	Period 4
Labour hours	12,755 hrs	16,263 hrs	18,495 hrs	15,944 hrs

 Question   Idle time

A product requires 10 labour hours for each unit. However 10% of working hours are idle time. How long must an employee be paid for in order to produce 20 units?

Answer

Standard time	20 units × 10 hours	200
Additional time	200 × 10/90	22
Total time required	20 × 10 × 100/90	222

5 Flexible budgets

FAST FORWARD

> Comparison of a fixed budget with the actual results for a different level of activity is of little use for control purposes. **Flexible budgets** should be used to show what cost and revenues should have been for the actual level of activity.

Key term

> A **flexible budget** is a budget which, by recognising different cost behaviour patterns, is designed to change as volume of activity changes.

If you previously studied F2, you will be familiar with this material.

5.1 Preparing a flexible budget

Step 1 The first step in the preparation of a flexible budget is the **determination of cost behaviour patterns**, which means **deciding whether costs are fixed, variable or semi-variable**.

Step 2 The second step in the preparation of a flexible budget is to calculate the **budget cost allowance** for each cost item.

Budget cost allowance = budgeted fixed cost* + (number of units × variable cost per unit)**

* nil for variable cost
** nil for fixed cost

Semi-variable costs therefore need splitting into their fixed and variable components so that the budget cost allowance can be calculated. One method for splitting semi-variable costs is the high/low method, which we covered in Chapter 10.

5.2 Example: preparing a flexible budget

(a) Prepare a budget for 20X6 for the direct labour costs and overhead expenses of a production department flexed at the activity levels of 80%, 90% and 100%, using the information listed below.

   (i) The direct labour hourly rate is expected to be $3.75.

   (ii) 100% activity represents 60,000 direct labour hours.

   (iii) *Variable costs*

Indirect labour	$0.75 per direct labour hour
Consumable supplies	$0.375 per direct labour hour
Canteen and other welfare services	6% of direct and indirect labour costs

   (iv) Semi-variable costs are expected to relate to the direct labour hours in the same manner as for the last five years.

Year	Direct labour hours	Semi-variable costs $
20X1	64,000	20,800
20X2	59,000	19,800
20X3	53,000	18,600
20X4	49,000	17,800
20X5	40,000 (estimate)	16,000 (estimate)

   (v) *Fixed costs*

	$
Depreciation	18,000
Maintenance	10,000
Insurance	4,000
Rates	15,000
Management salaries	25,000

   (vi) Inflation is to be ignored.

(b) Calculate the budget cost allowance (ie expected expenditure) for 20X6 assuming that 57,000 direct labour hours are worked.

Solution

(a)

	80% level 48,000 hrs $'000	90% level 54,000 hrs $'000	100% level 60,000 hrs $'000
Direct labour	180.00	202.50	225.0
Other variable costs			
Indirect labour	36.00	40.50	45.0
Consumable supplies	18.00	20.25	22.5
Canteen etc	12.96	14.58	16.2
Total variable costs ($5.145 per hour)	246.96	277.83	308.7
Semi-variable costs (W)	17.60	18.80	20.0
Fixed costs			
Depreciation	18.00	18.00	18.0
Maintenance	10.00	10.00	10.0
Insurance	4.00	4.00	4.0
Rates	15.00	15.00	15.0
Management salaries	25.00	25.00	25.0
Budgeted costs	336.56	368.63	400.7

Working

Using the high/low method:

		$
Total cost of 64,000 hours		20,800
Total cost of 40,000 hours		16,000
Variable cost of 24,000 hours		4,800
Variable cost per hour ($4,800/24,000)		$0.20

		$
Total cost of 64,000 hours		20,800
Variable cost of 64,000 hours (× $0.20)		12,800
Fixed costs		8,000

Semi-variable costs are calculated as follows.

			$
60,000 hours	(60,000 × $0.20) + $8,000	=	20,000
54,000 hours	(54,000 × $0.20) + $8,000	=	18,800
48,000 hours	(48,000 × $0.20) + $8,000	=	17,600

(b)   The budget cost allowance for 57,000 direct labour hours of work would be as follows.

		$
Variable costs	(57,000 × $5.145)	293,265
Semi-variable costs	($8,000 + (57,000 × $0.20))	19,400
Fixed costs		72,000
		384,665

5.3 Flexible budgets and performance management

Budgetary control involves drawing up budgets for the areas of responsibility for individual managers (for example production managers, purchasing managers and so on) and of regularly **comparing** actual results against expected results. The differences between actual results and expected results are called **variances** and these are used to provide a guideline for control action by individual managers.

Note that individual managers are held responsible for investigating differences between budgeted and actual results, and are then expected to take corrective action or amend the plan in the light of actual events.

The wrong approach to budgetary control is to compare actual results against a fixed budget. Suppose that a company manufactures a single product, Z. Budgeted results and actual results for June 20X2 are shown below.

	Budget	Actual results	Variance
Production and sales of the cloud (units)	2,000	3,000	
	$	$	$
Sales revenue (a)	20,000	30,000	10,000 (F)
Direct materials	6,000	8,500	2,500 (A)
Direct labour	4,000	4,500	500 (A)
Maintenance	1,000	1,400	400 (A)
Depreciation	2,000	2,200	200 (A)
Rent and rates	1,500	1,600	100 (A)
Other costs	3,600	5,000	1,400 (A)
Total costs (b)	18,100	23,200	5,100
Profit (a) – (b)	1,900	6,800	4,900 (F)

(a)   Here the variances are **meaningless** for control purposes. Costs were higher than budget because the output volume was also higher; variable costs would be expected to increase above the costs budgeted in the fixed budget. There is no information to show whether control action is needed for any aspect of costs or revenue.

(b)   For control purposes, it is necessary to know the following.

    (i)   Were actual costs higher than they should have been to produce and sell 3,000 Zs?
    (ii)   Was actual revenue satisfactory from the sale of 3,000 Zs?

The **correct approach to budgetary control** is as follows.

(a)   **Identify fixed and variable costs**
(b)   **Produce a flexible budget using marginal costing techniques**

Let's suppose that we have the following estimates of cost behaviour for the company.

(a)   Direct materials, direct labour and maintenance costs are variable.
(b)   Rent and rates and depreciation are fixed costs.
(c)   Other costs consist of fixed costs of $1,600 plus a variable cost of $1 per unit made and sold.

Now that the cost behaviour patterns are known, a budget cost allowance can be calculated for each item of expenditure. This allowance is shown in a **flexible budget** as the expected expenditure on each item for the relevant level of activity. The budget cost allowances are calculated as follows.

(a)   Variable cost allowances   = original budgets × (3,000 units/2,000 units)

    eg material cost allowance   = $6,000 × ³/₂ = $9,000

(b)   Fixed cost allowances   = as original budget

(c)   Semi-fixed cost allowances   = original budgeted fixed costs

                                      + (3,000 units × variable cost per unit)

    eg other cost allowances   = $1,600 + (3,000 × $1) = $4,600

The budgetary control analysis should be as follows.

	Fixed budget (a)	Flexible budget (b)	Actual results (c)	Budget variance (b) – (c)
Production and sales (units)	2,000	3,000	3,000	
	$	$	$	$
Sales revenue	20,000	30,000	30,000	0
Variable costs				
Direct materials	6,000	9,000	8,500	500 (F)
Direct labour	4,000	6,000	4,500	1,500 (F)
Maintenance	1,000	1,500	1,400	100 (F)
Semi-variable costs				
Other costs	3,600	4,600	5,000	400 (A)
Fixed costs				
Depreciation	2,000	2,000	2,200	200 (A)
Rent and rates	1,500	1,500	1,600	100 (A)
Total costs	18,100	24,600	23,200	1,400 (F)
Profit	1,900	5,400	6,800	1,400 (F)

Note. **(F) denotes a favourable variance** and **(A) an adverse or unfavourable variance.**

We can **analyse** the above as follows.

(a)   In selling 3,000 units the expected profit should have been, not the fixed budget profit of $1,900, but the flexible budget profit of $5,400. Instead, actual profit was $6,800 ie $1,400 more than we should have expected. One of the reasons for the improvement is that, **given output and sales** of 3,000 units, **costs were lower than expected** (and sales revenue exactly as expected).

	$
Direct materials cost variance	500 (F)
Direct labour cost variance	1,500 (F)
Maintenance cost variance	100 (F)
Other costs variance	400 (A)
Fixed cost variances	
Depreciation	200 (A)
Rent and rates	100 (A)
	1,400 (F)

(b) Another reason for the improvement in profit above the fixed budget profit is the **sales volume** (3,000 Zs were sold instead of 2,000).

	$	$
Sales revenue increased by		10,000
Variable costs increased by:		
Direct materials	3,000	
Direct labour	2,000	
Maintenance	500	
Variable element of other costs	1,000	
Fixed costs are unchanged		6,500
Profit increased by		3,500

Profit was therefore increased by $3,500 because sales volumes increased.

(c) A full variance analysis statement would be as follows.

	$	$
Fixed budget profit		1,900
Variances		
Sales volume	3,500 (F)	
Direct materials cost	500 (F)	
Direct labour cost	1,500 (F)	
Maintenance cost	100 (F)	
Other costs	400 (A)	
Depreciation	200 (A)	
Rent and rates	100 (A)	
		4,900 (F)
Actual profit		6,800

If management believes that any of these variances are large enough to justify it, they will investigate the reasons for them to see whether any corrective action is necessary or whether the plan needs amending in the light of actual events.

Question	Budget preparation

The budgeted and actual results of Crunch Co for September were as follows. The company uses a marginal costing system. There were no opening or closing stocks.

	Fixed budget		*Actual*	
Sales and production	1,000 units		700 units	
	$	$	$	$
Sales		20,000		14,200
Variable cost of sales				
Direct materials	8,000		5,200	
Direct labour	4,000		3,100	
Variable overhead	2,000		1,500	
		14,000		9,800
Contribution		6,000		4,400
Fixed costs		5,000		5,400
Profit/(loss)		1,000		(1,000)

Required

Prepare a budget that will be useful for management control purposes.

Answer

We need to prepare a **flexible budget for 700 units.**

	Budget 1,000 units	Per unit	Flexed budget 700 units	Actual 700 units	Variances
	$	$	$	$	$
Sales	20,000	(20)	14,000	14,200	200 (F)
Variable costs					
Direct material	8,000	(8)	5,600	5,200	400 (F)
Direct labour	4,000	(4)	2,800	3,100	300 (A)
Variable production overhead	2,000	(2)	1,400	1,500	100 (A)
	14,000	(14)	9,800	9,800	
Contribution	6,000		4,200	4,400	
Fixed costs	5,000	(N/A)	5,000	5,400	400 (A)
Profit/(loss)	1,000		(800)	(1,000)	200 (A)

By **flexing** the budget in the question above we **removed the effect on sales revenue of the difference between budgeted sales volume and actual sales volume.** But there is still a variance of $200 (F). This means that the actual *selling price* must have been different to the budgeted selling price, resulting in a $200 (F) **selling price variance**.

5.4 Factors to consider when preparing flexible budgets

The mechanics of flexible budgeting are, in theory, fairly straightforward but in practice there are a number of points to consider before figures are simply flexed.

(a)   Splitting mixed costs is not always straightforward.

(b)   Fixed costs may behave in a step-line fashion as activity levels increase/decrease.

(c)   Account must be taken of the assumptions upon which the original fixed budget was based. Such assumptions might include the constraint posed by limiting factors, the rate of inflation, judgements about future uncertainty, the demand for the organisation's products and so on.

(d)   By flexing a budget, a manager is effectively saying "If I knew then what I know now, this is the budget I would have set". It is a useful concept but can lead to some concern as managers can become confused and frustrated if faced with continually moving targets.

5.5 The need for flexible budgets

We have seen that flexible budgets may be prepared in order to plan for variations in the level of activity above or below the level set in the fixed budget. It has been suggested, however, that since many cost items in modern industry are fixed costs, the **value** of flexible budgets in planning is dwindling.

(a)   In many manufacturing industries, plant costs (depreciation, rent and so on) are a very large proportion of total costs, and these tend to be fixed costs.

(b)   Wage costs also tend to be fixed, because employees are generally guaranteed a basic wage for a working week of an agreed number of hours.

(c)   With the growth of service industries, labour (wages or fixed salaries) and overheads will account for most of the costs of a business, and direct materials will be a relatively small proportion of total costs.

Flexible budgets are nevertheless necessary, and even if they are not used at the planning stage, they must be used for budgetary control variance analysis.

6 The principle of controllability

The **principle of controllability** is that managers of responsibility centres should only be held accountable for costs over which they have some influence.

6.1 Budget centres

Budgetary control is based around a system of **budget centres**. Each budget centre will have its own budget and a manager will be responsible for managing the budget centre and ensuring that the budget is met.

The selection of budget centres in an organisation is therefore a key first step in setting up a control system. What should the budget centres be? What income, expenditure and/or capital employment plans should each budget centre prepare? And how will measures of performance for each budget centre be made?

A well-organised system of control should have the following features.

Feature	Explanation
A hierarchy of budget centres	If the organisation is quite large a hierarchy is needed. Subsidiary companies, departments and work sections might be budget centres. Budgets of each section would then be consolidated into a departmental budget, departmental budgets in turn would be consolidated into the subsidiary's budget, and the budgets of each subsidiary would be **combined into a master budget** for the group as a whole.
Clearly identified responsibilities for achieving budget targets	Individual managers should be made responsible for achieving the budget targets of a particular budget centre.
Responsibilities for revenues, costs and capital employed	Budget centres should be organised so that all the revenues earned by an organisation, all the costs it incurs, and all the capital it employs are made the responsibility of someone within the organisation, at an appropriate level of authority in the management hierarchy.

Budgetary control and budget centres are therefore part of the overall system of **responsibility accounting** within an organisation.

Key term

Responsibility accounting is a system of accounting that segregates revenue and costs into areas of personal responsibility in order to monitor and assess the performance of each part of an organisation.

6.2 Controllable costs

Controllable costs are items of expenditure which can be directly influenced by a given manager within a given time span.

Care must be taken to distinguish between controllable costs and uncontrollable costs in variance reporting. The **controllability principle** is that managers of responsibility centres should only be held accountable for costs over which they have some influence. From a **motivation** point of view this is important because it can be very demoralising for managers who feel that their performance is being judged on the basis of something over which they have no influence. It is also important from a **control** point of view in that control reports should ensure that information on costs is reported to the manager who is able to take action to control them.

Responsibility accounting attempts to associate costs, revenues, assets and liabilities with the managers most capable of controlling them. As a system of accounting, it therefore distinguishes between controllable and uncontrollable costs.

Most **variable costs** within a department are thought to be **controllable in the short term** because managers can influence the efficiency with which resources are used, even if they cannot do anything to raise or lower price levels.

A cost which is not controllable by a junior manager might be controllable by a senior manager. For example, there may be high direct labour costs in a department caused by excessive overtime working. The junior manager may feel obliged to continue with the overtime to meet production schedules, but his senior may be able to reduce costs by hiring extra full-time staff, thereby reducing the requirements for overtime.

A cost which is not controllable by a manager in one department may be controllable by a manager in another department. For example, an increase in material costs may be caused by buying at higher prices than expected (controllable by the purchasing department) or by excessive wastage (controllable by the production department) or by a faulty machine producing rejects (controllable by the maintenance department).

Some costs are **non-controllable**, such as increases in expenditure items due to inflation. Other costs are **controllable, but in the long term rather than the short term**. For example, production costs might be reduced by the introduction of new machinery and technology, but in the short term, management must attempt to do the best they can with the resources and machinery at their disposal.

6.2.1 The controllability of fixed costs

It is often assumed that all fixed costs are non-controllable in the short run. This is not so.

(a) **Committed fixed costs** are those costs arising from the possession of plant, equipment, buildings and an administration department to **support the long-term needs of the business**. These costs (depreciation, rent, administration salaries) are largely **non-controllable in the short term** because they have been committed by longer-term decisions affecting longer-term needs. When a company decides to cut production drastically, the long-term committed fixed costs will be reduced, but only after redundancy terms have been settled and assets sold.

(b) **Discretionary fixed costs**, such as advertising and research and development costs, are incurred as a result of a top management decision, but could be **raised or lowered at fairly short notice** (irrespective of the actual volume of production and sales).

6.2.2 Controllability and apportioned costs

Managers should only be held accountable for costs over which they have some influence. This may seem quite straightforward in theory, but it is not always so easy in practice to distinguish controllable from uncontrollable costs. **Apportioned overhead costs provide a good example.**

Suppose that a manager of a production department in a manufacturing company is made responsible for the costs of his department. These costs include **directly attributable overhead items** such as the costs of indirect labour employed and indirect materials consumed in the department. The department's overhead costs also include an apportionment of costs from other cost centres, such as rent and rates for the building it shares with other departments and a share of the costs of the maintenance department.

Should the production manager be held accountable for any of these apportioned costs?

(a) Managers should not be held accountable for costs over which they have no control. In this example, apportioned rent and rates costs would not be controllable by the production department manager.

(b) Managers should be held accountable for costs over which they have some influence. In this example, it is the responsibility of the maintenance department manager to keep maintenance costs within budget. But their costs will be partly variable and partly fixed, and the variable cost element will depend on the volume of demand for their services. If the production department's staff treat their equipment badly we might expect higher repair costs, and the production department manager should therefore be made accountable for the repair costs that his department makes the maintenance department incur on its behalf.

(c) Charging the production department with some of the costs of the maintenance department prevents the production department from viewing the maintenance services as 'free services'. Over-use would be discouraged and the production manager is more likely to question the activities of the maintenance department possibly resulting in a reduction in maintenance costs or the provision of more efficient maintenance services.

6.2.3 Controllability and dual responsibility

Quite often a particular cost might be the **responsibility of two or more managers**. For example, raw materials costs might be the responsibility of the purchasing manager (prices) and the production manager (usage). A **reporting system must allocate responsibility appropriately**. The purchasing manager must be responsible for any increase in raw materials prices whereas the production manager should be responsible for any increase in raw materials usage.

Attention!

> You can see that there are **no clear cut rules** as to which costs are controllable and which are not. Each situation and cost must be reviewed separately and a decision taken according to the control value of the information and its behavioural impact.

Chapter Roundup

- A **standard cost** is an estimated unit cost built up of standards for each cost element (standard resource price and standard resource usage).
  Standard costing is principally used to value inventories and cost production and to act as a control device.

- Standard costing is most suited to mass production and repetitive assembly work.

- The **responsibility for deriving standard costs** should be shared between **managers able to provide the necessary information** about levels of expected efficiency, prices and overhead costs.

- There are four **types of standard: ideal, attainable, current** and **basic**. These can have an impact on employee motivation.

- Budgets and standards are very similar and interrelated, but there are important differences between them.

- Comparison of a fixed budget with the actual results for a different level of activity is of little use for control purposes. **Flexible budgets** should be used to show what cost and revenues should have been for the actual level of activity.

- The **principle of controllability** is that managers of responsibility centres should only be held accountable for costs over which they have some influence.

- **Controllable costs** are items of expenditure which can be directly influenced by a given manager within a given time span.

Quick Quiz

1 Choose the appropriate words from those highlighted.

The **greatest/least** benefit from the use of standard costing can be gained if there is a degree of repetition in the production process.

Standard costing is therefore **most/less** suited to organisations which produce to customer demand and requirements and **most/less** suited to mass production.

2 *Match the type of standard with the correct definition.*

Types of standard	Definitions	
Ideal	(a)	Can be attained under perfect operating conditions
Attainable	(b)	Can be attained if production is carried out efficiently, machines are properly operated and/or materials are properly used
Basic		
Current	(c)	Based on current working conditions
	(d)	Remains unchanged over the years and is used to show trends

3 *Fill in the blanks.*

Standard costing is difficult in times of inflation but it is still worthwhile.

(a) .... and .... variances will still be meaningful.

(b) Inflation is .... : there is no reason why its effects cannot be removed.

(c) Standard costs can be .... , as long as this is not done ....

4 Provide three reasons why standard costing conflicts with schemes of continuous improvement and cost reduction programmes.

5 With what kind of standards is practical capacity associated?

6 Ideal standards are long-term targets.

☐ True   ☐ False

7 *Fill in the gaps.*

A flexible budget is a budget which, by recognising .... , is designed to .... as the level of activity changes.

8 An extract of the costs incurred at two different activity levels is shown. Classify the costs according to their behaviour patterns and show the budget cost allowance for an activity of 1,500 units.

	1,000 units	2,000 units	Type of cost	Budget cost allowance for 1,500 units
	$	$		$
Fuel	3,000	6,000	....	....
Photocopying	9,500	11,000	....	....
Heating	2,400	2,400	....	....
Direct wages	6,000	8,000	....	....

9 *Fill in the blanks.*

A well-organised system of control should have the following features.

(a) A hierarchy of ....

(b) Clearly identified .... for achieving budget targets

(c) Responsibilities for .... , ... and ....

10   Which of the following are not controllable by a production department manager?

    (a)   Direct labour rate

    (b)   Variable production overheads

    (c)   Apportioned canteen costs

    (d)   Increases in raw material costs due to inflation

    (e)   Increases in overall material costs due to high levels of wastage caused by poor supervision of production workers

    (f)   An increase in the level of idle time because of poorly-maintained machines

    (g)   Depreciation

    (h)   Advertising for production workers

Answers to Quick Quiz

1   greatest
     less
     most

2   Ideal   (a)   Basic   (d)
     Attainable   (b)   Current   (c)

3   (a)   Usage and efficiency variances will still be meaningful.
     (b)   Inflation is measurable: there is no reason why its effects cannot be removed.
     (c)   Standard costs can be reviewed, as long as this is not done too frequently.

4   (a)   Efforts to improve the efficiency of operations or reduce costs will alter quantities of inputs, prices and so on whereas standard costing is best used in a stable, standardised, repetitive environment.
     (b)   Predetermined standards conflict with a philosophy of continual improvement.
     (c)   Standard costs often incorporate a planned level of scrap in material standards. This is at odds with the aim of 'zero defects' inherent in continuous improvement programmes.

5   Attainable standards

6   True

7   cost behaviour patterns
     flex or change

8   Variable $4,500   Fixed $2,400
     Semi-variable $10,250   Semi-variable $7,000

9   (a)   budget centres   (c)   revenues
     (b)   responsibilities   costs
                                                    capital employed

10   (a)
     (c)
     (d)
     (f)   (if there is a maintenance department)
     (g)
     (h)

Now try the questions below from the Exam Question Bank

Number	Level	Marks	Time
Q16	Examination	20	36 mins

Variance analysis

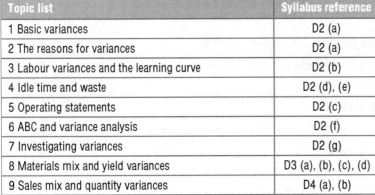

Topic list	Syllabus reference
1 Basic variances	D2 (a)
2 The reasons for variances	D2 (a)
3 Labour variances and the learning curve	D2 (b)
4 Idle time and waste	D2 (d), (e)
5 Operating statements	D2 (c)
6 ABC and variance analysis	D2 (f)
7 Investigating variances	D2 (g)
8 Materials mix and yield variances	D3 (a), (b), (c), (d)
9 Sales mix and quantity variances	D4 (a), (b)

Introduction

The **actual results** achieved by an organisation will, more than likely, be **different from the expected results** (the expected results being the standard costs and revenues which we looked at in the previous chapter). These differences are **variances** which you will have covered in your earlier studies.

We will revise the basic variances and their presentation in operating statements.

We will go on to look at more complicated variances which are more likely to be examined in F5. For example, when a product requires two or more materials in its make-up, the **materials usage variance** can be split into a materials **mix variance** and a materials **yield variance.** Similarly, the **sales volume variance** can be split into a sales **mix variance** and a sales **quantity variance.**

The management accountant would not stop at the calculation of variances. The next step would be to identify which warrant investigation and then to look into the reasons behind them. We suggest reasons for different types of variances and also highlight the way in which they inter-relate; the cause of a variance on one cost can often have an impact on another cost variance.

Study guide

		Intellectual level
D2	**Basic variances and operating statements**	
(a)	Calculate, identify the cause of and interpret basic variances: (i) Sales price and volume (ii) Materials total, price and usage (iii) Labour total, rate and efficiency (iv) Variable overhead total, expenditure and efficiency (v) Fixed overhead total, expenditure and, where appropriate, volume, capacity and efficiency	1
(b)	Explain the effect on labour variances where the learning curve has been used in the budget process	2
(c)	Produce full operating statements in both a marginal cost and full absorption costing environment, reconciling actual profit to budgeted profit	2
(d)	Calculate the effect of idle time and waste on variances including where idle time has been budgeted for	2
(e)	Explain the possible causes of idle time and waste and suggest methods of control	2
(f)	Calculate, using a simple situation, ABC-based variances	3
(g)	Explain the different methods available for deciding whether or not to investigate a variance cause	2
D3	**Material mix and yield variances**	
(a)	Calculate, identify the cause of, and explain mix and yield variances	2
(b)	Explain the wider issues involved in changing mix, eg cost, quality and performance measurement issues	2
(c)	Identify and explain the relationship of the material price variance with the material mix and yield variances	2
(d)	Suggest and justify alternative methods of controlling production processes	2
D4	**Sales mix and quantity variances**	
(a)	Calculate, identify the cause of, and explain sales mix and quantity variances	2
(b)	Identify and explain the relationship of the sales volume variances with the sales mix and quantity variances	2

Exam guide

The variance calculations set in this paper are likely to be the more complicated variances such as in the Pilot Paper and you will be required to **explain** them and **evaluate** performance.

One of the competencies you require to fulfil performance objective 14 of the PER is the ability to prepare regular variance analysis reports. You can apply the knowledge you obtain from this section of the text to help to demonstrate this competence.

1 Basic variances

- A **variance** is the difference between an actual result and an expected result.
- **Variance analysis** is the process by which the *total* difference between standard and actual results is analysed.
- When actual results are better than expected results, we have a **favourable variance (F).** If actual results are worse than expected results, we have an **adverse variance (A).**
- The **selling price variance** measures the effect on expected profit of a selling price different to the standard selling price. It is calculated as the difference between what the sales revenue should have been for the actual quantity sold, and what it was.
- The **sales volume variance** measures the increase or decrease in expected profit as a result of the sales volume being higher or lower than budgeted. It is calculated as the difference between the budgeted sales volume and the actual sales volume multiplied by the standard profit per unit.
- The material **total variance** is the difference between what the output actually cost and what it should have cost, in terms of material. It can be divided into the following two sub-variances.
- The **material price variance** is the difference between what the material did cost and what it should have cost.
- The **material usage variance** is the difference between the standard cost of the material that should have been used and the standard cost of the material that was used.
- The **labour total variance** is the difference between what the output should have cost and what it did cost, in terms of labour. It can be divided into two sub-variances.
- The **labour rate variance** is the difference between what the labour did cost and what it should have cost.
- The **labour efficiency variance** is the difference between the standard cost of the hours that should have been worked and the standard cost of the hours that were worked.
- **The variable production overhead total variance** is the difference between what the output should have cost and what it did cost, in terms of variable production overhead. It can be divided into two sub-variances.
- The **variable production overhead expenditure variance** is the difference between the amount of variable production overhead that should have been incurred in the actual hours actively worked, and the actual amount of variable production overhead incurred.
- The **variable production overhead efficiency variance** is the difference between the standard cost of the hours that should have been worked for the number of units actually produced, and the standard cost of the actual number of hours worked.
- **Fixed production overhead total variance** is the difference between fixed production overhead incurred and fixed production overhead absorbed. In other words, it is the under– or over-absorbed fixed production overhead.
- **Fixed production overhead expenditure variance** is the difference between the budgeted fixed production overhead expenditure and actual fixed production overhead expenditure.
- **Fixed production overhead volume variance** is the difference between actual and budgeted production/volume multiplied by the standard absorption rate per *unit*.
- **Fixed production overhead volume efficiency variance** is the difference between the number of hours that actual production should have taken, and the number of hours actually taken (that is, worked) multiplied by the standard absorption rate per *hour*.
- **Fixed production overhead volume capacity variance** is the difference between budgeted hours of work and the actual hours worked, multiplied by the standard absorption rate per *hour*.

A company produces and sells one product only, the Thing, the standard cost for one unit being as follows.

	$
Direct material A – 10 kilograms at $20 per kg	200
Direct material B – 5 litres at $6 per litre	30
Direct wages – 5 hours at $6 per hour	30
Fixed production overhead	50
Total standard cost	310

The fixed overhead included in the standard cost is based on an expected monthly output of 900 units. Fixed production overhead is absorbed on the basis of direct labour hours.

During April the actual results were as follows.

Production	800 units
Material A	7,800 kg used, costing $159,900
Material B	4,300 litres used, costing $23,650
Direct wages	4,200 hours worked for $24,150

Fixed production overhead $47,000

Required

(a)   Calculate price and usage variances for each material.

(b)   Calculate labour rate and efficiency variances.

(c)   Calculate fixed production overhead expenditure and volume variances and then subdivide the volume variance.

Answer

(a)   **Price variance – A**

	$
7,800 kgs should have cost (× $20)	156,000
but did cost	159,900
Price variance	3,900 (A)

Usage variance – A

800 units should have used (× 10 kgs)	8,000 kgs
but did use	7,800 kgs
Usage variance in kgs	200 (F)
× standard cost per kilogram	× $20
Usage variance in $	$4,000 (F)

Price variance – B

	$
4,300 litres should have cost (× $6)	25,800
but did cost	23,650
Price variance	2,150 (F)

Usage variance – B

800 units should have used (× 5 l)	4,000 l
but did use	4,300 l
Usage variance in litres	300 (A)
× standard cost per litre	× $6
Usage variance in $	$1,800 (A)

(b) **Labour rate variance**

	$
4,200 hours should have cost (× $6)	25,200
but did cost	24,150
Rate variance	1,050 (F)

Labour efficiency variance

800 units should have taken (× 5 hrs)	4,000 hrs
but did take	4,200 hrs
Efficiency variance in hours	200 (A)
× standard rate per hour	× $6
Efficiency variance in $	$1,200 (A)

(c) **Fixed overhead expenditure variance**

	$
Budgeted expenditure ($50 × 900)	45,000
Actual expenditure	47,000
Expenditure variance	2,000 (A)

Fixed overhead volume variance

	$
Budgeted production at standard rate (900 × $50)	45,000
Actual production at standard rate (800 × $50)	40,000
Volume variance	5,000 (A)

Fixed overhead volume efficiency variance

	$
800 units should have taken (× 5 hrs)	4,000 hrs
but did take	4,200 hrs
Volume efficiency variance in hours	200 (A)
× standard absorption rate per hour	× $10
Volume efficiency variance	$2,000 (A)

Fixed overhead volume capacity variance

Budgeted hours	4,500 hrs
Actual hours	4,200 hrs
Volume capacity variance in hours	300 (A)
× standard absorption rate per hour ($50 ÷ 5)	× $10
	$3,000 (A)

2 The reasons for variances   6/08, 12/09

Knowledge brought forward from earlier studies

In an examination question you should review the information given and use your imagination and common sense to suggest possible reasons for variances.

Variance	Favourable	Adverse	Calculation
Material price	Unforeseen discounts received Greater care in purchasing Change in material standard	Price increase Careless purchasing Change in material standard	Price $ Based on actual purchases What should it have cost? X What did it cost? (X) X
Material usage	Material used of higher quality than standard More effective use made of material Errors in allocating material to jobs	Defective material Excessive waste Theft Stricter quality control Errors in allocating material to jobs	Usage Kgs Based on actual production What should have been used? X What was used? (X) X Difference valued at $X standard cost per kg
Labour rate	Use of workers at a rate of pay lower than standard	Wage rate increase	Rate $ Based on actual hours paid What should it have cost? X What did it cost? (X) X
Idle time	Possible if idle time has been built into the budget	Machine breakdown Non-availability of material Illness or injury to worker	Idle time Hrs Hours worked X Hours paid (X) Difference valued at $X standard rate per hour
Labour efficiency	Output produced more quickly than expected, because of work motivation, better quality of equipment or materials, better learning rate Errors in allocating time to jobs	Lost time in excess of standard allowed Output lower than standard set because of lack of training, sub-standard material etc Errors in allocating time to jobs	Efficiency Hrs Based on actual production How long should it have taken? X How long did it take? (X) X Difference valued at $X standard rate per hour
**Overhead expenditure	Savings in costs incurred More economical use of services	Increase in cost of services Excessive use of services Change in type of services used	Based on actual hours worked $ What should it have cost? X What did it cost? (X) X
Overhead volume	Production or level of activity greater than budgeted.	Production or level of activity less than budgeted	Units Budgeted units X Actual units (X) X Difference valued at $X OAR per unit

Variance	Favourable	Adverse	Calculation	
Fixed overhead capacity	Production or level of activity greater than budgeted	Production or level of activity less than budgeted		Hrs
			Budgeted hrs worked	X
			Actual hrs worked	(X)
				X
			Difference valued at OAR per hour	X
Selling price	Unplanned price increase	Unplanned price reduction		$
			For the quantity sold	
			What revenue should have been generated	X
			Actual revenue	(X)
				X
Sales volume	Additional demand	Unexpected fall in demand Production difficulties		Units
			Budgeted sales	X
			Actual sales	(X)
				X
			Difference valued at standard profit per unit	X

3 Labour variances and the learning curve

Care must be taken when interpreting labour variances where the **learning curve** has been used in the budget process.

In Chapter 9 we looked at how the **learning curve** can be used for forecasting production time and labour costs in certain circumstances where the workforce as a whole improves in efficiency with experience.

Companies that use standard costing for much of their production output cannot apply standard times to output where a learning effect is taking place. This problem can be overcome in practice by:

(a) Establishing **standard times** for output, once the learning effect has worn off or become insignificant; and

(b) Introducing a **'launch cost'** budget for the product for the duration of the learning period.

When learning is still taking place, it would be unreasonable to compare actual times with the standard times that ought eventually to be achieved so **allowances must be made** when interpreting labour efficiency variances. Standard costs should reflect the point that has been reached on the learning curve. When learning has become **insignificant**, standards set on the basis of this **'steady state'** will be different to when learning was taking place. If the learning rate has been wrongly calculated, this must be allowed for in the variance calculations.

3.1 Example: labour variances and the learning curve

A new product has been introduced for which an 80% learning curve is expected to apply. The standard labour information has been based on estimates of the time needed to produce the first unit which is 200 hours at $50 per hour.

The first four units took 700 hours to produce at a cost of $37,500.

Required

(a) The original labour rate and efficiency variances.

(b) The labour rate and efficiency variances which take into account the learning effect.

Solution

(a) **Labour rate variance**

	$	
700 hours should have cost (× $50)	35,000	
but did cost	37,500	
Labour rate variance	2,500	(A)

Labour efficiency variance

Four units should have taken (× 200 hrs)	800	hours
but did take	700	hours
Efficiency variance in hours	100	hours (F)
× standard rate per hour	× $50	
Efficiency variance in $	$5,000	(F)

(b) **Incorporating the learning curve effect**

Average standard time per unit for 4 units

$$= 200 \times 0.8 \times 0.8$$
$$= 128 \text{ hours}$$

Total expected time for 4 units

$$= 128 \times 4$$
$$= 512 \text{ hours}$$

Labour efficiency variance

Four units should have taken	512	hours
but did take	700	hours
	188	hours (A)
× standard rate per hour	× $50	
	$9,400	(A)

The labour rate variance does not change but a favourable labour efficiency variance is now adverse once the learning effect has been incorporated.

4 Idle time and waste   6/08

In the previous chapter we looked at the meaning of **waste** and **idle time** and how they can be allowed for in standards and budgets. We now need to calculate their effect on variances.

4.1 Idle time variance

Idle time may be caused by machine breakdowns or not having work to give to employees, perhaps because of bottlenecks in production or a shortage of orders from customers. When it occurs, the labour force is still paid wages for time at work, but no actual work is done. Such time is unproductive and therefore inefficient. In variance analysis, idle time is an **adverse efficiency variance**.

Key term

> The **idle time variance** is the number of hours that labour were idle valued at the standard rate per hour.

The idle time variance is shown as a separate part of the total labour efficiency variance. The remaining efficiency variance will then relate only to the productivity of the labour force during the hours spent actively working.

In Chapter 10 we discussed how budgets can be prepared which **incorporate** expected idle time. An adverse variance will only result from idle time in **excess** of what was expected.

4.2 Example: Labour variances with idle time

During period 5, 1,500 units of product X were made and the cost of grade Z labour was $17,500 for 3,080 hours. A unit of product X is expected to use 2 hours of grade Z labour at a standard cost of $5 per labour hour. During the period, however, there was a shortage of customer orders and 100 hours were recorded as idle time.

Required

Calculate the following variances.

(a)   The labour total variance
(b)   The labour rate variance
(c)   The idle time variance
(d)   The labour efficiency variance

Solution

(a)   **The labour total variance**

	$
1,500 units of product X should have cost (× $10)	15,000
but did cost	17,500
Labour total variance	2,500 (A)

Actual cost is greater than standard cost. The variance is therefore adverse.

(b)   **The labour rate variance.** This is a comparison of what the hours paid should have cost and what they did cost.

	$
3,080 hours of grade Z labour should have cost (× $5)	15,400
but did cost	17,500
Labour rate variance	2,100 (A)

Actual cost is greater than standard cost. The variance is therefore adverse.

(c)   **The idle time variance**. This is the hours of idle time, valued at the standard rate per hour.

Idle time variance = 100 hours (A) × $5 = $500 (A)

(d)   **The labour efficiency variance.** This considers the hours actively worked (the difference between hours paid for and idle time hours) and is calculated by taking the amount of output produced and comparing the time it should have taken to make them, with the actual time spent *actively* making them (3,080 – 100 = 2,980 hours). The variance in hours is valued at the standard rate per labour hour.

1,500 units of product X should take (× 2 hrs)	3,000 hrs
but did take (3,080 – 100)	2,980 hrs
Labour efficiency variance in hours	20 hrs (F)
× standard rate per hour	× $5
Labour efficiency variance in $	$100 (F)

(e)   **Summary**

	$
Labour rate variance	2,100 (A)
Idle time variance	500 (A)
Labour efficiency variance	100 (F)
Labour total variance	2,500 (A)

Remember that, if idle time is recorded, the actual hours used in the efficiency variance calculation are the **hours worked** and not the hours paid for.

4.3 Example: Idle time in the budget

Bruno's budget for April includes total budgeted machine time of 3,800 hours. This includes productive hours and non productive (idle time) hours. Due to inevitable delays for set-ups, idle time of 10% is allowed. The standard variable machine cost per hour is $270. In practice in April, actual non productive machine hours were 430 hours.

Required

(a) Calculate the idle time variance.
(b) Suggest why this variance has arisen and what could be done to control excess idle time.

Solution

(a)

		Hours
Actual idle time		430
Standard idle time	10% of 3,800	380
Excess idle time		50
Variance × standard rate ($270)		13,500 (A)

(b) There is an adverse variance due to excess idle time. Idle time of 10% is expected for machine set-up delays and this has presumably taken longer than usually expected. This could be due to faulty machinery or problems with staff trained to do the set-ups. Management needs to investigate why the idle time was excessive and take action to prevent re-occurrence.

4.4 Wastage and material variances

In the same way as idle time, a certain amount of expected wastage may be built into the material usage standard. A variance therefore needs to be calculated comparing the actual results with a standard that has been adjusted for expected wastage.

4.4.1 Example

(a) Capella has prepared standard material specifications for each of products A and B as follows.

    (i) Each finished unit of product A and product B contains 2 units and 6 units of component X respectively.

    (ii) The standard input requirements for both products must also allow for losses during processing of 10% of the units of component X.

    (iii) The standard purchase price for component X is $8 per unit.

Customer demand for period 2 for products A and B is budgeted at 2,280 units and 2,925 units respectively. It is budgeted that returns from customers of products A and B requiring free replacement will be 5% and 2.5% respectively of goods delivered to customers. No stocks of raw material, work-in-progress or finished goods are planned.

Required

    (i) Calculate the material purchase budget for period 2 (units and $) for component X.

    (ii) Comment on the usefulness of standard specifications in the compilation of the material budget for Capella rather than using the following actual information for period 1.

	Product A	Product B
Sales to customers (units)	2,500	2,750
Purchases of component X (units)	6,250	19,250

Solution

(a) (i) **Losses and returns**

The figure of two units of X required for product A represents (1 − 0.1) = 0.9 (or 90%) of the requirement, because of losses. Likewise the demand figure of 2,280 represents 95% of the production needs, because of returns.

Material purchases budget for period 2

	A	B
Demand (units)	2,280	2,925
Returns (as decimal)	0.05	0.025
Demand allowing for returns (eg 2,925 × 1/(1 − 0.025)) (units)	2,400	3,000
Free replacements (units)	120	75

	A	B
Standard input of X (units)	2	6
Losses (as decimal)	0.1	0.1
Standard input allowing for losses (eg 2 × 1/(1 − 0.1)) (units)	2.2222	6.6667

	A Units	B Units
Standard units of component X required (eg 3,000 × 6)	4,800	18,000
Losses in process (balance)	533	2,000
Actual units of component X required (eg 2,400 × 2.2222)	5,333	20,000

	$
Cost for product A (5,333 × $8)	42,664
Cost for product B (20,000 × $8)	160,000
Total cost	202,664

(ii) **Usefulness of standard specifications**

With sales of 2,500 units of product A the **standard input** figure suggests that only **5,000 units of component X need be purchased**. In fact **6,250 units were required**. Likewise for product B: the standard suggests that 16,500 units of X would have been needed but actual needs were 19,250 units.

It could be argued that the **current standard** is **misleading**, and could lead to **under-purchasing** of component X, and **inability to meet demand** or **additional emergency purchasing,** at above average cost, later in the period. It might be better to **revise** the standard to reflect the actual figures 6,250/2,500 = **2.5 units** for product A and 19,250/2,750 = **7 units** for product B.

On the other hand it could be **argued** that such a **revision sends the wrong signals** to management. The **losses** in process and **returns** are undesirable, and it may be possible to **reduce** them or **eliminate** them entirely. From this point of view the **current standards** have been set at a level that will **give rise to variances**: this will continually **draw management attention** to inefficiencies, and give management a **target** to aim at.

The **period 2 budget** prepared for part (a)(i) illustrates this: effectively it sets management a period 2 **target** of reducing requirements for component X from 2.5 units to 2.2 units (product A), and from 7 units to 6.6 units (product B).

The standard specifications are thus quite in keeping with the principles of **Total Quality Management**.

5 Operating statements

- An **operating statement** is a regular report for management which compares actual costs and revenues with budgeted figures and shows variances.
- There are several ways in which an operating statement may be presented. Perhaps the most common format is one which **reconciles budgeted profit to actual profit**. Sales variances are reported first, and the total of the budgeted profit and the two sales variances results in a figure for 'actual sales minus the standard cost of sales'. The cost variances are then reported, and an actual profit calculated.

Question

Operating statement

A company manufactures one product, and the entire product is sold as soon as it is produced. There are no opening or closing inventories and work in progress is negligible. The company operates a standard costing system and analysis of variances is made every month. The standard cost card for the product, a widget, is as follows.

STANDARD COST CARD – WIDGET

		$
Direct materials	0.5 kilos at $4 per kilo	2.00
Direct wages	2 hours at $2.00 per hour	4.00
Variable overheads	2 hours at $0.30 per hour	0.60
Fixed overhead	2 hours at $3.70 per hour	7.40
Standard cost		14.00
Standard profit		6.00
Standing selling price		20.00

Budgeted output for January was 5,100 units. Actual results for January were as follows.

Production of 4,850 units was sold for $95,600
Materials consumed in production amounted to 2,300 kilos at a total cost of $9,800
Labour hours paid for amounted to 8,500 hours at a cost of $16,800
Actual operating hours amounted to 8,000 hours
Variable overheads amounted to $2,600
Fixed overheads amounted to $42,300

Required

Calculate all variances and prepare an operating statement for January.

		$
(a)	2,300 kg of material should cost (× $4)	9,200
	but did cost	9,800
	Material price variance	600 (A)
(b)	4,850 Widgets should use (× 0.5 kgs)	2,425 kg
	but did use	2,300 kg
	Material usage variance in kgs	125 kg (F)
	× standard cost per kg	× $4
	Material usage variance in $	$ 500 (F)
(c)	8,500 hours of labour should cost (× $2)	17,000
	but did cost	16,800
	Labour rate variance	200 (F)
(d)	4,850 Widgets should take (× 2 hrs)	9,700 hrs
	but did take (active hours)	8,000 hrs
	Labour efficiency variance in hours	1,700 hrs (F)
	× standard cost per hour	× $2
	Labour efficiency variance in $	$3,400 (F)
(e)	Idle time variance 500 hours (A) × $2	$1,000 (A)
(f)	8,000 hours incurring variable o/hd expenditure should cost (× $0.30)	2,400
	but did cost	2,600
	Variable overhead expenditure variance	200 (A)
(g)	Variable overhead efficiency variance is the same as the labour efficiency variance:	
	1,700 hours (F) × $0.30 per hour	$ 510 (F)
(h)	Budgeted fixed overhead (5,100 units × 2 hrs × $3.70)	37,740
	Actual fixed overhead	42,300
	Fixed overhead expenditure variance	4,560 (A)
(i)	Actual production at standard rate (4,850 units × $7.40)	35,890
	Budgeted production at standard rate (5,100 units × $7.40)	37,740
	Fixed overhead volume variance	1,850 (A)
(j)	4,850 Widgets should have sold for (× $20)	97,000
	but did sell for	95,600
	Selling price variance	1,400 (A)
(k)	Budgeted sales volume	5,100 units
	Actual sales volume	4,850 units
	Sales volume variance in units	250 units
	× standard profit per unit	× $6 (A)
	Sales volume variance in $	$1,500 (A)

	$	$
Budgeted profit (5,100 units × $6 profit)		30,600
Selling price variance	1,400	(A)
Sales volume variance	1,500	(A)
		2,900 (A)
Actual sales ($95,600) less the standard cost of sales (4,850 × $14)		27,700

OPERATING STATEMENT FOR JANUARY

	$	$	$
Budgeted profit			30,600
Sales variances: price		1,400 (A)	
volume		1,500 (A)	
			2,900 (A)
Actual sales minus the standard cost of sales			27,700

Cost variances

	(F) $	*(A)* $	$
Material price		600	
Material usage	500		
Labour rate	200		
Labour efficiency	3,400		
Labour idle time		1,000	
Variable overhead expenditure		200	
Variable overhead efficiency	510		
Fixed overhead expenditure		4,560	
Fixed overhead volume		1,850	
	4,610	8,210	3,600 (A)
Actual profit for January			24,100

Check

	$	$
Sales		95,600
Materials	9,800	
Labour	16,800	
Variable overhead	2,600	
Fixed overhead	42,300	
		71,500
Actual profit		24,100

5.1 Operating statements in a marginal cost environment

Knowledge brought forward from earlier studies

- There are two main differences between the variances calculated in an absorption costing system and the **variances calculated in a marginal costing system**. In a marginal costing system the only fixed overhead variance is an expenditure variance and the sales volume variance is valued at standard contribution margin, not standard profit margin.

Question

Marginal cost operating statement

Returning to the question above, now assume that the company operates a marginal costing system.

Required

Recalculate any variances necessary and produce an operating statement.

Answer

(a) There is no fixed overhead volume variance.

(b) The standard contribution per unit is $(20 – 6.60) = $13.40, therefore the sales volume variance of 250 units (A) is valued at (× $13.40) = $3,350 (A).

The other variances are unchanged, therefore an operating statement might appear as follows.

OPERATING STATEMENT FOR JANUARY

	$	$	$
Budgeted profit		30,600	
Budgeted fixed production costs		37,740	
Budgeted contribution		68,340	
Sales variances: volume		3,350 (A)	
price		1,400 (A)	
			4,750 (A)
Actual sales ($95,600) minus the standard			
variable cost of sales (4,850 × $6.60)			63,590

	(F)	(A)	
Variable cost variances	$	$	$
Material price		600	
Material usage	500		
Labour rate	200		
Labour efficiency	3,400		
Labour idle time		1,000	
Variable overhead expenditure		200	
Variable overhead efficiency	510		
	4,610	1,800	
			2,810 (F)
Actual contribution			66,400
Budgeted fixed production overhead		37,740	
Expenditure variance		4,560 (A)	
Actual fixed production overhead			42,300
Actual profit			24,100

Note. The profit here is the same on the profit calculated by standard absorption costing because there were no changes in inventory levels. Absorption costing and marginal costing do not always produce an identical profit figure.

One of the competencies you require to fulfil performance objective 12 of the PER is the ability to summarise and present financial information in an appropriate format for management purposes. You can apply the knowledge you obtain from this section of the text to help to demonstrate this competence.

6 ABC and variance analysis

Within an **ABC system, efficiency variances for longer-term variable overheads** are the difference between the level of activity that should have been needed and the actual activity level, valued at the standard rate per activity.

All overheads within an **ABC system** are **treated as variable** costs, varying either with production levels in the short term or with some other activity. The traditional method of calculating fixed overhead variances is therefore not taken. The calculation of ABC overhead variances is either **the same as the traditional approach for variable overheads** (if the overhead varies with production level) or **extremely similar** (if it varies with some other activity).

6.1 Approach for longer-term variable overheads

Expenditure variances are the difference between what expenditure should have been for the actual level of activity and actual expenditure.

Efficiency variances are the difference between the level of activity that should have been needed and the actual activity level, valued at the standard rate per activity.

6.2 Example: Simple ABC overhead variance analysis

The following information relates to B's ordering activity during control period 2.

Budget

Output	10,000 units
Activity level	2,000 orders
Total cost of activity	$90,000

Actual

Output	10,500 units
Activity level	1,800 orders
Total cost of activity	$84,000

Required

Calculate the overhead expenditure and efficiency variances relating to the ordering activity.

Solution

Expenditure variance

This is the difference between how much 1,800 orders should have cost and how much they did cost.

Each order should cost $90,000/2,000 = $45. This is the **cost driver rate**.

	$
1,800 orders should have cost (× $45)	81,000
but did cost	84,000
Expenditure variance	3,000 (A)

Efficiency variance

This is the difference between what the level of activity should have been for the output of 10,500 units, and what it was, valued at the standard rate per order (the cost driver rate).

Each unit of output should use 2,000/10,000 = 0.2 of an order

Activity level for 10,500 units should have been (× 0.2)	2,100 orders
but was	1,800 orders
Variance in orders	300 orders (F)
× standard rate per order	× $45
Efficiency variance	$13,500 (F)

6.3 Usefulness of this analysis

Given the lack of relevant management information provided by traditionally-analysed fixed overhead variances, the **results using ABC** analysis are of **more use**. It is clear in the example above that one reason why the cost of the ordering activity was greater than it should have been given the level of production was because the **cost per order was above budget**. The **main difference** was because it **took more orders than planned** given the actual level of production, however. The analysis has highlighted the efficiency of the ordering process for investigation.

7 Investigating variances

FAST FORWARD

> **Materiality**, **controllability**, the **type** of standard being used, variance **trend**, **interdependence** and **costs** should be taken into account when deciding on the significance of a variance.

> One of the competencies you require to fulfil performance objective 14 of the PER is the ability to give explanations and make recommendations based on variance analysis. You can apply the knowledge you obtain from this section of the text to help to demonstrate this competence.

7.1 The decision whether or not to investigate

Before management decide whether or not to investigate the reasons for the occurrence of a particular variance, there are a number of factors which should be considered in assessing the significance of the variance.

7.1.1 Materiality

Because a standard cost is really only an *average* expected cost, small variations between actual and standard are bound to occur and are unlikely to be significant. Obtaining an 'explanation' of the reasons why they occurred is likely to be time consuming and irritating for the manager concerned. The explanation will often be 'chance', which is not, in any case, particularly helpful. For such variations **further investigation is not worthwhile** since such variances are not controllable.

7.1.2 Controllability

This must also influence the decision about whether to investigate. If there is a general worldwide increase in the price of a raw material there is nothing that can be done internally to control the effect of this. If a central decision is made to award all employees a 10% increase in salary, staff costs in division A will increase by this amount and the variance is not controllable by division A's manager. **Uncontrollable variances call for a change in the plan, not an investigation into the past.**

7.1.3 The type of standard being used

The efficiency variance reported in any control period, whether for materials or labour, will depend on the **efficiency level set**. If, for example, an ideal standard is used, variances will always be adverse. A similar problem arises if average price levels are used as standards. If **inflation** exists, favourable price variances are likely to be reported at the beginning of a period, to be offset by adverse price variances later in the period.

7.1.4 Variance trend

Although small variations in a single period are unlikely to be significant, small variations that occur consistently may need more attention. Variance trend is probably more important that a single set of variances for one accounting period. The trend **provides an indication of whether the variance is fluctuating within acceptable control limits or becoming out of control.**

(a)   If, say, an efficiency variance is $1,000 adverse in month 1, the obvious conclusion is that the process is out of control and that corrective action must be taken. This may be correct, but what if the same variance is $1,000 adverse every month? The *trend* indicates that the process is in control and the standard has been wrongly set.

(b)   Suppose, though, that the same variance is consistently $1,000 adverse for each of the first six months of the year but that production has steadily fallen from 100 units in month 1 to 65 units by month 6. The variance trend in absolute terms is constant, but relative to the number of units produced, efficiency has got steadily worse.

Individual variances should therefore not be looked at in isolation; variances should be scrutinised for a number of successive periods if their full significance is to be appreciated.

7.1.5 Interdependence between variances

Individual variances should not be looked at in isolation. One variance might be inter-related with another, and much of it might have occurred only because the other variance occurred too. **When two variances are interdependent (interrelated) one will usually be adverse and the other one favourable.** Here are some examples.

Interrelated variances	Explanation
Materials price and usage	If **cheaper materials** are purchased for a job in order to obtain a favourable price variance, materials wastage might be **higher** and an **adverse usage variance** may occur. If the cheaper materials are more difficult to handle, there might be an **adverse labour efficiency variance** too. If more expensive materials are purchased, the **price variance** will be **adverse** but the **usage variance** might be **favourable** if the material is easier to use or of a higher quality.
Labour rate and efficiency	If employees are paid higher rates for experience and skill, using a highly skilled team might lead to an **adverse rate variance** and a **favourable efficiency variance** (experienced staff are less likely to waste material, for example). In contrast, a favourable rate variance might indicate a larger-than-expected proportion of inexperienced workers, which could result in an **adverse labour efficiency variance**, and perhaps **poor materials handling and high rates of rejects** too (and hence an adverse materials usage variance).
Selling price and sales volume	A reduction in the selling price might stimulate bigger sales demand, so that an **adverse selling price variance** might be counterbalanced by a **favourable sales volume variance**. Similarly, a price rise would give a **favourable price variance**, but possibly cause an **adverse sales volume variance**.

7.1.6 Costs of investigation

The costs of an investigation should be weighed against the benefits of correcting the cause of a variance.

Exam focus point

When asked to provide a commentary on variances you have calculated, make sure that you *interpret* your calculations rather than simply detail them.

7.2 Variance investigation models

FAST FORWARD

The **rule-of-thumb** and **statistical significance** variance investigation models and/or statistical **control charts** can be used to determine whether a variance should be investigated.

7.2.1 Rule-of-thumb model

This involves **deciding a limit** and if the size of a **variance is within the limit**, it should be considered **immaterial**. Only if it exceeds the limit is it considered materially significant, and worthy of investigation.

In practice many managers believe that this approach to deciding which variances to investigate is perfectly adequate. However, it has a number of **drawbacks**.

(a)   Should variances be investigated if they exceed 10% of standard? Or 5%? Or 15%?

(b)   Should a **different fixed percentage be applied to favourable and unfavourable variances**?

(c) Suppose that the fixed percentage is, say, 10% and an important category of expenditure has in the past been very closely controlled so that adverse variances have never exceeded, say, 2% of standard. Now if adverse variances suddenly shoot up to, say, **8% or 9%** of standard, there might well be **serious excess expenditures incurred that ought to be controlled**, but with the fixed percentage limit at 10%, the variances would not be 'flagged' for investigation.

(d) **Unimportant categories** of low-cost expenditures might be loosely controlled, with variances commonly exceeding 10% in both a favourable and adverse direction. These would be regularly – and **unnecessarily – flagged for investigation**.

(e) Where actual expenditures have **normal and expected wide fluctuations** from period to period, but the 'standard' is a fixed expenditure amount, variances will be **flagged for investigation unnecessarily often**.

(f) There is **no attempt to consider the costs and potential benefits of investigating variances** (except insofar as the pre-set percentage is of 'material significance').

(g) The **past history of variances in previous periods is ignored**. For example, if the pre-set percentage limit is set at 10% and an item of expenditure has regularly exceeded the standard by, say, 6% per month for a number of months in a row, in all probability there is a situation that ought to warrant control action. Using the pre-set percentage rule, however, the variance would never be flagged for investigation in spite of the cumulative adverse variances.

Some of the difficulties can be overcome by **varying the pre-set percentage from account to account** (for example 5% for direct labour efficiency, 2% for rent and rates, 10% for salesmen's expenditure, 15% for postage costs, 5% for direct materials price, 3% for direct materials usage and so on). On the other hand, some difficulties, if they are significant, can only be overcome with a different cost-variance investigation model.

7.2.2 Statistical significance model

Historical data are used to **calculate** both a standard as **an expected average** and the **expected standard deviation** around this average when the process is under control. An **in-control process** (process being material usage, fixed overhead expenditure and so on) is one in which any resulting **variance is simply due to random fluctuations** around the expected outcome. An **out-of-control process**, on the other hand, is one in which **corrective action can be taken to remedy any variance**.

By assuming that variances that occur are normally distributed around this average, a **variance will be investigated if it is *more* than a distance from the expected average that the estimated normal distribution suggests is likely if the process is in control**. (Note that such a variance would be deemed significant.)

The statistical significance rule has two principal **advantages** over the rule of thumb approach.

(a) **Important costs** that normally vary by only a small amount from standard will be **signalled for investigation if variances increase significantly**.

(b) Costs that **usually fluctuate by large amounts will not be signalled** for investigation unless variances are extremely large.

The main **disadvantage** of the statistical significance rule is the problem of assessing standard deviations in expenditure.

7.2.3 Statistical control charts

By marking variances and control limits on a control chart, **investigation** is signalled not only when a particular **variance exceeds the control limit** (since it would be non-random and worth investigating) but also when the **trend of variances shows a progressively worsening movement** in actual results (even though the variance in any single control period has not yet overstepped the control limit).

The $\bar{x}$ **control chart** is based on the principle of the statistical significance model. For each cost item, a chart is kept of monthly variances and **tolerance limits are set at 1, 2 or 3 standard deviations**.

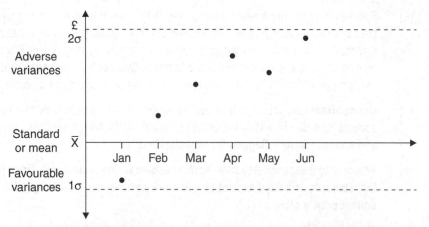

In this example, variances do not exceed the tolerance limits in any month, but the chart shows a worsening of variances over time, and so management might decide that an investigation is warranted, perhaps when it exceeds an inner warning limit.

Using a **cusum chart, the cumulative sum of variances** over a long period of time **is plotted**. If the variances are not significant, these 'sums' will simply fluctuate in a random way above and below the average to give a total or cumulative sum of zero. But if significant variances occur, the cumulative sum will start to develop a positive or negative drift, and when it exceeds a set tolerance limit, the situation must be investigated.

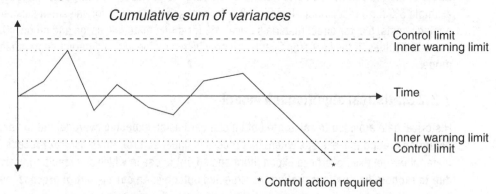

The **advantage** of the multiple period approach over the single period approach is that **trends are detectable earlier**, and control action would be introduced sooner than might have been the case if only current-period variances were investigated.

7.3 Possible control action

FAST FORWARD

Measurement errors and **out of date standards**, as well as **efficient/inefficient operations** and **random fluctuations**, can cause differences between standard and actual performance.

There are few basic reasons why variances occur and the **control action which may be taken will depend on the reason why the variance occurred**.

7.3.1 Measurement errors

In exam questions there is generally no question of the information that you are given being wrong. In practice, however, it may be extremely difficult to establish that 1,000 units of product A used 32,000 kg of raw material X. Scales may be misread, the pilfering or wastage of materials may go unrecorded, items may be wrongly classified (as material X3, say, when material X8 was used in reality), or employees may make 'cosmetic' adjustments to their records to make their own performance look better than it really was. An investigation may show that **control action is required to improve the accuracy of the recording system** so that measurement errors do not occur.

7.3.2 Out of date standards

Price standards are likely to become out of date quickly when frequent changes to the costs of material, power, labour and so on occur, or in **periods of high inflation**. In such circumstances an **investigation of variances is likely to highlight a general change in market prices** rather than efficiencies or inefficiencies in acquiring resources. Standards may also be out of date where operations are subject to **technological development** or if **learning curve effects** have not been taken into account. Investigation of this type of variance will provide information about the inaccuracy of the standard and **highlight the need to frequently review and update standards.**

7.3.3 Efficient or inefficient operations

Spoilage and better quality material/more highly skilled labour than standard are all likely to affect the efficiency of operations and hence cause variances. **Investigation** of variances in this category should **highlight the cause of the inefficiency or efficiency and will lead to control action to eliminate the inefficiency being repeated** or action to **compound the benefits of the efficiency**. For example, stricter supervision may be required to reduce wastage levels and the need for overtime working. The purchasing department could be encouraged to continue using suppliers of good quality materials.

7.3.4 Random or chance fluctuations

A standard is an average figure and so **actual results are likely to deviate unpredictably within the predictable range.** As long as the variance falls within this range, it will be classified as a random or chance fluctuation and **control action will not be necessary.**

8 Materials mix and yield variances   6/10

FAST FORWARD ⟫

The **materials usage variance** can be subdivided into a materials **mix** variance and a materials **yield** variance when more than one material is used in the product.

Exam focus point

The February 2010 edition of *Student Accountant* contained an article on material **mix** and **yield** variances written by the **examiner**. Ensure that you are familiar with this article.

Manufacturing processes often require that a number of different materials are combined to make a unit of finished product. When a product requires two or more raw materials in its make-up, it is often possible to **sub-analyse the materials usage variance into a materials mix and a materials yield variance**.

Adding a greater proportion of one material (therefore a smaller proportion of a different material) might make the materials mix **cheaper or more expensive**. For example the standard mix of materials for a product might consist of the following.

	$
(²/₃) 2 kg of material A at $1.00 per kg	2.00
(¹/₃) 1 kg of material B at $0.50 per kg	0.50
	2.50

It may be possible to change the mix so that one kilogram of material A is used and two kilograms of material B. The new mix would be cheaper.

	$
(¹/₃) 1 kg of material A	1
(²/₃) 2 kg of material B	1
	2

By changing the proportions in the mix, the **efficiency** of the combined material usage may change. In our example, in making the proportions of A and B cheaper, at 1:2, the product may now require more than three kilograms of input for its manufacture, and the new materials requirement per unit of product might be 3.6 kilograms.

		$
(¹⁄₃) 1.2 kg of material A at $1.00 per kg		1.20
(²⁄₃) 2.4 kg of material B at $0.50 per kg		1.20
		2.40

In establishing a materials usage standard, management may therefore have to balance the **cost** of a particular mix of materials with the **efficiency** of the yield of the mix.

Once the standard has been established it may be possible for management to exercise control over the materials used in production by calculating and reviewing mix and yield variances.

Key terms

A **mix variance** occurs when the materials are not mixed or blended in standard proportions and it is a measure of whether the actual mix is cheaper or more expensive than the standard mix.

A **yield variance** arises because there is a difference between what the input should have been for the output achieved and the actual input.

8.1 Calculating the variances

The **mix variance** is calculated as the **difference between** the **actual total quantity used** in **the standard mix** and the **actual quantities used in the actual mix, valued at standard costs**.

The **yield variance** is calculated as the **difference between the standard input for what was actually output, and the actual total quantity input (in the standard mix), valued at standard costs**.

8.2 When to calculate the mix and yield variance

A mix variance and yield variance are only appropriate in the following situations.

(a) **Where proportions of materials in a mix are changeable and controllable**

(b) Where the **usage variance of individual materials is of limited value because of the variability of the mix**, and a combined yield variance for all the materials together is more helpful for control

It would be totally inappropriate to calculate a mix variance where the materials in the 'mix' are discrete items. A chair, for example, might consist of wood, covering material, stuffing and glue. These materials are separate components, and it would not be possible to think in terms of controlling the proportions of each material in the final product. The usage of each material must be controlled separately.

8.3 Example: Materials usage, mix and yield variances

A company manufactures a chemical, Dynamite, using two compounds Flash and Bang. The standard materials usage and cost of one unit of Dynamite are as follows.

		$
Flash	5 kg at $2 per kg	10
Bang	10 kg at $3 per kg	30
		40

In a particular period, 80 units of Dynamite were produced from 500 kg of Flash and 730 kg of Bang.

Required

Calculate the materials usage, mix and yield variances.

Solution

(a) **Usage variance**

	Std usage for actual output kgs	Actual usage kgs	Variance kgs	Standard cost per kg $	Variance $
Flash	400	500	100 (A)	2	200 (A)
Bang	800	730	70 (F)	3	210 (F)
	1,200	1,230	30 (A)		10 (F)

The total usage variance of $10 (F) can be analysed into a mix variance and a yield variance.

(b) **Mix variance**

To calculate the mix variance, it is first necessary to decide how the total quantity of materials used (500 kg + 730 kg) should have been divided between Flash and Bang. In other words, we need to **calculate the standard mix of the actual quantity of materials used.**

	kg
Total quantity used (500 + 730)	1,230

	kg
Standard mix of actual use: ⅓ Flash	410
⅔ Bang	820
	1,230

The differences between what should have been used in the mix (as calculated above) and what was actually used is the mix variance (in kg) which should be converted into money values at standard cost.

	Actual quantity standard mix	Actual quantity actual mix	Variance	Standard cost per kg	Variance
	kgs	kgs	kgs	$	$
Flash	410	500*	90 (A)	2	180 (A)
Bang	820	730	90 (F)	3	270 (F)
	1,230	1,230	–		90 (F)

* When actual use exceeds standard use the variance is always adverse.

Note that the **total mix variance in quantity is zero**. This must always be the case since the expected mix is based on the total quantity actually used and hence the difference between the total expected and total actual is zero.

The favourable money variance is due to the greater use in the mix of the relatively cheap material, Flash.

(c) **Yield variance**

The yield variance can be calculated in total or for each individual material input.

In total

Each unit of output (Dynamite) requires	5 kg of Flash, costing	$10
	10 kg of Bang, costing	$30
	15 kg	$40

1,230 kg should have yielded (÷ 15 kg)	82 units of Dynamite
but did yield	80 units of Dynamite
Yield variance in units	2 units (A)

× standard cost per unit of output	× $40
Yield variance in $	$80 (A)

The adverse yield variance is due to the output from the input being less than standard.

For individual materials

This is calculated as the **difference between what the usage should have been for the output actually achieved and the actual usage in the standard mix**, converted into money values at standard cost.

	Standard quantity standard mix	Actual quantity standard mix	Variance	Standard cost per kg	Variance
	kgs	kgs	kgs	$	$
Flash	400	410	10 (A)	2	20 (A)
Bang	800	820	20 (A)	3	60 (A)
	1,200	1,230	30 (A)		80 (A)

Question

The standard materials cost of product D456 is as follows.

		$
Material X	3 kg at $2.00 per kg	6
Material Y	5 kg at $3.60 per kg	18
		24

During period 2, 2,000 kgs of material X (costing $4,100) and 2,400 kgs of material Y (costing $9,600) were used to produce 500 units of D456.

Required

Calculate the following variances.

(a) Price variances
(b) Mix variances
(c) Yield variances – in total and for each individual material

Answer

(a)

	$
2,000 kg of X should cost (× $2)	4,000
but did cost	4,100
Material X price variance	100 (A)

	$
2,400 kg of Y should cost (× $3.60)	8,640
but did cost	9,600
Material Y price variance	960 (A)

(b)

	kg
Total quantity used (2,000 + 2,400) kgs	4,400

		kg
Standard mix for actual use:	3/8 X	1,650
	5/8 Y	2,750
		4,400

	Actual quantity standard mix	Actual quantity actual mix	Variance	Standard cost per kg	Variance
	kgs	kgs	kgs	$	$
X	1,650	2,000	350 (A)	2.00	700 (A)
Y	2,750	2,400	350 (F)	3.60	1,260 (F)
	4,400	4,400	–		560 (F)

(c) **In total**

Each unit of D456 requires		
3 kg of X, costing		$6
5 kg of Y, costing		$18
8 kg		$24

4,400 kg should have yielded (÷ 8 kg)	550 units
But did yield	500 units
Yield variance in units	50 units (A)
× standard cost per unit of output	× $24
Yield variance in $	$1,200 (A)

For individual materials

	Standard quantity standard mix kgs	Actual quantity standard mix kgs	Variance kgs	Standard cost per kg $	Variance $
X	1,500	1,650	150 (A)	2.00	300 (A)
Y	2,500	2,750	250 (A)	3.60	900 (A)
	4,000	4,400	400 (A)		1,200 (A)

Exam focus point

> With all variance calculations, it is vital that you do not simply learn formulae. You must have a thorough understanding of what your calculations are showing. This is especially true of the variances we will look at in this section and in section 9.

8.4 Example: Losses, mix and yield

Coope and Sorcerer Co make product T42 in a continuous process, for which standard and actual quantities in month 10 were as follows.

	Standard			Actual		
	Quantity kg	Price per kg $	Value $	Quantity kg	Price per kg $	Std cost of actual usage $
Material P	40,000	2.50	100,000	34,000	2.50	85,000
Material Q	20,000	4.00	80,000	22,000	4.00	88,000
	60,000		180,000	56,000		173,000

Losses occur at an even rate during the processing operation and are expected to be 10% of materials input. Actual output during the month was 53,000 kgs.

Required

Calculate total usage, mix and yield variances.

Solution

Usage variance

Output of 53,000 kgs should have used input of 53,000/90% = 58,889 kgs.

∴ Standard input should have been as follows.

			Kg
P	$^2/_3 \times 58,889$ =		39,259
Q	$^1/_3 \times 58,889$ =		19,630
			58,889

	P	Q
53,000 kg of T42 should need	39,259 kg	19,630 kg
but did need	34,000 kg	22,000 kg
Usage variance in kg	5,259 kg (F)	2,370 kg (A)
× standard price per kg	× $2.50	× $4
Usage variance in $	$13,148 (F)	$9,480 (A)
Total usage variance	$3,668 (F)	

Yield variance

Each kg of T42 requires (1 × 100/90) kg of input costing $3.33 ($180,000/(60 ,000 × 90%))

56,000 kg should have yielded (÷ 100/90)		50,400 kg
but did yield		53,000 kg
Yield variance in kgs		2,600 kg (F)
× standard cost per kg of T42		× $3.33
Yield variance in $		$8,667 (F)

Mix variance

Total quantity used		56,000.00 kg

Standard mix for actual use:	2/3 P	37,333.33 kg
	1/3 Q	18,666.67 kg
		56,000.00 kg

	P	Q
Mix should have been	37,333.33 kg	18,666.67 kg
but was	34,000.00 kg	22,000.00 kg
Mix variance in kg	3,333.33 kg (F)	3,333.33 kg (A)
× standard cost per kg	× $2.50	× $4.00
Mix variance in $	$8,333.00 (F)	$13,333.00 (A)
Total mix variance	$5,000 (A)	

(Note that there is a difference between the sum of the mix and yield variances and the usage variance due to rounding.)

8.5 The issues involved in changing the mix

The materials mix variance indicates the **cost** of a change in the mix of materials and the yield variance indicates the **productivity** of the manufacturing process. A change in the mix can have wider implications. For example, rising raw material prices may cause pressure to change the mix of materials. Even if the yield is not affected by the change in the mix, the **quality** of the final product may change. This can have an adverse effect on sales if customers do not accept the change in quality. The production manager's performance may be measured by mix and yield variances but these **performance measures** may fail to indicate problems with falling quality and the impact on other areas of the business. **Quality targets** may also be needed.

8.6 Alternative methods of controlling production processes

In a modern manufacturing environment with an emphasis on quality management, using mix and yield variances for control purposes may not be possible or may be inadequate. Other control methods could be more useful.

- Rates of wastage
- Average cost of input calculations
- Percentage of deliveries on time
- Customer satisfaction ratings
- Yield percentage calculations or output to input conversion rates

We will be considering performance measures in more detail in Chapter 13.

9 Sales mix and quantity variances

FAST FORWARD

The **sales volume variance** can also be analysed further into a sales mix variance and a sales quantity variance.

9.1 Sales volume variance

You should be familiar with how to calculate the sales volume variance from your earlier studies. It measures the increase or decrease in the standard profit or contribution as a result of the sales volume being higher or lower than budgeted. It is calculated as the difference between actual sales units and budgeted sales units, multiplied by the standard profit per unit.

9.2 Sales mix and quantity variances

If a company **sells more than one product**, it is possible to analyse the overall sales volume variance into a sales mix variance and a sales quantity variance.

Key terms

The **sales mix variance** occurs when the proportions of the various products sold are different from those in the budget.

The **sales quantity variance** shows the difference in contribution/profit because of a change in sales volume from the budgeted volume of sales.

9.3 When to calculate the mix and quantity variances

A sales mix variance and a sales quantity variance are only meaningful where management can control the proportions of the products sold.

In particular, sales mix variances are only of use if there is some kind of link between the products in question.

(a) Complementary products, such as pancake mix and lemon juice
(b) Substitute products, such as branded and 'own-label' goods
(c) Same products, different sizes
(d) Products produced within a limiting factor environment

9.4 The units method of calculation

The sales mix variance is calculated as the difference between the actual quantity sold in the standard mix and the actual quantity sold in the actual mix, valued at standard margin per unit. The sales quantity variance is calculated as the difference between the actual sales volume in the budgeted proportions and the budgeted sales volumes, multiplied by the standard margin.

9.5 Example: sales mix and quantity variances

Just Desserts Limited makes and sells two products, Chocolate Crunch and Strawberry Sundae. The budgeted sales and profit are as follows.

	Sales Units	Revenue $	Costs $	Profit $	Profit per unit $
Chocolate Crunch	400	8,000	6,000	2,000	5
Strawberry Sundae	300	12,000	11,100	900	3
				2,900	

Actual sales were 280 units of Chocolate Crunch and 630 units of Strawberry Sundae. The company management is able to control the relative sales of each product through the allocation of sales effort, advertising and sales promotion expenses.

Required

Calculate the sales volume variance, the sales mix variance and the sales quantity variance.

Solution

(a) **Volume profit variance**

	Chocolate Crunch	Strawberry Sundae
Budgeted sales	400 units	300 units
Actual sales	280 units	630 units
Sales volume variance in units	120 units (A)	330 units (F)
× standard margin per unit	× $5	× $3
Sales volume variance in $	$600 (A)	$990 (F)
Total **sales volume variance**		$390 (F)

The favourable sales volume variance indicates that a potential increase in profit was achieved as a result of the change in sales volume compared with budgeted volume. Now we will see how to analyse this favourable variance into its mix and quantity elements.

(b) **Mix variance**

When we look at the mix of sales in this example it is apparent that a bigger proportion than budgeted of the less profitable Strawberry Sundae has been sold, therefore the **sales mix variance** will be adverse. The method for calculating the variance is as follows.

(i) Take the **actual total of sales** and **convert** this total into a **standard or budgeted mix**, on the assumption that sales should have been in the budgeted proportions or mix.

(ii) The difference between actual sales and 'standard mix' sales for each product is then converted into a variance by multiplying by the standard margin.

		Units
Total quantity sold (280 + 630)		910
Budgeted mix for actual sales:	4/7 Chocolate Crunch	520
	3/7 Strawberry Sundae	390
		910

	'Should' mix Actual quantity Standard mix	'Did' mix Actual quantity Actual mix	Difference	× Standard margin	Variance
Chocolate Crunch	520 units	280 units	240 (A)	× $5	$1,200 (A)
Strawberry Sundae	390 units	630 units	240 (F)	× $3	$720 (F)
	910 units	910 units	–		$480 (A)

The profit would have been $480 higher if the 910 units had been sold in the budgeted mix of 4:3.

(c) **Quantity variance**

The sales quantity variance is calculated as follows.

	Actual sales Standard mix	Standard sales Standard mix	Difference in units	× Standard profit	Variance
Chocolate Crunch	520 units	400 units	120 units (F)	× $5	$600 (F)
Strawberry Sundae	390 units	300 units	90 units (F)	× $3	$270 (F)
	910 units	700 units	210 units		$870 (F)

(d)   **Summary**

	$
Sales mix variance	480 (A)
Sales quantity variance	870 (F)
Sales volume variance	390 (F)

If an organisation uses standard marginal costing instead of standard absorption costing then standard contribution rather than standard profit margin is used in the calculations.

Exam focus point

Try not to confuse the sales volume profit variance with the sales quantity profit variance.

Chapter Roundup

- Care must be taken when interpreting labour variances where the **learning curve** has been used in the budget process.

- Within an **ABC system, efficiency variances for longer-term variable overheads** are the difference between the level of activity that should have been needed and the actual activity level, valued at the standard rate per activity.

- **Materiality**, **controllability**, the **type** of standard being used, variance **trend**, **interdependence** and **costs** should be taken into account when deciding on the significance of a variance.

- The **rule-of-thumb** and **statistical significance** variance investigation models and/or statistical **control charts** can be used to determine whether a variance should be investigated.

- **Measurement errors** and **out of date standards**, as well as **efficient/inefficient operations** and **random fluctuations**, can cause differences between standard and actual performance.

- The **materials usage variance** can be subdivided into a materials **mix** variance and a materials **yield** variance when more than one material is used in the product.

- The **sales volume variance** can also be analysed further into a **sales mix variance** and a **sales quantity variance**.

1   *Fill in the blanks.*

The material price variance is the difference between .... and ....

The material usage variance is the difference between .... and ....

2   If closing inventories of raw materials are valued at standard cost, the material price variance is calculated on material purchases in the period.

True ☐   False ☐

3   *Choose the appropriate words from those highlighted.*

The idle time variance is an **efficiency/price** variance which is **adverse/favourable**.

4   Are variable production overhead variances based on hours paid or hours worked?

5   *Fill in the boxes in the diagram with the names of the variances and add the appropriate definition number from the list below.*

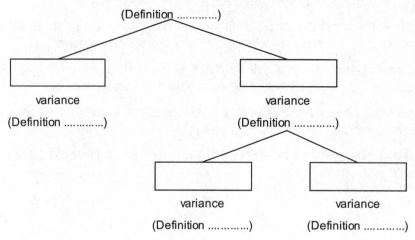

Fixed production overhead total variance
(Definition ....)

variance
(Definition ....)

variance
(Definition ....)

variance
(Definition ....)

variance
(Definition ....)

Definitions

1   The difference between actual and budgeted production, multiplied by the standard absorption rate per unit

2   The difference between budgeted hours of work and the actual hours worked, multiplied by the standard absorption rate per hour

3   The under or over absorption of fixed production overhead

4   The difference between budgeted fixed production overhead expenditure and actual fixed production overhead expenditure

5   The difference between the number of hours that actual production should have taken, and the number of hours actually taken, multiplied by the standard absorption rate per hour

6   The sales volume variance is valued at the standard selling price per unit.

True ☐   False ☐

7   *Match the following causes of variances to the appropriate variance.*

Variances		Causes	
(a)	Favourable labour efficiency	(1)	Inexperienced staff in the purchasing department
(b)	Adverse sales volume	(2)	Materials of higher quality than standard
(c)	Adverse material price	(3)	Unexpected slump in demand
(d)	Adverse selling price	(4)	Production difficulties
(e)	Adverse fixed production overhead volume	(5)	Strike
(f)	Idle time	(6)	Poor machine maintenance

8   *Match the three pairs of interrelated variances.*

(a)	Adverse selling price	(e)	Adverse materials price
(b)	Favourable labour rate	(f)	Favourable materials usage
(c)	Adverse materials usage	(g)	Adverse sales volume
(d)	Favourable sales volume	(h)	Idle time

9   *Fill in the blanks.*

If an organisation uses standard marginal costing, there will be no .... variance and the
.... variance will be valued at ....

10   *Choose the appropriate words from those highlighted.*

The materials mix variance is calculated as the difference between the **standard/actual** total quantity used in the **standard/actual** mix and the **standard/actual** quantities used in the **standard/actual** mix, valued at **standard/actual** costs.

11   *Choose the appropriate words from those highlighted.*

The materials yield variance is calculated on the difference between the **standard/actual** input for **standard/actual** output, and the **standard/actual** total quantity input (in the **standard/actual** mix), valued at **standard/actual** costs.

12   The total yield variance in quantity is zero.

     True [ ]   False [ ]

13   *Choose the appropriate words from those highlighted*

The sales mix variance is calculated as the difference between the **standard/actual** quantity sold in the **standard/actual** mix and the **standard/actual** quantity sold in the **standard/actual** mix, valued at **standard/actual** margin per unit.

14   *Choose the appropriate words from those highlighted*

The sales quantity variance is calculated as the difference between the **standard/actual** sales volume in the budgeted proportions and the budgeted sales volumes, multiplied by the **standard/actual** margin.

Answers to Quick Quiz

1   The material price variance is the difference between what the material did cost and what it should have cost.

The material usage variance is the difference between the standard cost of the material that should have been used and the standard cost of the material that was used.

2   True

3   The idle time variance is an adverse efficiency variance, which is adverse.

4   Variable production overhead variances are based on hours worked.

5

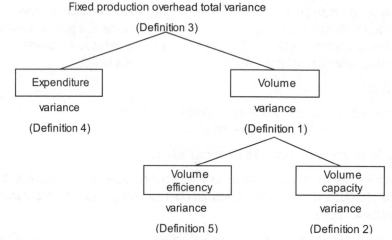

6   False. It is valued at the standard profit margin per unit.

7   (a)   (2)   (d)   (3)
    (b)   (3) or (4) or (5)   (e)   (4) or (5) or (6)
    (c)   (1)   (f)   (5) or (6)

8   (a) and (d)
    (b) and (c)
    (e) and (f)

9   There will be no fixed production overhead volume variance and the sales volume variance will be valued at standard contribution margin.

10   The materials mix variance is calculated as the difference between the actual total quantity used in the standard mix, and the actual quantities used in the actual mix, valued at standard costs.

11   The materials yield variance is calculated as the difference between the standard input for actual output, and the actual total quantity input (in the standard mix), valued at standard costs.

12   False. It is the total mix variance in quantity which is zero.

13   The sales mix variance is calculated as the difference between the actual quantity sold in the standard mix and the actual quantity sold in the actual mix, valued at standard margin per unit.

14   The sales quantity variance is calculated as the difference between the actual sales volume in the budgeted proportions and the budgeted sales volumes, multiplied by the standard margin.

Now try the question below from the Exam Question Bank

Number	Level	Marks	Time
Q17	Examination	20	36 mins

13

Behavioural aspects of standard costing

Topic list	Syllabus reference
1 Planning and operational variances	D5 (a), (b), (c), (d)
2 Behavioural aspects of standard costing	D6 (a), (b), (c)

Introduction

In this chapter we discuss the effects of standard costs and variances on staff motivation and action.

Managers' acceptance of the use of variances for performance measurement, and their **motivation**, is likely to increase if they know they will not be held responsible for poor planning and faulty standard setting. **Planning and operational variances** are used to highlight those variances which are **controllable** and those which are **non-controllable.**

We also discuss the problems of using standard costing in the modern, rapidly changing business environment.

Study guide

		Intellectual level
D5	**Planning and operational variances**	
(a)	Calculate a revised budget	2
(b)	Identify and explain those factors that could and could not be allowed to revise an original budget	2
(c)	Calculate planning and operational variances for sales, including market size and market share, materials and labour	2
(d)	Explain the manipulation issues in revising budgets	2
D6	**Behavioural aspects of standard costing**	
(a)	Describe the dysfunctional nature of some variances in the modern environment of JIT and TQM	2
(b)	Discuss the behavioural problems resulting from using standard costs in rapidly changing environments	2
(c)	Discuss the effect that variances have on staff motivation and action	2

Exam guide

Planning and operational variances are highly examinable and behavioural aspects of standard costing may form the discussion part of a question.

1 Planning and operational variances

FAST FORWARD

A planning and operational approach to variance analysis divides the total variance into those variances which have arisen because of inaccurate planning or faulty standards (**planning variances**) and those variances which have been caused by adverse or favourable operational performance, compared with a standard which has been revised in hindsight (**operational variances**).

So far in this text we have been looking at variances which are calculated using what we will call the conventional approach to variance analysis, whereby an actual cost is compared with an original standard cost. In this section of the chapter we will be examining planning and operational variances. They are not really alternatives to the conventional approach, they merely provide a much more detailed analysis.

Basically, the planning and operational approach attempts to divide a total variance (which has been calculated conventionally) into a group of variances which have arisen because of **inaccurate planning** or **faulty standards** (planning variances) and a group of variances which have been caused by adverse or favourable **operational performance** (operational variances, surprisingly enough!).

Planning and operational variances may seem confusing if you do not have a really good grasp of the conventional approach and so, before you go any further, make sure that you understand everything that we covered so far in this Text. Go back over any areas you are unsure about. Only when you are happy that you have mastered the basics should you begin on this section.

Key terms

A **planning variance** (or **revision variance**) compares an original standard with a revised standard that should or would have been used if planners had known in advance what was going to happen.

An **operational variance** (or **operating variance**) compares an actual result with the revised standard.

Planning and operational variances are based on the principle that variances ought to be reported by taking as the **main starting point**, not the original standard, but a **standard** which can be seen, in hindsight, to be the **optimum** that should have been **achievable**.

Exponents of this approach argue that the monetary value of variances ought to be a realistic reflection of what the **causes** of the variances have cost the organisation. In other words they should show the cash (and profit) gained or lost as a consequence of operating results being different to what should have been achieved. Variances can be valued in this way by **comparing actual results with a realistic standard or budget**. Such variances are called **operational variances**.

Planning variances arise because the **original standard and revised more realistic standards are different** and have nothing to do with operational performance. In most cases, it is unlikely that anything could be done about planning variances: they are **not controllable by operational managers but by senior management**.

In other words the **cause of a total variance** might be one or both of:

- Adverse or favourable operational performance (**operational variance**)
- Inaccurate planning, or faulty standards (**planning variance**)

1.1 Calculating total planning and operational variances

We will begin by looking at how to split a total cost variance into its planning and operational components.

1.1.1 Example: Total cost planning and operational variances

At the beginning of 20X0, WB set a standard marginal cost for its major product of $25 per unit. The standard cost is recalculated once each year. Actual production costs during August 20X0 were $304,000, when 8,000 units were made.

With the benefit of hindsight, the management of WB realises that a more realistic standard cost for current conditions would be $40 per unit. The planned standard cost of $25 is unrealistically low.

Required

Calculate the planning and operational variances.

Solution

With the benefit of hindsight, the **realistic standard should have been $40**. The variance caused by favourable or adverse **operating** performance should be calculated by comparing actual results against this realistic standard.

	$
Revised standard cost of actual production (8,000 × $40)	320,000
Actual cost	304,000
Total **operational** variance	16,000 (F)

The variance is favourable because the actual cost was lower than would have been expected using the revised basis.

The **planning** variance reveals the extent to which the original standard was at fault.

		$
Revised standard cost	8,000 units × $40 per unit	320,000
Original standard cost	8,000 units × $25 per unit	200,000
Planning variance		120,000 (A)

It is an adverse variance because the original standard was too optimistic, overestimating the expected profits by understating the standard cost. More simply, it is adverse because the revised cost is much higher than the original cost.

	$
Planning variance	120,000 (A)
Operational variance	16,000 (F)
Total	104,000 (A)

If **traditional variance analysis** had been used, the total cost variance would have been the same, but all the **'blame'** would appear to lie on actual results and operating inefficiencies (rather than some being due to faulty planning).

	$
Standard cost of 8,000 units (× $25)	200,000
Actual cost of 8,000 units	304,000
Total cost variance	104,000 (A)

Question	Planning and operational variances

Suppose a budget is prepared which includes a raw materials cost per unit of product of $2 (2 kg of copper at $1 per kg). Due to a rise in world prices for copper during the year, the average market price of copper rises to $1.50 per kg. During the year, 1,000 units were produced at a cost of $3,250 for 2,200 kg of copper.

What are the planning and operational variances?

Answer

Operational variance

	$
Actual cost (for 1,000 units)	3,250
Revised standard cost (for 1,000 units) (2,000 kg × $1.50)	3,000
Total operational variance	250 (A)

Planning variance

	$
Revised standard cost (1,000 × 2 kg × $1.50)	3,000
Original standard cost (1,000 × 2 kg × $1)	2,000
Total planning variance	1,000 (A)

1.2 Operational price and usage variances

So far we have only considered planning and operational variances in total, without carrying out the usual two-way split. In the question above, for instance, we identified a total operational variance for materials of $250 without considering whether this operational variance could be split between a usage variance and a price variance.

This is not a problem so long as you retain your grasp of knowledge you already possess. You know that a **price** variance measures the difference between the actual amount of money paid and the amount of money that should have been paid for that quantity of materials (or whatever). Thus, in our example:

	$
Actual price of actual materials (2,200 kg)	3,250
Revised standard price of actual materials ($1.50 × 2,200 kg)	3,300
Operational price variance	50 (F)

The variance is favourable because the materials were purchased more cheaply than would have been expected.

Similarly, a **usage** variance measures the difference between the actual physical quantity of materials used or hours taken and the quantities that should have been used or taken for the actual volume of production. Those physical differences are then converted into money values by applying the appropriate standard cost.

In our example we are calculating **operational variances**, so we are not interested in planning errors. This means that the **appropriate standard cost is the revised standard cost** of $1.50.

Actual quantity should have been		2,000 kgs
but was		2,200 kgs
Operational usage variance in kgs		200 kgs (A)
× revised standard cost per kg		× $1.50
Operational usage variance in $		$300 (A)

The two variances of course reconcile to the total variance as previously calculated.

	$	
Operational price variance	50	(F)
Operational usage variance	(300)	(A)
Total operational variance	250	(A)

1.3 Planning price and usage variances

We can also split the total planning variance into two. For example, if two planning errors have been made, one affecting price and one usage, the effect of each can be analysed.

1.3.1 Example planning price and usage variances

The standard materials cost of a product is 5 kgs × $7.50 per kg = $37.50. Actual production of 10,000 units used 54,400 kgs at a cost of $410,000. In retrospect it was realised that the standard materials cost should have been 5.3 kgs per unit at a cost of $8 per kg.

Required

Calculate the materials planning variances in as much detail as possible.

Solution

Calculate the **total** materials planning variance first, to give you a point of reference.

Total materials planning variance

		$
Original flexed budget cost	(10,000 × $37.50)	375,000
Revised flexed budget cost	(10,000 × 5.3 kgs × $8)	424,000
		49,000 (A)

Planning price variance

Actual units × revised standard usage × (original standard price – revised standard price)

= 10,000 units × 5.3 kgs × ($7.50 – $8.00) = $26,500 (A)

Planning usage variance

Actual units × original standard price × (original standard usage – revised standard usage)

= 10,000 units × $7.50 × (5 kgs – 5.3 kgs) = $22,500 (A)

Planning price variance + planning usage variance = total planning variance

$26,500 + £22,500 = $49,000 (A)

1.4 Operational variances for labour and overheads

Precisely the same argument applies to the calculation of operational variances for labour and overheads, and the examples already given should be sufficient to enable you to do the next question.

Question

A new product requires three hours of labour per unit at a standard rate of $6 per hour. In a particular month the budget is to produce 500 units. Actual results were as follows.

Hours worked	1,700
Production	540 units
Wages cost	$10,500

Within minutes of production starting it was realised that the job was extremely messy and the labour force could therefore claim an extra 25c per hour in 'dirty money'.

Required

Calculate planning and operational variances in as much detail as possible.

Answer

Keep calm and calculate the *total* variance in the normal way to begin with. Then you will understand what it is that you have to analyse. Next follow through the workings shown above, substituting the figures in the exercise for those in the example.

Total labour variance

	$
540 units should have cost (× 3 hrs × $6)	9,720
But did cost	10,500
	780 (A)

Planning variance

	$
Revised standard cost (540 × 3 hrs × $6.25)	10,125
Original standard cost (540 × 3 hrs × $6.00)	9,720
	405 (A)

Operational rate variance

	$
Actual cost of actual units	10,500
Revised cost of actual units (1,700 × $6.25)	10,625
	125 (F)

Operational efficiency variance

540 units should have taken (× 3 hrs)	1,620 hrs
but did take	1,700 hrs
Operational efficiency variance in hours	80 hrs
× revised standard rate per hour	× $6.25
Operational efficiency variance in $	$500 (A)

1.5 Planning and operational sales variances   12/07

Our final calculations in this section deal with planning and operational sales variances.

1.5.1 Example: Planning and operational sales variances

Dimsek budgeted to make and sell 400 units of its product, the role, in the four-week period no 8, as follows.

	$
Budgeted sales (100 units per week)	40,000
Variable costs (400 units × $60)	24,000
Contribution	16,000
Fixed costs	10,000
Profit	6,000

At the beginning of the second week, production came to a halt because inventories of raw materials ran out, and a new supply was not received until the beginning of week 3. As a consequence, the company lost one week's production and sales. Actual results in period 8 were as follows.

	$
Sales (320 units)	32,000
Variable costs (320 units × $60)	19,200
Contribution	12,800
Fixed costs	10,000
Actual profit	2,800

In retrospect, it is decided that the optimum budget, given the loss of production facilities in the third week, would have been to sell only 300 units in the period.

Required

Calculate appropriate planning and operational variances.

Solution

The **planning** variance **compares the revised budget** with the **original budget**.

Revised sales volume, given materials shortage	300 units
Original budgeted sales volume	400 units
Planning variance in units of sales	100 units(A)
× standard contribution per unit	× $40
Planning variance in $	$4,000 (A)

Arguably, **running out of raw materials is an operational error** and so the loss of sales volume and contribution from the materials shortage is an opportunity cost that could have been avoided with better purchasing arrangements. The operational variances are variances calculated in the usual way, except that actual results are compared with the revised standard or budget. There is a sales volume variance which is an **operational variance**, as follows.

Actual sales volume	320 units
Revised sales volume	300 units
Operational sales volume variance in units	20 units (F)
(possibly due to production efficiency or marketing efficiency)	
× standard contribution per unit	× $40
	$800 (F)

These variances can be used as **control information** to reconcile budgeted and actual profit.

	$	$
Operating statement, period 8		
Budgeted profit		6,000
Planning variance	4,000 (A)	
Operational variance – sales volume	800 (F)	
		3,200 (A)
Actual profit in period 8		2,800

You will have noticed that in this example sales volume variances were **valued at contribution forgone**, and there were no fixed cost volume variances. This is because contribution forgone, in terms of lost revenue or extra expenditure incurred, is the nearest equivalent to **opportunity cost** which is readily available to management accountants (who assume linearity of costs and revenues within a relevant range of activity).

KSO budgeted to sell 10,000 units of a new product during 20X0. The budgeted sales price was $10 per unit, and the variable cost $3 per unit.

Although actual sales in 20X0 were 10,000 units and variable costs of sales were $30,000, sales revenue was only $5 per unit. With the benefit of hindsight, it is realised that the budgeted sales price of $10 was hopelessly optimistic, and a price of $4.50 per unit would have been much more realistic.

Required

Calculate planning and operational variances.

Answer

The only variances are selling price variances.

Planning (selling price) variance

	Total
	$
Revised budget (10,000 × $4.50)	45,000
Original budget (10,000 × $10.00)	100,000
Planning variance	55,000 (A)

The original variance was too optimistic and so the planning variance is an adverse variance.

Operational (selling price) variance

	$
Actual sales (10,000 × $5)	50,000
Revised sales (10,000 × $4.50)	45,000
Operational (selling price) variance	5,000 (F)

The total difference between budgeted and actual profit of $50,000 (A) is therefore analysed as follows.

	$
Operational variance (selling price)	5,000 (F)
Planning variance	55,000 (A)
	50,000 (A)

PG budgeted sales for 20X8 were 5,000 units. The standard contribution is $9.60 per unit. A recession in 20X8 meant that the market for PG's products declined by 5%. PG's market share also fell by 3%. Actual sales were 4,500 units.

Required

Calculate planning and operational variances for sales volume.

Answer

Planning variance

	Units
Original budgeted sales	5,000
Revised budget sales (–5%)	4,750
	250 A
@ Contribution per unit of $9.60	$2,400

Operational variance

	Units
Revised budget sales	4,750
Actual sales	4,500
	250 A
@ Contribution per unit of $9.60	$2,400

The fall in **market size** is uncontrollable by the management of PG and therefore results in a **planning** variance. The fall in **market share** is controllable and forms part of the **operational** variance.

Exam focus point

The examiner is very keen that candidates should understand the practical problems involved with these variances and do not just concentrate on the mechanics of the calculations.

1.6 Calculating a revised budget   12/07

The syllabus requires you to be able to calculate a revised budget, which could involve revising standards for sales, materials and/or labour so that only operational variances are highlighted when actual results are compared to the revised budget.

1.6.1 Example: revised budget

A company produces Widgets and Splodgets which are fairly standardised products. The following information relates to period 1.

The standard selling price of Widgets is $50 each and Splodgets $100 each. In period 1, there was a special promotion on Splodgets with a 5% discount being offered. All units produced are sold and no inventory is held.

To produce a Widget they use 5 kg of X and in period 1, their plans were based on a cost of X of $3 per kg. Due to market movements the actual price changed and if they had purchased efficiently the cost would have been $4.50 per kg. Production of Widgets was 2,000 units.

A Splodget uses raw material Z but again the price of this can change rapidly. It was thought that Z would cost $30 per tonne but in fact they only paid $25 per tonne and if they had purchased correctly the cost would have been less as it was freely available at only $23 per tonne. It usually takes 1.5 tonnes of Z to produce 1 Splodget and 500 Splodgets are usually produced.

Each Widget takes 3 hours to produce and each Splodget 2 hours. Labour is paid $5 per hour. At the start of period 1, management negotiated a job security package with the workforce in exchange for a promised 5% increase in efficiency – that is, that the workers would increase output per hour by 5%.

Fixed overheads are usually $12,000 every period and variable overheads are $3 per labour hour.

Required

Produce the original budget and a revised budget allowing for controllable factors in a suitable format.

Solution

Original budget for Period 1

	$
Sales revenue ((2,000 × $50) + (500 × $100))	150,000
Material costs X (2,000 × 5kg × $3)	30,000
Material costs Z (500 × $30 × 1.5)	22,500
Labour costs ((2,000 × 3 × $5) + (500 × 2 × $5))	35,000
Variable overheads ((2,000 × 3 × $3) + (500 × 2 × $3))	21,000
Fixed overheads	12,000
Profit	29,500

Revised budget for Period 1

	$
Sales revenue ((2,000 × $50) + (500 × $95))	147,500
Material costs X (2,000 × 5kg × $4.5)	45,000
Material costs Z (500 × $23 × 1.5)	17,250
Labour costs ((2,000 × 3 × $5) + (500 × 2 × $5)) × 0.95	33,250
Variable overheads ((2,000 × 3 × $3) + (500 × 2 × $3)) × 0.95	19,950
Fixed overheads	12,000
Profit	20,050

1.6.2 When should budget revisions be allowed?

A budget revision should be allowed if something has happened which is **beyond the control** of the organisation or individual manager and which makes the original budget unsuitable for use in performance management.

Any adjustment should be **approved by senior management** who should look at the issues involved **objectively** and **independently**. **Operational issues** are the issues that a budget is attempting to control so they should **not** be subject to revision. However, it can be very **difficult to establish** what is due to operational problems (controllable) and what is due to planning (uncontrollable).

1.7 The value of planning and operational variances

Advantages of a system of planning and operational variances

- The analysis highlights those variances which are **controllable** and those which are **non-controllable**.
- **Managers' acceptance** of the use of variances for performance measurement, and their **motivation**, is likely to increase if they know they will not be held responsible for poor planning and faulty standard setting.
- The **planning and standard-setting processes** should improve; standards should be more accurate, relevant and appropriate.
- Operational variances will provide a **'fairer' reflection of actual performance**.

The limitations of planning and operational variances, which must be overcome if they are to be applied in practice.

- It is difficult to **decide in hindsight** what the **realistic standard** should have been.
- It may become **too easy to justify all the variances as being due to bad planning**, so no operational variances will be highlighted.
- Establishing realistic revised standards and analysing the total variance into planning and operational variances can be a **time consuming** task, even if a spreadsheet package is devised.
- Even though the intention is to provide more meaningful information, **managers may be resistant** to the very idea of variances and refuse to see the virtues of the approach. Careful presentation and explanation will be required until managers are used to the concepts.

2 Behavioural aspects of standard costing

The **role of standards and variances** in the modern business environment is open to question.

2.1 Standard costing and new technology

Standard costing has traditionally been associated with labour-intensive operations, but it can be applied to capital-intensive production too.

It is quite possible that with advanced manufacturing technology variable overheads are incurred in relation to machine time rather than labour time, and **standard costs should reflect this** where appropriate.

With **computer aided design/computer aided manufacture (CADCAM)** systems, the planning of manufacturing requirements can be computerised, so that standard costs can be constructed by computer, saving administrative time and expense while providing far **more accurate standards**.

2.2 Total quality management (TQM)

FAST FORWARD

In the context of **TQM**, quality means getting it right first time and improving continuously.

Key term

Total quality management (TQM) is the process of applying a zero defects philosophy to the management of all resources and relationships within an organisation as a means of developing and sustaining a culture of continuous improvement which focuses on meeting customers' expectations.

Mark Lee Inman listed 'eight requirements of quality' in an ACCA *Students' Newsletter* article, which could be seen as the **characteristics of total quality management programmes**.

(a)   Organisation wide there must be acceptance that the only thing that matters is the customer.

(b)   There should be recognition of the all-pervasive nature of the customer-supplier relationship, including internal customers; passing sub-standard material to another division is not satisfactory

(c)   Instead of relying on inspection to a predefined level of quality, the cause of the defect in the first place should be prevented.

(d)   Each employee or group of employees must be personally responsible for defect-free production or service in their domain.

(e)   There should be a move away from 'acceptable' quality levels. Any level of defects must be unacceptable.

(f)   All departments should try obsessively to get thing right first time; this applies to misdirected phone calls and typing errors as much as to production.

(g)   Quality certification programmes should be introduced.

(h)   The cost of poor quality should be emphasised; good quality generates savings.

2.3 Standard costing and TQM

Standard costing concentrates on **quantity** and ignores other factors contributing to effectiveness. In a **total quality environment**, however, quantity is not an issue; quality is. Effectiveness in such an environment therefore centres on high quality output (produced as a result of high quality input and the elimination of non-value adding activities) and the cost of failing to achieve the required level of effectiveness is measured not in variances, but in terms of **internal and external failure costs**, neither of which would be identified by a traditional standard costing analysis.

Standard costing systems might measure, say, **labour efficiency** in terms of individual tasks and level of **output.** In a total quality environment, labour is more likely to be viewed as a number of **multi-task** teams who are responsible for the completion of a part of the production process. The effectiveness of such a team is more appropriately measured in terms of **re-working** required, **returns** from customers, **defects** identified in subsequent stages of production and so on.

Traditional feedback control would seek to eliminate an adverse material price variance by requiring managers to source cheaper, possibly lower quality supplies. This may run counter to the aim of maximising quality of output.

2.3.1 Can standard costing and TQM co-exist?

Arguably, there is little point in running both a total quality management programme and a standard costing system simultaneously.

(a) Predetermined standards are at odds with the philosophy of **continual improvement** inherent in a total quality management programme.

(b) Continual improvements are likely to alter methods of working, prices, quantities of inputs and so on, whereas standard costing is most appropriate in a stable, standardised and repetitive environment.

(c) Material standard costs often incorporate a planned level of scrap. This is at odds with the TQM aim of **zero defects** and there is no motivation to 'get it right first time'.

(d) Attainable standards, which make some allowance for wastage and inefficiencies are commonly set. The use of such standards conflicts with the **elimination of waste** which is such a vital ingredient of a TQM programme.

(e) Standard costing control systems make individual managers **responsible** for the variances relating to their part of the organisation's activities. A TQM programme, on the other hand, aims to make **all personnel** aware of, and responsible for, the importance of supplying the customer with a quality product.

Question
TQM and variance analysis

One of the basic tenets of total quality management is 'get it right first time'. Is variance reporting a help or a hindrance in this respect?

Answer

In theory it should not be of any relevance at all, because variances will not occur. In practice an organisation will not get everything right first time and variance reporting may still draw attention to areas for improvement – **if the standard and 'being right' are the same thing.**

2.4 Standard costing and new philosophy

It has been argued that traditional variance analysis is unhelpful and **potentially misleading** in the modern organisation, and can make managers focus their attention on the wrong issues, for example **over-producing** and stockpiling finished goods, because higher production volumes mean that overheads are spread over more units. Here are two examples.

(a) **Efficiency variance**. Adverse efficiency variances should be avoided, which means that managers should try to prevent idle time and to keep up production. In a TQM environment using just-in-time manufacturing, action to eliminate idle time could result in the manufacture of unwanted products that must be held in store and might eventually be scrapped. Efficiency variances could focus management attention on the wrong problems.

(b) **Materials price variance**. In a JIT environment, the key issues with materials purchasing are supplier reliability, materials quality, and delivery in small order quantities. Purchasing managers shouldn't be shopping around every month looking for the cheapest price. Many JIT systems depend on long-term contractual links with suppliers, which means that material price variances are not relevant for control purposes.

The **role of standards and variances in the modern business environment** is viewed as follows by George Brown (a previous ACCA examiner).

'The rate of change in product type and design due to technological improvement, customer requirements and increased competition has led to rapid change in how businesses operate. The need to respond to customer demands for speedy availability of products, shortening product life cycles and higher quality standards has contributed to a number of changes in the way businesses operate…just-in-time systems…total quality programmes…..greater emphasis on the value chain…..accurate product costing and pricing information……improved speed and flexibility of information availability…' ('Standard costing – a status check')

Standard costing, on the other hand, is most appropriate in a stable, standardised and repetitive environment and one of the main objectives of standard costing is to ensure that processes conform to standards, that they do not vary, and that variances are eliminated. This may seem **restrictive and inhibiting in the business environment of the twenty first century**. (In fact, in the article referred to above, George Brown attempts to show that concerns about the restrictive and inhibiting nature of standard costing have been raised since it was first used and that efforts have continuously been made (such as planning and operating variances) to redesign standards and variances to maintain their relevance in an environment of change.)

2.5 Other problems with using standard costing in today's environment

(a)   Variance analysis concentrates on only a **narrow range of costs**, and does not give sufficient attention to issues such as quality and customer satisfaction.

(b)   Standard costing places **too much emphasis on direct labour costs**. Direct labour is only a small proportion of costs in the modern manufacturing environment and so this emphasis is not appropriate.

(c)   Many of the variances in a standard costing system focus on the control of **short-term variable costs**. In most modern manufacturing environments, the majority of costs, including direct labour costs, tend to be fixed in the short run.

(d)   The use of standard costing relies on the existence of **repetitive operations** and relatively **homogeneous** output. Nowadays many organisations are forced continually to respond to customers' changing requirements, with the result that output and operations are not so repetitive.

(e)   Standard costing systems were **developed** when the **business environment** was more **stable** and **less prone to change**. The current business environment is more dynamic and it is not possible to assume stable conditions.

(f)   Standard costing systems **assume** that **performance to standard is acceptable**. Today's business environment is more focused on continuous improvement.

(g)   Most standard costing systems produce **control statements weekly or monthly**. The modern manager needs much more prompt control information in order to function efficiently in a dynamic business environment.

2.6 The role in modern business of standards and variances

Two surveys ((Puxty and Lyall (1989) and Drury *et al* (1993)) have confirmed the **continued wide use of standard costing systems**. Drury *et al*, for instance, showed that 76% of the responding organisations operated a standard costing system.

- **Planning**. Even in a TQM environment, budgets will still need to be quantified. For example, the planned level of prevention and appraisal costs needs to be determined. Standards, such as returns of a particular product should not exceed 1% of deliveries during a budget period, can be set.

- **Control**. Cost and mix changes from plan will still be relevant in many processing situations.

- **Decision making**. Existing standards can be used as the starting point in the construction of a cost for a new product.

- **Performance measurement**. If the product mix is relatively stable, performance measurement may be enhanced by the use of a system of planning and operational variances.

- **Product pricing**. Target costs may be compared with current standards, and the resulting 'cost gap' investigated with a view to reducing it or eliminating it using techniques such as value engineering.

- **Improvement and change**. Variance trends can be monitored over time.

- **Accounting valuations**. Although the operation of a JIT system in conjunction with backflush accounting will reduce the need for standard costs and variance analysis, standards may be used to value residual inventory and the transfers to cost of sales account.

 **Question**

AB Co has been receiving an increasing number of customer complaints about a general weakness in the quality of its products in recent months. The company believes that its future success is dependent on product quality and it is therefore determined to improve it.

Required

Describe the contribution that variance analysis can make towards the aim of improved product quality.

Answer

Variance analysis can be used to enhance product quality and to keep track of quality control information. This is because variance analysis measures both the planned use of resources and the actual use of resources in order to compare the two.

As variance analysis is generally expressed in terms of purely quantitative measures, such as quantity of raw materials used and price per unit of quantity, issues of quality would appear to be excluded from the reporting process. Quality would appear to be an excuse for spending more time, say, or buying more expensive raw materials.

Variance analysis, as it currently stands, therefore needs to be **adapted** to take account of quality issues.

(a) Variance analysis reports should routinely include **measures such as defect rates**. Although zero defects will be most desirable, such a standard of performance may not be reached at first. However there should be an expected rate of defects: if this is exceeded then management attention is directed to the excess.

(b) The **absolute number of defects** should be measured *and* **their type**. If caused by certain materials and components this can shed light on, say, a favourable materials price variance which might have been caused by substandard materials being purchased more cheaply. Alternatively, if the defects are caused by shoddy assembly work this can shed light on a favourable labour efficiency variance if quality is being sacrificed for speed.

(c) It should also be possible to provide **financial measures for the cost of poor quality**. These can include direct costs such as the wages of inspection and quality control staff, the cost of time in rectifying the defects, and the cost of the materials used in rectification.

(d) Measures could be built into materials price and variance analysis, so that the **materials price variance** as currently reported includes a **factor reflecting the quality of materials purchased**.

 Question

Can you think of some ways in which a standard costing system could be adapted so that it is useful in the modern business environment?

Answer

Here are some ideas.

(a) **Non-financial measures** can be included within management control reports. Examples include number of defects, percentage of on-time deliveries, and so on.

(b) Even when output is not standardised, it may be possible to identify a number of **standard components and activities** whose costs may be controlled effectively by the setting of standard costs and identification of variances.

(c) The use of computer power enables standards to be **updated rapidly** and more frequently, so that they remain useful for the purposes of control by comparison.

(d) The use of **ideal standards** and **more demanding performance levels** can combine the benefits of **continuous improvement** and standard costing control.

(e)   **Information**, particularly of a non-financial nature, can be **produced more rapidly** with the assistance of **computers**. For example the use of on-line data capture can enable the continuous display of real time information on factors such as hours worked, number of components used and number of defects.

Chapter Roundup

- A planning and operational approach to variance analysis divides the total variance into those variances which have arisen because of inaccurate planning or faulty standards (**planning variances**) and those variances which have been caused by adverse or favourable operational performance, compared with a standard which has been revised in hindsight (**operational variances**).

- The **role of standards and variances** in the modern business environment is open to question.

- In the context of **TQM**, quality means getting it right first time and improving continuously.

Quick Quiz

1   A planning variance compares what with what?

2   If a planning efficiency variance is valued at an original standard rate, the planning rate variance is valued at the original efficiency level.

   True ☐   False ☐

3   Complete the table below to show a possible response to each of the traditional performance measures and a consequence of that response.

Measurement	Response	Consequence of action
Purchase price variance		
Labour efficiency variance		
Cost of scrap		
Scrap factor included in standard costs		

4   *Fill in the missing words.*

   (a)   Standard costing concentrates on ………………….….... whereas the issue in TQM is
   ………………..………… .

   (b)   Using standard costing, the cost of failing to achieve the required level of effectiveness is measured in ………………………... ; in TQM, it is measured in terms of …………………..………… .

   (c)   Standard costing systems might measure labour efficiency in terms of …………………………... .
   In a TQM environment, effectiveness is more appropriately measured in terms of
   ……………………….. .

Answers to Quick Quiz

1   A planning variance compares an original standard with a revised standard that should or would have been used if planners had known in advance what was going to happen.

2   False. It is valued at the revised efficiency level.

3

Measurement	Response	Consequence of action
Purchase price variance	Buy in greater bulk to reduce unit price	Excess stocks Higher holding costs Quality and reliability of delivery times ignored
Labour efficiency variance	Encourage greater output	Possibly excess stocks of the wrong products
Cost of scrap	Rework items to reduce scrap	Production flow held up by re-working
Scrap factor included in standard costs	Supervisor aims to achieve actual scrap = standard scrap	No motivation to get it right first time

4   (a)   quantity   (c)   individual tasks and level of output
              quality   reworking required, returns, defects

      (b)   variances
              internal and external failure costs

Now try the questions below from the Exam Question Bank

Number	Level	Marks	Time
Q18	Introductory	14	25 mins

Performance measurement and control

Performance measurement

Topic list	Syllabus reference
1 Performance measurement	E1
2 Financial performance indicators	E1 (a)
3 Non-financial performance indicators	E1 (b)
4 Short-termism and manipulation	E1 (c)
5 The balanced scorecard	E1 (d)
6 Building Block model	E1 (d), (e)

Introduction

Performance measurement and control is the final section in this Study Text. This chapter begins by introducing the term **performance measurement** and then describes the various performance measures that are used by various types of entity. Variances are an important measure of performance that you have already met.

It is important that the performance of an organisation is monitored, and this is most commonly done by calculating a number of ratios.

The chapter concludes by considering alternative views of performance measurement such as the **balanced scorecard** and **building blocks** which offer a contrast to the more **traditional** approaches.

Study guide

		Intellectual level
E1	**The scope of performance measurement**	
(a)	Describe, calculate and interpret financial performance indicators (FPIs) for profitability, liquidity and risk in both manufacturing and service businesses. Suggest methods to improve these measures	2
(b)	Describe, calculate and interpret non-financial performance indicators (NFPIs) and suggest methods to improve the performance indicated	2
(c)	Explain the causes and problems created by short-termism and financial manipulation of results and suggest methods to encourage a long term view	2
(d)	Explain and interpret the Balanced Scorecard, and the Building Block model proposed by Fitzgerald and Moon	2
(e)	Discuss the difficulties of target setting in qualitative areas	2

Exam guide

You must be able to **explain** as well as calculate performance indicators and **apply** your analysis to the organisation in the question. This has been a feature of all of the F5 exams so far. The organisations will not necessarily be limited companies.

There is an article on interpreting financial data in *Student Accountant*, April 2008.

1 Performance measurement   6/08

FAST FORWARD

> **Performance measurement** aims to establish how well something or somebody is doing in relation to a plan.
>
> Performance measures may be divided into two groups.
>
> - Financial performance indicators
> - Non-financial performance indicators

Exam focus point

> The July 2010 issue of *Student Accountant* contains an article on **performance management** written by the **examiner**. Ensure that you are familiar with this article.

Performance measurement aims to establish how well something or somebody is doing in relation to a plan. The 'thing' may be a machine, a factory, a subsidiary company or an organisation as a whole. The 'body' may be an individual employee, a manager or a group of people.

Performance measurement is a **vital part of** the **control process.**

1.1 Performance measures

Different measures are appropriate for different businesses. Factors to consider:

(a) **Measurement needs resources** – people, equipment and time to collect and analyse information. The costs and benefits of providing resources to produce a performance indicator must be carefully weighed up.

(b) **Performance must be measured in relation to something**, otherwise measurement is meaningless. Overall performance should be measured against the **objectives** of the organisation and the **plans** that result from those objectives. If the organisation has no clear objectives, the first step in performance measurement is to set them. The second is to identify the factors that are critical to the success of those objectives.

(c) **Measures must be relevant**. This means finding out what the organisation does and how it does it so that measures reflect what actually occurs.

(d) **Short** and **long-term achievement** should be measured. Short-term targets can be valuable, but exclusive use of them may direct the organisation away from opportunities that will mean success for the business in the long-term.

(e) Measures should be **fair.** They should only include factors which managers can control by their decisions, and for which they can be held **responsible**. Measuring controllable costs, revenues and assets may prove controversial however.

(f) A **variety** of measures should be used. Managers may be able to find ways to distort a single measure, but should not be able to affect a variety of measures. The balanced scorecard (Section 5) provides a method of measuring performance from a number of perspectives.

(g) **Realistic estimates** may be required for measures to be employed. These include estimates of financial items whose value is not certain, such as the cost of capital, and estimates of the impact of non-financial items.

(h) Measurement needs **responses,** above all managers to make decisions in the best interests of the organisation. Managers will only respond to measures that they find useful. The management accountant therefore needs to adopt a modern marketing philosophy to the provision of performance measures: satisfy customer wants, not pile 'em high and sell 'em cheap.

Once suitable performance measures have been selected they must be **monitored on a regular basis** to ensure that they are providing useful information. There is little point in an organisation devoting considerable resources to measuring market share if an increase in market share is not one of the organisation's objectives.

1.2 Quantitative and qualitative performance measures

Quantitative information is capable of being expressed in numbers. Qualitative information is not numeric. Qualitative information can sometimes be converted into numeric through tools such as ranking scales. For example 1 = Good, 2 = Average, 3 = Poor.

(a) An example of a **quantitative** performance measure is 'You have been late for work **twice** this week and it's only Tuesday!'.

(b) An example of a **qualitative** performance measure is 'My bed is **very** comfortable'.

The first measure is likely to find its way into a **staff appraisal report**. The second would feature in a bed manufacturer's **customer satisfaction survey**. Both are indicators of whether their subjects are doing as good a job as they are required to do.

Qualitative measures are by nature **subjective** and **judgmental** but they can still be useful. They are especially valuable when they are derived from several **different sources**, as the likelihood of an unreliable judgement is reduced.

Consider the statement.

'Seven out of ten customers think our beds are very comfortable.'

This is a **quantitative measure** of customer satisfaction (7 out of 10), as well as a **qualitative measure** of the perceived performance of the beds (very comfortable).

2 Financial performance indicators (FPIs)

Pilot paper, 12/07, 12/08,12/09

> **Financial performance indicators** analyse profitability, liquidity and risk.

Financial indicators (or **monetary** measures) include:

Measure	Example
Profit	**Profit** is the commonest measure of all. Profit maximisation is usually cited as the main objective of most business organisations: 'ICI increased pre-tax profits to $233m'; 'General Motors... yesterday reported better-than-expected first-quarter net income of $513m.. Earnings improved $680m from the first quarter of last year when GM lost $167m.
Revenue	'the US businesses contributed $113.9m of total group turnover of $409m'.
Costs	'Sterling's fall benefited pre-tax profits by about $50m while savings from the cost-cutting programme instituted in 1991 were running at around $100m a quarter'; 'The group interest charge rose from $48m to $61m'.
Share price	'The group's shares rose 31p to 1,278p despite the market's fall'.
Cash flow	'Cash flow was also continuing to improve, with cash and marketable securities totalling $8.4bn on March 31, up from $8bn at December 31'.

Note that the monetary amounts stated are **only given meaning in relation to something else**. Financial results should be compared against a **yard-stick** such as:

- Budgeted **sales**, **costs** and **profits**
- **Standards** in a standard costing system
- The **trend** over time (last year/this year, say)
- The results of **other parts of the business**
- The results of **other businesses**
- The **economy** in general
- **Future potential** (for example the performance of a new business may be judged in terms of nearness to breaking even).

Exam focus point

> Knowledge of how to calculate and interpret key ratios is a weak point for many students. Make sure it is one of your strong points.

2.1 Profitability

A company ought of course to be profitable, and there are obvious checks on **profitability**.

(a) Whether the company has made a profit or a loss on its ordinary activities.
(b) By how much this year's profit or loss is bigger or smaller than last year's profit or loss.

It is probably better to consider separately the profits or losses on exceptional items if there are any. Such gains or losses should not be expected to occur again, unlike profits or losses on normal trading.

Profitability

A company has the following summarised income statements for two consecutive years.

	Year 1	Year 2
	$	$
Turnover	70,000	100,000
Less cost of sales	42,000	55,000
Gross profit	28,000	45,000
Less expenses	21,000	35,000
Net profit	7,000	10,000

Although the net profit margin is the same for both years at 10%, the gross profit margin is not.

$$\text{Year 1} \quad \frac{28,000}{70,000} = 40\% \qquad\qquad \text{Year 2} \quad \frac{45,000}{100,000} = 45\%$$

Is this good or bad for the business?

Answer

An increased profit margin must be good because this indicates a wider gap between selling price and cost of sales. Given that the net profit ratio has stayed the same in the second year, however, expenses must be rising. In year 1 expenses were 30% of turnover, whereas in year 2 they were 35% of turnover. This indicates that administration, selling and distribution expenses or interest costs require tight control.

Percentage analysis of profit between year 1 and year 2

	Year 1	Year 2
	%	%
Cost of sales as a % of sales	60	55
Gross profit as a % of sales	40	45
	100	100
Expenses as a % of sales	30	35
Net profit as a % of sales	10	10
Gross profit as a % of sales	40	45

Profit on ordinary activities before taxation is generally thought to be a **better** figure to use than profit after taxation, because there might be unusual variations in the tax charge from year to year which would not affect the underlying profitability of the company's operations.

Another profit figure that should be calculated is **PBIT: profit before interest and tax**. This is the amount of profit which the company earned **before having to pay interest to the providers of loan capital**. By providers of loan capital, we usually mean longer-term loan capital, such as debentures and medium-term bank loans, which will be shown in the balance sheet as 'Payables: amounts falling due after more than one year.' This figure is of particular importance to bankers and lenders.

PBIT = profit on ordinary activities before taxation + interest charges on long-term loan capital

2.1.1 Sales margin

Key term

Sales margin is turnover less cost of sales.

Look at the following examples.

(a) **Wyndeham Press, a printer**

	20X5
	$'000
Turnover	89,844
Cost of sales	(60,769)
Gross profit	29,075
Distribution expenses	(1,523)
Administrative expenses	(13,300)
Goodwill amortisation	(212)
Operating profit (15.6%)	14,040
(Interest etc)	

Cost of sales comprises **direct material** cost, such as paper, and **direct labour**. Distribution and administrative expenses include depreciation. **Sales margin = 32%**.

Sales margin at least shows the contribution that is being made, especially when direct variable costs are very significant.

(b) **Arriva, a bus company**

	20X4
	$m
Turnover	1,534.3
Cost of sales	1,282.6
Gross profit	251.7
Net operating expenses	133.8
Operating profit (7.6%)	117.9
(Interest etc)	

Sales margin = 16%. Clearly a higher percentage of costs are operating costs.

(c) **Lessons to be learnt**

(i)   Sales margin as a measure is **not really any use in comparing different industries**.

(ii) Sales margin is **influenced** by the level of **fixed costs**.

(iii) **Trends** in sales margin are of interest. A falling sales margin suggests an organisation has not been able to pass on input price rises to customers.

(iv) **Comparisons** with similar companies are of interest. If an organisation has a lower sales margin than a similar business, this suggests problems in controlling input costs.

In short, the value of sales margin as a measure of performance depends on the **cost structure** of the industry and the **uses** to which it is put.

2.1.2 Earnings per share (EPS)

EPS is a convenient measure as it shows how well the shareholder is doing.

EPS is widely used as a **measure of a company's performance**, especially in **comparing** results over a period **of several years**. A company must be able to sustain its earnings in order to pay dividends and re-invest in the business so as to achieve future growth. Investors also look for **growth in the EPS** from one year to the next.

Key term

> **Earnings per share (EPS)** is defined as the profit attributable to each equity (ordinary) share.

Question   EPS

Walter Wall Carpets made profits before tax in 20X8 of $9,320,000. Tax amounted to $2,800,000.

The company's share capital is as follows.

	$
Ordinary share (10,000,000 shares of $1)	10,000,000
8% preference shares	2,000,000
	12,000,000

Required

Calculate the EPS for 20X8.

Answer

	$
Profits before tax	9,320,000
Less tax	2,800,000
Profits after tax	6,520,000
Less preference dividend (8% of $2,000,000)	160,000
Earnings	6,360,000
Number of ordinary shares	10,000,000
EPS	63.6c

EPS on its own does not really tell us anything. It must be seen **in context**.

(a)   EPS is used for comparing the results of a company **over time**. Is its EPS growing? What is the rate of growth? Is the rate of growth increasing or decreasing?

(b)   EPS should not be used blindly to compare the earnings of one company with another. For example, if A plc has an EPS of 12c for its 10,000,000 10p shares and B plc has an EPS of 24c for its 50,000,000 25c shares, we must take account of the numbers of shares. When **earnings are used to compare one company's shares with another**, this is done **using the P/E ratio or perhaps the earnings yield**.

(c)   If EPS is to be a reliable basis for comparing results, it **must be calculated consistently**. The EPS of one company must be directly comparable with the EPS of others, and the EPS of a company in one year must be directly comparable with its published EPS figures for previous years. Changes in the share capital of a company during the course of a year cause problems of comparability.

(d)   EPS is a figure based on past data, and it is easily manipulated by changes in accounting policies and by mergers or acquisitions. **The use of the measure in calculating management bonuses makes it particularly liable to manipulation.** The attention given to EPS as a performance measure by City analysts is arguably disproportionate to its true worth. Investors should be more concerned with **future earnings**, but of course estimates of these are more difficult to reach than the readily available figure.

2.1.3 Profitability and return: the return on capital employed (ROCE)

It is impossible to assess profits or profit growth properly without relating them to the amount of funds (the capital) employed in making the profits. An important profitability ratio is therefore **return on capital employed (ROCE)**, which states the profit as a **percentage of the amount of capital employed**.

Key terms

> **Return on Capital Employed** = $\dfrac{\text{PBIT}}{\text{Capital employed}}$
>
> **Capital employed** = Shareholders' funds *plus* 'payables: amounts falling due after more than one year' *plus* any long-term provisions for liabilities.
>
> = Total assets less current liabilities.

What does a company's ROCE tell us? What should we be looking for? There are three **comparisons** that can be made.

(a)   The change in ROCE from **one year to the next**

(b)   The ROCE being earned by **other companies**, if this information is available

(c)   A comparison of the ROCE with **current market borrowing rates**

   (i)   What would be the cost of extra borrowing to the company if it needed more loans, and is it earning an ROCE that suggests it could make high enough profits to make such borrowing worthwhile?

   (ii)   Is the company making an ROCE which suggests that it is making profitable use of its current borrowing?

2.1.4 Analysing profitability and return in more detail: the secondary ratios

We may analyse the ROCE, to find out why it is high or low, or better or worse than last year. There are two factors that contribute towards a return on capital employed, both related to turnover.

(a)   **Profit margin**. A company might make a high or a low profit margin on its sales. For example, a company that makes a profit of 25c per $1 of sales is making a bigger return on its turnover than another company making a profit of only 10c per $1 of sales.

(b)   **Asset turnover**. Asset turnover is a measure of how well the assets of a business are being used to generate sales. For example, if two companies each have capital employed of $100,000, and company A makes sales of $400,000 a year whereas company B makes sales of only $200,000 a year, company A is making a higher turnover from the same amount of assets and this will help company A to make a higher return on capital employed than company B. Asset turnover is expressed as 'x times' so that assets generate x times their value in annual turnover. Here, company A's asset turnover is 4 times and company B's is 2 times.

Profit margin and asset turnover together explain the ROCE, and if the ROCE is the primary profitability ratio, these other two are the secondary ratios. The relationship between the three ratios is as follows.

Profit margin	×	**asset turnover**	=	**ROCE**
$\dfrac{\text{PBIT}}{\text{Sales}}$	×	$\dfrac{\text{Sales}}{\text{Capital employed}}$	=	$\dfrac{\text{PBIT}}{\text{Capital employed}}$

It is also worth commenting on the **change in turnover** from one year to the next. Strong sales growth will usually indicate volume growth as well as turnover increases due to price rises, and volume growth is one sign of a prosperous company.

2.2 Gearing

The assets of a business must be financed somehow, and when a business is growing, the additional assets must be financed by additional capital. **Capital structure** refers to the **way in which an organisation** is **financed**, by a combination of long-term capital (ordinary shares and reserves, preference shares, debentures, bank loans, convertible bonds and so on) and short-term liabilities, such as a bank overdraft and trade payables.

2.2.1 Debts and financial risk

There are two main **reasons why companies should keep their debt burden under control**.

(a)   When a company is heavily in debt, and seems to be getting even more heavily into debt, banks and other would-be lenders are very soon likely to refuse further borrowing and the company might well find itself in trouble.

(b)   When a company is earning only a modest profit before interest and tax, and has a heavy debt burden, there will be very little profit left over for shareholders after the interest charges have been paid. And so if interest rates were to go up or the company were to borrow even more, it might soon be incurring interest charges in excess of PBIT. This might eventually lead to the liquidation of the company.

A high level of debt creates **financial risk**. Financial risk can be seen from different points of view.

(a)   **The company** as a whole. If a company builds up debts that it cannot pay when they fall due, it will be forced into liquidation.

(b) **Payables**. If a company cannot pay its debts, the company will go into liquidation owing creditors money that they are unlikely to recover in full.

(c) **Ordinary shareholders**. A company will not make any distributable profits unless it is able to earn enough profit before interest and tax to pay all its interest charges, and then tax. The lower the profits or the higher the interest-bearing debts, the less there will be, if there is anything at all, for shareholders.

When a company has preference shares in its capital structure, ordinary shareholders will not get anything until the preference dividend has been paid.

2.3 Gearing ratios

Gearing ratios measure the financial **risk** of a company's capital structure. Business risk can be measured by calculating a company's operational gearing.

Key term

Financial leverage/gearing is the use of debt finance to increase the return on equity by using borrowed funds in such a way that the return generated is greater than the cost of servicing the debt. If the return on borrowed funds is less than the cost of servicing the debt, the effect of gearing is to reduce the return on equity.

Gearing measures the **relationships between shareholders' capital plus reserves, and debt**. Debt is any loans which pay fixed interest and are secured. In this exam, overdrafts do not form part of debt in a gearing ratio.

There are a number of gearing ratios which can be used but in this exam:

$$\text{Gearing} = \frac{\text{Debt}}{\text{Debt plus equity}}$$

A gearing ratio of over 50% indicates **high** gearing.

There is **no absolute limit** to what a **gearing ratio** ought to be. Many companies are highly geared, but if a highly geared company is increasing its gearing, it is likely to have difficulty in the future when it wants to borrow even more, unless it can also boost its shareholders' capital, either with retained profits or with a new share issue.

2.3.1 The effect of gearing on earnings

The level of gearing has a considerable effect on the earnings attributable to the ordinary shareholders. A **highly geared** company must **earn enough profits to cover its interest charges before anything is available for equity**. On the other hand, if borrowed funds are invested in projects which provide returns in excess of the cost of debt capital, then shareholders will enjoy increased returns on their equity.

Gearing, however, also **increases the probability of financial failure** occurring through a company's inability to meet interest payments in poor trading circumstances.

2.3.2 Example: gearing

Suppose that two companies are identical in every respect except for their gearing. Both have assets of $20,000 and both make the same operating profits (profit before interest and tax: PBIT). The only difference between the two companies is that Nonlever Co is all-equity financed and Lever Co is partly financed by debt capital, as follows.

	Nonlever Co	Lever Co
	$	$
Assets	20,000	20,000
10% Bonds	0	(10,000)
	20,000	10,000
Ordinary shares of $1	20,000	10,000

Because Lever has $10,000 of 10% bonds it must make a profit before interest of at least $1,000 in order to pay the interest charges. Nonlever, on the other hand, does not have any minimum PBIT requirement because it has no debt capital. A company, which is lower geared, is considered less **risky** than a higher geared company because of the greater likelihood that its PBIT will be high enough to cover interest charges and make a profit for equity shareholders.

2.3.3 Operating gearing

Financial risk, as we have seen, can be measured by financial gearing. **Business risk** refers to the **risk of making only low profits**, or even losses, **due to the nature of the business** that the company is involved in. One way of measuring business risk is by calculating a company's **operating gearing** or **'operational gearing'**.

Key term

$$\text{Operating gearing or leverage} = \frac{\text{Contribution}}{\text{Profit before interest and tax (PBIT)}}$$

If contribution is high but PBIT is low, fixed costs will be high, and only just covered by contribution. **Business risk**, as measured by operating gearing, will be **high**. If contribution is not much bigger than PBIT, fixed costs will be low, and fairly easily covered. Business risk, as measured by operating gearing, will be low.

2.4 Liquidity

FAST FORWARD

A company can be profitable but at the same time get into cash flow problems. Liquidity ratios (**current** and **quick**) and **working capital turnover ratios** give some idea of a company's liquidity.

Profitability is of course an important aspect of a company's performance, and debt or gearing is another. Neither, however, addresses directly the key issue of liquidity. A company needs liquid assets so that it can meet its debts when they fall due.

Key term

Liquidity is the amount of cash a company can obtain quickly to settle its debts (and possibly to meet other unforeseen demands for cash payments too).

2.4.1 Liquid assets

Liquid funds include:

(a) Cash
(b) Short-term investments for which there is a ready market, such as investments in shares of other companies (NB **not** subsidiaries or associates)
(c) Fixed-term deposits with a bank or building society, for example six month deposits with a bank
(d) Trade receivables
(e) Bills of exchange receivable

Some assets are more liquid than others. Inventories of goods are fairly liquid in some businesses. Inventories of finished production goods might be sold quickly, and a supermarket will hold consumer goods for resale that could well be sold for cash very soon. Raw materials and components in a manufacturing company have to be used to make a finished product before they can be sold to realise cash, and so they are less liquid than finished goods. Just how liquid they are depends on the speed of inventory turnover and the length of the production cycle.

Non-current assets are not liquid assets. A company can sell off non-current assets, but unless they are no longer needed, or are worn out and about to be replaced, they are necessary to continue the company's operations. Selling non-current assets is certainly not a solution to a company's cash needs, and so although there may be an occasional non-current asset item which is about to be sold off, probably because it is going to be replaced, it is safe to disregard non-current assets when measuring a company's liquidity.

In summary, **liquid assets are current asset items that will or could soon be converted into cash, and cash** itself. Two common definitions of liquid assets are **all current assets** or **all current assets with the exception of inventories.**

The main source of liquid assets for a trading company is sales. A company can obtain cash from sources other than sales, such as the issue of shares for cash, a new loan or the sale of non-current assets. But a company cannot rely on these at all times, and in general, obtaining liquid funds depends on making sales and profits.

2.4.2 The current ratio

The **current ratio** is the standard test of liquidity.

Key term

$$\text{Current ratio} = \frac{\text{Current assets}}{\text{Current liabilities}}$$

A company should have enough current assets that give a promise of 'cash to come' to meet its commitments to pay its current liabilities. Obviously, a ratio in **excess of 1** should be expected. In practice, a ratio comfortably in excess of 1 should be expected, but what is 'comfortable' varies between different types of businesses.

Companies are not able to convert all their current assets into cash very quickly. In particular, some manufacturing companies might hold large quantities of raw material inventories, which must be used in production to create finished goods. Finished goods might be warehoused for a long time, or sold on lengthy credit. In such businesses, where inventory turnover is slow, most inventories are not very liquid assets, because the cash cycle is so long. For these reasons, we calculate an additional liquidity ratio, known as the quick ratio or acid test ratio.

2.4.3 The quick ratio

Key term

$$\text{Quick ratio or acid test ratio} = \frac{\text{Current assets less inventories}}{\text{Current liabilities}}$$

This ratio should ideally be **at least 1** for companies with a **slow inventory turnover**. For companies with a **fast inventory turnover**, a quick ratio can be **less than 1** without suggesting that the company is in cash flow difficulties.

Do not forget the other side of the coin. The current ratio and the quick ratio can be bigger than they should be. A company that has large volumes of inventories and receivables might be over-investing in working capital, and so tying up more funds in the business than it needs to. This would suggest poor management of receivables or inventories by the company.

2.4.4 The accounts receivable payment period

Key term

$$\text{Accounts receivable days or accounts receivable payment period} = \frac{\text{Trade receivables}}{\text{Credit sales turnover}} \times 365 \text{ days}$$

This is a rough measure of the average length of time it takes for a company's accounts receivable to pay what they owe.

The trade accounts receivable are not the *total* figure for accounts receivable in the balance sheet, which includes prepayments and non-trade accounts receivable. The trade accounts receivable figure will be itemised in an analysis of the total accounts receivable, in a note to the accounts.

The estimate of accounts receivable days is only approximate.

(a)   The **balance sheet value** of accounts receivable might be **abnormally high** or low compared with the 'normal' level the company usually has. This may apply especially to smaller companies, where the size of year-end accounts receivable may largely depend on whether a few or even a single large customer pay just before or just after the year-end.

(b)   Turnover in the income statement excludes sales tax, but the accounts receivable figure in the balance sheet includes sales tax. We are not strictly comparing like with like.

2.4.5 The inventory turnover period

Key term

$$\text{Inventory days} = \frac{\text{Inventory}}{\text{Cost of sales}} \times 365 \text{ days}$$

This indicates the average number of days that items of inventory are held for. As with the average accounts receivable collection period, this is only an approximate figure, but one which should be reliable enough for finding changes over time.

A lengthening inventory turnover period indicates:

(a)   A **slowdown** in **trading**, or

(b)   A **build-up** in **inventory levels**, perhaps suggesting that the investment in inventories is becoming excessive

If we add together the inventory days and the accounts receivable days, this should give us an indication of how soon inventory is convertible into cash, thereby giving a further indication of the **company's liquidity**.

2.4.6 The accounts payable payment period

Key term

$$\text{Accounts payable payment period} = \frac{\text{Average trade payables}}{\text{Credit purchases or Cost of sales}} \times 365 \text{ days}$$

The accounts payable payment period often helps to assess a company's liquidity; an increase in accounts payable days is often a sign of lack of long-term finance or poor management of current assets, resulting in the use of extended credit from suppliers, increased bank overdraft and so on.

All the ratios calculated above will **vary by industry**; hence **comparisons** of ratios calculated with other similar companies in the same industry are important.

One of the competencies you require to fulfil performance objective 12 of the PER is the ability to provide analysis of performance against key financial performance indicators (KPIs). You can apply the knowledge you obtain from this section of the text to help to demonstrate this competence.

 Question

Calculate liquidity and working capital ratios from the accounts of a manufacturer of products for the construction industry, and comment on the ratios.

	20X8	20X7
	$m	$m
Turnover	2,065.0	1,788.7
Cost of sales	1,478.6	1,304.0
Gross profit	586.4	484.7
Current assets		
Inventories	119.0	109.0
Receivables (note 1)	400.9	347.4
Short-term investments	4.2	18.8
Cash at bank and in hand	48.2	48.0
	572.3	523.2
Payables: amounts falling due within one year		
Loans and overdrafts	49.1	35.3
Corporation taxes	62.0	46.7
Dividend	19.2	14.3
Payables (note 2)	370.7	324.0
	501.0	420.3
	$m	$m
Net current assets	71.3	102.9
Notes		
1 Trade receivables	329.8	285.4
2 Trade payables	236.2	210.8

Answer

	20X8	20X7
Current ratio	572.3/501.0 = 1.14	523.2/420.3 = 1.24
Quick ratio	453.3/501.0 = 0.90	414.2/420.3 = 0.99
Receivables' payment period	329.8/2,065.0 × 365 = 58 days	285.4/1,788.7 × 365 = 58 days
Inventory turnover period	119.0/1,478.6 × 365 = 29 days	109.0/1,304.0 × 365 = 31 days
Payables' turnover period	236.2/1,478.6 × 365 = 58 days	210.8/1,304.0 × 365 = 59 days

As a manufacturing group serving the construction industry, the company would be expected to have a comparatively lengthy receivables' turnover period, because of the relatively poor cash flow in the construction industry. It is clear that the company compensates for this by ensuring that they do not pay for raw materials and other costs before they have sold their inventories of finished goods (hence the similarity of receivables' and payables' turnover periods).

The company's current ratio is a little lower than average but its quick ratio is better than average and very little less than the current ratio. This suggests that inventory levels are strictly controlled, which is reinforced by the low inventory turnover period. It would seem that working capital is tightly managed, to avoid the poor liquidity which could be caused by a high receivables' turnover period and comparatively high payables.

3 Non-financial performance indicators (NFPIs)

Pilot paper, 12/07, 6/09

FAST FORWARD Changes in cost structures, the competitive environment and the manufacturing environment have led to an **increased use of non-financial performance indicators** (NFPIs).

There has been a growing emphasis on NFPIs for a number of reasons.

(a) **Concentration on too few variables**. If performance measurement systems focus entirely on those items which can be expressed in monetary terms, managers will concentrate on only those variables and ignore other important variables that cannot be expressed in monetary terms.

(b) **Lack of information on quality.** Traditional responsibility accounting systems fail to provide information on the quality or importance of operations.

(c) **Changes in cost structures.** Modern technology requires massive investment and product life cycles have got shorter. A greater proportion of costs are sunk and a large proportion of costs are planned, engineered or designed into a product/service before production/delivery. At the time the product/service is produced/delivered, it is therefore too late to control costs.

(d) **Changes in competitive environment.** Financial measures do not convey the full picture of a company's performance, especially in a modern business environment.

(e) **Changes in manufacturing environment**. New manufacturing techniques and technologies focus on minimising throughput times, inventory levels and set-up times. But managers can reduce the costs for which they are responsible by increasing inventory levels through maximising output. If a performance measurement system focuses principally on costs, managers may concentrate on cost reduction and ignore other important strategic manufacturing goals.

(f) **NFPIs are a better indicator of future prospects**. Financial performance indicators tend to focus on the short term. They can give a positive impression of what is happening now but problems may be looming. For example, falling quality will ultimately damage profitability.

3.1 The value of NFPIs

Unlike traditional variance reports, NFPIs can be provided **quickly** for managers, per shift, daily or even hourly as required. They are likely to be easy to calculate, and easier for non-financial managers to **understand** and therefore to **use effectively**.

The beauty of non-financial indicators is that **anything can be compared** if it is **meaningful** to do so. The measures should be **tailored** to the circumstances so that, for example, number of coffee breaks per 20 pages of Study Text might indicate to you how hard you are studying!

Many suitable measures combine elements from the chart shown below. The chart is not intended to be prescriptive or exhaustive.

Errors/failure	Time	Quantity	People
Defects	Second	Range of products	Employees
Equipment failures	Minute	Parts/components	Employee skills
Warranty claims	Hour	Units produced	Customers
Complaints	Shift	Units sold	Competitors
Returns	Cycle	Services performed	Suppliers
Stockouts	Day	kg/litres/metres	
Lateness/waiting	Month	m^2/m^3	
Misinformation	Year	Documents	
Miscalculation		Deliveries	
Absenteeism		Enquiries	

Traditional measures derived from these lists like 'kg (of material) per unit produced' or 'units produced per hour' are fairly obvious, but what may at first seem a fairly **unlikely combination** may also be very revealing. 'Absenteeism per customer', for example, may be of no significance at all or it may reveal that a particularly difficult customer is being avoided, and hence that some action is needed.

There is clearly a need for the information provider to work more closely with the managers who will be using the information to make sure that their needs are properly understood. The measures used are likely to be **developed and refined over time**. It may be that some will serve the purpose of drawing attention to areas in need of improvement but will be of no further relevance once remedial action has been taken. A flexible, responsive approach is essential.

Question   NFPIs

Using the above chart make up five non-financial indicators and explain how each might be useful.

Answer

Here are five indicators, showing you how to use the chart, but there are many other possibilities.

(a)   Services performed late v total services performed
(b)   Total units sold v total units sold by competitors (indicating market share)
(c)   Warranty claims per month
(d)   Documents processed per employee
(e)   Equipment failures per 1,000 units produced

Don't forget to explain how the ones that you chose might be useful.

3.2 NFPIs in relation to employees

FAST FORWARD NFPIs can usefully be applied to **employees** and product/service **quality**.

One of the many criticisms of traditional accounting performance measurement systems is that they **do not measure the skills, morale and training of the workforce**, which can be as **valuable to an organisation as its tangible assets**. For example if employees have not been trained in the manufacturing practices required to achieve the objectives of the new manufacturing environment, an organisation is unlikely to be successful.

Employee attitudes and morale can be measured by **surveying** employees. Education and skills levels, promotion and training, absenteeism and labour turnover for the employees for which each manager is responsible can also be monitored.

3.3 Performance measurement in a TQM environment

Total Quality Management is a highly significant trend in modern business thinking. Because **TQM embraces every activity** of a business, performance measures cannot be confined to the production process but must also cover the work of sales and distribution departments and administration departments, the efforts of external suppliers, and the reaction of external customers.

In many cases the measures used will be non-financial ones. They may be divided into three types.

(a)   **Measuring the quality of incoming supplies.** Quality control should include procedures for acceptance and inspection of goods inwards and measurement of rejects.

(b)   **Monitoring work done as it proceeds.** 'In-process' controls include statistical process controls and random sampling, and measures such as the amount of scrap and reworking in relation to good production. Measurements can be made by product, by worker or work team, by machine or machine type, by department, or whatever is appropriate.

(c)   **Measuring customer satisfaction.** This may be monitored in the form of letters of complaint, returned goods, penalty discounts, claims under guarantee, or requests for visits by service engineers. Some companies adopt a more pro-active approach to monitoring customer satisfaction by surveying their customers on a regular basis. They use the feedback to obtain an index of customer satisfaction which is used to identify quality problems before they affect profits.

3.4 Quality of service

Service quality is measured principally by **qualitative measures**, as you might expect, although some quantitative measures are used by some businesses.

(a) If it were able to obtain the information, a retailer might use number of lost customers in a period as an indicator of service quality.

(b) Lawyers use the proportion of time spent with clients.

3.4.1 Measures of customer satisfaction

You have probably filled in **questionnaires** in fast food restaurants or on aeroplanes without realising that you were completing a customer attitude survey for input to the organisation's management information system.

Other possible measures of customer satisfaction include:

(a) Market research information on customer preferences and customer satisfaction with specific product features

(b) Number of defective units supplied to customers as a percentage of total units supplied

(c) Number of customer complaints as a percentage of total sales volume

(d) Percentage of products which fail early or excessively

(e) On-time delivery rate

(f) Average time to deal with customer queries

(g) New customer accounts opened

(h) Repeat business from existing customers

4 Short-termism and manipulation

6/08

FAST FORWARD

Short-termism is when there is a bias towards short-term rather than long-term performance. It is often due to the fact that managers' performance is measured on short-term results.

Key term

Short-termism is when there is a bias towards short-term rather than long-term performance.

Organisations often have to make a trade-off between short-term and long-term objectives. Decisions which involve the **sacrifice of longer-term objectives** include the following.

(a) Postponing or abandoning capital expenditure projects, which would eventually contribute to growth and profits, in order to protect short term cash flow and profits.

(b) Cutting R&D expenditure to save operating costs, and so reducing the prospects for future product development.

(c) Reducing quality control, to save operating costs (but also adversely affecting reputation and goodwill).

(d) Reducing the level of customer service, to save operating costs (but sacrificing goodwill).

(e) Cutting training costs or recruitment (so the company might be faced with skills shortages).

Managers may also **manipulate** results, especially if rewards are linked to performance. This can be achieved by changing the timing of capital purchases, building up inventories and speeding up or delaying payments and receipts.

4.1 Methods to encourage a long-term view

Steps that could be taken to encourage managers to take a long-term view, so that the 'ideal' decisions are taken, include the following.

(a) **Making short-term targets realistic**. If budget targets are unrealistically tough, a manager will be forced to make trade-offs between the short and long term.

(b)   **Providing sufficient management information** to allow managers to see what trade-offs they are making. Managers must be kept aware of long-term aims as well as shorter-term (budget) targets.

(c)   **Evaluating managers' performance** in terms of contribution to long-term as well as short-term objectives.

(d)   **Link managers' rewards to share price**. This may encourage goal congruence.

(e)   **Set quality based targets** as well as financial targets. Multiple targets can be used.

5 The balanced scorecard

FAST FORWARD

The **balanced scorecard** approach to performance measurement focuses on four different perspectives and uses financial and non-financial indicators.

Although segments of a business may be measured by a single performance indicator such as ROI, profit, or cost variances, it might be more suitable to use multiple measures of performance where each measure reflects a **different aspect of achievement**. Where multiple measures are used, several may be **non-financial**.

The most popular approach in current management thinking is the use of a **'balanced scorecard'** consisting of a variety of indicators both financial and non-financial.

Key term

The **balanced scorecard** approach emphasises the need to provide management with a set of information which covers all relevant areas of performance in an objective and unbiased fashion. The information provided may be both financial and non-financial and cover areas such as profitability, customer satisfaction, internal efficiency and innovation.

5.1 Perspectives

The balanced scorecard focuses on **four different perspectives**, as follows.

Perspective	Question	Explanation
Customer	What do existing and new customers value from us?	Gives rise to targets that matter to customers: cost, quality, delivery, inspection, handling and so on.
Internal	What processes must we excel at to achieve our financial and customer objectives?	Aims to improve internal processes and decision making.
Innovation and learning	Can we continue to improve and create future value?	Considers the business's capacity to maintain its competitive position through the acquisition of new skills and the development of new products.
Financial	How do we create value for our shareholders?	Covers traditional measures such as growth, profitability and shareholder value but set through talking to the shareholder or shareholders direct.

Performance targets are set once the key areas for improvement have been identified, and the balanced scorecard is the main monthly report.

The scorecard is **'balanced'** as managers are required to think in terms of **all four** perspectives, to prevent improvements being made in one area at the expense of another.

Important features of this approach are as follows.

(a)   It looks at both **internal and external** matters concerning the organisation.

(b)   It is related to the key elements of a company's **strategy**.

(c)   **Financial and non-financial** measures are linked together.

5.2 Example

An example of how a balanced scorecard might appear is offered below.

Balanced Scorecard

Financial Perspective

GOALS	MEASURES
Survive	Cash flow
Succeed	Monthly sales growth and operating income by division
Prosper	Increase market share and ROI

Customer Perspective

GOALS	MEASURES
New products	Percentage of sales from new products
Responsive supply	On-time delivery (defined by customer)
Preferred supplier	Share of key accounts' purchases
	Ranking by key accounts
Customer partnership	Number of cooperative engineering efforts

Internal Business Perspective

GOALS	MEASURES
Technology capability	Manufacturing configuration vs competition
Manufacturing excellence	Cycle time
	Unit cost
	Yield
Design productivity	Silicon efficiency
	Engineering efficiency
New product introduction	Actual introduction schedule vs plan

Innovation and Learning Perspective

GOALS	MEASURES
Technology leadership	Time to develop next generation of products
Manufacturing learning	Process time to maturity
Product focus	Percentage of products that equal 80% sales
Time to market	New product introduction vs competition

5.3 Example: Balanced scorecard and not-for-profit organisations

Not-for-profit organisations such as charities are likely to have significantly different goals in comparison to profitable businesses. The following are goals that may be relevant to a charity.

Financial perspective

- Increase income from charitable donations
- Improve margins

Internal business perspective

- Reduce overheads
- Claim back tax on gift aid

Customer perspective

- Continued donor support
- Donor involvement in initiatives

Innovation and learning perspective

- More projects supported
- More fundraisers
- More money pledged

Required

Suggest some performance measures for each of the goals outlined above.

Solution

The balanced scorecard for the charity may appear as follows.

Financial perspective

GOALS	MEASURES (KPI)
Income from charitable donations	Donations received
Improved margins	Lower costs and/or increased income from all sources

Customer perspective

GOALS	MEASURES (KPI)
Continued donor support	Pledges given and direct debits set up
Donor involvement in initiatives	Fundraising and charity dinners

Internal business perspective

GOALS	MEASURES (KPI)
Reduce overheads	Lower overheads measured by monitoring and accounts
Claim back tax on gift aid	Improved reclaim times for gift aided donation

Innovation and learning perspective

GOALS	MEASURES (KPI)
More projects supported	Number of projects given support
More fundraisers	Number of fundraisers recruited
More money pledged	Amount of donations promised

Question	Balanced scorecard

Spotlight Productions has in the past produced just one fairly successful product. Recently, however, a new version of this product has been launched. Development work continues to add a related product to the product list. Given below are some details of the activities during the month of November.

Units produced	– existing product	25,000
	– new product	5,000
Cost of units produced	– existing product	$375,000
	– new product	$70,000
Sales revenue	– existing product	$550,000
	– new product	$125,000
Hours worked	– existing product	5,000
	– new product	1,250
Development costs		$47,000

Required

(a) Suggest and calculate performance indicators that could be calculated for each of the four perspectives on the balanced scorecard.

(b) Suggest how this information would be interpreted.

Answer

(a) **Customer**

- Percentage of sales represented by new products $= \dfrac{\$125,000}{\$550,000 + \$125,000} \times 100$

  $= 18.5\%$

Internal

- Productivity – existing product $= \dfrac{25{,}000 \text{ units}}{5{,}000 \text{ units}}$

  $= 5 \text{ units per hour}$

  – new product $= \dfrac{5{,}000 \text{ units}}{1{,}250 \text{ units}}$

  $= 4 \text{ units per hour}$

- Unit cost – existing product $= \dfrac{\$375{,}000}{25{,}000 \text{ units}}$

  $= \$15 \text{ per unit}$

  – new product $= \dfrac{\$70{,}000}{5{,}000 \text{ units}}$

  $= \$14 \text{ per unit}$

Financial

- Gross profit – existing product $= \dfrac{\$550{,}000 - 375{,}000}{\$550{,}000}$

  $= 32\%$

  – new product $= \dfrac{\$125{,}000 - 70{,}000}{\$125{,}000}$

  $= 44\%$

Innovation and learning

- Development costs as % of sales $= \dfrac{\$47{,}000}{\$675{,}000}$

  $= 7\%$

(b)   Using a range of performance indicators will allow Spotlight Productions to look at the success of the new product in wider terms than just its profitability. For example, productivity is lower for the new product than the existing product, so managers may wish to examine the processes involved in order to make improvements. Sales of the new product look very promising but some additional measure of customer satisfaction could provide a better view of long-term prospects.

6 Building Block model

FAST FORWARD

Fitzgerald and Moon's **building blocks** for **dimensions, standards** and **rewards** attempt to overcome the problems associated with performance measurement of service businesses.

Question

Services v manufacturing

In Chapter 2b we looked at five major characteristics of services that distinguish services from manufacturing. Can you relate them to the provision of a haircut?

Answer

(a) **Intangibility**. A haircut is intangible in itself, and the performance of the service comprises many other intangible factors, like the music in the salon, the personality of the hairdresser.

(b) **Simultaneity/inseparability**. The production and consumption of a haircut are simultaneous, and so cannot be inspected for quality in advance, nor returned if it is not what was required.

(c) **Perishability**. Haircuts are perishable, so they cannot be stored. You cannot buy them in bulk, and the hairdresser cannot do them in advance and keep them in stock in case of heavy demand.

(d) **Heterogeneity/variability**. A haircut is heterogeneous and so the exact service received will vary each time: not only will Justin and Nigel cut hair differently, but Justin will not consistently deliver the same standard of haircut.

(e) **No transfer of ownership.** A haircut does not become the property of the customer.

Performance measurement in service businesses has sometimes been perceived as difficult because of the five factors listed above, but the modern view is that if something is difficult to measure this is because it has not been clearly enough defined. Fitzgerald & Moon provide **building blocks** for **standards, rewards** and **dimensions** for performance measurement systems in service businesses.

6.1 Standards

These are **ownership**, **achievability** and **equity**.

(a) To ensure that employees take **ownership** of standards, they need to **participate** in the budget and standard-setting processes. They are then more likely to **accept** the standards, feel more **motivated** as they perceive the standards to be achievable and **morale** is improved. The disadvantage to participation is that it offers the opportunity for the introduction of **budgetary slack**.

(b) Standards need to be set **high enough** to ensure that there is some **sense of achievement** in attaining them, but **not so high** that there is a **demotivating** effect because they are unachievable. It is management's task to find a **balance** between what the organisation perceives as achievable and what employees perceive as achievable.

(c) It is vital that **equity** is seen to occur when applying standards for performance measurement purposes. The performance of different business units should not be measured against the same standards if some units have an inherent advantage unconnected with their own efforts. For example, divisions operating in different countries should not be assessed against the same standards.

6.2 Rewards

The reward structure of the performance measurement system should guide individuals to work towards standards. Three issues need to be considered if the performance measurement system is to operate successfully: **clarity**, **motivation** and **controllability**.

(a) The organisation's objectives need to be **clearly understood** by those whose performance is being appraised ie they need to know what goals they are working towards.

(b) Individuals should be **motivated** to work in pursuit of the organisation's strategic objectives. Goal clarity and participation have been shown to contribute to higher levels of motivation to achieve targets, providing managers accept those targets. Bonuses can be used to motivate.

(c) Managers should have a certain level of **controllability** for their areas of responsibility. For example they should not be held responsible for costs over which they have no control.

6.3 Dimensions

(a) **Competitive performance**, focusing on factors such as sales growth and market share.

(b) **Financial performance**, concentrating on profitability, capital structure and so on.

(c) **Quality of service** looks at matters like reliability, courtesy and competence.

(d) **Flexibility** is an apt heading for assessing the organisation's ability to deliver at the right speed, to respond to precise customer specifications, and to cope with fluctuations in demand.

(e) **Resource utilisation**, not unsurprisingly, considers how efficiently resources are being utilised. This can be problematic because of the complexity of the inputs to a service and the outputs from it and because some of the inputs are supplied by the customer (he or she brings their own hair, for example). Many measures are possible, however, for example 'number of customers per hairdresser'. Performance measures can be devised easily if it is known what activities are involved in the service.

(f) **Innovation** is assessed in terms of both the innovation process and the success of individual innovations.

These dimensions can be divided into two sets.

- The **results** (measured by financial performance and competitiveness)
- The **determinants** (the remainder)

Focus on the examination and improvement of the determinants should lead to improvement in the results.

There is no need to elaborate on **competitive performance**, **financial performance** and **quality of service** issues, all of which have been covered already. The other three dimensions deserve more attention.

6.3.1 Flexibility

Flexibility has three aspects.

(a) **Speed of delivery**
Punctuality is vital in some service industries like passenger transport: indeed punctuality is currently one of the most widely publicised performance measures in the UK, because organisations like railway companies are making a point of it. **Measures** include waiting time in queues, as well as late trains. In other types of service it may be more a question of **timeliness**. Does the auditor turn up to do the annual audit during the appointed week? Is the audit done within the time anticipated by the partner or does it drag on for weeks? These aspects are all easily measurable in terms of **'days late'**. Depending upon the circumstances, 'days late' may also reflect an inability to cope with fluctuations in demand.

(b) **Response to customer specifications**
The ability of a service organisation to respond to **customers' specifications** is one of the criteria by which Fitzgerald *et al* distinguish between the three different types of service. Clearly a professional service such as legal advice and assistance must be tailored exactly to the customer's needs. Performance is partly a matter of customer perception and so **customer attitude surveys** may be appropriate. However it is also a matter of the diversity of skills possessed by the service organisation and so it can be measured in terms of the **mix of staff skills** and the amount of time spent on **training**. In **mass service** business customisation is not possible by the very nature of the service.

(c) **Coping with demand**
This is clearly measurable in quantitative terms in a mass service like a railway company which can ascertain the extent of **overcrowding**. It can also be very closely monitored in service shops: customer **queuing** time can be measured in banks and retailers, for example. Professional services can measure levels of **overtime** worked: excessive amounts indicate that the current demand is too great for the organisation to cope with in the long term without obtaining extra human resources.

6.3.2 Resource utilisation measures

Resource utilisation is usually measured in terms of **productivity**. The ease with which this may be measured varies according to the service being delivered.

The main resource of a firm of accountants, for example, is the **time** of various grades of staff. The main output of an accountancy firm is **chargeable hours**.

In a restaurant it is not nearly so straightforward. Inputs are highly **diverse**: the ingredients for the meal, the chef's time and expertise, the surroundings and the customers' own likes and dislikes. A **customer attitude survey** might show whether or not a customer enjoyed the food, but it could not ascribe the enjoyment or lack of it to the quality of the ingredients, say, rather than the skill of the chef.

Here are some of the resource utilisation ratios listed by Fitzgerald *et al*.

Business	Input	Output
Ernst & Young Consulting	Man hours available	Chargeable hours
Commonwealth Hotels	Rooms available	Rooms occupied
Railway companies	Train miles available	Passenger miles
Barclays Bank	Number of staff	Number of accounts

6.3.3 Innovation

In a modern environment in which product quality, product differentiation and continuous improvement are the order of the day, a company that can find innovative ways of satisfying customers' needs has an important **competitive advantage**.

Fitzgerald *et al* suggest that **individual innovations** should be measured in terms of whether they bring about **improvements in the other five 'dimensions'**.

The innovating **process** can be measured in terms of how much it **costs** to develop a new service, how **effective** the process is (that is, how innovative is the organisation, if at all?), and how **quickly** it can develop new services. In more concrete terms this might translate into the following.

(a)   The amount of **R&D** spending and whether (and how quickly) these costs are recovered from new service sales

(b)   The proportion of **new** services to **total** services provided

(c)   The time between **identification** of the need for a new service and making it **available**

 | Question | Competitiveness and resource utilisation

A service business has collected some figures relating to its year just ended.

		Budget	Actual
Customer enquiries:	New customers	6,000	9,000
	Existing customers	4,000	3,000
Business won:	New customers	2,000	4,000
	Existing customers	1,500	1,500
Types of services performed:	Service A	875	780
	Service B	1,575	1,850
	Service C	1,050	2,870
Employees:	Service A	5	4
	Service B	10	10
	Service C	5	8

Required

Calculate figures that illustrate competitiveness and resource utilisation.

Answer

Competitiveness can only be measured from these figures by looking at how successful the organisation is at converting enquiries into firm orders.

Percentage of enquiries converted into firm orders

	Budget	Actual
New customers (W1)	33%	44%
Existing customers (W1)	37.5%	50%

Resource utilisation can be measured by looking at average services performed per employee.

	Budget	Actual	Rise
Service A (W2)	175	195	+11.4%
Service B (W2)	157.5	185	+17.5%
Service C (W2)	210	358.75	+70.8%

Workings

1   For example 2,000/6,000 = 33%
2   For example 875/5 = 175

What comments would you make about these results? How well is the business doing?

Exam focus point

Be prepared to think up performance measures for different areas of an organisation's business. Remember to make the measures relevant to the organisation in question. There is little point in suggesting measures such as waiting times in queues to assess the quality of the service provided by an educational establishment.

Question

Performance indicators

Suggest two separate performance indicators that could be used to assess each of the following areas of a fast food chain's operations.

(a)   Food preparation department
(b)   Marketing department

Answer

Here are some suggestions.

(a)   Material usage per product   (b)   Market share
       Wastage levels   Sales revenue per employee
       Incidences of food poisoning   Growth in sales revenue

Chapter Roundup

- **Performance measurement** aims to establish how well something or somebody is doing in relation to a plan.

  Performance measures may be divided into two groups.

  - Financial performance indicators
  - Non-financial performance indicators

- **Financial performance indicators** analyse profitability, liquidity and risk.

- **Gearing ratios** measure the financial **risk** of a company's capital structure. Business risk can be measured by calculating a company's operational gearing.

- A company can be profitable but at the same time get into cash flow problems. Liquidity ratios (**current** and **quick**) and **working capital turnover ratios** give some idea of a company's liquidity.

- Changes in cost structures, the competitive environment and the manufacturing environment have lead to an **increased use of non-financial performance indicators** (NFPIs).

- NFPIs can usefully be applied to **employees** and product/service **quality**.

- **Short-termism** is when there is a bias towards short-term rather than long-term performance. It is often due to the fact that managers' performance is measured on short-term results.

- The **balanced scorecard** approach to performance measurement focuses on four different perspectives and uses financial and non-financial indicators.

- Fitzgerald and Moon's **building blocks** for **dimensions, standards** and **rewards** attempt to overcome the problems associated with performance measurement of service businesses.

1   Give five examples of a financial performance measure.

     •   ....   •   ....

     •   ....   •   ....

     •   ....

2   How do quantitative and qualitative performance measures differ?

3   Choose the correct words from those highlighted.

     In general, a current ratio **in excess of 1/less than 1/approximately zero** should be expected.

4   **Service quality** is measured principally by quantitative measures.

     True   ☐   False   ☐

5   *Fill in the blanks.*

     NFPIs are less likely to be .... than traditional profit-related measures and they should therefore offer a means of counteracting ....

6   What are the three most important features of the balanced scorecard approach?

7   *Fill in the blanks.*

     The five characteristics of a service business are .... , ..., ..., ... and ....

8   Fitzgerald and Moon's standards for performance measurement systems are ownership, achievability and controllability. *True or false?*

9   *Fill in the gaps.*

     Fitzgerald and Moon's dimensions can be divided into the results (............................... and ....) and the determinants (................................ , ..., ... and ....) .

1
- Profit
- Revenue
- Costs
- Share price
- Cash flow

2 Quantitative measures are expressed in numbers whereas qualitative measures are not.

3 in excess of 1

4 False. Service quality is measured principally by **qualitative** measures.

5 manipulated
short termism

6
- It looks at both internal and external matters concerning the organisation
- It is related to the key elements of a company's strategy
- Financial and non-financial measures are linked together

7 Heterogeneity/variability
Perishability
Intangibility

Simultaneity/inseparability
No transfer of ownership

8 False. They are ownership, achievability and equity.

9 *Results*

Financial performance
Competitive performance

Determinants

Quality   Innovation
Flexibility   Resource utilisation

Now try the questions below from the Exam Question Bank

Number	Level	Marks	Time
Q19	Examination	20	36 mins

15

Divisional performance measures

Topic list	Syllabus reference
1 Divisionalisation	E2
2 Return on investment (ROI)	E2 (c)
3 Residual income (RI)	E2 (c), (d)
4 Transfer pricing	E2 (a), (b)

Introduction

This chapter looks at **divisional performance** and **transfer pricing** which is a system of charging other divisions of your organisation when you provide them with your division's goods or services.

In a **divisionalised organisation** structure of any kind, if one division does work that is used by another division, transfer pricing may be required. Do not be misled by the term 'price': there is not necessarily any suggestion of **profit** as there usually is with an external selling price. But as we shall see, transfer pricing is particularly appropriate where divisions are designated as **profit centres**.

Study guide

		Intellectual level
E2	**Divisional performance and transfer pricing**	
(a)	Explain the basis for setting a transfer price using variable cost, full cost and the principles behind allowing for intermediate markets	2
(b)	Explain how transfer prices can distort the performance assessment of divisions and decisions made	2
(c)	Explain the meaning of, and calculate, Return on Investment (ROI) and Residual Income (RI), and discuss their shortcomings	2
(d)	Compare divisional performance and recognise the problems of doing so	2

Exam guide

You may be required to calculate transfer prices in this exam. You must be able to explain how and why they are used and the problems they can create.

1 Divisionalisation

FAST FORWARD
> There are a number of advantages and disadvantages to **divisionalisation**.

In general, a large organisation can be **structured in one of two ways: functionally** (all activities of a similar type within a company, such as production, sales, research, are under the control of the appropriate departmental head) or **divisionally** (split into divisions in accordance with the products or services made or provided).

Divisional managers are therefore responsible for all operations (production, sales and so on) relating to their product, the functional structure being applied to each division. It is possible, of course, that only part of a company is divisionalised and activities such as administration are structured centrally on a functional basis with the responsibility of providing services to *all* divisions.

1.1 Decentralisation

In general, a **divisional structure will lead to decentralisation** of the decision-making process and divisional managers may have the freedom to set selling prices, choose suppliers, make product mix and output decisions and so on. Decentralisation is, however, a matter of degree, depending on how much freedom divisional managers are given.

1.2 Advantages of divisionalisation

(a) Divisionalisation can **improve** the **quality of decisions** made because divisional managers (those taking the decisions) know local conditions and are able to make more informed judgements. Moreover, with the personal incentive to improve the division's performance, they ought to take decisions in the division's best interests.

(b) **Decisions should be taken more quickly** because information does not have to pass along the chain of command to and from top management. Decisions can be made on the spot by those who are familiar with the product lines and production processes and who are able to react to changes in local conditions quickly and efficiently.

(c) The authority to act to improve performance should **motivate divisional managers**.

(d) Divisional organisation **frees top management** from detailed involvement in day-to-day operations and allows them to devote more time to strategic planning.

(e) Divisions provide **valuable training grounds for future members of top management** by giving them experience of managerial skills in a less complex environment than that faced by top management.

(f) In a large business organisation, the **central head office will not have the management resources or skills to direct operations closely enough itself**. Some authority must be delegated to local operational managers.

1.3 Disadvantages of divisionalisation

(a) A danger with divisional accounting is that the business organisation will divide into a number of self-interested segments, each acting at times against the wishes and interests of other segments. Decisions might be taken by a divisional manager in the best interests of his own part of the business, but against the best interest of other divisions and possibly against the interests of the organisation as a whole.

A task of **head office** is therefore to try to **prevent dysfunctional decision making** by individual divisional managers. To do this, head office must reserve some power and authority for itself so that divisional managers cannot be allowed to make entirely independent decisions. A **balance** ought to be kept **between decentralisation** of authority to provide incentives and motivation, **and retaining centralised authority** to ensure that the organisation's divisions are all working towards the same target, the benefit of the organisation as a whole (in other words, **retaining goal congruence** among the organisation's separate divisions).

(b) It is claimed that the **costs of activities that are common** to all divisions such as running the accounting department **may be greater** for a divisionalised structure than for a centralised structure.

(c) **Top management**, by delegating decision making to divisional managers, may **lose control** since they are not aware of what is going on in the organisation as a whole. (With a good system of performance evaluation and appropriate control information, however, top management should be able to control operations just as effectively.)

1.4 Responsibility accounting

FAST FORWARD

Responsibility accounting is the term used to describe decentralisation of authority, with the performance of the decentralised units measured in terms of accounting results.

With a system of responsibility accounting there are three types of **responsibility centre: cost centre; profit centre; investment centre**.

The creation of divisions allows for the operation of a system of **responsibility accounting**. There are a number of types of responsibility accounting unit, or responsibility centre that can be used within a system of responsibility accounting.

In the weakest form of decentralisation a system of **cost centres** might be used. As decentralisation becomes stronger the responsibility accounting framework will be based around **profit centres**. In its strongest form **investment centres** are used.

Type of responsibility centre	Manager has control over ...	Principal performance measures
Cost centre	Controllable costs	Variance analysis Efficiency measures
Revenue centre	Revenues only	Revenues
Profit centre	Controllable costs Sales prices (including transfer prices)	Profit

Type of responsibility centre	Manager has control over ...	Principal performance measures
Contribution centre	As for profit centre except that expenditure is reported on a marginal cost basis	Contribution
Investment centre	Controllable costs Sales prices (including transfer prices) Output volumes Investment in non-current assets and working capital	Return on investment Residual income Other financial ratios

2 Return on investment (ROI)   12/08

FAST FORWARD

The performance of an investment centre is usually monitored using either or both of **return on investment (ROI)** and **residual income (RI)**.

ROI is generally regarded as the **key performance measure**. The main reason for its **widespread use** is that it **ties in directly with the accounting process**, and is identifiable from the income statement and balance sheet. However it does have limitations, as we will see later in this chapter.

Key term

Return on investment (ROI) shows how much profit has been made in relation to the amount of capital invested and is calculated as (profit/capital employed) × 100%.

For example, suppose that a company has two investment centres A and B, which show results for the year as follows.

	A $	B $
Profit	60,000	30,000
Capital employed	400,000	120,000
ROI	15%	25%

Investment centre A has made double the profits of investment centre B, and in terms of profits alone has therefore been more 'successful'. However, B has achieved its profits with a much lower capital investment, and so has earned a much higher ROI. This suggests that B has been a more successful investment than A.

2.1 Measuring ROI

FAST FORWARD

There is no generally agreed method of calculating ROI and it can have **behavioural implications** and lead to dysfunctional decision making when used as a guide to investment decisions. It focuses attention on short-run performance whereas investment decisions should be evaluated over their full life.

ROI can be measured in different ways.

2.1.1 Profit after depreciation as a % of net assets employed

This is probably the **most common method**, but it does present a problem. If an investment centre maintains the same annual profit, and keeps the same assets without a policy of regular replacement of non-current assets, its ROI will increase year by year as the assets get older. This **can give a false impression of improving performance over time**.

For example, the results of investment centre X, with a policy of straight-line depreciation of assets over a 5-year period, might be as follows.

Year	Non-current assets at cost $'000	Depreciation in the year $'000	NBV (mid year) $'000	Working capital $'000	Capital employed $'000	Profit $'000	ROI
0	100			10	110		
1	100	20	90	10	100	10	10.0%
2	100	20	70	10	80	10	12.5%
3	100	20	50	10	60	10	16.7%
4	100	20	30	10	40	10	25.0%
5	100	20	10	10	20	10	50.0%

This table of figures is intended to show that an investment centre can **improve its ROI** year by year, simply **by allowing its non-current assets to depreciate**, and there could be a **disincentive to** investment centre managers to **reinvest in new or replacement assets**, because the centre's ROI would probably fall.

This example has used a mid year NBV but a year end or start of year NBV can also be used.

Exam focus point

In December 2008, the examiner only gave information on net assets at the start of the year so this could be used without any further calculations.

Question

ROI calculation (1)

A new company has non-current assets of $460,000 which will be depreciated to nil on a straight line basis over 10 years. Net current assets will consistently be $75,000, and annual profit will consistently be $30,000. ROI is measured as return on net assets.

Required

Calculate the company's ROI in years 2 and 6.

Answer

Year 2 – 6.8%
Year 6 – 11.6%

A further disadvantage of measuring ROI as profit divided by net assets is that, for similar reasons, it is not **easy to compare** fairly the **performance of investment centres**.

For example, suppose that we have two investment centres.

	Investment centre P		Investment centre Q	
	$	$	$	$
Working capital		20,000		20,000
Non-current assets at cost	230,000		230,000	
Accumulated depreciation	170,000		10,000	
Net book value		60,000		220,000
Capital employed		80,000		240,000
Profit		$24,000		$24,000
ROI		30%		10%

Investment centres P and Q have the same amount of working capital, the same value of non-current assets at cost, and the same profit. But P's non-current assets have been depreciated by a much bigger amount (presumably P's non-current assets are much older than Q's) and so P's ROI is three times the size of Q's ROI. The conclusion might therefore be that P has performed much better than Q. This comparison, however, would not be 'fair', because the difference in performance might be entirely attributable to the age of their non-current assets.

The arguments for using net book values for calculating ROI

(a)   It is the **'normally accepted'** method of calculating ROI.

(b)   Organisations are continually buying new non-current assets to replace old ones that wear out, and so on the whole, the **total net book value** of all non-current assets together **will remain fairly constant** (assuming nil inflation and nil growth).

2.1.2 Profit after depreciation as a % of gross assets employed

Instead of measuring ROI as return on net assets, we could measure it as return on gross assets ie before depreciation. This would **remove the problem of ROI increasing over time as non-current assets get older**.

If a company acquired a non-current asset costing $40,000, which it intends to depreciate by $10,000 pa for 4 years, and if the asset earns a profit of $8,000 pa after depreciation, ROI might be calculated on net book values or gross values, as follows.

Year	Profit	NBV(mid-year value)	ROI based on NBV	Gross value	ROI based on gross value
	$	$		$	
1	8,000	35,000	22.9%	40,000	20%
2	8,000	25,000	32.0%	40,000	20%
3	8,000	15,000	53.3%	40,000	20%
4	8,000	5,000	160.0%	40,000	20%

The ROI based on **net book value** shows an **increasing trend over time**, simply because the asset's value is falling as it is depreciated. The ROI based on gross book value suggests that the asset has **performed consistently** in each of the four years, which is probably a more valid conclusion.

Question
ROI calculation (2)

Repeat **Question: ROI calculation (1)**, measuring ROI as return on gross assets.

Answer

Year 2 – 5.6%
Year 6 – 5.6%

However, using gross book values to measure ROI has its **disadvantages**. Most important of these is that measuring ROI as return on gross assets ignores the age factor, and **does not distinguish between old and new assets**.

(a)   **Older non-current assets** usually **cost more to repair and maintain**, to keep them running. An investment centre with old assets may therefore have its profitability reduced by repair costs, and its ROI might fall over time as its assets get older and repair costs get bigger.

(b)   **Inflation** and **technological change alter the cost of non-current assets**. If one investment centre has non-current assets bought ten years ago with a gross cost of $1 million, and another investment centre, in the same area of business operations, has non-current assets bought very recently for $1 million, the quantity and technological character of the non-current assets of the two investment centres are likely to be very different.

2.1.3 Constituent elements of the investment base

Although we have looked at how the investment base should be valued, we need to consider its appropriate constituent elements.

(a)   If a **manager's performance is being evaluated**, only those **assets** which can be **traced directly to the division** and are **controllable by the manager should be included**. Head office assets or investment centre assets controlled by head office should not be included. So, for example, only those cash balances actually maintained within an investment centre itself should be included.

(b)   If it is the performance of the investment centre that is being appraised, **a proportion of the investment in head office assets would need to be included** because an investment centre could not operate without the support of head office assets and administrative backup.

2.1.4 Profits

We have looked at how to define the asset base used in the calculations but what about profit? If the **performance of the investment centre manager is being assessed** it should seem reasonable to **base profit on the revenues and costs controllable by the manager** and exclude service and head office costs except those costs specifically attributable to the investment centre. If it is the **performance of the investment centre that is being assessed, however, the inclusion of general service and head office costs would seem reasonable**.

The profit figure for ROI should always be the amount before any interest is charged.

2.1.5 Massaging the ROI

If a manager's large bonus depends on ROI being met, the manager may feel pressure to massage the measure. The **asset base** of the ratio can be **altered** by increasing/decreasing payables and receivables (by speeding up or delaying payments and receipts).

2.2 ROI and new investments

If investment centre performance is judged by ROI, we should expect that the managers of investment centres will probably decide to undertake new capital investments **only if these new investments are likely to increase the ROI of their centre**.

Suppose that an investment centre, A, currently makes a return of 40% on capital employed. The manager of centre A would probably only want to undertake new investments that promise to yield a return of 40% or more, otherwise the investment centre's overall ROI would fall.

For example, if investment centre A currently has assets of $1,000,000 and expects to earn a profit of $400,000, how would the centre's manager view a new capital investment which would cost $250,000 and yield a profit of $75,000 pa?

	Without the new investment	With the new investment
Profit	$400,000	$475,000
Capital employed	$1,000,000	$1,250,000
ROI	40%	38%

The **new investment** would **reduce the investment centre's ROI** from 40% to 38%, and so the investment centre manager would probably decide **not to undertake** the new investment.

If the group of companies of which investment centre A is a part has a target ROI of, say, 25%, the new investment would presumably be seen as **beneficial for the group as a whole**. But even though it promises to yield a return of 75,000/250,000 = 30%, which is above the group's target ROI, it would still make investment centre A's results look worse. The manager of investment centre A would, in these circumstances, be motivated to do not what is best for the organisation as a whole, but what is **best for his division.**

ROI should not be used to guide investment decisions but there is a difficult **motivational** problem. If management performance is measured in terms of ROI, any decisions which benefit the company in the long term but which reduce the ROI in the immediate short term would reflect badly on the manager's reported performance. In other words, good investment decisions would make a manager's performance seem **worse** than if the wrong investment decision were taken instead.

3 Residual income (RI)

> RI can sometimes give results that avoid the **behavioural** problem of **dysfunctionality**. Its weakness is that it does not facilitate comparisons between investment centres nor does it relate the size of a centre's income to the size of the investment.

An alternative way of measuring the performance of an investment centre, instead of using ROI, is residual income (RI). **Residual income is a measure of the centre's profits after deducting a notional or imputed interest cost**.

(a) The centre's profit is **after deducting depreciation** on capital equipment.

(b) The imputed cost of capital might be the organisation's cost of borrowing or its weighted average cost of capital.

Key term

> **Residual income** is a measure of the centre's profits after deducting a notional or imputed interest cost.

Question

RI

A division with capital employed of $400,000 currently earns an ROI of 22%. It can make an additional investment of $50,000 for a 5 year life with nil residual value. The average net profit from this investment would be $12,000 after depreciation. The division's cost of capital is 14%.

What are the residual incomes before and after the investment?

Answer

	Before investment	After investment
	$	$
Divisional profit ($400,000 x 22%)	88,000	100,000
Imputed interest		
(400,000 × 0.14)	56,000	
(450,000 × 0.14)		63,000
Residual income	32,000	37,000

3.1 The advantages and weaknesses of RI compared with ROI

The advantages of using RI

(a) Residual income will **increase** when investments earning above the cost of capital are undertaken and investments earning below the cost of capital are eliminated.

(b) Residual income is **more flexible** since a different cost of capital can be applied to investments with **different risk** characteristics.

The **weakness** of RI is that it **does not facilitate comparisons** between investment centres nor **does it relate the size of a centre's income to the size of the investment**.

3.2 RI versus ROI: marginally profitable investments

Residual income will increase if a new investment is undertaken which earns a profit in excess of the imputed interest charge on the value of the asset acquired. Residual income will go up even if the investment only just exceeds the imputed interest charge, and this means that 'marginally profitable' investments are likely to be undertaken by the investment centre manager.

In contrast, when a manager is judged by ROI, a marginally profitable investment would be less likely to be undertaken because it would reduce the average ROI earned by the centre as a whole.

3.2.1 Example: ROI versus residual income

Suppose that Department H has the following profit, assets employed and an imputed interest charge of 12% on operating assets.

	$	$
Operating profit	30,000	
Operating assets		100,000
Imputed interest (12%)	12,000	
Return on investment		30%
Residual income	18,000	

Suppose now that an additional investment of $10,000 is proposed, which will increase operating income in Department H by $1,400. The effect of the investment would be:

	$	$
Total operating income	31,400	
Total operating assets		110,000
Imputed interest (12%)	13,200	
Return on investment		28.5%
Residual income	18,200	

If the Department H manager is made responsible for the department's performance, he would **resist the new investment if he were to be judged on ROI**, but would **welcome the investment if he were judged according to RI**, since there would be a marginal increase of $200 in residual income from the investment, but a fall of 1.5% in ROI.

The marginal investment offers a return of 14% ($1,400 on an investment of $10,000) which is above the 'cut-off rate' of 12%. Since the original return on investment was 30%, the marginal investment will reduce the overall divisional performance. Indeed, any marginal investment offering an accounting rate of return of less than 30% in the year would reduce the overall performance.

Exam focus point

> Examination questions on residual income may focus on the sort of behavioural aspects of investment centre measurement that we have discussed above, for example why it is considered necessary to use residual income to measure performance rather than ROI, and why residual income might influence an investment centre manager's investment decisions differently.

4 Transfer pricing   6/10

> Transfer prices are a way of promoting **divisional autonomy**, ideally without prejudicing the **measurement of divisional performance** or discouraging **overall corporate profit maximisation**.
>
> Transfer prices should be set at a level which ensures that profits for the organisation as a whole are maximised.

Transfer pricing is used when divisions of an organisation need to charge other divisions of the same organisation for goods and services they provide to them. For example, subsidiary A might make a component that is used as part of a product made by subsidiary B of the same company, but that can also be sold to the external market, including makers of rival products to subsidiary B's product. There will therefore be two sources of revenue for A.

(a)   External sales revenue from sales made to other organisations.

(b)   Internal sales revenue from sales made to other responsibility centres within the same organisation, valued at the transfer price.

A **transfer price** is the price at which goods or services are transferred from one department to another, or from one member of a group to another.

4.1 Problems with transfer pricing

4.1.1 Maintaining the right level of divisional autonomy

Transfer prices are particularly appropriate for **profit centres** because if one profit centre does work for another the size of the transfer price will affect the costs of one profit centre and the revenues of another.

However, as we have seen, a danger with profit centre accounting is that the business organisation will **divide into a number of self-interested segments**, each acting at times against the wishes and interests of other segments. Decisions might be taken by a profit centre manager in the best interests of his own part of the business, but against the best interests of other profit centres and possibly the organisation as a whole.

4.1.2 Ensuring divisional performance is measured fairly

Profit centre managers tend to put their own profit performance above everything else. Since profit centre performance is measured according to the profit they earn, no profit centre will want to do work for another and incur costs without being paid for it. Consequently, profit centre managers are likely to dispute the size of transfer prices with each other, or disagree about whether one profit centre should do work for another or not. Transfer prices **affect behaviour and decisions** by profit centre managers.

4.1.3 Ensuring corporate profits are maximised

When there are disagreements about how much work should be transferred between divisions, and how many sales the division should make to the external market, there is presumably a **profit-maximising level of output and sales for the organisation as a whole**. However, unless each profit centre also maximises its own profit at this same level of output, there will be inter-divisional disagreements about output levels and the profit-maximising output will not be achieved.

4.1.4 The ideal solution

Ideally a transfer price should be set at a level that overcomes these problems.

(a) The transfer price should provide an 'artificial' selling price that enables the **transferring division to earn a return for its efforts**, and the **receiving division to incur a cost for benefits received**.

(b) The transfer price should be set at a level that enables **profit centre performance** to be **measured 'commercially'**. This means that the transfer price should be a fair commercial price.

(c) The transfer price, if possible, should encourage profit centre managers to agree on the amount of goods and services to be transferred, which will also be at a level that is consistent with the aims of the organisation as a whole such as **maximising company profits**.

In practice it is difficult to achieve all three aims.

Question

Benefits of transfer pricing

The transfer pricing system operated by a divisional company has the potential to make a significant contribution towards the achievement of corporate financial objectives.

Required

Explain the potential benefits of operating a transfer pricing system within a divisionalised company.

Potential benefits of operating a transfer pricing system within a divisionalised company include the following.

(a)   It can lead to **goal congruence** by motivating divisional managers to make decisions, which improve divisional profit and improve profit of the organisation as a whole.

(b)   It can prevent **dysfunctional decision making** so that decisions taken by a divisional manager are in the best interests of his own part of the business, other divisions and the organisation as a whole.

(c)   Transfer prices can be set at a level that enables divisional performance to be measured 'commercially'. A transfer pricing system should therefore report a level of divisional profit that is a **reasonable measure of the managerial performance** of the division.

(d)   It should ensure that **divisional autonomy** is not undermined. A well-run transfer pricing system helps to ensure that a balance is kept between divisional autonomy to provide incentives and motivation, and centralised authority to ensure that the divisions are all working towards the same target, the benefit of the organisation as a whole.

4.2 General rules

FAST FORWARD

The **limits within which transfer prices should fall** are as follows.

- **The minimum**. The sum of the supplying division's marginal cost and opportunity cost of the item transferred.
- **The maximum**. The lowest market price at which the receiving division could purchase the goods or services externally, less any internal cost savings in packaging and delivery.

The **minimum** results from the fact that the **supplying division will not agree to transfer if the transfer price is less than the marginal cost + opportunity cost of the item transferred** (because if it were the division would incur a loss).

The **maximum** results from the fact that the **receiving division will buy the item at the cheapest price possible**.

4.2.1 Example: general rules

Division X produces product L at a marginal cost per unit of $100. If a unit is transferred internally to division Y, $25 contribution is foregone on an external sale. The item can be purchased externally for $150.

- **The minimum**. Division X will not agree to a transfer price of less than $(100 + 25) = $125 per unit.
- **The maximum**. Division Y will not agree to a transfer price in excess of $150.

The difference between the two results ($25) represents the savings from producing internally as opposed to buying externally.

4.2.2 Opportunity cost

The **opportunity cost** included in determining the lower limit will be one of the following.

(a)   The maximum contribution forgone by the supplying division **in transferring internally rather than selling goods externally**.

(b)   The contribution forgone by **not using the same facilities** in the producing division **for their next best alternative use**.

If there is **no external market** for the item being transferred, and **no alternative uses for** the division's facilities, the **transfer price = standard variable cost of production**.

If there is an **external market** for the item being transferred and **no alternative**, **more profitable use** for the facilities in that division, the **transfer price = the market price**.

4.2.3 Example: The transfer price at full and spare capacity

The factors that influence the transfer price charged when divisions are operating at **full capacity** and **spare capacity** are best illustrated using an example.

Until recently, Strike Ltd focused exclusively on making soles for work boots and football boots. It sold these rubber soles to boot manufacturers. Last year the company decided to take advantage of its strong reputation by expanding into the business of making football boots. As a consequence of this expansion, the company is now structured as two independent divisions, the Boot Division and the Sole Division.

The Sole Division continues to make rubber soles for both football boots and work boots and sells these soles to other boot manufacturers. The Boot division manufactures leather uppers for football boots and attaches these uppers to rubber soles. During its first year the Boot Division purchased its rubber soles from outside suppliers so as not to disrupt the operations of the Sole Division.

Strike management now wants the Sole Division to provide at least some of the soles used by the Boot Division. The table below shows the contribution margin for each division when the Boot Division purchases from an outside supplier.

	Boot Division $		Sole Division $
Selling price of football boot	100	Selling price of sole	28
Variable cost of making boot (not including sole)	45	Variable cost per sole	21
Cost of sole purchased from outside suppliers	25		
Contribution margin per unit	30	Contribution margin per unit	7

The information above indicates that the total contribution margin per unit is $37 ($30 + $7).

Required

What would be a fair transfer price if the Sole Division sold 10,000 soles to the Boot Division?

Solution

The answer depends on how busy the Sole Division is – that is, whether it has **spare capacity**.

No spare capacity

As indicated above, the Sole Division charges $28 and derives a contribution margin of $7 per sole. The Sole Division has **no spare capacity** and produces and sells 80,000 units (soles) to outside customers. Therefore, the Sole Division must receive from the Boot Division a payment that will at least cover its variable cost per sole **plus** its lost contribution margin per sole (the **opportunity cost**). If the Sole Division can not cover that amount (the **minimum** transfer price), it should not sell soles to the Boot Division. The minimum transfer price that would be acceptable to the Sole Division is$28, as shown below.

$21 (variable cost) + $7 (opportunity cost) = $28

Spare capacity

The minimum transfer price is different if a division has spare capacity. Assume the Sole Division produces 80,000 soles but can only sell 70,000 to the open market. As a result, it has available capacity of 10,000 units. In this situation, the Sole Division does not lose its contribution margin of $7 per unit, and therefore the minimum price it would now accept is $21 as shown below.

$21 (variable cost) + $0 (opportunity cost) = $21

In this case the Boot Division and the Sole Division should **negotiate** a transfer price within the range of $21 and $25 (cost from outside supplier).

4.3 The use of market price as a basis for transfer prices

If an **external market price exists** for transferred goods, profit centre managers will be aware of the price they could obtain or the price they would have to pay for their goods on the external market, and they would inevitably **compare** this price **with the transfer price**.

4.3.1 Example: transferring goods at market value

A company has two profit centres, A and B. A sells half of its output on the open market and transfers the other half to B. Costs and external revenues in an accounting period are as follows.

	A	B	Total
	$	$	$
External sales	8,000	24,000	32,000
Costs of production	12,000	10,000	22,000
Company profit			10,000

Required

What are the consequences of setting a transfer price at market value?

Solution

If the transfer price is at market price, A would be happy to sell the output to B for $8,000, which is what A would get by selling it externally instead of transferring it.

	A		B		Total
	$	$	$	$	$
Market sales		8,000		24,000	32,000
Transfer sales		8,000		–	
		16,000		24,000	
Transfer costs		–	8,000		
Own costs	12,000		10,000		22,000
		12,000	18,000		
Profit		4,000		6,000	10,000

The **transfer sales of A are self cancelling with the transfer cost of B**, so that the total profits are unaffected by the transfer items. The transfer price simply spreads the total profit between A and B.

Consequences

(a)   A earns the same profit on transfers as on external sales. B must pay a commercial price for transferred goods, and both divisions will have their profit measured in a fair way.

(b)   A will be indifferent about selling externally or transferring goods to B because the profit is the same on both types of transaction. B can therefore ask for and obtain as many units as it wants from A.

A **market-based** transfer price therefore seems to be the **ideal** transfer price.

4.4 The merits of market value transfer prices

4.4.1 Divisional autonomy

In a decentralised company, divisional managers should have the **autonomy** to make output, selling and buying **decisions which appear to be in the best interests of the division's performance.** (If every division optimises its performance, the company as a whole must inevitably achieve optimal results.) Thus a **transferor division should be given the freedom to sell output on the open market,** rather than to transfer it within the company.

'Arm's length' transfer prices, which give profit centre managers the freedom to negotiate prices with other profit centres as though they were independent companies, will tend to result in a market-based transfer price.

4.4.2 Corporate profit maximisation

In most cases where the transfer price is at market price, **internal transfers** should be **expected**, because the **buying division** is likely to **benefit** from a better quality of service, greater flexibility, and dependability of supply. **Both divisions** may **benefit** from cheaper costs of administration, selling and transport. A market price as the transfer price would therefore **result in decisions which would be in the best interests of the company or group as a whole.**

4.4.3 Divisional performance measurement

Where a **market price exists**, but the **transfer price is a different amount** (say, at standard cost plus), divisional managers will **argue** about the volume of internal transfers.

For example, if division X is expected to sell output to division Y at a transfer price of $8 per unit when the open market price is $10, its manager will decide to sell all output on the open market. The manager of division Y would resent the loss of his cheap supply from X, and would be reluctant to buy on the open market. A wasteful situation would arise where X sells on the open market at $10, where Y buys at $10, so that administration, selling and distribution costs would have been saved if X had sold directly to Y at $10, the market price.

4.5 The disadvantages of market value transfer prices

Market value as a transfer price does have certain **disadvantages**.

(a)   The **market price may be a temporary one**, induced by adverse economic conditions, or dumping, or the market price might depend on the volume of output supplied to the external market by the profit centre.

(b)   A transfer price at market value might, under some circumstances, **act as a disincentive to use up any spare capacity** in the divisions. A price based on incremental cost, in contrast, might provide an incentive to use up the spare resources in order to provide a marginal contribution to profit.

(c)   Many products **do not have an equivalent market price** so that the price of a similar, but not identical, product might have to be chosen. In such circumstances, the option to sell or buy on the open market does not really exist.

(d)   There might be an **imperfect external market** for the transferred item, so that if the transferring division tried to sell more externally, it would have to reduce its selling price.

4.6 Cost-based approaches to transfer pricing

FAST FORWARD

> Problems arise with the use of **cost-based** transfer prices because one party or the other is liable to perceive them as unfair.

Cost-based approaches to transfer pricing are often used in practice, because in practice the following conditions are common.

(a)   There is **no external market** for the product that is being transferred.

(b)   Alternatively, although there is an external market it is an **imperfect** one because the market price is affected by such factors as the amount that the company setting the transfer price supplies to it, or because there is only a limited external demand.

In either case there will not be a suitable market price upon which to base the transfer price.

4.6.1 Transfer prices based on full cost

Under this approach, the **full cost** (including fixed overheads absorbed) incurred by the supplying division in making the 'intermediate' product is charged to the receiving division. The obvious drawback to this is that the division supplying the product **makes no profit** on its work so is not motivated to supply internally. Also, there are a number of alternative ways in which fixed costs can be accounted for. If a **full cost plus** approach is used a **profit margin** is also included in this transfer price. The supplying division will therefore gain some profit at the expense of the buying division.

4.6.2 Example: transfer prices based on full cost

Suppose a company has two profit centres, A and B. A can only sell half of its maximum output of 800 units externally because of limited demand. It transfers the other half of its output to B which also faces limited demand. Costs and revenues in an accounting period are as follows.

	A	B	Total
	$	$	$
External sales	8,000	24,000	32,000
Costs of production in the division	13,000	10,000	23,000
Profit			9,000

Division A's costs included fixed production overheads of $4,800 and fixed selling and administration costs of $1,000.

There are no opening or closing inventories. It does not matter, for this illustration, whether marginal costing or absorption costing is used. For the moment, we shall ignore the question of whether the current output levels are profit-maximising and congruent with the goals of the company as a whole.

If the transfer price is at full cost, A in our example would have 'sales' to B of $6,000 (($13,000 – 1,000) × 50%). Selling and administration costs are not included as these are not incurred on the internal transfers. This would be a cost to B, as follows.

		A		B	Company as a whole
	$	$	$	$	$
Open market sales		8,000		24,000	32,000
Transfer sales		6,000		–	
Total sales, inc transfers		14,000		24,000	
Transfer costs			6,000		
Own costs	13,000		10,000		23,000
Total costs, inc transfers		13,000		16,000	
Profit		1,000		8,000	9,000

The **transfer sales of A are self-cancelling with the transfer costs of B** so that total profits are **unaffected by the transfer items**. The transfer price simply spreads the total profit of $9,000 between A and B.

The obvious **drawback** to the transfer price at cost is that **A makes no profit** on its work, and the manager of division A would much prefer to sell output on the open market to earn a profit, rather than transfer to B, regardless of whether or not transfers to B would be in the best interests of the company as a whole. Division A needs a profit on its transfers in order to be motivated to supply B; therefore transfer pricing at cost is inconsistent with the use of a profit centre accounting system.

Key term

An **intermediate product** is one that is used as a component of another product, for example car headlights or food additives.

4.6.3 Transfer price at variable cost

A variable cost approach entails charging the variable cost (which we assume to be the same as the marginal cost) that has been incurred by the supplying division to the receiving division.

The problem is that with a transfer price at marginal cost the **supplying division does not cover its fixed costs.**

4.7 Identifying the optimal transfer price

Here are some guiding rules for identifying the optimal transfer price.

(a) The **ideal transfer price** should **reflect the opportunity cost** of sale to the supply division and the opportunity cost to the buying division. Unfortunately, full information about opportunity costs may not be easily obtainable in practice.

(b) Where a **perfect external market price exists and unit variable costs and unit selling prices are constant**, the **opportunity cost** of transfer will be **external market price** or **external market price less savings in selling costs.**

(c) In the **absence of a perfect external market price for the transferred item**, but when **unit variable costs are constant**, and the **sales price per unit of the end-product is constant**, the **ideal transfer price** should reflect the opportunity cost of the resources consumed by the supply division to make and supply the item and so should be at **standard variable cost + opportunity cost of making the transfer.**

(d) When **unit variable costs and/or unit selling prices are not constant,** there will be a **profit-maximising level of output** and the **ideal transfer price** will only be found by sensible **negotiation** and careful **analysis.**

   (i) Establish the output and sales quantities that will optimise the profits of the company or group as a whole.

   (ii) Establish the transfer price at which both profit centres would maximise their profits at this company-optimising output level.

   There may be a range of prices within which both profit centres can agree on the output level that would maximise their individual profits and the profits of the company as a whole. Any price within the range would then be 'ideal'.

4.8 Transfer pricing calculations

4.8.1 Sub-optimal decisions

Note that as the level of transfer price increases, its effect on a division within the organisation could lead to sub-optimalisation problems for the organisation as a whole.

4.8.2 Example: sub-optimal decisions

For example, suppose division B could buy the product from an outside supplier for $10 instead of paying $15 ($6,000/(800/2)) to division A. This transfer price would therefore force division B to buy the product externally at $10 per unit, although it could be manufactured internally for a variable cost of $(13,000 – 4,800 – 1,000)/800 = $9 per unit.

Although division B (the buying division) would save ($15 – $10) = $5 per unit by buying externally, the organisation as a whole would lose $400 as follows.

	Per unit
	$
Marginal cost of production	9
External purchase cost	10
Loss if buy in	1

The overall loss on transfer/purchase of 400 units is therefore 400 × $1 = $400.

This loss of $1 per unit assumes that any other use for the released capacity would produce a benefit of less than $400. If the 400 units could also be sold externally for $20 per unit, the optimal decision for the organisation as a whole would be to buy in the units for division B at $10 per unit.

	Per unit $
Market price	20
Marginal cost	9
Contribution	11
Loss if buy-in	(1)
Incremental profit	10

The overall incremental profit would therefore be 400 × $10 = $4,000.

4.8.3 Example: prices based on full cost plus

If the transfers are at cost plus a margin of, say, 10%, A's sales to B would be $6,600 ($13,000 −1,000) × 50% × 1.10).

	A		B		Total
	$	$	$	$	$
Open market sales		8,000		24,000	32,000
Transfer sales		6,600		–	
		14,600		24,000	
Transfer costs			6,600		
Own costs	13,000		10,000		23,000
		13,000		16,600	
Profit		1,600		7,400	9,000

Compared to a transfer price at cost, **A gains some profit** at the expense of B. However, A makes a bigger profit on external sales in this case because the profit mark-up of 10% is less than the profit mark-up on open market sales. The choice of 10% as a profit mark-up was arbitrary and unrelated to external market conditions.

The transfer price **fails on all three criteria** (divisional autonomy, performance measurement and corporate profit measurement) for judgement.

(a) Arguably, the transfer price does not give A fair revenue or charge B a reasonable cost, and so their profit **performance is distorted**. It would certainly be unfair, for example, to compare A's profit with B's profit.

(b) Given this unfairness it is likely that the **autonomy** of each of the divisional managers is **under threat**. If they cannot agree on what is a fair split of the external profit a decision will have to be imposed from above.

(c) It would seem to give A an incentive to sell more goods externally and transfer less to B. This may or **may not be in the best interests of the company as a whole**.

In fact we can demonstrate that the method is **flawed from the point of view of corporate profit maximisation**. Division A's total production costs of $12,000 include an element of fixed costs. Half of division A's total production costs are transferred to division B. However from the point of view of division B the cost is entirely variable.

The cost per unit to A is $15 ($12,000 ÷ 800) and this includes a fixed element of $6 ($4,800 ÷ 800), while division B's own costs are $25 ($10,000 ÷ 400) per unit, including a fixed element of $10 (say). The **total variable cost is really** $9 + $15 = **$24**, but from division **B's point of view** the **variable cost** is $15 + $(25 − 10) = **$30**. This means that division B will be unwilling to sell the final product for less than $30, whereas any price above $24 would make a contribution to overall costs. Thus, if external prices for the final product fall, B might be tempted to cease production.

4.8.4 Example: transfer prices based on variable or marginal cost

A variable or marginal cost approach entails charging the variable cost (which we assume to be the same as the marginal cost) that has been incurred by the supplying division to the receiving division. As above, we shall suppose that A's cost per unit is $15, of which $6 is fixed and $9 variable.

	A $	A $	B $	B $	Company as a whole $	Company as a whole $
Market sales		8,000		24,000		32,000
Transfer sales		3,600		–		
		11,600		24,000		
Transfer costs			3,600			
Own variable costs	7,200		6,000		13,200	
Own fixed costs	5,800		4,000		9,800	
Total costs and transfers		13,000		13,600		23,000
(Loss)/Profit		(1,400)		10,400		9,000

4.8.5 Divisional autonomy, divisional performance measurement and corporate profit maximisation

(a)   This result is **deeply unsatisfactory for the manager of division** A who could make an additional $4,400 ($(8,000 – 3,600)) profit if no goods were transferred to division B, but all were sold externally.

(b)   Given that the manager of division A would prefer to transfer externally, **head office** are likely to have to **insist** that internal transfers are made.

(c)   For the company overall, external transfers only would cause a large fall in profit, because division B could make no sales at all.

Point to note. Suppose no more than the current $8,000 could be earned from external sales and the production capacity used for production for internal transfer would remain idle if not used. Division A would be indifferent to the transfers at marginal cost as they do not represent any benefit to the division.

If more than the $8,000 of revenue could be earned externally (ie division A could sell more externally than at present), division A would have a strong disincentive to supply B at marginal cost.

Chapter Roundup

- There are a number of advantages and disadvantages to **divisionalisation**.

- **Responsibility accounting** is the term used to describe decentralisation of authority, with the performance of the decentralised units measured in terms of accounting results.

  With a system of responsibility accounting there are three types of **responsibility centre: cost centre; profit centre; investment centre**.

- The performance of an investment centre is usually monitored using either or both of **return on investment (ROI)** and **residual income (RI).**

- There is no generally agreed method of calculating ROI and it can have **behavioural implications** and lead to dysfunctional decision making when used as a guide to investment decisions. It focuses attention on short-run performance whereas investment decisions should be evaluated over their full life.

- RI can sometimes give results that avoid the **behavioural** problem of **dysfunctionality**. Its weakness is that it does not facilitate comparisons between investment centres nor does it relate the size of a centre's income to the size of the investment.

- Transfer prices are a way of promoting **divisional autonomy**, ideally without prejudicing the **measurement of divisional performance** or discouraging **overall corporate profit maximisation**.

  Transfer prices should be set at a level which ensures that profits for the organisation as a whole are maximised.

- The **limits within which transfer prices should fall** are as follows.

  - **The minimum**. The sum of the supplying division's marginal cost and opportunity cost of the item transferred.
  - **The maximum**. The lowest market price at which the receiving division could purchase the goods or services externally, less any internal cost savings in packaging and delivery.

- Problems arise with the use of **cost-based** transfer prices because one party or the other is liable to perceive them as unfair.

1   *Choose the correct words from those highlighted.*

    ROI based on profits as a % of net assets employed will (a) **increase/decrease** as an asset gets older and its book value (b) **increases/reduces**. This could therefore create an (c) **incentive/disincentive** to investment centre managers to reinvest in new or replacement assets.

2   An investment centre with capital employed of $570,000 is budgeted to earn a profit of $119,700 next year. A proposed fixed asset investment of $50,000, not included in the budget at present, will earn a profit next year of $8,500 after depreciation. The company's cost of capital is 15%. What is the budgeted ROI and residual income for next year, both with and without the investment?

	ROI	Residual income
Without investment	....	....
With investment	....	....

3   'The use of residual income in performance measurement will avoid dysfunctional decision making because it will always lead to the correct decision concerning capital investments.' True or false?

4   To prevent dysfunctional transfer price decision making, profit centres must be allowed to make autonomous decisions. *True or false?*

5   Which of the following is not a disadvantage of using market value as a transfer price?

    A   The market price might be a temporary one.
    B   Use of market price might act as a disincentive to use up spare capacity.
    C   Many products do not have an equivalent market price.
    D   The external market might be perfect.

6   *Fill in the blanks.*

    Ideally, a transfer price should be set that enables the individual divisions to maximise their profits at a level of output that maximises ....

    The transfer price which achieves this is unlikely to be a .... transfer price or a .... transfer price.

    If optimum decisions are to be taken, transfer prices should reflect ....

Answers to Quick Quiz

1   (a)   increase
    (b)   reduces
    (c)   disincentive

2
	ROI	Residual income
Without investment	21.0%	$34,200
With investment	20.7%	$35,200

3   False

4   False. They cannot be allowed to make entirely autonomous decisions.

5   D

6   profit for the company as a whole; market-based; cost-based; opportunity costs

Now try the questions below from the Exam Question Bank

Number	Level	Marks	Time
Q20	Examination	20	36 mins

16

Further performance management

Topic list	Syllabus reference
1 Not-for-profit organisations	E3 (a), (c)
2 Performance measurement in not-for-profit organisations	E3 (b)
3 Value for money	E3 (d)
4 External considerations	E4 (a), (b), (c)
5 Behaviour aspects of performance management	E4 (d)

Introduction

This final chapter on performance measurement looks at performance analysis in not for profit organisations and the public sector. The problems of having **non-quantifiable** and **multiple** objectives are discussed.

We then go on to consider how **external considerations** are allowed for in performance measurement and finally identify and explain the **behaviour aspects** of performance management.

Study guide

		Intellectual level
E3	**Performance analysis in not for profit organisations and the public sector**	
(a)	Comment on the problems of having non-quantifiable objectives in performance management	2
(b)	Explain how performance could be measured in this sector	2
(c)	Comment on the problems of having multiple objectives in this sector	2
(d)	Outline Value for Money (VFM) as a public sector objective	1
E4	**External considerations and behavioural aspects**	
(a)	Explain the need to allow for external considerations in performance management, including stakeholders, market conditions and allowance for competitors	2
(b)	Suggest ways in which external considerations could be allowed for in performance management	2
(c)	Interpret performance in the light of external considerations	2
(d)	Identify and explain the behaviour aspects of performance management	2

Exam guide

Scenarios in your exam may relate to not-for-profit organisations and the public sector and you need to understand their particular needs and issues. Always **apply** your answers to the specific organisation.

1 Not-for-profit organisations

FAST FORWARD

One possible definition of a **not-for-profit seeking organisation** is that its first objective is to be involved in non-loss operations to cover its costs, profits only being made as a means to an end.

Although most people would 'know one if they saw it', there is a surprising problem in clearly defining what counts as a not-for-profit organisation.

Bois has suggested that not-for-profit organisations are defined by recognising that their first objective is to be involved in **non-loss operations** in order to cover their costs and that profits are only made as a means to an end (such as providing a service, or accomplishing some socially or morally worthy objective).

Key term

A **not-for-profit organisation** is '... an organisation whose attainment of its prime goal is not assessed by economic measures. However, in pursuit of that goal it may undertake profit-making activities.' (*Bois*)

This may involve a number of different kinds of organisation with, for example, differing legal status – charities, statutory bodies offering public transport or the provision of services such as leisure, health or public utilities such as water or road maintenance.

1.1 Objectives and not-for-profit organisations

FAST FORWARD

Not-for-profit organisations have **multiple objectives** which are **difficult to define**.

A major problem with many not-for-profit organisations, particularly government bodies, is that it is extremely **difficult to define their objectives** at all. In addition they tend to have **multiple objectives**, so that even if they could all be clearly identified it is impossible to say which is the overriding objective.

Question
Objectives

What objectives might the following not-for-profit organisations have?

(a)　　An army
(b)　　A local council
(c)　　A charity

(d)　　A political party
(e)　　A college

Answer

Here are some suggestions.

(a)　　To defend a country
(b)　　To provide services for local people (such as the elderly)
(c)　　To help others/protect the environment
(d)　　To gain power/enact legislation
(e)　　To provide education

More general objectives for not-for-profit organisations include:

- Surplus maximisation (equivalent to profit maximisation)
- Revenue maximisation (as for a commercial business)
- Usage maximisation (as in leisure centre swimming pool usage)
- Usage targeting (matching the capacity available, as in the NHS)
- Full/partial cost recovery (minimising subsidy)
- Budget maximisation (maximising what is offered)
- Producer satisfaction maximisation (satisfying the wants of staff and volunteers)
- Client satisfaction maximisation (the police generating the support of the public)

It is difficult to judge whether **non-quantifiable objectives** have been met. For example, assessing whether a charity has improved the situation of those benefiting from its activities is difficult to research. Statistics related to product mix, financial resources, size of budgets, number of employees, number of volunteers, number of customers serviced and number and location of facilities are all useful for this task.

The primary objectives of commercial manufacturing and service organisations are likely to be fairly similar and centre on satisfying shareholders.

Exam focus point

> In an exam, if faced with a question on the public sector, remember that you are likely to have had extensive contact with a variety of public sector organisations and have seen something of how they work. Your greatest contact is likely to have been with the public education system, but you will probably have had contact with some local government authorities which provide a wide variety of services from street cleaning, to leisure facilities, to fire services. You may also have had contact with the health service.
>
> Think now about your experiences and use them in the exam.

2 Performance measurement in not-for-profit organisations

FAST FORWARD

There are a range of problems in measuring performance of not-for-profit organisations.

Commercial organisations generally have market competition and the profit motive to guide the process of managing resources economically, efficiently and effectively. However, not-for-profit organisations cannot by definition be **judged by profitability** and do **not** generally have to be **successful against competition,** so other methods of assessing performance have to be used.

As we have already said, a major problem with many not-for-profit organisations, particularly government bodies, is that it is extremely **difficult to define their objectives** at all, let alone find one which can serve a yardstick function in the way that profit does for commercial bodies.

Objectives for non-profit seeking organisations

One of the objectives of a local government body could be 'to provide adequate street lighting throughout the area'.

(a)   How could the 'adequacy' of street lighting be measured?

(b)   Assume that other objectives are to improve road safety in the area and to reduce crime. How much does 'adequate' street lighting contribute to each of these aims?

(c)   What is an excessive amount of money to pay for adequately lit streets, improved road safety and reduced crime? How much is too little?

Answer

Mull over these questions and discuss them in class or with colleagues if possible. It is possible to suggest answers, perhaps even in quantitative terms, but the point is that there are no **easy** answers, and no right or wrong answers.

You might consider (partly depending upon your political point of view) that it is therefore not necessary to measure performance in not-for-profit organisations. However, few would argue that such bodies should be given **whatever amount of money** they say they need to pursue their aims, with no **check** on whether it is spent well or badly.

(a)   Without information about what is being achieved (outputs) and what it is costing (inputs) it is impossible to make **efficient resource allocations**. These allocation decisions rely on a range of performance measures which, if unavailable, may lead managers to allocate resources based on subjective judgement, personal whim or in response to political pressure.

(b)   Without performance measures managers will not know the **extent to which operations are contributing to effectiveness and efficiency;** when diagnostic interventions are necessary; how the performance of their organisation **compares** with similar units elsewhere; and how their performance has **changed** over time.

(c)   **Government** may require performance information to decide how much to spend in the public sector and where, within the sector, it should be allocated. In particular they will be interested to know what results may be achieved as a consequence of a particular level of funding, or to decide whether or not a service could be delivered more effectively and efficiently in the private sector. Likewise **people who provide funds for** other kinds of not-for-profit organisations are entitled to know whether their money is being put to good use.

2.1 How can performance be measured?

Performance is judged in terms of inputs and outputs and hence the **value for money criteria** of **economy, efficiency** and **effectiveness.**

Performance is usually judged in terms of **inputs and outputs** and this ties in with the 'value for money' criteria that are often used to assess not-for-profit organisations (covered in Section 3).

*   **Economy** (spending money frugally)
*   **Efficiency** (getting out as much as possible for what goes in)
*   **Effectiveness** (getting done, by means of the above, what was supposed to be done)

More formal definitions are as follows.

Key terms

> **Effectiveness** is the relationship between an organisation's outputs and its objectives.
>
> **Efficiency** is the relationship between inputs and outputs.
>
> **Economy** is attaining the appropriate quantity and quality of inputs at lowest cost.

We will look at these concepts in more depth in Section 3.

2.2 Problems with performance measurement of not-for-profit organisations

(a) **Multiple objectives**

As we have said, they tend to have multiple objectives, so that even if they can all be clearly identified it is impossible to say which is the overriding objective.

(b) **Measuring outputs**

Outputs can seldom be measured in a way that is generally agreed to be meaningful. (For example, are good exam results alone an adequate measure of the quality of teaching?) Data collection can be problematic. For example, unreported crimes are not included in data used to measure the performance of a police force.

(c) **Lack of profit measure**

If an organisation is not expected to make a profit, or if it has no sales, indicators such as ROI and RI are meaningless.

(d) **Nature of service provided**

Many not-for-profit organisations provide services for which it is difficult to define a cost unit. For example, what is the cost unit for a local fire service? This problem does exist for commercial service providers but problems of performance measurement are made simple because profit can be used.

(e) **Financial constraints**

Although every organisation operates under financial constraints, these are more pronounced in not-for-profit organisations. For instance, a commercial organisation's borrowing power is effectively limited by managerial prudence and the willingness of lenders to lend, but a local authority's ability to raise finance (whether by borrowing or via local taxes) is subject to strict control by central government.

(f) **Political, social and legal considerations**

(i) Unlike commercial organisations, public sector organisations are subject to strong political influences. Local authorities, for example, have to carry out central government's policies as well as their own (possibly conflicting) policies.

(ii) The public may have higher expectations of public sector organisations than commercial organisations. A decision to close a local hospital in an effort to save costs, for example, is likely to be less acceptable to the public than the closure of a factory for the same reason.

(iii) The performance indicators of public sector organisations are subject to far more onerous legal requirements than those of private sector organisations. We consider this point in more detail in Section 6.

(iv) Whereas profit-seeking organisations are unlikely in the long term to continue services making a negative contribution, not-for-profit organisations may be required to offer a range of services, even if some are uneconomic.

2.3 Solutions

2.3.1 Inputs

Performance can be judged in terms of inputs. This is very common in everyday life. If somebody tells you that their suit cost $750, you would generally conclude that it was an extremely well-designed and good quality suit, even if you did not think so when you first saw it. The drawback is that you might also conclude that the person wearing the suit had been cheated or was a fool, or you may happen to be of the opinion that no piece of clothing is worth $750. So it is with the inputs and outputs of a not-for-profit organisations.

2.3.2 Judgement

A second possibility is to accept that performance measurement must to some extent be subjective. Judgements can be made by **experts** in that particular not-for-profit activity or by the **persons who fund the activity**.

2.3.3 Comparisons

We have said that most not-for-profit organisations do not face competition but this does not mean that all are unique. Bodies like local governments, health services and so on can judge their performance **against each other** and **against the historical results of their predecessors**. And since they are not competing with each other, there is less of a problem with confidentiality and so **benchmarking** is easier.

In practice, **benchmarking** usually encompasses:

- Regularly comparing aspects of performance (functions or processes) with best practitioners
- Identifying gaps in performance
- Seeking fresh approaches to bring about improvements in performance
- Following through with implementing improvements
- Following up by monitoring progress and reviewing the benefits

2.3.4 Quantitative measures

Unit cost measurements like 'cost per patient day' or 'cost of borrowing one library book' can fairly easily be established to allow organisations to assess whether they are doing better or worse than their counterparts.

Efficiency measurement of inputs and outputs is illustrated in three different situations as follows.

(a)   **Where input is fixed**

$$\frac{\text{Actual output}}{\text{Maximum output obtainable for a given input}}$$

25/30 miles per gallon = 83.3% efficiency

(b)   **Where output is fixed**

$$\frac{\text{Minimum input needed for a given output}}{\text{Actual input}}$$

55/60 hours to erect scaffolding = 91.7% efficiency

(c)   **Where input and output are both variable**

Actual output ÷ actual input
compared with
standard output ÷ standard input

$9,030/7,000 meals = $1.29 per meal

$9,600/7,500 meals = $1.28 per meal
Efficiency = 99.2%

As a further illustration, suppose that at a cost of $40,000 and 4,000 hours (inputs) in an average year two policemen travel 8,000 miles and are instrumental in 200 arrests (outputs). A large number of possibly meaningful measures can be derived from these few figures, as the table below shows.

	$40,000	4,000 hours	8,000 miles	200 arrests
Cost $40,000		$40,000/4,000 = $10 per hour	$40,000/8,000 = $5 per mile	$40,000/200 = $200 per arrest
Time 4,000 hours	4,000/$40,000 = 6 minutes patrolling per $1 spent		4,000/8,000 = ½ hour to patrol 1 mile	4,000/200 = 20 hours per arrest
Miles 8,000	8,000/$40,000 = 0.2 of a mile per $1	8,000/4,000 = 2 miles patrolled per hour		8,000/200 = 40 miles per arrest
Arrests 200	200/$40,000 = 1 arrest per $200	200/4,000 = 1 arrest every 20 hours	200/8,000 = 1 arrest every 40 miles	

These measures **do not necessarily identify cause and effect** (do teachers or equipment produce better exam results?) **or personal responsibility and accountability**. Actual performance needs to be compared as follows.

(a)   With standards, if there are any
(b)   With similar external activities
(c)   With similar internal activities

(d)   With targets
(e)   With indices
(f)   Over time, as trends

Not-for-profit organisations are forced to use a **wide range** of indicators and can be considered early users of a **balanced scorecard** approach (covered in Chapter 14).

3 Value for money

FAST FORWARD

> Public sector organisations are now under considerable pressure to prove that they operate economically, efficiently and effectively, and are encouraged from many sources to draw up action plans to achieve **value for money** as part of the continuing process of good management.

Although much has been written about value for money (VFM), there is no great mystique about the concept. The term is common in everyday speech and so is the idea.

Key term

> **Value for money** means providing a service in a way which is economical, efficient and effective.

To drive the point home, think of a bottle of Fairy Liquid. If we believe the advertising, Fairy is good 'value for money' because it washes half as many plates again as any other washing up liquid. Bottle for bottle it may be more expensive, but plate for plate it is cheaper. Not only this but Fairy gets plates 'squeaky' clean. To summarise, Fairy gives us VFM because it exhibits the following characteristics.

- **Economy** (more clean plates per pound)
- **Efficiency** (more clean plates per squirt)
- **Effectiveness** (plates as clean as they should be)

The assessment of economy, efficiency and effectiveness should be a part of the normal management process of any organisation, public or private.

(a)   Management should carry out **performance reviews** as a regular feature of their control responsibilities.
(b)   Independent assessments of management performance can be carried out by 'outsiders', perhaps an internal audit department, as **value for money audits (VFM audits).**

Value for money is important **whatever level of expenditure** is being considered. Negatively it may be seen as an approach to spreading costs in public expenditure fairly across services but positively it is necessary to ensure that the desired impact is achieved with the minimum use of resources.

3.1 Economy

Economy is concerned with the cost of inputs, and it is achieved by **obtaining those inputs at the lowest acceptable cost**. Economy **does not mean straightforward cost-cutting,** because resources must be acquired which are of a suitable **quality** to provide the service to the desired standard. Cost-cutting should not sacrifice quality to the extent that service standards fall to an unacceptable level. Economising by buying poor quality materials, labour or equipment is a 'false economy'.

3.2 Efficiency

Efficiency means the following.

(a)   **Maximising output for a given input**, for example maximising the number of transactions handled per employee or per $1 spent.

(b)   **Achieving the minimum input for a given output**. For example, a government department may be required to pay unemployment benefit to millions of people. Efficiency will be achieved by making these payments with the minimum labour and computer time.

3.3 Effectiveness

Effectiveness means ensuring that the **outputs** of a service or programme have the **desired impacts**; in other words, finding out whether they **succeed in achieving objectives**, and if so, to what extent.

3.4 Studying and measuring the three Es

Economy, efficiency and effectiveness can be studied and measured with reference to the following.

(a)   **Inputs**

  (i)   Money
  (ii) Resources – the labour, materials, time and so on consumed, and their cost

  For example, a VFM audit into state secondary education would look at the efficiency and economy of the use of resources for education (the use of schoolteachers, school buildings, equipment, cash) and whether the resources are being used for their purpose: what is the pupil/teacher ratio and are trained teachers being fully used to teach the subjects they have been trained for?

(b)   **Outputs**, in other words the **results of an activity**, measurable as the services actually produced, and the quality of the services.

  In the case of a VFM audit of secondary education, outputs would be measured as the number of pupils taught and the number of subjects taught per pupil; how many examination papers are taken and what is the pass rate; what proportion of students go on to further education at a university or college.

(c)   Impacts, which are the effect that the outputs of an activity or programme have in terms of achieving policy objectives.

Policy objectives might be to provide a minimum level of education to all children up to the age of 16, and to make education relevant for the children's future jobs and careers. This might be measured by the ratio of jobs vacant to unemployed school leavers. A VFM audit could assess to what extent this objective is being achieved.

As another example from education, suppose that there is a programme to build a new school in an area. The **inputs** would be the **costs of building** the school, and the resources used up; the **outputs** would be the **school building** itself; and the **impacts** would be the **effect that the new school has on education in the area** it serves.

4 External considerations

Performance management needs to allow for **external considerations** including stakeholders, market conditions and allowance for competitiors.

4.1 Stakeholders

Key term

> **Stakeholders** are groups of people or individuals who have a legitimate interest in the activities of an organisation. They include customers, employees, the community, shareholders, suppliers and lenders.

There are three broad types of stakeholder in an organisation.

- **Internal** stakeholders (employees, management)
- **Connected** stakeholders (shareholders, customers, suppliers, financiers)
- **External** stakeholders (the community, government, pressure groups)

The stakeholder approach suggests that **corporate objectives** are, or should be, **shaped** and **influenced** by **those** who have **sufficient involvement or interest** in the organisation's operational activities.

4.1.1 Internal stakeholders: employees and management

Because employees and management are so **intimately connected** with the company, their objectives are likely to have a **strong influence** on how it is run. They are interested in the following issues.

(a) The **organisation's continuation and growth**. Management and employees have a special interest in the organisation's continued existence.

(b) Managers and employees have **individual interests** and goals which can be harnessed to the goals of the organisation.

- Jobs/careers
- Money
- Benefits
- Satisfaction
- Promotion

For managers and employees, an organisation's social obligations will include the provision of safe working conditions and anti-discrimination policies.

4.1.2 Connected stakeholders

Increasing shareholder value should assume a **core role** in the strategic management of a business. If management performance is measured and rewarded by reference to changes in **shareholder value** then shareholders will be happy, because managers are likely to **encourage long-term share price growth**.

Connected stakeholder	Interests to defend	
Shareholders (corporate strategy)	• Increase in shareholder wealth, measured by profitability, P/E ratios, market capitalisation, dividends and yield • Risk	
Bankers (cash flows)	• Security of loan	• Adherence to loan agreements
Suppliers (purchase strategy)	• Profitable sales • Payment for goods	• Long-term relationship
Customers (product market strategy)	• Goods as promised	• Future benefits

Even though **shareholders** are deemed to be interested in return on investment and/or capital appreciation, many want to **invest** in **ethically-sound** organisations.

4.1.3 External stakeholders

External stakeholder groups – the government, local authorities, pressure groups, the community at large, professional bodies – are likely to have quite diverse objectives.

External stakeholder	Interests to defend
Government	• Jobs, training, tax
Interest/pressure groups / charities / 'civil society'	• Pollution • Rights • Other

It is external stakeholders in particular who **induce social and ethical obligations**.

4.1.4 Performance measures

Organisations may need to develop performance measures to ensure that the needs of stakeholders are met.

Stakeholder	Measure
Employees	Morale index
Shareholders	Share price, dividend yield
Government	Percentage of products conforming to environmental regulations
Customers	Warranty cost, percentage of repeat customers

There is a strong link here to the balanced scorecard approach and the need to have a range of non-financial performance indicators as well as financial performance indicators.

4.2 Economic environment

Economic growth

- Has the economy grown or is there a recession?
- How has demand for goods/services been affected?

Local economic trends

- Are local businesses rationalising or expanding?
- Are office/factory rents increasing/falling?
- In what direction are house prices moving?
- Are labour rates on the increase?

Inflation

(a) Is a high rate making it difficult to plan, owing to the uncertainty of future financial returns? Inflation and expectations of it help to explain short termism.
(b) Is the rate depressing consumer demand?
(c) Is the rate encouraging investment in domestic industries?
(d) Is a high rate leading employees to demand higher money wages to compensate for a fall in the value of their wages?

Interest rates

- How do these affect consumer confidence and liquidity, and hence demand?
- Is the cost of borrowing increasing, thereby reducing profitability?

Exchange rates

- What impact do these have on the cost of overseas imports?
- Are prices that can be charged to overseas customers affected?

Government fiscal policy

(a) Are consumers increasing/decreasing the amount they spend due to tax and government spending decisions?

(b) How is the government's corporation tax policy affecting the organisation?

(c) Is VAT affecting demand?

Government spending

Is the organisation a supplier to the government (such as a construction firm) and hence affected by the level of spending?

4.3 Competition

We considered the effects of competitors' behaviour in Chapter 5 when we looked at **pricing strategies**. Performance management must consider information on competitors' prices and cost structures and identify which features of an organisation's products add most value. Management accounting information has to be produced speedily and be up-to-date so that managers can react quickly and effectively to **changing market conditions**.

5 Behaviour aspects of performance management

It is generally considered to be unreasonable to assess managers' performance in relation to matters that are beyond their control. Therefore **management performance measures** should **only include those items that are directly controllable by the manager** in question.

If people **know** that their performance is being **measured** then this will **affect the standard** of their performance, particularly if they know that they will be **rewarded** for achieving a certain level of performance.

Ideally, performance **measures** will be devised that **reward behaviour** that **maximises the corporate good**. In practice, however, it is not quite so simple.

(a) There is a danger that managers and staff will **concentrate** only upon what they know is **being measured**. This is not a problem if every important issue has a measure attached to it, but such a system is difficult to devise and implement in practice.

(b) **Individuals** have their own goals, but good performance that satisfies their own sense of what is important will not necessarily work towards the **corporate good**. Each individual may face a **conflict** between taking action to ensure organisational goals and action to ensure personal goals.

Point (b) is the problem of **goal congruence.**

5.1 Example: performance measurement and behaviour

(a) As we saw in Chapter 15, a divisional manager whose performance is assessed on the basis of his division's ROI might reject a proposal that produces an ROI greater than the group's target return if it reduces his division's overall return.

(b) Traditional feedback control would seek to eliminate an adverse material price variance by requiring managers to source cheaper, possibly lower quality, suppliers. This may run counter to an organisational objective to implement a system of TQM with the aim of reducing quality costs.

5.2 Measuring managerial performance

It is difficult to devise performance measures that relate specifically to a manager to judge his or her performance as a manager. It is possible to calculate statistics to assess the manager as an employee like any other employee (days absent, professional qualifications obtained, personability and so on), but this is not the point. As soon as the issue of **ability as a manager** arises it is necessary to **consider him in relation to his area of responsibility**. If we want to know how good a manager is at marketing the only information there is to go on is the marketing performance of his division (which may or may not be traceable to his own efforts).

5.3 The controllability principle

As we have seen, the **controllability principle** is that managers of responsibility centres should only be held accountable for costs over which they have some influence. From a motivation point of view this is important because it can be very demoralising for managers who feel that their performance is being judged on the basis of something over which they have no influence. It is also important from a control point of view in that control reports should ensure that information on costs is reported to the manager who is able to take action to control them.

5.4 Reward schemes and performance measurement

In many organisations, senior management try to motivate managers and employees by offering organisational rewards (more pay and promotion) for the achievement of certain levels of performance. The conventional theory of reward structures is that if the organisation establishes procedures for formal measurement of performance, and **rewards individuals for good performance**, individuals will be more likely to direct their efforts towards achieving the organisation's goals.

5.4.1 Problems associated with reward schemes

(a)   A serious problem that can arise is that performance-related pay and performance evaluation systems can **encourage dysfunctional behaviour.** Many investigations have noted the tendency of managers to pad their budgets either in anticipation of cuts by superiors or to make subsequent variances more favourable.

(b)   Perhaps of even more concern are the numerous examples of managers making **decisions that are contrary to the wider purposes of the organisation.**

(c)   Schemes designed to **ensure long-term achievements** (that is, to combat short termism) **may not motivate** since efforts and reward are too distant in time from each other (or managers may not think they will be around that long!).

(d)   It is questionable whether any performance measures or set of measures can provide a **comprehensive assessment of what a single person achieves** for an organisation. There will always be the old chestnut of lack of goal congruence, employees being committed to what is measured, rather than the objectives of the organisation.

(e)   **Self-interested performance** may be encouraged at the **expense of team work**.

(f)   High levels of output (whether this is number of calls answered or production of product X) may be achieved at the expense of **quality**.

(g)   In order to make bonuses more accessible, **standards and targets may have to be lowered**, with knock-on effects on quality.

(h)   They **undervalue intrinsic rewards** (which reflect the satisfaction that an individual experiences from doing a job and the opportunity for growth that the job provides) given that they promote extrinsic rewards (bonuses and so on).

Chapter Roundup

- One possible definition of a **not-for-profit seeking organisation** is that its first objective is to be involved in non-loss operations to cover its costs, profits only being made as a means to an end.

- Not-for-profit organisations have **multiple objectives** which are **difficult to define**.

- There are a range of problems in measuring performance of not-for-profit organisations.

- Performance is judged in terms of inputs and outputs and hence the **value for money criteria** of **economy, efficiency** and **effectiveness.**

- Public sector organisations are now under considerable pressure to prove that they operate economically, efficiently and effectively, and are encouraged from many sources to draw up action plans to achieve **value for money** as part of the continuing process of good management.

- Performance management needs to allow for **external considerations** including stakeholders, market conditions and allowance for competitiors.

- It is generally considered to be unreasonable to assess managers' performance in relation to matters that are beyond their control. Therefore **management performance measures** should **only include those items that are directly controllable by the manager** in question.

Quick Quiz

1. What general objectives of non-profit seeking organisations are being described in each of the following?

    (a) Maximising what is offered
    (b) Satisfying the wants of staff and volunteers
    (c) Equivalent to profit maximisation
    (d) Matching capacity available

2. The public service funding system operates on the basis that performance against non-financial objectives leads to a reduction in the level of funding. *True or false?*

3. *Match the definition to the term.*

Terms		Definition	
(a)	Economy	(1)	Ensuring outputs succeed in achieving objectives
(b)	Efficiency	(2)	Getting out as much as possible for what goes in
(c)	Effectiveness	(3)	Spending money frugally

4. Economy means cost cutting. *True or false?*

5. Six problems of measuring performance in non-profit seeking organisations were described in this chapter. Which two are missing from the list below?

    (a) Multiple objectives   (c) Lack of profit measure
    (b) Measuring output   (d) Nature of service provided

1   (a)   Budget maximisation
    (b)   Producer satisfaction maximisation
    (c)   Surplus maximisation
    (d)   Usage targeting

2   False

3   (a) (3); (b) (2); (c) (1)

4   False

5   Financial constraints
    Political/social/legal considerations

Now try the questions below from the Exam Question Bank

Number	Level	Marks	Time
Q21	Examination	20	36 mins

Exam question and answer bank

1 Solo

Solo makes and sells a single product. The following data relate to periods 1 to 4.

	$
Variable cost per unit	30
Selling price per unit	55
Fixed costs per period	6,000

Normal activity is 500 units and production and sales for the four periods are as follows:

	Period 1 units	Period 2 units	Period 3 units	Period 4 units
Sales	500	400	550	450
Production	500	500	450	500

There were no opening inventories at the start of period 1.

The marginal costing operating statement for periods 1 to 4 is shown below.

Marginal costing operating statement

	Period 1 $	Period 1 $	Period 2 $	Period 2 $	Period 3 $	Period 3 $	Period 4 $	Period 4 $
Sales		27,500		22,000		30,250		24,750
Variable production costs	15,000		15,000		13,500		15,000	
Add: Opening inventory b/fwd					3,000			
Less: Closing inventory c/fwd	–		(3,000)		–		(1,500)	
Variable production cost of sales		15,000		12,000		16,500		13,500
Contribution		12,500		10,000		13,750		11,250
Fixed costs		6,000		6,000		6,000		6,000
Profit for period		6,500		4,000		7,750		5,250

Required

(a) Prepare the operating statements for *each* of the periods 1 to 4, based on absorption costing principles. **(5 marks)**

(b) Comment briefly on the results obtained in each period *and* in total by the two systems. **(5 marks)**

(Total = 10 marks)

2 Southcott

Southcott Ltd is a firm of financial consultants which offers short revision courses on taxation and auditing for professional examinations. The firm has budgeted annual overheads totalling $152,625. Until recently the firm has applied overheads on a volume basis, based on the number of course days offered. The firm has no variable costs and the only direct costs are the consultants' own time which they divide equally between their two courses. The firm is considering the possibility of adopting an activity based costing (ABC) system and has identified the overhead costs as shown below.

Details of overheads

	$
Centre hire	62,500
Enquiries administration	27,125
Brochures	63,000
Total	152,625

The following information relates to the past year and is expected to remain the same for the coming year.

Course	No of courses sold	Duration of course	No of enquiries per course	No of brochures printed per course
Auditing	50	2 days	175	300
Taxation	30	3 days	70	200

All courses run with a maximum number of students (30), as it is deemed that beyond this number the learning experience is severely diminished, and the same centre is hired for all courses at a standard daily rate. The firm has the human resources to run only one course at any one time.

Required

(a) Calculate the overhead cost per course for both auditing and taxation using traditional volume based absorption costing. **(3 marks)**

(b) Recalculate the overhead costs per course using activity based costing and explain your choice of cost driver in your answer. **(10 marks)**

(c) Discuss the results that you have obtained. **(5 marks)**

(Total = 18 marks)

3 Abkaber   36 mins

Abkaber assembles three types of motorcycle at the same factory: the 50cc Sunshine; the 250cc Roadster and the 1000cc Fireball. It sells the motorcycles throughout the world. In response to market pressures Abkaber has invested heavily in new manufacturing technology in recent years and, as a result, has significantly reduced the size of its workforce.

Historically, the company has allocated all overhead costs using total direct labour hours, but is now considering introducing Activity Based Costing (ABC). Abkaber's accountant has produced the following analysis.

	Annual output (units)	Annual direct labour Hours	Selling price ($ per unit)	Raw material cost ($ per unit)
Sunshine	2,000	200,000	4,000	400
Roadster	1,600	220,000	6,000	600
Fireball	400	80,000	8,000	900

The three cost drivers that generate overheads are:

Deliveries to retailers	–	the number of deliveries of motorcycles to retail showrooms
Set-ups	–	the number of times the assembly line process is re-set to accommodate a production run of a different type of motorcycle
Purchase orders	–	the number of purchase orders.

The annual cost driver volumes relating to each activity and for each type of motorcycle are as follows:

	Number of deliveries to retailers	Number of set-ups	Number of purchase orders
Sunshine	100	35	400
Roadster	80	40	300
Fireball	70	25	100

The annual overhead costs relating to these activities are as follows:

	$
Deliveries to retailers	2,400,000
Set-up costs	6,000,000
Purchase orders	3,600,000

All direct labour is paid at $5 per hour. The company holds no inventories.

At a board meeting there was some concern over the introduction of activity based costing.

The finance director argued: 'I very much doubt whether selling the Fireball is viable but I am not convinced that activity based costing would tell us any more than the use of labour hours in assessing the viability of each product.'

The marketing director argued: 'I am in the process of negotiating a major new contract with a motorcycle rental company for the Sunshine model. For such a big order they will not pay our normal prices but we need to at least cover our incremental costs. I am not convinced that activity based costing would achieve this as it merely averages costs for our entire production'.

The managing director argued: 'I believe that activity based costing would be an improvement but it still has its problems. For instance if we carry out an activity many times surely we get better at it and costs fall rather than remain constant. Similarly, some costs are fixed and do not vary either with labour hours or any other cost driver.'

The chairman argued: 'I cannot see the problem. The overall profit for the company is the same no matter which method of allocating overheads we use. It seems to make no difference to me.'

Required

(a) Calculate the total profit on each of Abkaber's three types of product using each of the following methods to attribute overheads:

(i) the existing method based upon labour hours; and

(ii) activity based costing. **(10 marks)**

(b) Write a report to the directors of Abkaber, as its management accountant. The report should:

(i) evaluate the labour hours and the activity based costing methods in the circumstances of Abkaber; and

(ii) examine the implications of activity based costing for Abkaber, and in so doing evaluate the issues raised by each of the directors.

Refer to your calculations in requirement (a) above where appropriate. **(10 marks)**

(Total = 20 marks)

4 Life cycle costing   31 mins

A company manufactures MP3 players. It is planning to introduce a new model and development will begin very soon. It expects the new product to have a life cycle of 3 years and the following costs have been estimated.

	Year 0	Year 1	Year 2	Year 3
Units manufactured and sold		25,000	100,000	75,000
Price per unit		$90	$80	$70
R&D costs	$850,000	$90,000	-	-
Production costs				
Variable cost per unit		$30	$25	$25
Fixed costs		$500,000	$500,000	$500,000
Marketing costs				
Variable cost per unit		$5	$4	$3
Fixed costs		$300,000	$200,000	$200,000
Distribution costs				
Variable cost per unit		$1	$1	$1
Fixed costs		$190,000	$190,000	$190,000
Customer service costs per unit		$3	$2	$2

Required

(a) Explain life cycle costing and state what distinguishes it from more traditional management accounting techniques. **(10 marks)**

(b) Calculate the cost per unit looking at the whole lifecycle and comment on the price to be charged. **(7 marks)**

(Total = 17 marks)

5 Bottlenecks

36 mins

F Co makes and sells two products, A and B, each of which passes through the same automated production operations. The following estimated information is available for period 1.

- **Product unit data**

	A	B
Direct material cost ($)	2	40
Variable production overhead cost ($)	28	4
Overall hours per product unit (hours)	0.25	0.15

- Original estimates of production/sales of products A and B are 120,000 units and 45,000 units respectively. The selling prices per unit for A and B are $60 and $70 respectively.

- Maximum demand for each product is 20% above the estimated sales levels.

- Total fixed production overhead cost is $1,470,000. This is absorbed by products A and B at an average rate per hour based on the estimated production levels.

One of the production operations has a maximum capacity of 3,075 hours which has been identified as a bottleneck which limits the overall estimated production/sales of products A and B. The bottleneck hours required per product unit for products A and B are 0.02 and 0.015 respectively.

Required

(a) Calculate the mix (in units) of products A and B which will maximise net profit and the value (in $) of the maximum net profit. **(6 marks)**

(b) F Co has now decided to determine the profit-maximising mix of products A and B based on the throughput accounting principle of maximising the throughput return per production hour of the bottleneck resource.

Given that the variable overhead cost, based on the value (in $) which applies to the original estimated production/sales mix, is now considered to be fixed for the short/intermediate term:

(i) Calculate the mix (of units) of products A and B which will maximise net profit and the value of that net profit. **(8 marks)**

(ii) Calculate the throughput accounting ratio for product B and comment on it. **(3 marks)**

(iii) It is estimated that the direct material cost per unit of product B may increase by 20% due to shortage of supply. Calculate the revised throughput accounting ratio for product B and comment on it. **(3 marks)**

(Total = 20 marks)

6 HYC

HYC makes three products H, Y and C. All three products must be offered for sale each month in order to be able to provide a complete market service. The products are fragile and their quality deteriorates rapidly once they are manufactured.

The products are produced on two types of machine and worked on by a single grade of direct labour. Five direct employees are paid $8 per hour for a guaranteed minimum of 160 hours each per month.

All of the products are first moulded on a machine type 1 and then finished and sealed on a machine type 2.

The machine hour requirements for each of the products are as follows.

	Product H	Product Y	Product C
	Hours per unit	Hours per unit	Hours per unit
Machine type 1	1.5	4.5	3.0
Machine type 2	1.0	2.5	2.0

The capacity of the available machines type 1 and 2 are 600 hours and 500 hours per month respectively.

Details of the selling prices, unit costs and monthly demand for the three products are as follows.

	Product H	Product Y	Product C
	$ per unit	$ per unit	$ per unit
Selling price	91	174	140
Component cost	22	19	16
Other direct material cost	23	11	14
Direct labour cost at $8 per hour	6	48	36
Overheads	24	62	52
Profit	16	34	22
Maximum monthly demand (units)	120	70	60

Although HYC uses marginal costing and contribution analysis as the basis for its decision making activities, profits are reported in the monthly management accounts using the absorption costing basis. Finished goods inventories are valued in the monthly management accounts at full absorption cost.

Required

(a) Calculate the machine utilisation rate for each machine each month and explain which of the machines is the bottleneck/limiting factor. **(4 marks)**

(b) Using the current system of marginal costing and contribution analysis, calculate the profit maximising monthly output of the three products. **(4 marks)**

(c) Explain why throughput accounting might provide more relevant information in HYC's circumstances. **(4 marks)**

(d) Using a throughput approach, calculate the throughput-maximising monthly output of the three products. **(4 marks)**

(e) Explain the throughput accounting approach to optimising the level of inventory and its valuation. Contrast this approach to the current system employed by HYC. **(4 marks)**

(Total = 20 marks)

7 BD Company

36 mins

For some time the BD company has sold its entire output of canned goods to supermarket chains which sell them as 'own label' products. One advantage of this arrangement is that BD incurs no marketing costs, but there is continued pressure from the chains on prices, and margins are tight.

As a consequence, BD is considering selling some of its output under the BD brand. Margins will be better but there will be substantial marketing costs.

The following information is available.

	Current year's results – 20X2 (adjusted to 20X3 cost levels)	Forecast for 20X3 (assuming all 'own label' sales)
Sales (millions of cans)	18	19
	$ million	$ million
Sales	5.94	6.27
Manufacturing costs	4.30	4.45
Administration costs	1.20	1.20
Profit	0.44	0.62

For 20X3 the unit contribution on BD brand sales is expected to be $33\frac{1}{3}\%$ greater than 'own label' sales, but variable marketing costs of 2c per can and fixed marketing costs of $400,000 will be incurred.

Required

(a) Prepare a contribution breakeven chart for 20X3 assuming that all sales will be 'own label'.

(7 marks)

(b) Prepare a contribution breakeven chart for 20X3 assuming that 50% of sales are 'own label' and 50% are of the BD brand. **(7 marks)**

Note. The breakeven points and margins of safety must be shown clearly on the charts.

(c) Comment on the positions shown by the charts and your calculations and discuss what other factors management should consider before making a decision. **(6 marks)**

Ignore inflation. **(Total = 20 marks)**

8 RAB Consulting

36 mins

RAB Consulting specialises in two types of consultancy project.

- Each Type A project requires twenty hours of work from qualified researchers and eight hours of work from junior researchers.

- Each Type B project requires twelve hours of work from qualified researchers and fifteen hours of work from junior researchers.

Researchers are paid on an hourly basis at the following rates:

Qualified researchers	$30/hour
Junior researchers	$14/hour

Other data relating to the projects:

Project type

	A	B
	$	$
Revenue per project	1,700	1,500
Direct project expenses	408	310
Administration*	280	270

* Administration costs are attributed to projects using a rate per project hour. Total administration costs are $28,000 per four-week period.

During the four-week period ending on 30 June 20X0, owing to holidays and other staffing difficulties the number of working hours available are:

Qualified researchers	1,344
Junior researchers	1,120

An agreement has already been made for twenty type A projects with XYZ group. RAB Consulting must start and complete these projects in the four-week period ending 30 June 20X0.

A maximum of 60 type B projects may be undertaken during the four-week period ending 30 June 20X0.

RAB Consulting is preparing its detailed budget for the four-week period ending 30 June 20X0 and needs to identify the most profitable use of the resources it has available.

Required

(a)   Calculate the contribution from each type of project.   **(2 marks)**

(b)   Determine the optimal production plan for the four week period ending 30 June 20X0, assuming that RAB is seeking to maximise the profit earned. You should use a linear programming graph, identify the feasible region and the optimal point and accurately calculate the maximum profit that could be earned using whichever equations you need.   **(12 marks)**

(c)   Explain the meaning of a shadow price and calculate the shadow price of qualified researcher time.   **(6 marks)**

                                            (Total = 20 marks)

9 Plastic tools   36 mins

A small company is engaged in the production of plastic tools for the garden.

Subtotals on the spreadsheet of budgeted overheads for a year reveal the following.

	Moulding department	Finishing department	General factory Overhead
Variable overhead $'000	1,600	500	1,050
Fixed overhead $'000	2,500	850	1,750
Budgeted activity			
Machine hours (000)	800	600	
Practical capacity			
Machine hours (000)	1,200	800	

For the purposes of reallocation of general factory overhead it is agreed that the variable overheads accrue in line with the machine hours worked in each department. General factory fixed overhead is to be reallocated on the basis of the practical machine hour capacity of the two departments.

It has been a long-standing company practice to establish selling prices by applying a mark-up on full manufacturing cost of between 25% and 35%.

A possible price is sought for one new product which is in a final development stage. The total market for this product is estimated at 200,000 units per annum. Market research indicates that the company could expect to obtain and hold about 10% of the market. It is hoped the product will offer some improvement over competitors' products, which are currently marketed at between $90 and $100 each.

The product development department have determined that the direct material content is $9 per unit. Each unit of the product will take two labour hours (four machine hours) in the moulding department and three labour hours (three machine hours) in finishing. Hourly labour rates are $5.00 and $5.50 respectively.

Management estimate that the annual fixed costs which would be specifically incurred in relation to the product are supervision $20,000, depreciation of a recently acquired machine $120,000 and advertising $27,000. It may be assumed that these costs are included in the budget given above. Given the state of development of this new product, management do not consider it necessary to make revisions to the budgeted activity levels given above for any possible extra machine hours involved in its manufacture.

Required

(a) Prepare full cost and marginal cost information which may help with the pricing decision.

(10 marks)

(b) Comment on the cost information and suggest a price range which should be considered.

(5 marks)

(c) Briefly explain the role of costs in pricing.

(5 marks)

(Total = 20 marks)

10 AB

36 mins

AB produces a consumable compound X, used in the preliminary stage of a technical process that it installs in customers' factories worldwide. An overseas competitor, CD, offering an alternative process which uses the same preliminary stage, has developed a new compound, Y, for that stage which is both cheaper in its ingredients and more effective than X.

At present, CD is offering Y only in his own national market, but it is expected that it will not be long before he extends its sales overseas. Both X and Y are also sold separately to users of the technical process as a replacement for the original compound that eventually loses its strength. This replacement demand amounts to 60% of total demand for X and would do so for Y. CD is selling Y at the same price as X ($64.08 per kg).

AB discovers that it would take 20 weeks to set up a production facility to manufacture Y at an incremental capital cost of $3,500 and the comparative manufacturing costs of X and Y would be:

	X $ per kg	Y $ per kg
Direct materials	17.33	4.01
Direct labour	7.36	2.85
	24.69	6.86

AB normally absorbs departmental overhead at 200% of direct labour: 30% of this departmental overhead is variable directly with direct labour cost. Selling and administration overhead is absorbed at one-half of departmental overhead.

The current sales of X average 74 kgs per week and this level (whether of X or of Y if it were produced) is not expected to change over the next year. Because the direct materials for X are highly specialised, AB has always had to keep large inventories in order to obtain supplies. At present, these amount to $44,800 at cost. Its inventory of finished X is $51,900 at full cost. Unfortunately, neither X nor its raw materials have any resale value whatsoever: in fact, it would cost $0.30 per kg to dispose of them.

Over the next three months AB is not normally busy and, in order to avoid laying off staff, has an arrangement with the trade union whereby it pays its factory operators at 65% of their normal rate of pay for the period whilst they do non-production work. AB assesses that it could process all its relevant direct materials into X in that period, if necessary.

There are two main options open to AB:

(a) to continue to sell X until all its inventories of X (both of direct materials and of finished inventory) are exhausted, and then start sales of Y immediately afterwards;

(b) to start sales of Y as soon as possible and then to dispose of any remaining inventories of X and/or its raw materials.

Required

(a) Recommend with supporting calculations, which of the two main courses of action suggested is the more advantageous from a purely cost and financial point of view. **(10 marks)**

(b) Identify three major non-financial factors that AB would need to consider in making its eventual decision as to what to do. **(6 marks)**

(c) Suggest one other course of action that AB might follow, explaining what you consider to be its merits and demerits when compared with your answer at (a) above. **(4 marks)**

(Total = 20 marks)

11 Stow Health Centre   36 mins

Stow Health Centre specialises in the provision of sports/exercise and medical/dietary advice to clients. The service is provided on a residential basis and clients stay for whatever number of days suits their needs.

Budgeted estimates for the year ending 31 June 20X1 are as follows.

(a) The maximum capacity of the centre is 50 clients per day for 350 days in the year.

(b) Clients will be invoiced at a fee per day. The budgeted occupancy level will vary with the client fee level per day and is estimated at different percentages of maximum capacity as follows.

Client fee per day	Occupancy level	Occupancy as percentage of maximum capacity
$180	High	90%
$200	Most likely	75%
$220	Low	60%

(c) Variable costs are also estimated at one of three levels per client day. The high, most likely and low levels per client day are $95, $85 and $70 respectively.

The range of cost levels reflects only the possible effect of the purchase prices of goods and services.

Required

(a) Prepare a summary which shows the budgeted contribution earned by Stow Health Centre for the year ended 30 June 20X1 for each of nine possible outcomes. **(6 marks)**

(b) State the client fee strategy for the year to 30 June 20X1 which will result from the use of each of the following decision rules.

(i) Maximax
(ii) Maximin
(iii) Minimax regret

Your answer should explain the basis of operation of each rule. Use the information from your answer to (a) as relevant and show any additional working calculations as necessary. **(10 marks)**

(c) The probabilities of variable cost levels occurring at the high, most likely and low levels provided in the question are estimated as 0.1, 0.6 and 0.3 respectively.

Using the information available, determine the client fee strategy which will be chosen where maximisation of expected value of contribution is used as the decision basis. **(4 marks)**

(Total = 20 marks)

12 Budgets and people

In his study of *The Impact of Budgets on People* Argyris reported inter alia the following comment by a financial controller on the practice of participation in the setting of budgets in his company.

'We bring in the supervisors of budget areas, we tell them that we want their frank opinion but most of them just sit there and nod their heads. We know they're not coming out with exactly how they feel. I guess budgets scare them.'

Required

Suggest reasons why managers may be reluctant to participate fully in setting budgets, and suggest also unwanted side effects which may arise from the imposition of budgets by senior management. **(12 marks)**

13 Zero based budgeting

27 mins

You work for a large multinational company which manufactures weedkillers. It has been decided to introduce zero based budgeting in place of the more traditional incremental budgeting. The manager of the research and development department has never heard of zero based budgeting.

Required

Write a report to the manager of the research and development department which explains the following.

(a)	How zero based budgeting techniques differ from traditional budgeting	**(5 marks)**
(b)	How ZBB may assist in planning and controlling discretionary costs	**(5 marks)**
(c)	How ZBB will help to control budgetary slack	**(5 marks)**

(Total = 15 marks)

14 Forecasting

32 mins

	Sales of article B ('000 units)			
	Q1	Q2	Q3	Q4 (Q = quarter)
20X3	24.8	36.3	38.1	47.5
20X4	31.2	42.0	43.4	55.9
20X5	40.0	48.8	54.0	69.1
20X6	54.7	57.8	60.3	68.9

(a) Look at the data. What sort of trend and seasonal pattern do you expect to emerge from the analysis of this data? **(3 marks)**

(b) Derive a regression equation from the data and forecast the trend in sales for the four quarters of 20X7. **(9 marks)**

(c) Discuss the usefulness of this method of forecasting. **(6 marks)**

(Total = 18 marks)

15 Dench

22 mins

Dench manufacturing has received a special order from Sands to produce 225 components to be incorporated into Sand's product. The components have a high cost, due to the expertise required for their manufacture. Dench produces the components in batches of 15, and as the ones required are to be custom-made to Sands' specifications, a 'prototype' batch was manufactured with the following costs:

		$
Materials		
4 kg of A, $7.50/kg		30
2 kg of B, $15/kg		30
Labour		
20 hrs skilled, $15/hr		300
5 hrs semi-skilled, $8/hr		40
Variable Overhead		
25 labour hours, $4/hr		100
		500

Additional information with respect to the workforce is noted below:

Skilled   Virtually a permanent workforce that has been employed by Dench for a long period of time. These workers have a great deal of experience in manufacturing components similar to those required by Sands, and turnover is virtually non-existent.

Semi-Skilled   Hired by Dench on an 'as needed' basis. These workers would have had some prior experience, but Dench management believe the level to be relatively insignificant. Past experience shows turnover rate to be quite high, even for short employment periods.

Dench's plans are to exclude the prototype batch from Sands' order. Management believes a 80% learning rate effect is experienced in this manufacturing process, and would like a cost estimate for the 225 components prepared on that basis.

Required

(a)   Prepare the cost estimate, assuming an 80% learning rate is experienced.   **(7 marks)**

(b)   Briefly discuss some of the factors that can limit the use of learning curve theory in practice.

(5 marks)

(Total = 12 marks)

16 McDreamy

36 mins

McDreamy is in an industry sector which is recovering from the recent recession. The directors of the company hope next year to be operating at 85% of capacity, although currently the company is operating at only 65% of capacity. 65% of capacity represents output of 10,000 units of the single product which is produced and sold. One hundred direct workers are employed on production for 200,000 hours in the current year.

The flexed budgets for the current year are as follows.

Capacity level	55%	65%	75%
	$	$	$
Direct materials	846,200	1,000,000	1,153,800
Direct wages	1,480,850	1,750,000	2,019,150
Production overhead	596,170	650,000	703,830
Selling and distribution overhead	192,310	200,000	207,690
Administration overhead	120,000	120,000	120,000
Total costs	3,235,530	3,720,000	4,204,470

Profit in any year is budgeted to be $16\frac{2}{3}\%$ of sales.

The following percentage increases in costs are expected for next year.

	Increase %
Direct materials	6.0
Direct wages	3.0
Variable production overhead	7.0
Variable selling and distribution overhead	7.0
Fixed production overhead	10.0
Fixed selling and distribution overhead	7.5
Administration overhead	10.0

Required

(a) Prepare for next year a flexible budget statement on the assumption that the company operates at 85% of capacity; your statement should show both contribution and profit. **(12 marks)**

(b) State *three* problems which may arise from the change in capacity level. **(3 marks)**

(c) Explain what is meant by the principle of controllability. **(5 marks)**

(Total = 20 marks)

Helping hand. Profit may be expressed either as a percentage of cost of sales (**mark-up**) or as a percentage of sales (**margin**).

- If profit is x% of sales (**margin**), then profit is also $\left(\dfrac{x}{100-x} \times 100\% \right)$ of cost of sales (**mark-up**)

- If profit is 16.67% of sales (**margin**), then profit is also 20% $\left(\dfrac{16.67}{100-16.67} \times 100\% \right)$ of cost of sales (**mark-up**)

---

17 ACCA-Chem Co

36 mins

(a) ACCA-Chem Co manufacture a single product, product W, and have provided you with the following information which relates to the period which has just ended.

Standard cost per unit of product W

Materials:

Material	Kilos	Price per kilo $	Total $
F	15	4	60
G	12	3	36
H	8	6	48
	35		144

Labour:	Hours	Rate per hour $	
Department P	4	10	40
Department Q	2	6	12
			196

Budgeted sales for the period are 4,500 units at $260 per unit. There were no budgeted opening or closing inventories of product W.

The actual materials and labour used was as follows.

Materials:

Material	Kilos	Price per kilo $	Total $
F	59,800	4.25	254,150
G	53,500	2.80	149,800
H	33,300	6.40	213,120

Labour:

	Hours	Rate per hour $	
Department P	20,500	10.60	217,300
Department Q	9,225	5.60	51,660

4,100 units of product W were produced and sold for $1,115,800.

Required

(i)   Calculate the following material variances.

     (1)   Price   (3)   Mix

     (2)   Usage   (4)   Yield   **(8 marks)**

(ii)   Calculate the following labour variances for each of the production departments.

     (1)   Cost   (3)   Rate

     (2)   Efficiency   **(4 marks)**

(iii)   Calculate the sales variances.   **(3 marks)**

(iv)   Comment on your findings to help explain what has happened to the yield variance.

                                                           (5 marks)

                                           (Total = 20 marks)

18 Milbao   25 mins

Milbao manufactures and sells electronic games. Each year it budgets for its profits, including detailed budgets for sales, materials and labour. Departmental managers are allowed to revise their budgets if they believe there have been planning errors.

The managing director has become concerned that recent budget revisions have meant that there are favourable operational variances but less profit than expected.

Two specific situations have recently arisen, for which budget revisions were sought:

Components

A supplier of an essential component was forced into liquidation. Milbao's buyer managed to find another supplier overseas at short notice. This second supplier charged more for the components and also a delivery charge. The buyer has said that he had to agree to the price as the component was needed urgently. Two months later, another, more competitive, local supplier was found.

A budget revision is being sought for the two months where higher prices had to be paid.

Labour

During the early part of the year, Milbao experienced problems with the quality of work being produced by the game designers. The departmental manager had complained in his board report that his team were complacent and had not attempted to keep up with new developments in the industry.

It was therefore decided, after discussion of the board report, that something had to be done. The company changed its policy so as to recruit designers with excellent reputations for innovation on short-term contracts. This has had the effect of pushing up the costs involved but increasing productivity.

The design departmental manager has requested a budget revision to cover the extra costs involved following the change of policy.

Required

(a)   Discuss each request for a budget revision, putting what you see as both sides of the argument and conclude whether a budget revision should be allowed.   **(8 marks)**

The standard marginal cost of the best selling game is $35 per unit. The standard cost is recalculated once each year. Actual production costs during July 20X1 were $425,600, when 11,200 units were made.

The management of Milbao has now accepted that a more realistic standard marginal cost would have been $55 per unit given current conditions.

Required

(b)   Calculate the planning and operational variances and comment on your results.   **(6 marks)**

(Total = 14 marks)

19 Spring   36 mins

At a recent board meeting of Spring, there was a heated discussion on the need to improve financial performance. The production director argued that financial performance could be improved if the company replaced its existing absorption costing approach with an activity-based costing system. He argued that this would lead to better cost control and increased profit margins. The managing director agreed that better cost control could lead to increased profitability, but informed the meeting that he believed that performance needed to be monitored in both financial and non-financial terms. He pointed out that sales could be lost due to poor product quality or a lack of after-sales service just as easily as by asking too high a price for Spring's products. He suggested that while the board should consider introducing activity-based costing, it should also consider ways in which the company could monitor and assess performance on a wide basis.

Required

(a)   Describe the key features of activity-based costing and discuss the advantages and disadvantages of adopting an activity-based approach to cost accumulation.   **(11 marks)**

(b)   Explain the need for the measurement of organisational and managerial performance, giving examples of the range of financial and non-financial performance measures that might be used.
          (9 marks)

(Total = 20 marks)

20 Divisional performance measures   36 mins

(a)   Compare and contrast the use of residual income and return on investment in divisional performance measurement, stating the advantages and disadvantages of each.   **(7 marks)**

(b)   Division Y of Chardonnay currently has capital employed of $100,000 and earns an annual profit after depreciation of $18,000. The divisional manager is considering an investment of $10,000 in an asset which will have a ten-year life with no residual value and will earn a constant annual profit after depreciation of $1,600. The cost of capital is 15%.

Calculate the following and comment on the results.

(i)   The return on divisional investment, before and after the new investment
(ii)   The divisional residual income before and after the new investment   **(8 marks)**

(c)   Explain the potential benefits of operating a transfer pricing system within a divisionalised company.   **(5 marks)**

(Total = 20 marks)

21 Non-profit seeking organisations

36 mins

(a)   The absence of the profit measure in non-profit seeking organisations causes problems for the measurement of their efficiency and effectiveness.

Required

(i)   Explain why the absence of the profit measure should be a cause of the problems referred to.   **(8 marks)**

(ii)   Explain how these problems extend to activities within business entities which have a profit motive. Support your answer with examples.   **(4 marks)**

(b)   A public health clinic is the subject of a scheme to measure its efficiency and effectiveness. Amongst a number of factors, the 'quality of care provided' has been included as an aspect of the clinic's service to be measured. Three features of 'quality of care provided' have been listed.

(i)   Clinic's adherence to appointment times

(ii)   Patients' ability to contact the clinic and make appointment without difficulty

(iii)   The provision of a comprehensive patient health monitoring programme

Required

(i)   Suggest a set of quantitative measures which can be used to identify the effective level of achievement of each of the features listed.   **(6 marks)**

(ii)   Indicate how these measures could be combined into a single 'quality of care' measure.
                                                                                                          (2 marks)

                                                                                            (Total = 20 marks)

1 Solo

Top tips. Remember that when inventory levels **increase**, absorption costing reports the **higher** profit figure because some of the fixed production overhead will be carried forward in closing inventory (which reduces the cost of sales and hence increases the profit).

			Marks
(a)	Operating statement		5
(b)	Calculation of differences	1	
	Comments for each period	3	
	Comments on total difference	1	
			5
			10

(a) Absorption costing operating statement

	Period 1		Period 2		Period 3		Period 4	
	$	$	$	$	$	$	$	$
Sales		27,500		22,000		30,250		24,750
Production costs								
Variable	15,000		15,000		13,500		15,000	
Fixed	6,000		6,000		5,400		6,000	
	21,000		21,000		18,900		21,000	
Add: Opening inventory b/fwd	–		–		4,200		–	
Less: Closing inventory c/fwd	–		*(4,200)		–		**(2,100)	
Production cost of sales	21,000		16,800		23,100		18,900	
Under-absorbed overhead	–		–		600		–	
Total production costs		21,000		16,800		23,700		18,900
Profit for period		6,500		5,200		6,550		5,850

The absorption rate for fixed costs is $\dfrac{\$6,000}{500\,\text{units}} = \$12$ per unit

Inventory is valued at $30 + $12 = $42 per unit
* 100 units at $42 per unit = $4,200
** 50 units at $42 per unit = $2,100

(b)

	Period 1 $	Period 2 $	Period 3 $	Period 4 $	Total $
Marginal costing profit	6,500	4,000	7,750	5,250	23,500
Absorption costing Profit	6,500	5,200	6,550	5,850	24,100
Difference (Absorption costing less marginal costing profits)	–	1,200	(1,200)	600	600

Period 1

Profits based on marginal costing and absorption costing principles are the same for period 1. This is because there is no change in inventory levels during this period.

Period 2

Profits based on absorption costing principles are $1,200 higher than those based on marginal costing principles. Inventory levels have increased by 100 units during this period, and the 100 units of closing inventory include absorbed fixed overheads of $1,200 (100 units × $12 per unit).

Period 3

During this period, inventory levels have fallen by 100 units. When inventory levels fall in a period, absorption costing profits are less than marginal costing profits by $1,200 (100 units × $12 per unit).

Period 4

The difference in profit in this period = change in inventory levels × fixed overhead absorbed per unit

= (opening inventory + production – sales) × $12
= (0 + 500 – 450) × $12
= 50 × $12
= $600

Since opening inventory is nil, and closing inventory is 50 units (0 + 500 – 450) then inventory levels have increased by 50 units. Absorption costing principles report higher profits than marginal costing principles when inventory levels increase in a period, therefore absorption costing profits are $600 greater than marginal costing profits during this period.

Total

Total absorption costing profits are $600 greater than total marginal costing profits in periods 1 – 4. This is because at the beginning of period 1, opening inventory was nil, and at the end of period 4, closing inventory was 50 units. The reasoning behind this is the same as for period 4 above.

2 Southcott

Top tips. Because ABC is new to you, this first ABC question in the bank is **not exam standard**. Nevertheless, you need to be able to provide a good answer as it tests the key skills you need for the topic.

Part (a) should have caused you no problems. The original absorption basis was course days and so you simply needed to calculate the number of course days (number of courses × duration of course) for each course and total the results. Dividing total overheads by this figure gives an overhead cost per course day. Overheads are included in the cost of a course on the basis of the course duration.

Part (b) provides an example of the application of ABC to a **service organisation**. The **principles** to apply are the **same** as those you would apply when dealing with a manufacturing organisation.

Step 1   Determine the cost driver for each category of overhead.
Step 2   Calculate a cost per cost driver (cost/number of cost drivers)
Step 3   Include overhead in the cost of a course on the basis of the number of cost drivers
           generated by a course.

Don't forget to provide **reasons** for your choice of cost drivers. A 'tag-on' requirement like this might be worth the three marks that can make the difference between a pass and a fail.

(a)

	Auditing	Taxation	Total
No of courses sold	50	30	
Duration of course (days)	2	3	
No of course days	100	90	190

Overhead cost per course day = $\dfrac{\$152,625}{190}$ = $803.29

Overhead cost per course

Auditing $803.29 × 2 days = $1,606.58
Taxation $803.29 × 3 days = $2,409.87

(b) **Overhead costs per course using activity based costing**

		Auditing $ per course		Taxation $ per course
Centre hire at $328.95 per day	(× 2)	657.90	(× 3)	986.85
Enquiries administration at $2.50 per enquiry	(× 175)	437.50	(× 70)	175.00
Brochures at $3 per brochure	(× 300)	900.00	(× 200)	600.00
Overhead cost per course		1,995.40		1,761.85

Workings

1   Centre hire cost per course day $= \dfrac{\$62,500}{190} = \$328.95$

2   Enquiries administration cost per enquiry $= \dfrac{\$27,125}{(50 \times 175) + (30 \times 70)} = \$2.50$

3   Brochure cost per brochure printed $= \dfrac{\$63,000}{(50 \times 300) + (30 \times 200)} = \$3$ per brochure

Reasons for the choice of cost drivers

(i)   The cost driver for centre hire costs is the number of course days, since the centre is hired at a standard daily rate.

(ii)   The cost driver for enquiries administration is the number of enquiries, since more enquiries would result in an increase in the cost of enquiries administration.

(iii)   The cost driver for brochure costs is the number of brochures printed, since an increase in the number of brochures printed would lead to a higher cost.

(c)   Using traditional absorption costing, taxation has a higher overhead cost per course. This is because the courses are longer so more overhead is absorbed on a cost per course day basis.

Using ABC, however, the results are reversed and taxation courses have a lower overhead cost per course. This is mainly due to the high number of enquiries for auditing courses which do not necessarily result in course bookings. This highlights the need for the firm to analyse the reasons for this and take action if possible.

3 Abkaber

> **Top tips.** Part (a) is fairly straightforward requiring the calculation of profit for the three products under both absorption costing and ABC. Under ABC make sure you calculate the costs per cost driver.
>
> Part (b) requires a discussion of the impact of ABC and an analysis of each of the directors' comments. It is important that you apply your understanding of ABC to each of these comments.

(a)   (i)   **Existing method**

	Sunshine $	Roadster $	Fireball $
Direct labour ($5 per hr) (W1)	1,000,000	1,100,000	400,000
Materials (W2)	800,000	960,000	360,000
Overheads (at $24) (W3)	4,800,000	5,280,000	1,920,000
Total costs	6,600,000	7,340,000	2,680,000
Output (Units)	2,000	1,600	400

	Sunshine	Roadster	Fireball
	$	$	$
Selling price	4,000	6,000	8,000
Cost per unit (W4)	3,300	4,587.5	6,700
	700	1,412.5	1,300
Total profit	$	$	$
(output in units × profit/unit)	1,400,000	2,260,000	520,000

Total profit = $4,180,000

Workings

1 Labour cost

Sunshine	200,000 hrs × $5 per hour =	1,000,000
Roadster	220,000 hrs × $5 per hour =	1,100,000
Fireball	80,000 hrs × $5 per hour =	400,000

2 Material cost

Sunshine	2,000 × 400 =	800,000
Roadster	1,600 × 600 =	960,000
Fireball	400 × 900 =	360,000

3 Overhead per labour hour

	$
Total overhead cost =	12,000,000
Total labour hours =	500,000 hrs

$$\text{Overhead per labour hour} = \frac{\$12,000,000}{500,000} = \$24$$

4 Cost per unit

Sunshine: $\dfrac{\text{Total costs}}{\text{Units produced}} = \dfrac{6,600,000}{2,000} = \$3,300$

Roadster: $\dfrac{\text{Total costs}}{\text{Units produced}} = \dfrac{7,340,000}{1,600} = \$4,587.50$

Fireball: $\dfrac{\text{Total costs}}{\text{Units produced}} = \dfrac{2,680,000}{400} = \$6,700$

(ii) **Activity based costing**

	Sunshine	Roadster	Fireball
	$	$	$
Direct labour ($5 per hr) (as (W1) above)	1,000,000	1,100,000	400,000
Materials (as (W2) above)	800,000	960,000	360,000
Overheads			
Deliveries (W5(a))	960,000	768,000	672,000
Set up costs (W5(b))	2,100,000	2,400,000	1,500,000
Purchase orders (W5(c))	1,800,000	1,350,000	450,000
	6,600,000	6,578,000	3,382,000
Output units	2,000	1,600	400
	$	$	$
Selling price	4,000	6,000	8,000
Cost per unit (W4)	3,330	4,111.25	8,455
Profit/(loss) per unit	670	1,888.75	(455)
Total profit/(loss)	$1,340,000	$3,022,000	($182,000)

Total profit = $4,580,000

Workings

5   **Overheads**

$

$$\frac{\text{Overhead cost of deliveries to retailers}}{\text{Total number of deliveries}} = \frac{2,400,000}{250} = \$9,600$$

$$\frac{\text{Overhead cost of set - ups}}{\text{Total number of set - ups}} = \frac{6,000,000}{100} = \$60,000$$

$$\frac{\text{Overhead cost of purchase orders}}{\text{Total number of purchase orders}} = \frac{3,600,000}{800} = \$4,500$$

5(a)   **Deliveries overheads**

Sunshine	$9,600 × 100 =	$960,000
Roadster	$9,600 × 80 =	$768,000
Fireball	$9,600 × 70 =	$672,000

5(b)   **Set-up cost overheads**

Sunshine	$60,000 × 35 =	$2,100,000
Roadster	$60,000 × 40 =	$2,400,000
Fireball	$60,000 × 25 =	$1,500,000

5(c)   **Purchase order overheads**

Sunshine	$4,500 × 400 =	$1,800,000
Roadster	$4,500 × 300 =	$1,350,000
Fireball	$4,500 × 100 =	$450,000

(b)   REPORT

To:	Directors, Abkaber
From:	Management accountant
Subject:	The implications of activity based costing
Date:	12.12.X2

(i)   **Labour hours and activity based costing allocation**

Labour hours

For the allocation of overheads on the basis of labour hours to be appropriate, there would need to be a direct relationship between overheads and labour hours. From the information available, this does not appear to be the case.

A traditional method of cost allocation, such as the one based on labour hours, was developed when an enterprise produced a narrow range of products which underwent similar operations and consumed similar proportions of overheads. Moreover, when such methods were being widely used, overhead costs were only a very small proportion of total costs, with direct labour and material costs accounting for the largest proportion of total costs.

Abkaber has invested in new technology and as a result has significantly reduced the size of its workforce. Direct labour costs now account for a relatively smaller proportion of total costs with overheads making up the highest single cost item. Allocation of overheads on the basis of labour costs would tend to allocate too great a proportion of overheads to the higher volume Sunshine than the lower volume Fireball, ignoring the fact that the lower volume product may require relatively more support services. It therefore seems likely that attributing overheads on the basis of labour hours may lead to inappropriate decisions.

Activity based costing

Activity based costing attempts to overcome this problem by identifying the factors which cause the costs of an organisation's major activities.

The idea behind activity based costing is that activities such as ordering, materials handling, deliveries and set up cause costs. Producing goods creates demand for activities. Costs are assigned to a product on the basis of the product's consumption of activities.

Supporters of ABC argue that it is activities that generate costs, not labour hours.

The accuracy of any ABC system will depend on the appropriateness of the activities as cost drivers. Each cost driver selected should be appropriate to the overheads to which it relates. There should be a direct and proportionate relationship between the relevant overhead costs and the cost driver selected.

The labour hours costing system and ABC result in markedly different profit figures, especially with respect to the Fireball which appears profitable under the first system but loss making under ABC.

The reason for this is that, although the Fireball uses twice as many hours per unit as the Sunshine, its low output volume of only 400 units (compared with 2,000 units of Sunshine) means that a proportionately lower amount of overheads is absorbed.

Under activity based costing, the Fireball shows a loss because ABC recognises the relatively high set-up costs, deliveries and purchase orders.

(ii) **Finance director's comments**

The finance director is questioning the viability of the Fireball, but doubts whether ABC provides more information than the labour hours costing method.

ABC helps the company focus on the fact that the low volumes of Fireball involve a disproportionate amount of set-up costs, deliveries and purchase orders, resulting in a relatively higher allocation of overheads.

It may be the case that a review of current activities relating to Fireball may reduce costs. There are also other, non-financial, considerations for continuing to produce the Fireball. As the more expensive of the three products, it may have brand value and help raise the reputation of the company as well as that of the other models.

Marketing director's comments

The marketing director is questioning the suitability of ABC in helping price a major new contract.

(1) The accuracy of ABC depends on the appropriateness of the cost drivers identified. Although more appropriate than the labour hours allocation basis, for the type of one-off decision the marketing director needs to make, an incremental cost approach may be better.

(2) There may be factors both financial and non-financial that ABC may not be able to capture. For example, there may be costs common to more than one product, interdependencies between costs and revenues, or interdependencies between the sales volumes of the different products.

   The relationship between costs and activities is based on historic observations which may not be a reliable guide to the future.

Managing director's comments

The MD is correct to question the fact that ABC assumes that the cost per activity is constant. In practice, the existence of a learning curve may mean that the costs per activity are going down as the activity is repeated.

The MD is correct in questioning the inclusion of fixed costs which do not vary with either labour hours or any cost driver and thus show no cause and effect relationship under ABC.

Chairman's comments

As (i) and (ii) above illustrate, the overall profit under the two methods is the same. However, it would not be appropriate to dismiss the two approaches as irrelevant.

(1) If the company carried inventory, then the method of cost allocation would affect the inventory valuation and consequently profit.

(2) It is important to understand both the strengths and limitations of ABC as a decision making tool. Although it may appear to be more appropriate than labour hours in the allocation of overheads there are financial and non-financial factors that ABC does not capture. A decision to discontinue production of the Fireball should not be made without the consideration of these factors. These may include:

- Existence of a learning curve
- The inclusion of fixed costs that do not vary with level of activity
- Interdependencies of cost and revenues
- Interdependencies of sales of the three products

Further considerations

Abkaber will need to continue evaluating the activities identified and the relationship between cost drivers and overheads.

4 Life cycle costing

Top tips. You can expect calculations to be combined with discussion in an exam question. Make sure you show your workings clearly and write full answers to the discussion parts.

(a) **Life cycle costs**

Life cycle costs are the **costs incurred on products and services from their design stage, through development to market launch, production and sales, and their eventual withdrawal from the market**. A product's life cycle costs might therefore be classified as follows.

(i) Acquisition costs (costs of research, design, testing, production and construction)

(ii) Product distribution costs (transportation and handling)

(iii) Maintenance costs (customer service, field maintenance and 'in-factory' maintenance)

(iv) Operation costs (the costs incurred in operations, such as energy costs, and various facility and other utility costs)

(v) Training costs (operator and maintenance training)

(vi) Inventory costs (the cost of holding spare parts, warehousing and so on)

(vii) Technical data costs (cost of purchasing any technical data)

(viii) Retirement and disposal costs (costs occurring at the end of the product's life)

Life cycle costing versus traditional management accounting systems

Traditional management accounting practice

This is, in general, to report costs at the physical production stage of the life cycle of a product; costs are not accumulated over the entire life cycle. Such practice does not, therefore, assess a product's profitability over its entire life but rather on a **periodic basis**. Costs tend to be accumulated according to function; research, design, development and customer service costs incurred on all products during a period are totalled and recorded as a period expense.

Life cycle costing

(i) Using **life cycle costing**, on the other hand, such costs are traced to individual products over **complete life cycles**. These accumulated costs are compared with the revenues attributable to each product and hence the **total profitability** of any given product can be

determined. Moreover, by gathering costs for each product, the relationship between the choice of design adopted and the resulting marketing and production costs becomes clear.

(ii)   The **control function** of life cycle costing lies in the **comparison of actual and budgeted life cycle costs for a product**. Such comparisons allow for the refinement of future decisions about product design, lead to more effective resource allocation and show whether expected savings from using new production methods or technology have been realised.

Life cycle costing and AMT environments

Research has shown that, for organisations operating within an **advanced manufacturing technology environment**, approximately **90%** of a product's life-cycle cost is determined by decisions made **early** within the life cycle. In such an environment there is therefore a need to ensure that the tightest cost controls are at the **design stage**, because the majority of costs are committed at this point. This necessitates the need for a management accounting system that assists in the planning and control of a product's life cycle costs, which monitors spending and commitments to spend during the early stages of a product's life cycle and which recognises the reduced life cycle and the subsequent challenge to profitability of products produced in an AMT environment. Life cycle costing is such a system.

Summary

Life cycle costing **increases the visibility of costs** such as those associated with research, design, development and customer service, and also enables **individual product profitability** to be more fully understood by attributing all costs to products. As a consequence, more **accurate feedback** information is available on the organisation's success or failure in **developing new products**. In today's **competitive environment**, where the ability to produce new and updated versions of products is of paramount importance to the survival of the organisation, this information is vital.

(b)   **Lifecycle costs**

		$'000
R&D (850 + 90)		940
Production	– variable (750 + 2,500 + 1,875)	5,125
	– fixed (500 × 3)	1,500
Marketing	– variable (125 + 400 + 225)	750
	– fixed (300 + 200 + 200)	700
Distribution	– variable (25 + 100 + 75)	200
	– fixed (190 × 3)	570
Customer service (75 + 200 + 150)		425
Total life cycle costs		10,210
Production ('000 units) (25 + 100 + 75)		÷ 200
Cost per unit		$51.05

The suggested price will therefore provide a profit over the complete lifecycle.

5 Bottlenecks

Top tips. This question will have given you useful practice of limiting factor analysis.

As you will see in the layout of our workings to part (b)(i), you can adopt the same approach as taken in (a) when dealing with a TA environment. You had to remember to deduct the 'variable' costs from the total throughput contribution, but otherwise there were some very easy marks available for part (b)(i).

Exam questions in F5 will tend to have more marks for interpretation than this question.

Easy marks. You should have got the full three marks for part (b)(ii) (provided you could remember how to calculate a TA ratio!).

Part (b)(iii) was a gift for three marks.

(a) We need to carry out **limiting factor analysis**.

Step 1 Establish scarce resources, if any

We are told that one of the production operations is the bottleneck, limiting production/sales.

Step 2 Rank products on the basis of contribution per unit of the limiting factor

	A	B
	$	$
Direct material cost	2	40
Variable production overhead cost	28	4
	30	44
Selling price	60	70
Contribution per unit	30	26
Bottleneck hours per unit	0.02	0.015
Contribution per bottleneck hour	$1,500	$1,733
Ranking	2	1

Step 3 Determine profit-maximising product mix

Product	Demand		Hours required	Hours available		Units of production
B	45,000 × 1.2 = 54,000	(× 0.015)	810	810	(÷ 0.015)	54,000
A	120,000 × 1.2 = 144,000	(× 0.02)	2,880	2,265 (bal)	(÷ 0.02)	113,250
			3,690	3,075		

Maximum profit calculation

Product	Units	Contribution per unit	Total contribution
			$
A	113,250	× $30	3,397,500
B	54,000	× $26	1,404,000
			4,801,500
Less: fixed production overhead			1,470,000
Maximum net profit			3,331,500

(b) (i) Throughput return per production hour of the bottleneck resource = (selling price − material cost)/hours on the bottleneck resource

Step 1 Rank products on the basis of throughput return per bottleneck hour

	A	B
	$	$
Selling price	60	70
Material cost	2	40
Throughput return	58	30
Bottleneck hours per unit	0.02	0.015
Return per bottleneck hour	$2,900	$2,000
Ranking	1	2

Step 2 Determine profit-maximising product mix

Product	Demand	Hours required	Hours available		Units of production
A	144,000	2,880	2,880	(÷ 0.02)	144,000
B	54,000	810	195 (bal)	(÷ 0.015)	13,000
		3,690	3,075		

Maximum profit calculation

Product	Units	Throughput return per unit	Total return $
A	144,000	× $58	8,352,000
B	13,000	× $30	390,000
Total throughput return			8,742,000
Less: overhead costs			
shown as variable in (a) ((120,000 × $28) + (45,000 × $4))			(3,540,000)
fixed			(1,470,000)
Maximum net profit			3,732,000

(ii)   TA ratio = throughput return per hour/conversion cost per hour

Conversion cost per hour = overhead costs/bottleneck hours
         = $(3,540,000 + 1,470,000)/3,075
         = $1,629.27

∴ TA ratio for B = $2,000/ $1,629.27 = 1.2275

Efforts should be made to improve the size of the TA ratio as follows.

(1)   Improving throughput ($) per unit by increasing selling price or reducing material cost per unit. Product B has a very high material cost element ($40).

(2)   Improving the throughput return per hour by reducing the time spent on the bottleneck resource. If product B spent 0.012 hours instead of 0.015 hours on the bottleneck resource, say, its TA ratio would improve.

The organisation's overall position can be improved by reducing conversion costs and/or by reducing or eliminating the impact of any bottlenecks.

Product B's TA ratio, at 1.2275, is greater than 1 and so the product is worth producing. Product A's ratio is 1.780 ($2,900/$1,629.27), however, and hence priority should be given to product A.

(iii)   If the direct material cost of B increases by 20%, its throughput return becomes $(70 − (40 × 120%)) = $22.

Its return per bottleneck hour is then $22 ÷ 0.015 = $1,467.

Its TA ratio becomes $1,467/$1,629.27 = 0.900.

The return from B is now less than the associated production cost through the bottleneck resource and so production of B is not worthwhile in a TA environment.

Product A is being produced to maximum demand, however, and the residual capacity used by product B has no incremental cost since all overhead cost is fixed in the short and intermediate term. In these circumstances, product B is still generating a positive cash flow of $1,467 per hour (or $22 per unit).

6 HYC

Top tips. Show your workings and use a clear layout. Make sure you spend an equal amount of time on the discussions as on the calculations.

(a)

		Product		
Machine hours required	H	Y	C	Total
Type 1	180	315	180	675
Type 2	120	175	120	415

Machine utilisation rate:

Machine type 1 = 675/600 = 112.5%
Machine type 2 = 415/500 = 83.0%

Machine type 1 has the highest utilisation rate and the rate is above 100 per cent. Therefore machine type 1 is the bottleneck/limiting factor.

(b)

	Product		
	H	Y	C
Contribution per unit	$40	$96	$74
Machine type 1 hours	1.5	4.5	3.0
Contribution per hour	$26.67	$21.33	$24.67
Ranking	1	3	2

Allocation of machine type 1 hours according to this ranking:

Product H	120 units using	180	hours
Product C	60 units using	180	hours
		360	hours used
Product Y (240/4.5) 53 units using		238.5	hours
		598.5	hours used

(c) A major concept underlying throughput accounting is that the majority of costs, with the exception of material and component costs, are fixed.

In HYC's case it is clear that the labour cost, which is treated as a variable cost in traditional marginal costing, is indeed a fixed cost. The employees are paid for a guaranteed 800 hours (160 × 5) each month, whereas the number of labour hours required to meet the maximum demand can be calculated as 780 hours as follows.

	Product			
	H	Y	C	Total
Labour hours per unit	0.75	6	4.5	
Maximum demand (units)	120	70	60	
Total hours required per month	90	420	270	780

Therefore labour is a fixed cost that will not alter within the relevant range of activity. Throughput accounting recognises this in the calculation of throughput.

Furthermore, given the perishable nature of HYC's products, the throughput accounting approach to inventory minimisation and maximisation of throughput would be more appropriate.

(d)

	Product		
	H	Y	C
	$ per unit	$ per unit	$ per unit
Sales revenue	91	174	140
Component cost	22	19	16
Other direct material	23	11	14
Throughput per unit	46	144	110
Machine type 1 hours	1.5	4.5	3.0
	$	$	$
Throughput per hour	30.67	32.00	36.76
Ranking	3	2	1

Allocation of machine type 1 hours according to this ranking:

Product C	60 units using	180 hours
Product Y	70 units using	315 hours
		495 hours used
Product H (105/1.5) 70 units using		105 hours
		600 hours used

(e) The conventional cost accounting approach used by HYC views inventory as an asset. In the throughput accounting approach inventory is not viewed as an asset, but rather as a result of unsynchronised manufacturing. The existence of inventory is thus viewed as a breakdown in synchronisation and a barrier to generating profits.

In throughput accounting the ideal inventory level is zero, with the exception that a buffer inventory should be held prior to the bottleneck machine.

As regards the valuation of inventory, the throughput philosophy is that no value is added to inventory items and no profit is earned until the items are actually sold. Thus inventory is valued at its material cost only until it is sold.

This approach to inventory valuation is in contrast to the full absorption costing system used by HYC. The latter approach encourages managers to produce output just to add to work in progress or finished goods inventory, since this helps with the absorption of overheads and boosts reported profits. This behaviour will be avoided and managers will be more likely to be willing to minimise inventory if it is valued at material cost only.

7 BD Company

Top tips. The F5 exam could include a full question on the topic so ensure you make a good attempt at this one.

To draw up a **contribution breakeven chart** you need to **know** three things.

- Selling price per can
- Variable cost per can
- Fixed costs

These can all be calculated from information in the question with varying degrees of difficulty/ease.

As CVP analysis is based on **marginal costing principles** and given that information in the question is provided for two time periods, you have a rather large hint that you need to split the manufacturing costs into fixed and variable components using the **high-low method**. It is safe to assume that the **administration** costs are **fixed** as they are the **same** in both time periods. Selling price per unit is a straightforward calculation.

You then have enough information to draw up the chart. You can always calculate breakeven point and margin of safety and compare them with your chart to ensure that you have marked them on the chart correctly. (Did you actually see the note in the requirements asking you to show them on the chart?)

Part (b) involves **multi-product** CVP analysis. The data for the chart is not difficult to derive, but the calculation of breakeven point must be based on contribution per mix, **the standard mix being one own label, one BD brand**.

An exam question will invariably ask for some written analysis, and this question is no exception. The points you need to make are not particularly technical, but are simply grounded in common sense. If option 2 shows the higher profit, **lower breakeven point** (so that **not so many sales are required to cover costs**) and a **higher margin of safety** (which means that the **difference between expected sales and breakeven sales is likely to be higher**), it should be the better option. There are, of course, **other factors** that might affect that decision.

Assumption. Manufacturing costs for the BD brand will be the same as for own label brands.

Initial workings

Manufacturing costs

We need to analyse the cost behaviour patterns by separating the manufacturing costs into their fixed and variable elements, using the high-low method.

	Sales Millions	Costs $ million
20X3	19	4.45
20X2	18	4.30
	1	0.15

Variable manufacturing cost per can = $0.15

Fixed manufacturing cost = $4.45 million – (19 million × $0.15)

= $1.6 million

Selling prices

Selling price per can in 20X3	= 6.27/19	= $0.33
∴ Unit contribution per can	= $0.33 – $0.15	= $0.18
∴ Contribution per can of BD brand	= $0.18 × 133 1/3%	= $0.24
Variable cost per can of BD brand	= $0.15 + $0.02	= $0.17
∴ Selling price per can of BD brand	= $0.17 + $0.24	= $0.41

(a) **Data for chart**

	$ million	$ million
Variable costs (19 million × $0.15)		2.85
Fixed costs: manufacturing	1.60	
administration	1.20	
		2.80
Total costs		5.65

$$\text{Breakeven point} = \frac{\text{fixed costs}}{\text{contribution}} = \frac{\$2.8m}{\$0.18}$$

= 15.55 million cans

= $5.13 million sales

Margin of safety = 19m – 15.55m = 3.45 million cans = $1.14 million sales

Breakeven chart for 20X3 - all 'own label' sales

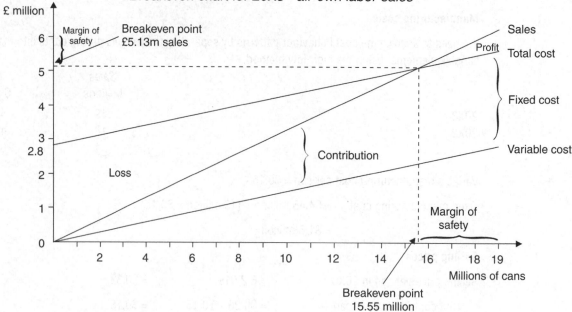

(b) **Data for chart**

		$ million	$ million
Variable costs:	own label (9.5m × $0.15)		1.425
	BD brand (9.5m × $0.17)		1.615
			3.040
Fixed costs:	manufacturing	1.600	
	administration	1.200	
	marketing	0.400	
			3.200
Total costs:			6.240
Sales value:	own label (9.5m × $0.33)		3.135
	BD brand (9.5m × $0.41)		3.895
			7.030

Our standard mix is 1 own label, 1 BD brand.

$$\text{Breakeven point} = \frac{\text{fixed costs}}{\text{contribution per mix}} = \frac{\$3.2m}{\$(0.18+0.24)} = \frac{\$3.2m}{\$0.42}$$

$$= 7.62 \text{ million mixes} = 15.24 \text{ million cans}$$

$$= 7.62 \times (\$(0.33 + 0.41)) \text{ million sales} = \$5.64 \text{ million sales}$$

Margin of safety = 19m – 15.24 million = 3.76 million cans = 1.88 million mixes

$$= 1.88 \times (\$(0.33 + 0.41)) \text{ million sales}$$

$$= \$1.39 \text{ million sales}$$

Profit = $7.03 million – $6.24 million = $790,000

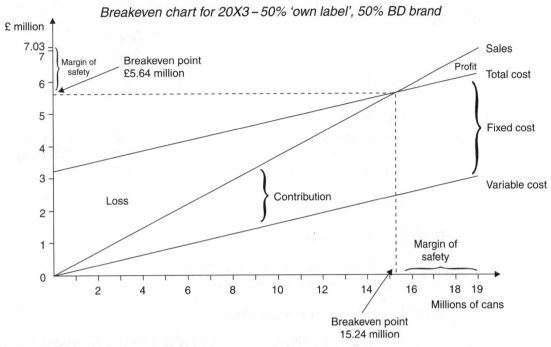

Breakeven chart for 20X3 – 50% 'own label', 50% BD brand

(c) The **first chart** shows a breakeven point of 15.55 million cans ($5.13m sales value) and a margin of safety of 3.45 million cans ($1.14m sales value). Forecast profit for sales of 19 million cans is $620,000.

The **second chart** shows a breakeven point of 15.24 million cans ($5.64m sales value) and a margin of safety of 3.76 million cans ($1.39m sales value). Forecast profit for sales of 19 million cans is $790,000.

Option 2 therefore results in a higher profit figure, as well as a lower breakeven point and increased margin of safety. On this basis it is the better of the two options.

Other factors which management should consider before making a decision

(i) The supermarket chains may put the same pressure on margins and prices of the BD brand as they do on the own label brands.

(ii) Customers may realise that the BD brand is the same product as the own label brand and may not be willing to pay the premium price.

(iii) If the mix of sales can be changed in favour of the BD brand then profits will improve still further.

8 RAB Consulting

Top tips. This is a straightforward linear programming question. The best way to approach graphical linear programming questions is to work through the **six steps** we recommend in the text.

- Define variables
- Establish objective function
- Establish constraints
- Graph the problem
- Define feasible area
- Determine optimal solution

Notice the approach we have taken to choosing our sample **iso-contribution line**. This is something that students often find difficult, so choose easy **numbers (related to the coefficients of the variables)**, making sure that the line then falls within the feasible area.

(a) (i)

		Type A $ per project		Type B $ per project
Revenue		1,700		1,500
Variable costs				
Labour				
– qualified researchers	(20 hrs × $30)	600	(12 hrs × $30)	360
– junior researchers	(8 hrs × $14)	112	(15 hrs × $14)	210
Direct project expenses		408		310
		1,120		880
Contribution		580		620

(b) **Step 1** Define variables

Let a = number of type A projects
Let b = number of type B projects

Step 2 **Establish objective function**

Maximise contribution (C) = 580a + 620b, subject to the constraints below.

Step 3 **Establish constraints**

Qualified researchers time:	$20a + 12b \leq 1{,}344$
Junior researchers time:	$8a + 15b \leq 1{,}120$
Agreement for type A:	$a \geq 20$
Maximum for type B:	$b \leq 60$
Non-negativity:	$a \geq 0, b \geq 0$

Step 4 **Graphing the problem**

Constraints

Qualified researcher time:	if a = 0, b = 112
	if b = 0, a = 67.2
Junior researcher time:	if a = 0, b = 74.67
	if b = 0, a = 140
Agreement for type A:	graph the line a = 20
Maximum for type B:	graph the line b = 60

Step 5 **Define feasible area**

Iso-contribution line

580a + 620b = 35,960 (where 35,960 = 58 × 62 × 10) goes through the points (62, 0) and (0, 58)

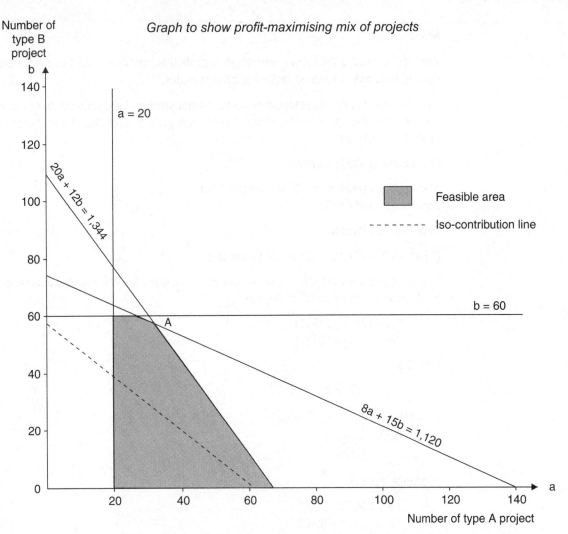

Graph to show profit-maximising mix of projects

Moving the iso-contribution line away from the origin, we see that it leaves the feasible area at the intersection of the two time constraints (point A).

Step 6   Determine optimal solution

Find the coordinates of A

$20a + 12b$	$= 1,344$	(1)
$8a + 15b$	$= 1,120$	(2)
$20a + 37.5b$	$= 2,800$	(3) (2) × 2.5
$25.5b$	$= 1,456$	(3) − (1)
b	$= 57.10$	
$20a + 685.02$	$= 1,344$	substitute into (1)
a	$= 32.94$	

The profit-maximising mix of projects is 32.94 of type A and 57.10 of type B.

Profit for profit-maximising mix

		$
Contribution from type A:	32.94 × $580	19,105
Contribution from type B:	57.10 × $620	35,402
Total contribution		54,507
Less: fixed costs		(28,000)
		26,507

(c)   **Shadow price**

The shadow price is the **extra contribution** or profit that may be earned if one more unit of a **binding resource** or **limiting factor** becomes available.

It can be used to inform managers of the **maximum price** that should be paid for more of a scarce resource over and above the basic rate. The shadow price of a constraint that is not binding at the optimal solution is zero.

Calculation of shadow prices

At the optimal solution, A = 32.94 and B = 57.10
Contribution = $54,507

Qualified researchers

$(32.94 \times 20) + (57.10 \times 12) = 1,344$ = availability

The constraint is **binding**. If one more hour of labour was available, the new optimal product mix would be at the intersection of the lines:

$$20a + 12b = 1,345 \ (1)$$
$$8a + 15b = 1,120 \ (2)$$

$(2) \times 2.5$

$$20a + 37.5b = 2,800 \ (3)$$

$(3) - (1)$

$$25.5b = 1,455$$
$$b = 57.06$$

Substitute into (1)

$$20a + 684.72 = 1,345$$
$$a = 33.01$$

Contribution = $(580 \times 33.01) + (620 \times 57.06) = \$54,523$

The **shadow price** of one hour of qualified researcher's time is the extra contribution generated which is $16.

9 Plastic tools

Top tips. The techniques required in part (a) are extremely **straightforward** (calculation of overhead absorption rates for example) so beware of making a silly arithmetical error.

In part (b), there is a lot of information that you can use when suggesting a suitable price range. Your **higher-level skills** are required, however. Make sensible comments on the various possible prices.

The most important point to make in (c) is that **cost is not the only factor to consider** when setting prices, although of course it must be considered.

(a) **Calculation of overhead absorption rates**

	Moulding dept $'000	Finishing dept $'000	General factory overhead $'000
Variable overhead			
Initial allocation	1,600	500	1,050
Reapportion general overhead (800:600)	600	450	(1,050)
Total variable overhead	2,200	950	–
Budgeted machine hours	800	600	
Variable overhead rate per hour	$2.75	$1.58	

	$'000	$'000	$'000
Fixed overhead			
Initial allocation	2,500	850	1,750
Reapportion general overhead (1,200:800)	1,050	700	(1,750)
Total fixed overhead	3,550	1,550	–
Budgeted machine hours	800	600	
Fixed overhead rate per hour	$4.44	$2.58	

Information to assist with the pricing decision

	$ per unit	$ per unit
Direct material		9.00
Direct labour: moulding dept (2 × $5)	10.00	
finishing dept (3 × $5.50)	16.50	
		26.50
Variable overhead: moulding dept (4 × $2.75)	11.00	
finishing dept (3 × $1.58)	4.74	
		15.74
Variable manufacturing cost		51.24
Fixed overhead: moulding dept (4 × $4.44)	17.76	
finishing dept (3 × $2.58)	7.74	
		25.50
Full manufacturing cost		76.74

A **full-cost plus price** will be **based on this cost** of $76.74 **plus a mark-up** of between 25% and 35%. Taking a high, low and average mark-up, the potential prices are as follows.

	25% mark-up $ per unit	30% mark-up $ per unit	35% mark-up $ per unit
Full manufacturing cost	76.74	76.74	76.74
Mark-up	19.19	23.02	26.86
Full cost-plus price	95.93	99.76	103.60

Certain incremental or specific fixed costs have been identified, however, and these should be borne in mind for a well-informed pricing decision.

Product cost based on incremental fixed costs

	$'000	$ per unit
Variable manufacturing cost		51.24
Incremental fixed costs: supervision	20	
depreciation	120	
advertising	27	
	167	
Incremental fixed cost per unit (÷ 20,000 (W))		8.35
Incremental total cost per unit		59.59

Working

Total market = 200,000 units per annum

Ten per cent market share = 20,000 units per annum

(b)   The cost information provides a range of bases for a pricing decision.

Variable manufacturing cost

The variable manufacturing cost is $51.24 per unit. At a price below this level there would be no contribution to fixed overheads. Since the prevailing market price is between $90 and $100 each, such a low price might suggest that the product is of inferior quality.

Incremental total cost

The incremental total cost per unit is $59.59. Management must select a price above this level to be sure of covering all costs associated with this product. This unit rate depends on achieving an annual volume of 20,000 units.

Full manufacturing cost

The full manufacturing cost per unit is $76.74. A price based on this cost will ensure that all costs are covered in the long run, if the annual volume of 20,000 units is achieved. Since competitors' prices range between $90 and $100 it seems possible that the company can compete with a price calculated on a full cost-plus basis.

The range of prices suggested, using the company's usual mark-up of between 25 per cent and 35 per cent, is $95.93 to $103.60 per unit.

Given the current price range of the competitors' products and the fact that the product is expected to offer some improvement over competitors' products, a price towards the upper end of the suggested range would be appropriate.

(c)   In general, the **price charged** for a product should **exceed its cost**. There are a number of different cost-based approaches to pricing, however, and each is appropriate in different circumstances.

Full-cost plus pricing involves adding a profit margin to the fully absorbed total cost of a product. In certain situations, for example if an organisation has spare capacity, it may be appropriate to use **marginal cost** as the basis for pricing. Alternatively if the lowest possible price is sought, perhaps for strategic reasons, a **minimum** price based on **relevant costs** may be used as the basis for a pricing decision. Management must not lose sight of the need to cover fixed costs in the long run, however.

Whichever cost basis is used, it is important to appreciate that a cost-based price merely provides a **starting point for informed management decisions and pricing negotiations.**

Cost is **only one of the factors to bear in mind** when making a price-setting decision. Other factors to consider will include the organisation's objectives, the market in which the organisation operates and the effect which price has on the volume of demand for its goods.

10 AB

(a)   **Full cost of production per kg of X**

	$
Direct materials	17.33
Direct labour	7.36
Production overhead (200% of labour)	14.72
	39.41

The quantity of inventory-in-hand is therefore $51,900/$39.41 = 1,317 kg

At a weekly sales volume of 74 kg, this represents 1,317/74 = about 18 weeks of sales

It will take 20 weeks to set up the production facility for Y, and so inventory in hand of finished X can be sold before any Y can be produced. This **finished inventory** is therefore **irrelevant** to the decision under review; it will be sold whatever decision is taken.

The problem therefore centres on the inventory in hand of direct materials. Assuming that there is no loss or wastage in manufacture and so 1 kg of direct material is needed to produce 1 kg of X then inventory in hand is $44,800/$17.33 = 2,585 kg.

This would be converted into 2,585 kg of X, which would represent sales volume for 2,585/74 = 35 weeks.

If AB sells its existing inventories of finished X (in 18 weeks) there are **two options**.

(i)   To produce enough X from raw materials for 2 more weeks, until production of Y can start, and then dispose of all other quantities of direct material – ie 33 weeks' supply.

(ii)   To produce enough X from raw materials to use up the existing inventory of raw materials, and so delay the introduction of Y by 33 weeks.

The relevant costs of these two options

(i)   **Direct materials**. The relevant cost of existing inventories of raw materials is $(0.30). In other words the 'cost' is a benefit. By using the direct materials to make more X, the company would save $0.30 per kg used.

(ii)   **Direct labour**. It is assumed that if labour is switched to production work from non-production work in the next three months, they must be paid at the full rate of pay, and not at 65% of normal rate. The *incremental* cost of labour would be 35% of the normal rate (35% of $7.36 = $2.58 per kg produced).

Relevant cost of production of X

	$
Direct materials	(0.30)
Direct labour	2.58
Variable overhead (30% of full overhead cost of $14.72)	4.42
Cost per kg of X	6.70

Relevant cost per kg of Y

	$
Direct materials	4.01
Direct labour	2.85
Variable overhead (30% of 200% of $2.85)	1.71
	8.57

(*Note.* Y cannot be made for 20 weeks, and so the company cannot make use of spare labour capacity to produce any units of Y.)

It is cheaper to use up the direct material inventories and make X ($6.70 per kg) than to introduce Y as soon as possible, because there would be a saving of ($8.57 – $6.70) = $1.87 per kg made.

AB must sell X for at least 20 weeks until Y could be produced anyway, but the introduction of Y could be delayed by a further 33 weeks until all inventories of direct material for X are used up. The saving in total would be about $1.87 per kg × 74 kg per week × 33 weeks = $4,567.

(b) **Non-financial factors that must be considered in reaching the decision**

    (i)   **The workforce**. If the recommended course of action is undertaken, the workforce will produce enough units of X in the next 13 weeks to satisfy sales demand over the next year, (with 18 weeks' supply of existing finished goods inventories and a further 35 weeks' supply obtainable from direct materials inventories). When production of Y begins, the direct labour content of production will fall to $2.85 per kg – less than 40% of the current effort per kg produced – but sales demand will not rise. The changeover will therefore mean a big drop in labour requirements in production. Redundancies seem inevitable, and might be costly. By switching to producing Y as soon as possible, the redundancies might be less immediate, and could be justified more easily to employees and their union representatives than a decision to produce enough X in the next 3 months to eliminate further production needs for about 9 months.

    (ii)   **Customers' interests**. Product Y is a superior and 'more effective' compound than X. It would be in customers' interests to provide them with this improved product as soon as possible, instead of delaying its introduction until existing inventories of direct materials for X have been used up.

    (iii)   **Competition**. CD is expected to start selling Y overseas, and quite possibly in direct competition with AB. CD has the advantage of having developed Y itself, and appears to use it in the preliminary stage of an alternative technical process. The competitive threat to AB is two-fold:

        (1)   CD might take away some of the replacement demand for Y from AB so that AB's sales of X or Y would fall.

        (2)   CD might compete with AB to install its total technical process into customers' factories, and so the competition would be wider than the market for compound Y.

(c) **Alternative course of action**

    (i)   Produce enough units of X in the next 13 weeks to use up existing inventories of direct materials.

    (ii)   Start sales of Y as soon as possible, and offer customers the choice between X and Y. Since X is an inferior compound, it would have to be sold at a lower price than Y.

Merits of this course of action

(i)   The workforce would be usefully employed for the next 13 weeks and then production of Y would begin at once. Although redundancies would still seem inevitable, the company would be creating as much work as it could for its employees.

(ii)   AB's customers would be made aware of the superiority of Y over X in terms of price, and of AB's commitment to the new compound. AB's marketing approach would be both 'honest' and would also give customers an attractive choice of buying the superior Y or, for a time, an inferior X but at a lower price. This might well enhance AB's marketing success.

Demerits of this course of action

(i)   It is unlikely to be a profit-maximising option, because selling X at a discount price would reduce profitability.

(ii)   Customers who get a discount on X might demand similar discounts on Y.

(iii)   Some customers might query the technical differences between X and Y, and question why AB has been selling X at such a high price in the past – this might lead to some customer relations difficulties.

(iv)   AB must decide when to reduce the price of X, given that Y cannot be made for 20 weeks. The timing of the price reduction might create some difficulties with customers who buy X just before the price is reduced.

11 Stow Health Centre

Top tips Did you get confused in part (a)? The occupancy level will vary with the client fee per day, while the variable cost per client day is independent. In other words, at each of the **three different levels of client fee** per day, there are **three possible levels of variable cost** per client and so 3 × 3 = **9 possible levels of contribution per client day.**

The most tricky aspect of part (b) was dealing with the **minimax regret decision rule**. This rule involves choosing the strategy which will **minimise the maximum regret** (ie drop in contribution) from choosing one option instead of the best option. This requires you to draw up an **opportunity loss table**. This will show the **drop in contribution** at **each level of variable cost** from **choosing a level of client fee which is not the best option**. For example, at a variable cost of $95 per day, the best strategy would be a client fee of $200 per day. The opportunity loss from using a fee of $180 would be the difference between the contributions at the two fee levels.

For part (c) you simply need to **calculate an EV of variable cost per day**. You are then faced with a situation of one level of client fee per day and one level of variable cost per day at each level of 'demand'.

(a)   We need to calculate budgeted contribution and so the summary will need to show the various income (fee) and variable cost levels.

		Client fee per day	
Variable cost per day	$180	£200	£220
$	$	$	$
95	1,338,750	1,378,125	1,312,500
85	1,496,250	1,509,375	1,417,500
70	1,732,500	1,706,250	1,575,000

Workings

Number of client days:
Maximum capacity = 50 × 350 = 17,500
High occupancy level = 90% × 17,500 = 15,750
Most likely occupancy level = 75% × 17,500 = 13,125
Low occupancy level = 60% × 17,500 = 10,500

Number of client days × contribution per client day (fee – variable cost) = contribution

(b) (i) The **maximax** decision rule involves choosing the outcome with the **best possible result**, in this instance choosing the outcome which **maximises contribution**. The decision maker would therefore choose a **client fee of $180 per day**, which could result in a contribution of $1,732,500.

(ii) The **maximin** decision rule involves choosing the outcome that offers the **least unattractive worst outcome,** in this instance choosing the outcome which **maximises the minimum contribution**. The decision maker would therefore choose a **client fee of $200 per day**, which has a lowest possible contribution of $1,378,125. This is better than the worst possible outcomes from client fees per day of $180 and $220, which would provide contributions of $1,338,750 and $1,312,500 respectively.

(iii) The **minimax regret** decision rule involves choosing the **outcome that minimises the maximum regret** from making the wrong decision, in this instance choosing the outcome which minimises the opportunity lost from making the wrong decision.

We can use the calculations performed in (a) to draw up an **opportunity loss table.**

	Variable cost per day			Maximum regret
Client fee per day	$95	$85	$70	
$	$	$	$	$
180	39,375 (W1)	13,125 (W4)	0 (W7)	39,375
200	0 (W2)	0 (W5)	26,250 (W8)	26,250
220	65,625 (W3)	91,875 (W6)	157,500 (W9)	157,500

The minimax regret decision strategy would be to **choose a client fee of $200** to minimise the maximum regret at $26,250.

Workings

1 At a variable cost of $95 per day, the best strategy would be a client fee of $200 per day. The opportunity loss from using a fee of $180 would be $(1,378,125 – 1,338,750) = $39,375.

2 The opportunity loss in this case is $(1,378,125 – 1,378,125) = $0.

3 The opportunity loss in this case is $(1,378,125 – 1,312,500) = $65,625.

4 At a variable cost of $85 per day, the best strategy would be a client fee of $200 per day. The opportunity loss from using a fee of $180 would be $(1,509,375 – 1,496,250)= $13,125.

5 The opportunity loss in this case is $(1,509,375 – 1,509,375) = 0.

6 The opportunity loss in this case is $(1,509,375 – 1,417,500) = $91,875.

7 At a variable cost of $70 per day, the best strategy would be client fee of $180 per day. The opportunity loss from using a fee of $180 would be $(1,732,500 – 1,732,500) = $0.

8 The opportunity loss in this case is $(1,732,500 – 1,706,250) = $26,250.

9 The opportunity loss in this case is $(1,732,500 – 1,575,000) = $157,500.

(c) **Expected value of variable costs** = $(0.1 \times \$95) + (0.6 \times \$85) + (0.3 \times \$70) = \$81.50$.

We can now calculate an expected value of budgeted contribution at each client fee per day level.

	Client fee per day		
Variable cost	$180	$200	$220
$81.50	1,551,375	1,553,312.50	1,454,250

If **maximisation of EV of contribution is used as the decision basis**, a **client fee of $200 per day** will be selected, with an EV of contribution of $1,555,312.50 (although this is *very* close to the EV of contribution which results from a client fee of $180).

12 Budgets and people

There is one major **reason why managers may be reluctant to participate** fully in setting up budgets and that is a **lack of education in the purposes of the budgeting process**. The budget's major role is to communicate the various motivations that exist among management so that everybody sees, understands and co-ordinates the goals of the organisation.

Specific reasons for the reluctance of managers to participate are as follows.

(a) Managers view budgets as **too rigid a constraint on their decision making.** For example, a manager may be unable to sanction an item of expenditure if it has not been budgeted for. The natural reaction to this supposed restriction of their autonomy is resistance and self defence.

(b) Managers feel that the top management **goals expressed by the budget will interfere with their personal goals** (for example their desire to 'build an empire' with substantial resources under their control, large personal income and so on). A successful budgetary system will harmonise the budget goals with the managers' personal goals, but it is by no means easy to achieve a successful system.

(c) Managers imagine that the purpose of budgets is to provide senior management with a **rod** with which to chastise those who do not stay within budget. They will be unwilling to help in the construction of such a rod.

(d) Managers view the budgeting process as one in which they must **fight for a fair share** of the organisation's **resources** in competition with colleagues with other responsibilities.

(e) Managers misinterpret the **control function** of the budgeting system to be a method whereby **blame** can be **attached**. By not participating in the budget setting process, they are able to blame an 'unattainable' or 'unrealistic' budget for any poor results they may have.

As a reaction to these uneducated notions, the behaviour of managers involved in budget preparation can conflict with the desires of senior management. Such behaviour is often described as **dysfunctional**; it is counter-productive because it is **not goal congruent.**

The **unwanted side effects** which may arise from the **imposition of budgets** by senior management (for example under an authoritative rather than a participative budgetary system) are examples of **dysfunctional behaviour** and include the following.

(a) There may be a **reluctance to reduce costs** for fear that future budget allowances may be reduced as a consequence of successful cost cutting.

(b) Managers may **spend up to their budget** in order to justify levels of expenditure. This is particularly the case in local government circles where there is a tendency to spend any available cash at the end of a financial year.

(c) There may be **padding**, whereby managers request inflated allowances. In turn senior management may cut budgets where they suspect padding exists. Padding is sometimes called slack and represents the difference between the budget allowance requested and the realistic costs necessary to accomplish the objective.

(d) In extreme cases of authoritative budgeting, the **'emotional' responses** of managers can be highly detrimental to the goals of the organisation, for example non-cooperation.

13 Zero based budgeting

REPORT

To: R&D manager
From: Management accountant
Date: 01.01.X3
Subject: Zero based budgeting

(a)   **Zero based budgeting and traditional budgeting**

The traditional approach to budgeting works from the premise that last year's activities will continue at the same level or volume, and that next year's budget can be based on last year's costs plus an extra amount to allow for expansion and inflation. The term 'incremental' budgeting is often used to describe this approach.

Zero based budgeting (ZBB) quite literally works from a zero base. The approach recognises that every activity has a cost and insists that there must be quantifiable benefits to justify the spending. ZBB expects managers to choose the best method of achieving each task by comparing costs and benefits. Activities must be ranked in order of priority.

(b)   A **discretionary cost** is not vital to the continued existence of an organisation in the way that, say, raw materials are to a manufacturing business. ZBB was developed originally to help management with the difficult task of allocating resources in precisely such areas. **Research and development** is a frequently cited example; others are **advertising** and **training**.

Within a research and development department ZBB will establish priorities by ranking the projects that are planned and in progress. Project managers will be forced to consider the benefit obtainable from their work in relation to the costs involved. The result may be an overall increase in R&D expenditure, but only if it is justified.

(c)   **Budgetary slack** may be defined as the difference between the minimum necessary costs and the costs built into the budget or actually incurred. One of the reasons why, under traditional budgeting, an extra amount is added to last year's budget may be because managers are overestimating costs to avoid being blamed in the future for overspending and to make targets easier to achieve. Slack is a protective device and it is self-fulfilling because managers will subsequently ensure that their actual spending rises to meet the (overestimated) budget, in case they are blamed for careless budgeting.

In an R&D department a further incentive to include slack is the nature of the work. Managers may well have 'pet' projects in which their personal interest is so strong that they tend to ignore the benefit or lack of benefit to the organisation which is funding them.

The **ZBB approach**, as described in (a) above, clearly will not accept this approach: all expenditure has (in theory) to be justified in cost-benefit terms in its entirety in order to be included in next year's budget. In practice it is more likely that managers will start from their current level of expenditure as usual, but ZBB requires them to work **downwards**, asking what would happen if any particular element of current expenditure and current operations were removed from the budget.

14 Forecasting

> **Top tips.** This question gives you practice at using the linear regression formulae that will be given to you in your exam. They look daunting but a methodical approach and practice will make them straightforward. You should always be prepared to answer questions on the usefulness or otherwise of quantitative techniques.

(a)   For every quarter, each year shows an increase in sales, so an **increasing trend** is expected. Also, there is a **regular seasonal pattern** with a steady increase in sales from Q1 to Q4.

(b) Letting $X = t$ and $y = T$

x	y	xy	x^2
1	24.8	24.8	1
2	36.3	72.6	4
3	38.1	114.3	9
4	47.5	190.0	16
5	31.2	156.0	25
6	42.0	252.0	36
7	43.4	303.8	49
8	55.9	447.2	64
9	40.0	360.0	81
10	48.8	488.0	100
11	54.0	594.0	121
12	69.1	829.2	144
13	54.7	711.1	169
14	57.8	809.2	196
15	60.3	904.5	225
16	68.9	1,102.4	256
136	772.8	7,359.1	1,496

$$b = \frac{n\Sigma xy - \Sigma x\Sigma y}{n\Sigma x^2 - (\Sigma x)^2} = \frac{(16 \times 7,359.1) - (136 \times 772.8)}{(16 \times 1,496) - 136^2} = 2.3244$$

$$a = \frac{\Sigma y}{n} - \frac{b\Sigma x}{n} = \frac{772.8}{16} - 2.3244 \times \frac{136}{16} = 28.54$$

The trend equation is therefore:

T = 28.54 + 2.3244t

In 20X7, t takes values 17–20, giving trend forecasts as follows:

Q1	t = 17	T = 28.54 + (2.3244 x 17) = 68.0548
Q2	t = 18	T = 70.3792
Q3	t = 19	T = 72.7036
Q4	t = 20	T = 75.028

(c) Linear regression analysis requires that certain conditions should apply and these conditions may not necessarily be realistic.

(i)   A **linear relationship** is assumed. This assumption can be tested by measures of reliability, such as the correlation coefficient.

(ii)   When calculating a line of best fit, we have to assume that the variables behave in the same way outside the range of x values used to establish the line.

(iii) In order for this method of forecasting to be useful, management should either be **confident that conditions** which have existed in the past **will continue into the future or amend the estimates** of cost produced by the linear regression analysis to **allow for expected changes** in the future.

As with any forecasting process, the **amount of data available is very important**. Even if correlation is high, if we have fewer than about ten pairs of data, we must regard any forecast as being somewhat unreliable.

It must be **assumed** that the value of one variable, y, can be predicted or estimated from the value of one other variable, x.

All forecasts are subject to error, but the likely errors vary from case to case.

- The **further into the future** the forecast is for, the **more unreliable** it is likely to be
- The **less data** available on which to base the forecast, the **less reliable** the forecast
- The historic **pattern** of trend and seasonal variations **may not continue** in the future
- **Random variations** may upset the pattern of trend and seasonal variation

15 Dench

(a) **Cost estimate for 225 components is based upon the following assumptions:**

(1) The first batch of 15 is excluded from the order (and total cost for first batch is likewise excluded); and

(2) The 80% learning rate only applies to the skilled workforce, (and related variable overhead) due to their high level of expertise/low turnover rate.

Cumulative Batches	Cumulative Units	Total Time Hours	Cum ave time/batch Hours
1	15	20	20
2	30	32	16
4	60	51.2	12.8
8	120	81.92	10.24
16	240	131.072	8.192

Total cost for 16 batches (240 components)

		$
Material A:	$30 batch	480
Material B:	$30/batch	480
Labour:	Skilled 131.072 hr @ $15/hr	1,966
	Semi-skilled $40/batch	640
Variable OH:	131.072 hr @ $4/hr	524
	5 hr/batch at $4/hr	320
		4,410
Less: Cost for 1st batch (15 components)		(500)
∴ cost for 225 components		3,910

(b) The limited use of learning curve theory is due to several factors:

(i) The learning curve phenomenon is not always present.

(ii) It assumes stable conditions at work (eg of the labour force and labour mix) which will enable learning to take place. This is not always practicable (eg because of labour turnover).

(iii) It must also assume a certain degree of motivation amongst employees.

(iv) Extensive breaks between production of items must not be too long, or workers will 'forget' and the learning process would have to begin all over again.

(v) It is difficult to obtain enough accurate data to decide what the learning curve is.

16 McDreamy

Top tips. Make sure you read the question carefully especially on the calculation of capacity levels. Note that at 65% capacity 10,000 units are produced.

Part (b) requires you to apply your knowledge and part (c) is a straightforward regurgitation of text book knowledge.

(a) **Flexible budget statement for next year operating at 85% capacity**

	Workings		
Output	1	13,077 units	
		$	$
Sales revenue	9		5,911,484
Variable costs			
Direct materials	2	1,386,162	
Direct wages	3	2,357,129	
Variable production overhead	4	489,734	
Variable selling and distribution overhead	5	69,962	
			4,302,987
Contribution			1,608,497
Fixed costs			
Production overhead	6	330,000	
Selling and distribution overhead	7	161,250	
Administration overhead	8	132,000	
			623,250
Profit			985,247

Workings

1   65% of capacity = 10,000 units
∴ 100% of capacity = 10,000 ÷ 0.65 = 15,385 units
∴ 85% of capacity = (10,000 ÷ 0.65) × 0.85 = 13,077 units
∴ 75% of capacity = 11,538
∴ 55% of capacity = 8,462

2   Current direct material cost per unit   = $1,000,000 ÷ 10,000
= $100 per unit

∴ Flexible budget allowance for next year = $100 × 1.06 × 13,077
= $1,386,162

3   Current direct wages cost per unit   = $1,750,000 ÷ 10,000
= $175 per unit

∴ Flexible budget allowance for next year = $175 × 1.03 × 13,077
= $2,357,129

4   Production overhead increases by $53,830 for an increase in activity of (10,000 – 8,462) units

∴ Variable production overhead per unit = $35
∴ Variable overhead allowance for 85% capacity   = 13,077 × $35   = $457,695
Plus 7% increase $32,039
Total allowance $489,734

5   Selling overhead increases by $7,690 for an increase in activity of (10,000 – 8,462) units.

∴ Variable cost per unit = $5
∴ Variable overhead allowance for 85% capacity   = 13,077 × $5   = $65,385
Plus 7% increase $4,577
Total allowance $69,962

6

	$
Total production overhead at 65% activity	650,000
Less variable overhead (10,000 × $35 (W4))	350,000
Fixed overhead this year	300,000
Plus 10% increase	30,000
Total allowance	330,000

7

	$
Total selling overhead at 65% activity	200,000
Less variable overhead (10,000 × $5 (W5))	50,000
Fixed overhead this year	150,000
Plus 7.5% increase	11,250
Total allowance	161,250

8   Administration overhead = $120,000 × 1.1 = $132,000

9   The cost and selling price structure is as follows.

	%
Sales price	100.00
Profit	16.67
Cost	83.33

∴ Profit as a percentage of cost = $\dfrac{16.67}{83.33} \times 100\% = 20\%$ of cost

	$
Total cost ($4,302,987 + $623,250)	4,926,237
Profit at 20% of cost	985,247
∴ Sales value	5,911,484

(b)   Three **problems** which may **arise from the change in capacity level** are as follows.

(i)   There is likely to be a requirement for **additional cash for working capital**, for example inventory levels and debtors will probably increase. This additional cash may not be available.

(ii)   It will probably be necessary to **recruit more direct labour**. The activities involved in advertising, interviewing and training may lead to increased costs.

(iii)   It may be necessary to **reduce the selling price** to sell the increased volume. This could have an **adverse effect on profits**.

(c)   **The principle of controllability** is that managers of responsibility centres should only be held accountable for costs over which they have some influence.

Budgetary control is based around a system of **budget centres**. Each budget centre will have its own budget and a manager will be responsible for managing the budget centre and ensuring that the budget is met.

Budgetary control and budget centres are therefore part of the overall system of **responsibility accounting** within an organisation.

Controllable costs are items of expenditure which can be directly influenced by a given manager within a given time span.

Care must be taken to distinguish between controllable costs and uncontrollable costs in variance reporting. The **controllability principle** is that managers of responsibility centres should only be held accountable for costs over which they have some influence. From a **motivation** point of view this is important because it can be very demoralising for managers who feel that their performance is being judged on the basis of something over which they have no influence. It is also important from a **control** point of view in that control reports should ensure that information on costs is reported to the manager who is able to take action to control them.

Responsibility accounting attempts to associate costs, revenues, assets and liabilities with the managers most capable of controlling them. As a system of accounting, it therefore distinguishes between controllable and uncontrollable costs.

Most **variable costs** within a department are thought to be **controllable in the short term** because managers can influence the efficiency with which resources are used, even if they cannot do anything to raise or lower price levels.

A cost which is not controllable by a junior manager might be controllable by a senior manager. For example, there may be high direct labour costs in a department caused by excessive overtime working. The junior manager may feel obliged to continue with the overtime to meet production schedules, but his senior may be able to reduce costs by hiring extra full-time staff, thereby reducing the requirements for overtime.

A cost which is not controllable by a manager in one department may be controllable by a manager in another department. For example, an increase in material costs may be caused by buying at higher prices than expected (controllable by the purchasing department) or by excessive wastage (controllable by the production department) or by a faulty machine producing rejects (controllable by the maintenance department).

Some costs are **non-controllable**, such as increases in expenditure items due to inflation. Other costs are **controllable, but in the long term rather than the short term**. For example, production costs might be reduced by the introduction of new machinery and technology, but in the short term, management must attempt to do the best they can with the resources and machinery at their disposal.

17 ACCA-Chem Co

Top tips. There are quite a lot of calculations in this question. Whilst it's easy to say that you should split your time so that you spend enough time on the written elements, written element (a) (iv) is dependent upon your answer to the earlier calculations.

Work through (a) (iv) carefully, and make sure you understand the link between the different variances.

(a)   (i)   (1)   **Price variances**

	$	$
Material F		
59,800 kgs should have cost (× $4)	239,200	
but did cost (× $4.25)	254,150	
		14,950 (A)
Material G		
53,500 kgs should have cost (× $3)	160,500	
but did cost (× $2.80)	149,800	
		10,700 (F)
Material H		
33,300 kgs should have cost (× $6)	199,800	
but did cost (× $6.40)	213,120	
		13,320 (A)
Total material price variance		17,570 (A)

(2)   **Usage variances**

	F	G	H
4,100 units of output of product W should need	61,500 kgs	49,200 kgs	32,800 kgs
but did need	59,800 kgs	53,500 kgs	33,300 kgs
Usage variance in kgs	1,700 kgs(F)	4,300 kgs (A)	500 kgs (A)
× standard price per kg	× $4	× $3	× $6
Usage variance in $	$6,800 (F)	$12,900 (A)	$3,000 (A)

Total material usage variance = $9,100 (A)

Mix variances

Total kgs used = 146,600 kgs

Standard mix for actual use

		kgs
F	$^{15}/_{35} \times 146,600 =$	62,829
G	$^{12}/_{35} \times 146,600 =$	50,263
H	$^{8}/_{35} \times 146,600 =$	33,508
		146,600

	Actual quantity standard mix	Actual quantity actual mix	Variance	Standard cost per kg	Variance
	Kgs	Kgs	Kgs	$	$
F	62,829	59,800	3,029 (F)	4	12,116 (F)
G	50,263	53,500	3,237 (A)	3	9,711 (A)
H	33,508	33,300	208 (F)	6	1,248 (F)
	146,600	146,600	–		3,653 (F)

Total mix variance = $3,653 (F)

(4) Yield variance

The yield variance can be calculated in total or for each material input.

In total

146,600 kg input should yield (/35)	4188.57 units	
146,600 kg input did yield	4100.00 units	
	88.57 (A)	
@ $144 per unit	$12,754 (A)	

	Standard quantity standard mix	Actual quantity standard mix	Variance	Standard cost per kg	Variance
	Kgs	Kgs	Kgs	$	$
F	61,500	62,829	1,329 (A)	4	5,316 (A)
G	49,200	50,263	1,063 (A)	3	3,189 (A)
H	32,800	33,508	708 (A)	6	4,248 (A)
	143,500	146,600	442 (A)		12,753 (A)

(ii) (1)

		Dept P		Dept Q	Total
		$		$	$
4,100 units should have cost	(× $40)	164,000	(× $12)	49,200	213,200
but did cost		217,300		51,660	268,960
Labour cost variance		53,300 (A)		2,460 (A)	55,760 (A)

(2)

		Dept P		Dept Q	Total
4,100 units should have taken	(× 4)	16,400 hrs	(× 2)	8,200 hrs	
but did take		20,500 hrs		9,225 hrs	
		4,100 hrs (A)		1,025 hrs (A)	
× standard rate per hour		× $10		× $6	
Labour efficiency variance		41,000 (A)		$6,150 (A)	$47,150 (A)

(3)

		Dept P $		Dept Q $	Total $
20,500 hrs/9,225 hrs should have cost	(× $10)	205,000	(× $6)	55,350	260,350
but did cost		217,300		51,660	268,960
Labour rate variance		12,300 (A)		3,690 (F)	8,610 (A)

(iii)

	$
4,100 units should have sold for (× $260)	1,066,000
but did sell for	1,115,800
Selling price variance	49,800 (F)
Budgeted sales for period	44,500 units
Actual sales volume	4,100 units
Volume variance in kgs	400 units(A)
× standard profit per kg ($(260 − 196))	× $64
Sales volume profit variance	$25,600 (A)

(iv) **Adverse yield variance**

An analysis of the materials mix variance (see (a)(i)(3)) shows that 3,029 kgs of F and 208 kgs of H (the more expensive materials) were replaced by 3,237 kgs of G (the cheapest material). This **substitution of cheaper material** could have led to the adverse yield variance. It is **also** possible that the yield variance was because the material G that was used was of a **lower than standard quality** since it was purchased at a price below its standard price.

Adverse efficiency variance

The adverse labour efficiency variance may have been due to Material G taking longer to process than normal because it was of a poor quality. Alternatively, the fact that in Department Q the **actual rate was less than the standard rate could mean that less skilled labour was used** than provided for in the standard, and that this then **lowered productivity** with the result that the **yield was lower than expected**.

18 Milbao

Top tips. Part (a) does not require detailed technical knowledge but should be based on your knowledge of how budgets and control systems can operate effectively.

The variance calculations in part (b) are very straightforward but don't forget to comment on your results.

(a) **Components**

Arguments for a revision

The problem arose due to a liquidation of a supplier which is **outside the control** of the buyer who is unlikely to have been aware it was going to happen.

The buyer will expect this revision to be allowed as it is outside his control and is likely to be demoralised and demotivated if it is refused.

Arguments against a revision

The buyer accepted the deal with the new supplier **without attempting to negotiate**. This may have been a panicked reaction to the immediate problem which has increased Milbao's costs.

The buyer is responsible for sourcing the cheapest materials and this could have been achieved with an alternative local supplier. A more **considered, careful approach** would have achieved a better deal.

A buyer should also have a good knowledge of his supplier's circumstances and it could be argued that some advance knowledge of liquidity problems could have been expected.

Conclusion

The budget revision should not be allowed. Although the liquidation was outside the control of the buyer, he could have achieved a better price.

Labour

Arguments for a revision

The Board made the decision to change the recruitment policy and this decision was outside the **control** of the departmental manager. The departmental manager is therefore not responsible for the extra cost.

Arguments against a revision

The **organisation as a whole** is in control of this decision so the cost is controllable.

The departmental manager **requested** a change in recruitment so is responsible for the extra cost involved.

The **productivity increases** have benefited the department involved so it should also be charged with the costs involved.

Conclusion

This was an **operational decision** that the departmental manager requested and agreed to. It has had the desired effects so no budget revision should be allowed.

(b)   The variance caused by favourable or adverse **operating** performance should be calculated by comparing actual results against the realistic standard of $55 per unit.

	$
Revised standard cost of actual production (11,200 × $55)	616,000
Actual cost	425,600
Total **operational** variance	190,400 (F)

The variance is favourable because the actual cost was lower than would have been expected using the revised basis.

The **planning** variance reveals the extent to which the original standard was at fault.

		$
Revised standard cost	11,200 units × $55 per unit	616,000
Original standard cost	11,200 units × $35 per unit	392,000
Planning variance		224,000 (A)

It is an adverse variance because the original standard was too optimistic, overestimating the expected profits by understating the standard cost.

	$
Planning variance	224,000 (A)
Operational variance	190,400 (F)
Total	33,600 (A)

If **traditional variance analysis** had been used, the total cost variance would have been the same, but all the **'blame'** would appear to lie on actual results and operating inefficiencies (rather than some being due to faulty planning).

	$
Standard cost of 11,200 units (× $35)	392,000
Actual cost of 11,200 units	425,600
Total cost variance	33,600 (A)

19 Spring

(a) **Activity based costing** (ABC) involves the identification of the factors which cause the costs of an organisation's major activities. Support overheads are charged to products on the basis of their usage of the factor causing the overheads. The major ideas behind activity based costing are as follows.

   (1) **Activities cause costs**. Activities include ordering, materials handling, machining, assembly, production scheduling and despatching.

   (2) Producing products creates demand for the activities.

   (3) Costs are assigned to a product on the basis of the product's consumption of the activities.

   The principal idea of ABC is to focus attention on what causes costs to increase, ie the cost drivers. Those costs that do vary with production volume, such as power costs, should be traced to products using production volume-related cost drivers as appropriate, such as direct labour hours or direct machine hours. Overheads which do not vary with output but with some other activity should be traced to products using transaction-based cost drivers, such as number of production runs and number of orders received. Traditional costing systems allow overheads to be related to products in rather more arbitrary ways producing, it is claimed, less accurate product costs.

   An ABC system involves the following features.

   Step 1   Identify an organisation's major activities.

   Step 2   Identify the factors which determine the size of the costs of an activity/cause the costs of an activity. These are the cost drivers.

   Step 3   Collect the costs associated with each cost driver into what are known as cost pools.

   Step 4   Charge costs to products on the basis of their usage of the activity.

   ### Advantages of ABC

   The complexity of manufacturing has increased, with wider product ranges, shorter product life cycles and more complex production processes. ABC recognises this complexity with its multiple cost drivers.

   In a more competitive environment, companies must be able to assess product profitability realistically. ABC facilitates a good understanding of what drives overhead costs.

   In modern manufacturing systems, overhead functions include a lot of non-factory-floor activities such as product design, quality control, production planning and customer services. ABC is concerned with all overhead costs and so goes beyond 'traditional' factory floor boundaries.

   ### Disadvantages of ABC

   It has however been suggested by critics that activity based costing has some serious flaws. Some measure of (arbitrary) cost apportionment may still be required at the cost pooling stage for items like rent, rates and building depreciation.

   Unless costs are caused by an activity that is measurable in quantitative terms and which can be related to production output, cost drivers will not be usable. What drives the cost of the annual external audit, for example?

   ABC is sometimes introduced because it is fashionable, not because it will be used by management to provide meaningful product costs or extra information. If Spring's management is not going to use ABC information, an absorption costing system may be simpler to operate. Put another way, the cost of implementing and maintaining an ABC system can exceed the benefits of improved accuracy.

Implementing ABC is often problematic. Recent journal articles have highlighted the following issues.

(i)   An incorrect belief that ABC can solve all an organisation's problems
(ii)   Lack of the correct type of data
(iii)   Difficulty in determining appropriate cost drivers

(b)   **Performance measurement** is a part of the system of financial control of an enterprise, as well as being important to investors. Managerial performance and organisational performance are linked, since the decisions that managers make will influence how well or otherwise the organisation performs. This performance needs to be measured as part of the **control process**. The key elements of such a process are as follows.

Step 1   **Plans and targets are set for the future**. These could be long-, medium- or short-term plans. Examples include budgets, profit targets and standard costs.

Step 2   **Plans are put into operation**. As a consequence, materials and labour are used, and other expenses are incurred.

Step 3   **Actual results are recorded and analysed**.

Step 4   **Information about actual results is fed back** to the management concerned, often in the form of accounting reports.

Step 5   **The feedback is used by management to compare** actual results with the plan or targets.

Step 6   By comparing actual and planned results, management can then do one of three things, depending on how they see the situation.

(a)   **They can take control action**. By identifying what has gone wrong, and then finding out why, corrective measures can be taken.

(b)   **They can decide to do nothing**. This could be the decision when actual results are going better than planned, or when poor results were caused by something which is unlikely to happen again in the future.

(c)   **They can alter the plan or target** if actual results are different from the plan or target, and there is nothing that management can do (or nothing, perhaps, that they want to do) to correct the situation.

The usual assumption in financial management for the private sector is that the primary financial objective of the company is to maximise shareholders' wealth. Financial targets may include targets for earnings; earnings per share; dividend per share; gearing levels; profit retention and operating profitability.

There are a variety of ways that such performance can be measured. As part of the system of financial control in an organisation, it will be necessary to have ways of measuring the progress of the enterprise, so that managers know how well the company is doing. A common means of doing this is through ratio analysis, which is concerned with comparing and quantifying relationships between financial variables, such as those variables found in the balance sheet and profit and loss account of the enterprise.

Ratios can be grouped into the following four categories: profitability and return; debt and gearing; liquidity: control of cash and other working capital items; shareholders' investment ratios ('stock market ratios'). The ratios can be seen to be interrelated.

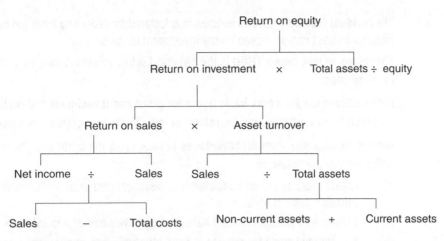

Such ratios help in providing for an overall management plan to achieve profitability, and allow the interrelationships between ratios to be checked.

There is a danger, however, in focusing excessively on financial performance measures which can be easily quantified, thus placing an undue emphasis on maximising short-term performance even if this conflicts with maximising long-term performance. Non-financial objectives may include employee welfare; management welfare; the welfare of society; service provision objectives and the fulfilment of responsibilities to customers and suppliers.

It is therefore important that a range of non-financial indicators be developed to provide better predictors for the attainment of long-term profitability goals. Here are some examples.

- Quality
- Number of customer complaints
- Lead times

- Delivery to time
- Non-productive hours
- System (machine) down time

Unlike traditional variance reports, measures such as these can be provided quickly for managers, per shift or on a daily or hourly basis. They are likely to be easy to calculate, and easier for non-financial managers to understand and therefore to use effectively.

A popular approach in current management thinking to performance measurement (for service and non-service organisations) is the use of what is called a 'balanced scorecard'. The balanced scorecard approach aims to provide management with information covering all relevant areas of performance. The information provided may include both financial and non-financial elements. The scorecard is 'balanced' in the sense that managers are required to think in terms of all four perspectives (customer perception, innovation capability, internal processes and financial measures), to prevent improvements being made in one area at the expense of another. The method had the advantages of looking at both internal and external matters concerning the organisation and of linking together financial and non-financial measures.

20 Divisional performance measures

Top tips. Parts (a) and (b) require you to demonstrate knowledge you should have picked up directly from the text. No application skills are required at all in this instance.

That being said, it is vital that you do not learn the advantages and disadvantages of ROI and RI in a parrot fashion as they underlie the very core of the chapter. You **must understand how and why ROI affects managerial behaviour**, for example. You are just as likely to get a written question on this area as a calculation-based one.

The calculations required in (b) should not have caused you any problems.

Part (c) is **basic book knowledge** and so you should have been able to score quite a few of the marks available.

(a)   The **residual income (RI)** for a division is calculated by deducting from the divisional profit an imputed interest charge, based on the investment in the division.

The **return on investment (ROI)** is the divisional profit expressed as a percentage of the investment in the division.

Both methods use the **same basic figure for profit and investment**, but **residual income** produces an **absolute** measure whereas the **return on investment** is expressed as a **percentage**.

Both methods suffer from **disadvantages** in measuring the profit and the investment in a division which include the following.

(i)   Assets must be valued consistently at historical cost or at replacement cost. Neither valuation basis is ideal.

(ii)   Divisions might use different bases to value inventory and to calculate depreciation.

(iii)   Any charges made for the use of head office services or allocations of head office assets to divisions are likely to be arbitrary.

In addition, **return on investment** suffers from the following **disadvantages**.

(i)   Rigid adherence to the need to maintain ROI in the short term can discourage managers from investing in new assets, since average divisional ROI tends to fall in the early stages of a new investment. Residual income can overcome this problem by highlighting projects which return more than the cost of capital.

(ii)   It can be difficult to compare the percentage ROI results of divisions if their activities are very different: residual income can overcome this problem through the use of different interest rates for different divisions.

(b)   (i)   **Return on divisional investment (ROI)**

	Before investment	After investment
Divisional profit	$18,000	$19,600
Divisional investment	$100,000	$110,000
Divisional ROI	18.0%	17.8%

The ROI will fall in the short term if the new investment is undertaken. This is a problem which often arises with ROI, as noted in part (a) of this solution.

(ii)   **Divisional residual income**

	Before investment	After investment
	$	$
Divisional profit	18,000	19,600
Less imputed interest: $100,000 × 15%	15,000	
$110,000 × 15%		16,500
Residual income	3,000	3,100

The residual income will increase if the new investment is undertaken. The use of residual income has highlighted the fact that the new project returns more than the cost of capital (16% compared with 15%).

(c)   **Potential benefits of operating a transfer pricing system within a divisionalised company**

(i)   It can lead to **goal congruence** by motivating divisional managers to make decisions, which improve divisional profit and improve profit of the organisation as a whole.

(ii)   It can prevent **dysfunctional decision making** so that decisions taken by a divisional manager are in the best interests of his own part of the business, other divisions and the organisation as a whole.

(iii)   Transfer prices can be set at a level that enables divisional performance to be measured 'commercially'. A transfer pricing system should therefore report a level of divisional profit that is a **reasonable measure of the managerial performance** of the division.

(iv)   It should ensure that **divisional autonomy** is not undermined. A well-run transfer pricing system helps to ensure that a balance is kept between divisional autonomy to provide incentives and motivation, and centralised authority to ensure that the divisions are all working towards the same target, the benefit of the organisation as a whole.

21 Non-profit seeking organisations

(a) (i) **Effectiveness** refers to the use of resources so as to achieve desired ends or objectives or outputs.

In a profit-making organisation, objectives can be expressed financially in terms of a target profit or return. The organisation, or profit centres within the organisation, can be judged to have operated effectively if they have achieved a target profit within a given period.

In non-profit seeking organisations, effectiveness cannot be measured in this way. The organisation's objectives cannot be expressed in financial terms at all, and non-financial objectives need to be established. The effectiveness of performance could be measured in terms of whether targeted non-financial objectives have been achieved, but there are several **problems** involved in trying to do this.

(1) The organisation might have several **different objectives** which are difficult to reconcile with each other. Achieving one objective might only be possible at the expense of failing to achieve another. For example, schools have the objective of providing education. They teach a certain curriculum, but by opting to educate students in some subjects, there is no time available to provide education in other subjects.

(2) A non-profit seeking organisation will invariably be **restricted in what it can achieve by the availability of funds**. The health service, for example, has the objective of providing health care, but since funds are restricted there is a limit to the amount of care that can be provided, and there will be competition for funds between different parts of the service.

(3) The objectives of non-profit seeking organisations are also difficult to establish because the **quality** of the service provided will be a significant feature of their service. For example, a local authority has, amongst its various different objectives, the objective of providing a rubbish collection service. The effectiveness of this service can only be judged by establishing what standard or quality of service is required.

(4) With differing objectives, none of them directly comparable, and none that can be expressed in profit terms, **human judgement** is likely to be involved in deciding whether an organisation has been effective or not. This is most clearly seen in government organisations where political views cloud opinion about the government's performance.

Efficiency refers to the rate at which resources are consumed to achieve desired ends. Efficiency measurements compare the output produced by the organisation with the resources employed or used up to achieve the output. They are used to control the consumption of resources, so that the maximum output is achieved by a given amount of input resources, or a certain volume of output is produced within the minimum resources being used up.

In profit-making organisations, the efficiency of the organisation as a whole can be measured in terms of return on capital employed. Individual profit centres or operating units within the organisation can also have efficiency measured by relating the quantity of output produced, which has a **market value** and therefore a quantifiable financial value, to the resources (and their costs) required to make the output.

In non-profit seeking organisations, output does not usually have a market value, and it is therefore more difficult to measure efficiency. This difficulty is compounded by the fact that since these organisations often have **several different objectives**, it is difficult to compare the efficiency of one operation with the efficiency of another. For example, with the police force, it might be difficult to compare the efficiency of a serious crimes squad with the efficiency of the traffic police, because each has its own 'outputs' that are not easily comparable in terms of 'value achieved'.

In spite of the difficulties of measuring effectiveness and efficiency, control over the performance of non-profit seeking organisations can only be satisfactorily achieved by assessments of **'value for money'** (economy, efficiency and effectiveness).

(ii) The same problems extend to **support activities** within profit-motivated organisations, where these activities are not directly involved in the creation of output and sales. Examples include research and development, the personnel function, the accountancy function and so on.

(1) Some of the outputs of these functions **cannot be measured in market values**.

(2) The **objectives** of the functions are **not easily expressed** in quantifiable terms.

Examples

(1) Within the personnel department, outputs from activities such as training and some aspects of recruitment can be given market price values by estimating what the same services would cost if provided by an external organisation. Other activities, however, do not have any such market valuation. Welfare is an example. Its objective is to provide support for employees in their personal affairs, but since this objective cannot easily be expressed as quantifiable targets, and does not have a market price valuation, the effectiveness and efficiency of work done by welfare staff cannot be measured easily.

(2) Within the accountancy department, outputs from management accountants are management information. This does not have an easily-measured market value, and information's value depends more on quality than quantity. The contribution of management accounting to profitability is difficult to judge, and so the efficiency and effectiveness of the function are difficult to measure.

(b) (i) To measure effectiveness, we need to establish objectives or targets for performance. Since these cannot be expressed financially, **non-financial targets** must be used. The effective level of achievement could be measured by comparing actual performance against target.

Adherence to appointment times

(1) Percentage of appointments kept on time
(2) Percentage of appointments no more than 10 minutes late
(3) Percentage of appointments kept within 30 minutes of schedule
(4) Percentage of cancelled appointments
(5) Average delay in appointments

A **problem** with these measures is that there is an implied assumption that all patients will be at the clinic by their appointed time. In practice, this will not always be the case.

Patients' ability to contact the clinic and make appointments

(1)   Percentage of patients who can make an appointment at their first preferred time, or at the first date offered to them

(2)   Average time from making an appointment to the appointment date

(3)   Number of complaints about failure to contact the clinic, as a percentage of total patients seen

(4)   If the telephone answering system provides for queuing of calls, the average waiting-for-answer times for callers and the percentage of abandoned calls

Comprehensive monitoring programme

Measures might be based on the definition of each element or step within a monitoring programme for a patient, It would then be possible to measure the following.

(1)   Percentage of patients receiving every stage of the programme (and percentage receiving every stage but one, every stage but two, and so on)

(2)   If each stage has a scheduled date for completion, the average delay for patients in the completion of each stage

(ii)   A **single quality of care** measure would call for subjective judgements about the following.

(1)   The key **objective**/objectives for each of the three features of service
(2)   The relative **weighting** that should be given to each

The objectives would have to be measured on comparable terms, and since money values are inappropriate, an index based on percentage or a points-scoring system of measurement might be used. A target index or points score for achievement could then be set, and actual results compared against the target.

Index

BPP
LEARNING MEDIA

Review Form & Free Prize Draw – Paper F5 Performance Management (11/10)

All original review forms from the entire BPP range, completed with genuine comments, will be entered into one of two draws on 31 July 2011 and 31 January 2012. The names on the first four forms picked out on each occasion will be sent a cheque for £50.

Name: _____   Address: _____

_____

_____

How have you used this Text?	During the past six months do you recall seeing/receiving any of the following?
(Tick one box only)	(Tick as many boxes as are relevant)

How have you used this Text?
(Tick one box only)

☐ Home study (book only)

☐ On a course: college _____

☐ With 'correspondence' package

☐ Other _____

Why did you decide to purchase this Text? (Tick one box only)

☐ Have used BPP Texts in the past

☐ Recommendation by friend/colleague

☐ Recommendation by a lecturer at college

☐ Saw advertising

☐ Saw information on BPP website

☐ Other _____

During the past six months do you recall seeing/receiving any of the following?
(Tick as many boxes as are relevant)

☐ Our advertisement in *ACCA Student Accountant*

☐ Our advertisement in *Pass*

☐ Our advertisement in *PQ*

☐ Our brochure with a letter through the post

☐ Our website www.bpp.com

Which (if any) aspects of our advertising do you find useful?
(Tick as many boxes as are relevant)

☐ Prices and publication dates of new editions

☐ Information on Text content

☐ Facility to order books off-the-page

☐ None of the above

Which BPP products have you used?

Text	☑	*Success CD*	☐	*Learn Online*	☐
Kit	☐	*i-Learn*	☐	*Home Study Package*	☐
Passcard	☐	*i-Pass*	☐	*Home Study PLUS*	☐

Your ratings, comments and suggestions would be appreciated on the following areas.

	Very useful	Useful	Not useful
Introductory section (Key study steps, personal study)	☐	☐	☐
Chapter introductions	☐	☐	☐
Key terms	☐	☐	☐
Quality of explanations	☐	☐	☐
Case studies and other examples	☐	☐	☐
Exam focus points	☐	☐	☐
Questions and answers in each chapter	☐	☐	☐
Fast forwards and chapter roundups	☐	☐	☐
Quick quizzes	☐	☐	☐
Question Bank	☐	☐	☐
Answer Bank	☐	☐	☐
Index	☐	☐	☐

Overall opinion of this Study Text   Excellent ☐   Good ☐   Adequate ☐   Poor ☐

Do you intend to continue using BPP products?   Yes ☐   No ☐

On the reverse of this page are noted particular areas of the text about which we would welcome your feedback.
The BPP author of this edition can be e-mailed at: ianblackmore@bpp.com

Please return this form to: Lesley Buick, ACCA Publishing Manager, BPP Learning Media Ltd, FREEPOST, London, W12 8BR

Review Form & Free Prize Draw (continued)

TELL US WHAT YOU THINK

Free Prize Draw Rules

1 Closing date for 31 July 2011 draw is 30 June 2011. Closing date for 31 January 2012 draw is 31 December 2011.

2 Restricted to entries with UK and Eire addresses only. BPP employees, their families and business associates are excluded.

3 No purchase necessary. Entry forms are available upon request from BPP Learning Media Limited. No more than one entry per title, per person. Draw restricted to persons aged 16 and over.

4 Winners will be notified by post and receive their cheques not later than 6 weeks after the relevant draw date.

5 The decision of the promoter in all matters is final and binding. No correspondence will be entered into.